THE WONDERLAND OF KNOWLEDGE

·

*The New
Pictorial Encyclopedia*

INDUSTRY'S INFERNO

No spectacle in industry is more awe-inspiring than the blast furnace of a steel mill at night. Here, the iron ore is melted at a high temperature and is then drawn off to the sand bed in front of the furnace. The white-hot metal is drawn into the forms, called "pigs," where it hardens, giving rise to the term "pig iron." It is a colorful sight, for when the metal runs off it is a fiery white, and as it cools it changes to orange and then to red.

THE WONDERLAND OF KNOWLEDGE

•

The New Pictorial Encyclopedia

Chairman, Editorial Board

GORDON J. LAING, Ph.D., LL. D., Litt. D.

Former Dean of the Division of the Humanities,
the University of Chicago

Associate Editors

HARRY ORRIN GILLET, B.S.

RODERICK M. GRANT, A.B.

Managing Editor

BERTHA MAUDE WHITE, A.B.

Assistant Editor

EUNICE W. THOMPSON, M.A.

Picture Editors

CHESTER H. LAWRENCE

CROSBY J. LISKE   JAMES POYNTON, Ph.B.

1947

WONDERLAND OF KNOWLEDGE CORPORATION

JUST TO SATISFY YOUR *Curiosity*

How did basket ball get its name?

When the game was invented in 1891, by Dr. James Naismith, the object was to cage the ball in peach baskets. Later, the baskets were replaced by hoops, which permitted the ball to fall back to the floor, but the name remained the same. See BASKET BALL.

What is the highest score possible in bowling?

A perfect score is 300, which consists of twelve consecutive strikes. See BOWLING.

What is an uppercut?

An uppercut is a short, upward-swinging punch, delivered at close quarters and usually aimed at the jaw. See BOXING.

What great American poem was written by a youth in his teens?

Thanatopsis, the first important work of William Cullen Bryant, was written when he was seventeen. This was the first notable poem of America's first great poet. See BRYANT, WILLIAM CULLEN.

What great plant breeder developed a variety of potato that brought millions of dollars to American farmers?

Luther Burbank originated a variety of potato that more than doubled the former yield per acre. See BURBANK, LUTHER.

What were the fastest ships in the world before the era of steam?

The famous Yankee "clipper" ships, pride of American shipbuilders in the middle of the nineteenth century, could outdistance any vessel on the seas at that time. See BOAT.

Where do bicycles sell in greater numbers than do automobiles?

There are more bicycles in Europe than there are automobiles, and in European capitals, thousands of people ride to work on "velos" and "wheels." See BICYCLE.

What does a "falling glass" on shipboard tell the captain?

"Falling of the glass" means that the mercury in the barometer is falling, a sign of stormy weather. The fall of the mercury indicates decreasing air pressure. See BAROMETER.

What is the longest suspension bridge in the world?

The longest suspension bridge in the world is the one connecting San Francisco and Oakland, on opposite sides of San Francisco Bay. This bridge is eight and one-fourth miles in length, including approaches. See BRIDGE.

Why did the ancient Babylonians use bricks for their buildings?

Wood and stone were scarce in Babylonia, and it was necessary to use some other material. Clay was molded into bricks and these were baked or dried in the sun. See BRICK AND BRICKLAYING.

What is the difference between a weed and a flower?

The only thing that distinguishes a weed from a flower is its usefulness. The daisy is regarded as a charming flower in the florist shop, but it is a weed when it grows in a farm field. See BOTANY.

Can life come from lifeless things?

Science tells us that life comes only from life; non-living things have no power to produce living things. At one time, even scientists believed that the flies they saw crawling on decayed meat were produced by the meat itself. The French bacteriologist, Louis Pasteur, proved the falsity of this belief. See BIOLOGY.

What is the King James version of the Bible?

This is the English translation made by a group of scholars in 1611, at the request of King James I of England. It is the version most widely used among Protestants, and its beautiful phraseology has become a part of our literary speech. A few revisions of the King James version are also in use. See BIBLE.

What Bible character tricked his father into giving him the blessing due the eldest son?

Jacob, younger twin brother of Esau, received from the patriarch Isaac the farewell blessing that belonged to his brother. See BIBLE STORIES.

Why is Boston, Mass., called "The Hub"?

This name is derived from the term "hub of the solar system." The latter was applied to the city humorously by Oliver Wendell Holmes, the poet and essayist. Because Boston has been the center of so many literary and historical events, "The Hub" still seems an appropriate nickname. See BOSTON, MASS.

What is the Bill of Rights?

In the United States, the Bill of Rights consists of the first ten amendments to the Constitution, guaranteeing to the people freedom of speech and press, trial by jury, and other rights of a free nation. In England it is an act of Parliament which states certain fundamentals of English liberty. It was passed in 1689, after the revolution which forced King James II from the throne. France has several bills of rights. See BILL OF RIGHTS.

What is the difference between the British Empire and the British Commonwealth of Nations?

The British Commonwealth of Nations is composed of the dominions of Canada, Australia, Union of South Africa, New Zealand, and the United Kingdom of Great Britain and Northern Ireland. The British Empire consists of the Commonwealth, the Indian Empire, the colonies, and other possessions of England. See BRITISH COMMONWEALTH OF NATIONS; BRITISH EMPIRE.

Copyright 1937, 1940, 1942, 1944, 1945, 1947
PUBLISHERS PRODUCTIONS, INC.
Chicago

Printed in U.S.A.

NORTHERN EUROPE'S WATER HIGHWAY—THE BALTIC SEA

BAL'TIC SEA. A water highway for all Northern Europe, the Baltic Sea connects eight European nations directly by water. To Latvia, Germany, Lithuania, Denmark, Estonia, Russia, Finland, and Sweden, it is a life line to the outside world in time of peace.

Four hundred miles in width and 950 miles long at its greatest dimensions, the Baltic is the outlet for more than 250 rivers, whose fresh-water flow has caused that sea to be only about one-third as salty as the ocean. Its various shallows and stormy winds make the Baltic a hazardous passageway for the vast shipping traffic for which it is famous.

The Baltic is divided into two sections by a chain of islands; the northern section includes the Gulf of Bothnia, whose entrance is controlled by Russia. The southern portion is connected with the North Sea by the Kiel Canal across North Germany. Because they hold these strategic points, Germany and Soviet Russia could easily control the entire Baltic Sea in wartime.

BALTIMORE, *bawl'ti more,* MD. Associated with Southern traditions, the Revolution, and the writing of the *Star-Spangled Banner,* home of Johns Hopkins University, and metropolis of Maryland, Baltimore is a city possessing interest and distinction. Situated on the north shore of the Patapsco River, fourteen miles from Chesapeake Bay, it is an Atlantic port of major rank, for the river is a wide and deep estuary of the bay. The city is ninety-four miles south of Philadelphia and forty-two miles northeast of Washington, and is conveniently located with respect to ocean commerce, Middle West and Eastern markets, and trade by way of the Panama Canal.

Founded in 1729 and named for the pioneers of Maryland colony, George Calvert and his son Cecil (Lords Baltimore), the city was incorporated in 1796. Between the War of 1812 and the Civil War, the fast "Baltimore clippers" were making the place a great shipping center. Baltimore enjoyed steady growth after the war, and

BRIGHT-COLORED SONGSTERS

Two Baltimore orioles (top and center) and an orchard oriole.

at the census of 1940, with a population of 859,100, it was the seventh city in the United States.

BALTIMORE ORIOLE, HANGBIRD, FIREBIRD, or GOLDEN ROBIN. Related to the blackbird family, the Baltimore oriole is about seven inches long. Its head, back, wings, and tail are black, but the rest of its body is a brilliant orange. The bird is commonly found in the United States and in Southern Canada. The female builds a long, pouch-like nest of string and plant fibers, while Mr. Oriole sits and sings his clear, sweet song. The nest is so well made that no rain can enter it, and even strong winds will not shake it from the limb to which it is attached. The bird received the name Baltimore because he wears the orange and black colors of Lord Baltimore.

BALUCHISTAN, *ba lu chi stahn'.* Rugged and mountainous, a land of sandy deserts and few water holes, Baluchistan lies to the west of India in a direct line with Persia. Asiatic tribes, led by powerful native chiefs, roam its hills; a "khan," or native ruler, is given a certain amount of authority by the British government.

Since the nineteenth century, British commissioners have been sent to Baluchistan, although until the latter part of the century the country was always regarded as independent. Since then it has been under the influence of Great Britain and is governed as a province of India. From Quetta, the capital city, the British rule directly over one-third of the land. The remainder of the country is governed through the tribal chieftains. Although there is much waste land, considerable cotton, indigo, and a variety of fruits are raised. Date palms are found in quantity in the southwest. The area of the country is 134,002 square miles. The total population is about 858,000, over ninety per cent of whom are Mohammedans.

BAMBOO'. Anyone who has fished or pole-vaulted is familiar with bamboo. Strong and flexible, it is the largest member of the grass family, growing in abundance in tropical countries.

Although bamboo is used in northern countries to a large extent, it is in the tropics that it has its greatest usefulness. Some bamboo stems grow to ten inches in diameter and from 50 to 125 feet in height. These larger stems are hard enough and strong enough to be used in building houses. Natives also use bamboo for bridges, water pipes, tables, stools, toys, masts for boats, floor mats, boxes, ladders, fences, paper and baskets.

In America and Europe, bamboo is used to manufacture special kinds of paper, walking sticks, and sports equipment. The seeds of certain species of bamboo can be eaten, and in some countries the

Courtesy United Fruit Co.

THE GERM-PROOF HEALTH FRUIT—FROM TREE TO TABLE

Bananas grow in huge, upthrusting bunches on big-leafed tropic plants (right). They are carried out of the jungle-like plantations on pack mules (upper left), which take them to the railways. Later, thousands of miles away, bananas make an appetizing centerpiece (lower left).

young shoots are pickled for food. They are often used in chop suey.

Bamboo is found growing in the Philippine Islands, Southern Asia, Japan, the East Indies, and in parts of South America and Africa. Some varieties have been successfully grown in California and Florida. The root from which the round, jointed stalks grow is long, thick, and creeping. From the joints spring several shoots with one or two rigid spines. Flowers grow in large clusters from the joints of the stalk. The leaves are oval, and are eight or nine inches long.

BANANA, *ba nah'na*. Here is a fruit that is germ-proof and dirt-proof. The skin of the banana keeps out all bacteria. If it were not for this protective covering, people living outside the tropics might not be able to enjoy this fruit. In fact, the banana was long unknown in America because shippers believed the fruit would spoil before it arrived.

Shortly after the end of the Civil War, a New England ship captain brought the first shipment of bananas to the United States. At Jamaica he loaded his ship with green bananas. When he landed at Boston, after a fast trip, the fruit was a golden yellow. Thus began an important trade, for now the people of the United States and Canada consume about 70,000,000 bunches of bananas a year. The bulk of the banana crop is produced in the West Indies and in Central and South America.

The banana plant is not a tree but an herb with an underground stem. The trunk, which may be thirty feet high, is not really a trunk but a sheath of leaves with a channel in the center, up which the flower grows. The bud which forms the fruit grows from the top of the plant and bends down toward the ground. A person who has seen bananas hanging in a grocery store might be surprised to know that the bananas on the plant grow in the opposite direction. He might say that the bananas grow upside down; but it is the grocer who changes things, for he hangs the bananas with the tops down.

When bananas reach the proper size, but while they are still green, a man slits the trunk with a sharp knife. The weight of the fruit slowly bends the trunk until the worker can reach the fruit. He then cuts off the bunch and places it on a cart to be sent to market. In this way it is possible to market the fruit without damaging it. Each plant bears just one bunch of fruit. After the fruit is removed, the plant is cut down.

Unlike other fruits, bananas have no particular season. They ripen the year round because a new plant begins to grow from the stem of the one that has been cut down. A new plant completes its growth and bears fruit in less than two years.

Whether eaten cooked or raw, the banana is a delicious, healthful food. A green banana, however, should never be eaten raw, because it is very hard to digest and has an unpleasant flavor. When the yellow skin is flecked with brown, the banana is sweet and easily digested. It is rich in fruit sugars.

Courtesy United Fruit Co.

THE BEGINNING AND THE END OF A BANANA PLANT

This shapeless mass of earth and rootlets (left) is the rhizome, or rootstock, of a banana plant. It will produce a large number of fruitful shoots, but usually only two or three are allowed to develop, to prevent crowding. Each plant produces just one bunch like the one the boy (right) is carrying.

Music
on the
March ~

BAND. Everyone loves a parade. There are few things more thrilling than a column of men or women marching to the strains of stirring music, or the line of colorful, decorated floats passing down the street. But try to imagine a parade without a band! There would be no gay, brilliant drum major with his high hat and twirling baton; no throbbing beat of the drum or blaring trumpets.

Of course, bands do more than march in parades, but the real purpose of a band is to play while moving, and it is this that distinguishes it from an orchestra. Since it would not be easy for musicians to play their violins, 'cellos, and bass viols while walking, the band ensemble uses only instruments that can be blown, like cornets, tubas, saxophones, trombones, French horns, and clarinets, and those that can be beaten, like snare drums, bass drums, cymbals, and chimes.

The most famous American band is the United States Marine Band of Washington, D. C. It plays on such important occasions as the President's inauguration and special services. In England are the Royal Artillery and Royal Marine bands. For many years the Queen's Own Band of Toronto was a leading Canadian organization. Some bands are mounted on horseback, presenting a spectacular sight whenever they parade. In Holland there is an army band on bicycles.

CRASHING CYMBALS, THROBBING DRUMS, AND SOFT REEDS

Drums and cymbals keep the rhythm and reed instruments lend fullness to the modern band. The bassoon and clarinet (left) are wood-wind instruments, while the saxophone is a combination of brass and reed, blown like a clarinet, but possessing a louder and fuller tone. The sarrusophone (right) also combines the reed with brass.

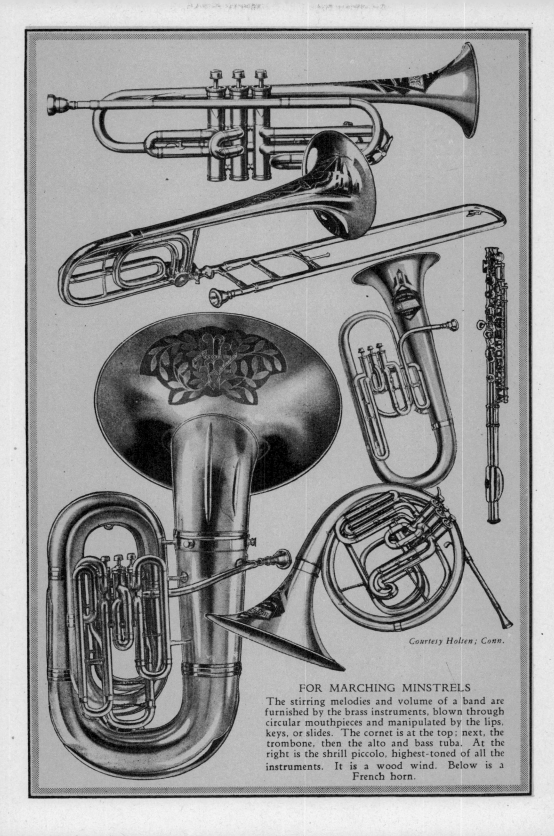

Courtesy Holten; Conn.

FOR MARCHING MINSTRELS

The stirring melodies and volume of a band are
furnished by the brass instruments, blown through
circular mouthpieces and manipulated by the lips,
keys, or slides. The cornet is at the top; next, the
trombone, then the alto and bass tuba. At the
right is the shrill piccolo, highest-toned of all the
instruments. It is a wood wind. Below is a
French horn.

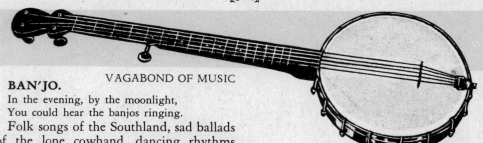

VAGABOND OF MUSIC

BAN'JO.

In the evening, by the moonlight,
You could hear the banjos ringing.

Folk songs of the Southland, sad ballads of the lone cowhand, dancing rhythms from "Tin Pan Alley," all find sympathetic support in the strumming of this friendly musical instrument.

The banjo has a drumlike head resembling a heavy tambourine, and a fretted neck, like a guitar's. It is played by stopping the five to nine strings with the fingers of one hand, and plucking or striking them with thumb and fingers of the other hand. Sometimes a celluloid pick is used to sound the strings. In this way, melody and harmonization can be played, singly or combined. Banjos cost from a few dollars for an acceptable instrument up to a thousand dollars for one used by professional experts, depending on the workmanship and tone.

Young moderns find it quite easy to acquire considerable skill on the banjo, without the help of a teacher, and so contribute substantially to their own good times.

BANK OF ENGLAND. See BANKS AND BANKING.

BANK OF THE UNITED STATES. Today, every American town of any size has one or more banks. There are thousands of such institutions throughout the country, and their total resources run well over 100 billion dollars. All of them are privately owned, by individuals or groups, and are regulated by state and national laws. But in the first years of independence, when the United States was a young and struggling nation, a means of paying its debts and issuing sound money was urgently needed. There were only three banks in the United States at that time, and they were not prepared to handle all the banking business of the nation.

Alexander Hamilton, the first Secretary of the Treasury, decided that a bank, chartered and supported by the Federal government, would solve the problem. In 1791, despite opposition, a Bank of the United States, in Philadelphia, was chartered for twenty years. It had a capital of $10,000,000, one-fifth supplied by the government, and had the power to issue national currency. Branches were formed in eight cities. Opposition to the bank continued, however, and at the end of twenty years the charter was not renewed.

After the War of 1812, American finances were again in disorder. Paper money had lost much of its value and business demanded another Bank of the United States. A second bank was chartered in 1816, with a capital of $35,000,000 and twenty-five branches. It operated successfully until Andrew Jackson, President of the United States, vetoed the act to renew its charter, in 1832. During Van Buren's administration, the present independent Treasury system was adopted and took over the work of handling government funds.

BANKS, SAVINGS. See SAVINGS BANKS.

BANKS AND BANKING. One of the most important institutions in any community is the bank. Through it, stores, factories, farms, and railroads can borrow money—cash and credit to tide them over poor seasons, meet emergency expenses, make improvements. The bank helps new businesses to get started. It provides a safe place for savings and securities and a convenient system for exchanging money; it helps administer estate and other affairs.

MASSIVE COLUMNS SYMBOLIC OF STABILITY

The modern bank building is an architectural monument to security.

TEMPLES OF FINANCE

Banks line historic Lombard Street in London (left), financial center of the British Empire. The shield is the ancient emblem of a long-established house. Above, the Bank of England, called "The Old Lady of Threadneedle Street."

In addition, many banks issue money under the regulation of the national government.

When banks fail, the business life of a community slows up, resulting in hardship for its citizens. When banks are open and loaning money, business life in the community thrives. Business depends on banks, and banks, in turn, depend on the faith of the people of the community.

Three Kinds of Banks. There are three types of banks in the United States: the *national* bank, the *state* bank, and the *private* bank. The national bank is an institution organized by five or more persons granted authority to issue bank notes on condition of investing their capital stock in United States government bonds. In towns having a population of 3,000 or less, national banks must have a fund of at least $25,000, which is called the *capital stock*. Large city banks must have a minimum capital of $100,000. National banks are inspected regularly by examiners who act under the supervision of the Federal Comptroller of the Currency.

State banks are chartered by the state and regulated by its laws. They are examined by employes of the state. Some states do not allow private banks because of the difficulty of supervision by state authorities. This type of bank is owned by one person, or a group of persons.

Forerunners of Modern Banks. As long as men have engaged in trade and used money, there have been banks. The earliest institutions, however, were different from modern banks, for they merely exchanged money. The first bank we have definite knowledge of was the Bank of Venice, founded in 1171, which existed for more than 600 years. As time went on, banks were founded in most important cities of Europe and they expanded their functions. They began to accept money for safekeeping, and paid a fee to the person entrusting it to them for its use. This gave rise to the practice of paying interest to depositors.

Courtesy First National Bank of Atlanta

TWENTIETH-CENTURY TREASURE CHEST

Tons of steel and concrete guard valuables stored in the vault seen through the circular opening. Nothing can open this ponderous armored door once it has been closed, for the machinery which moves its great bolts operates by a time clock set for a certain hour.

They also loaned money and charged the person who borrowed it a fee based upon the amount of money he borrowed. This was the way loaning at interest began. The modern system of issuing checks and drafts was started about the beginning of the seventeenth century.

Domestic Developments. The first bank chartered in the United States opened in 1780, but it was rechartered by Pennsylvania the following year. The first real national bank was the Bank of the United States. Since 1863 banks and the government have been separated, except for examination and regulation. The National Banking Act of that year was for the purpose of selling United States bonds and stabilizing money. For fifty years this act

proved sufficient for the banks of the country. In 1913 the Federal Reserve System was created in order that there might be better control of bank reserves and a more flexible money system.

Under the act of 1913, twelve Federal Reserve districts were formed with a bank for each. Each national bank was required to buy stock in the Reserve Bank, which had a fixed capital of $4,000,000. The purpose of the Reserve Banks is to serve as a depository for the funds of its member banks. Each Reserve Bank is managed by a board of nine directors. Over all is the Board of Governors of the Federal Reserve system, composed of the Secretary of the Treasury, the Comptroller of Currency, and five other members appointed

"SPOOK" OF THE FOREST

Like an eery denizen of a haunted wilderness, the banyan tree looks as if it were created by a witch's wand. It is, in fact, almost like a story-book tree, for its branches take root, forming a twisted maze of trunks.

by the President for fourteen-year terms, each at a salary of $15,000 per year.

Banking laws were changed again in 1933 to provide more stability for banks and greater security for depositors. The two most important provisions of the act were that commercial banks were prohibited from dealing in securities, and that bank deposits would be insured by the Federal government. Deposits up to $5,000 are insured 100 per cent.

Banks Abroad. Banks are much the same all over the world, although each country has an individual system. In England the Bank of England is the most important institution. It was incorporated in 1694, and received the power to issue money and to handle all the banking business of the country through branch banks. The gold of the government is stored in its vaults.

The Bank of France is similar to the Bank of England. Founded in 1800, it has the sole right to issue paper money in France, and has often aided the government in times of distress. Banks of other countries in Europe follow systems resembling the French.

BANTU, *bahn'too.* This is the general name given to a language group of Negroid tribes which includes the Kaffirs, Zulus, Bechuanas, and others of Central and Southeastern Africa. There are more than 270 Bantu dialects, spoken by 50,000,000 people, or more than a third of the continent's population.

BAN'YAN, or BAN'IAN. Not all trees grow from the ground up; in India there is a strange variety of fig tree whose branches send out shoots which grow downward and take root in the ground. The supports thus formed enlarge into trunks which grow more branches, and the same process is repeated. These are the banyan trees, each one covering a large area of ground. On the island of Ceylon there is a single tree which has 350 major trunks and more than 3,000 minor ones. It is said that some specimens form a natural circular temple, 1,000 feet in diameter. Although the wood is of little value, gum lac comes from the bark.

BAP'TISM. One of the great religious ceremonies of the Christian Church is baptism, in which a person is symbolically purified by being dipped in water or washed or sprinkled with it. The rite represents admittance to the Church or the removal of the stain of sin from the soul, and is performed in different ways by different sects. It is thought to have been first used by the Jews, before the time of Jesus. Although Jesus Himself never baptized converts, He ordered His disciples to do so (*Matt.* XXVIII, 19).

The person to be baptized in the primitive Church was dipped in a river or vessel, "in the name of the Father, and of the Son, and of the Holy Ghost." Sprinkling was used only for persons unable to leave their beds. Now, however, most Protestant sects allow pouring or sprinkling. The Baptists are an exception, requiring that baptism be complete immersion for those who can make a personal confession of faith. The Greek Church and various Eastern sects also retain the custom of complete immersion.

Courtesy Canadian Pacific

WHERE WINTER NEVER COMES

Tiny Barbados, an island lying off the northeastern coast of South America, is the most densely populated land in the world, excepting China. Its climate is warm the year around, one of the reasons for its 184,000 inhabitants.

BAP'TISTS. This is the name of a large division of the Protestant Church whose members hold that baptism should be given only to those who have made a personal confession of faith. Another, and perhaps better known, teaching which distinguishes the Baptist Church is that complete immersion is the only true baptism.

The first Baptist organization in America was founded by Roger Williams, at Providence, R. I., in 1639. Since then this sect has grown to be one of the largest religious groups in the United States, with an estimated membership of more than 10,000,000 communicants.

BARBADOS, *bahr ba' doze.* Sugar cane, coffee, and tobacco come from densely populated Barbados, easternmost island of the British West Indies. It has been a British possession since 1625, and at present is headquarters for the English West India forces. In the year 1752, Bar-

bados was visited by George Washington and his invalid brother, Lawrence.

The soil on the island is very fertile, and produces important crops of cotton, indigo, and arrowroot, as well as sugar cane. Leading industries are sugar refining and the manufacture of rum. Fisheries are also important. Barbados is governed by an elected assembly and a staff appointed by the king, including a governor, an executive committee, and a legislative council. Bridgetown is the capital. According to recent estimates, Barbados has a population of about 202,000, with colored inhabitants predominating. Its area is 166 square miles.

BAR'BARY. In all the history of the sea, there were few pirates more fierce and treacherous than the Moors who preyed upon ships off the Barbary coast of North Africa until the beginning of the nineteenth century. Vessels sailing the blue

Ewing Galloway

IN CATALONIA'S CAPITAL

waters of the Mediterranean Sea were constantly plagued by the pirate ships, and many merchant sailors were killed trying to protect valuable cargoes. All during the sixteenth, seventeenth, and eighteenth centuries this condition existed, and exceptional was the crew that was not warned as it sailed into the Mediterranean, "Beware of the Barbary pirates!"

At last, after many American cargo ships had been seized by the pirates and tribute exacted for the release of hostages, the United States declared war on the pirates. Commodore Stephen Decatur was dispatched to their ports in command of a naval squadron of nine ships and, in 1815, succeeded in making their leaders sign treaties of peace. From that time on, the Barbary coast was safe for American ships.

This territory of North Africa, known as Barbary, took its name from the Berbers, who are the original inhabitants. The countries include Morocco, Algeria, Tunisia, and Libya, controlled largely by Spain, France, and Italy. In addition to the Berbers and Moors, there are many Arabs, Jews, Turks, and some European colonists. Barbary was a rich territory in the time of Carthaginian power, under Roman provincial rule, and during the supremacy of the Italian states. See DECATUR, STEPHEN.

BARCELONA, *bahr se lo'nah,* SPAIN. The ancient city of Barcelona is located in Northeastern Spain, on the Mediterranean coast. It is the greatest seaport and industrial center in the country, and before the Spanish Civil War it was the largest city of the republic. Its chief manufactures include cotton, woolen, and silk goods, chemicals, glass, and metal products. The population is estimated at about 1,400,000.

In medieval times, Barcelona was the capital of the kingdom of Catalonia. After the Spanish revolution of 1932, the city was the capital of the autonomous region of Catalonia; and in 1937, during the Civil War, it became the Loyalist capital. Although it was so heavily besieged by General Franco's forces that much of the city was destroyed, Barcelona resisted capture for two years. After the war, the new Fascist government began to rebuild the city.

BARD. Long before Wales and the other parts of the British Isles united, there were men in Britain who composed and sang verses to honor the chiefs of their tribes. They sang of brave deeds and battles to the accompaniment of a harp, and many of their songs became known throughout the land. The bards were very popular at banquets and courts, and their art of entertaining was passed on from father to son.

In the thirteenth century, Wales was conquered by King Edward I of England, who is said to have hanged all Welsh bards because their songs inspired the people with a spirit of rebellion. It was upon this incident that Thomas Gray based his famous poem, *The Bard.* Some ancient Welsh ballads still exist, furnishing a bright chapter in the history of English literature. Bards also lived in Gaul before the time of Christ, but none of their songs are known today.

BA′RIUM. A soft, yellowish metal of many uses, barium is necessary to the manufacture of peroxide, a bleach and disinfectant. Its products also are used in the manufacture of automobile tires, paper, printer's ink, rat poison, high-grade optical glass, dyes, photographic material, fireworks, detonators, and railroad signals. Formations of lime deposits in water are often prevented through the use of barium hydrate. The metal is found naturally only in compounds, and was first isolated from other elements by Sir Humphry Davy in 1808. Its symbol is *Ba*.

ESKIMO OF THE GRAINS
Because it is hardy, barley is grown farther north than other cereals.

BAR′LEY. An important cereal grain, barley has been known for thousands of years. Kernels of it have been found in ancient Egyptian tombs. In fact, it is probable that barley was known to man long before the dawn of history. It is grown farther north than any other cereal, as, for example, in Iceland and Alaska; and it is also grown in countries of the world farther south, as in India and North Africa. The grain in appearance greatly resembles wheat.

Barley has long been used in Europe as a bread grain and also as feed for horses, cattle, and pigs. It is also one of the chief grains used in brewing beer. In the United States barley was seldom used as a food until Americans had to save their wheat supply for the soldiers fighting in France during the World War. Barley contains much starch and is very nourishing.

The United States produces about one-eighth of the world's barley crop, California, Minnesota, North Dakota, Wisconsin, and South Dakota being the chief barley-producing states. Russia, Germany, Austria, and Hungary are the leading European producers, though England grows the best barley for malting.

BAR′NACLE. Every reader of sea stories has heard of ships covered with barnacles. These little shell-covered, saltwater animals are found attached to ship bottoms, sunken timber, shells, and other submerged objects. Barnacles live almost everywhere in salt seas, but are not found in fresh waters. They feed on small animals of the sea brought within their reach by the water. Some of the larger barnacles are edible.

SEA NUISANCES
Barnacles, which thrive in salt water, are troublesome pests to ships, despite their minute size.

BARN'UM. PHINEAS TAYLOR (1810-1891). The greatest showman of his time, Barnum believed that the American people loved to be "humbugged," and upon this principle he earned great sums and a reputation as a natural-born promoter. No one since his time has been his equal in the art of coaxing dollars from the credulous public. Barnum's plan was to create public interest by advertising, and then to satisfy the patron's curiosity by whatever means available. His varied career represents a mixture of boldness, astuteness, and good fortune.

Barnum was born at Bethel, Conn., the son of a tavern keeper. As a boy he was constantly playing tricks upon his father's customers. As a young man he devoted himself to the lottery business and newspaper editing. In 1834 he first entered the show business by buying Joyce Heth, a negro slave that Barnum advertised as George Washington's nurse, 160 years old. With her and a small company he toured the country giving exhibitions, and made a large profit. When Joyce died, two years later, it was found that she was not older than seventy.

After losing most of his money, Barnum, in 1841, managed to buy Scudder's American Museum in New York. He became wealthy again by exhibiting in the museum various false freaks and curiosities, and also the famous dwarf, Charles Stratton, whom Barnum "ballyhooed" as General Tom Thumb. In 1844 Barnum toured Europe exhibiting this miniature man.

Barnum's next find was Jenny Lind, the Swedish soprano, with whom he went on a successful tour across the United States. He paid her $1,000 a night to sing for 150 nights, making for himself a profit of $700,000. Sometimes the admission tickets were sold at auctions and brought almost unbelievable prices. Poverty and riches again alternated, and Barnum also tried his luck at politics. There he was unsuccessful.

In 1871 the American public was startled by announcements of the "Greatest Show on Earth." This huge spectacle consisted of a traveling museum, menagerie, and circus, requiring 500 men and horses and 100 railroad cars to move it around the country. The famous "Barnum and Bailey's," beloved of children the country over, represented the merger, in 1881, of the Barnum spectacle and the circus of a successful imitator, J. A. Bailey. In 1907 the "Greatest Show on Earth" was sold to Ringling Brothers. Millions of people have seen this show, and the public never seems to tire of it.

Barnum wrote a story of his life in which he revealed many of the ways in which he had tricked the public. An entertaining biography entitled *Barnum,* by M. R. Werner, was the basis of the moving picture, *The Great Barnum.*

Courtesy Taylor Instrument Co.

ANEROID BAROMETER

BAROM'ETER. In stories of the sea, we sometimes read of the captain's anxiety as he watches the steady "falling of the glass." What is referred to is the falling of mercury in the barometer, a device that foretells the approach of a storm by recording changes in air pressure. The barometer is not only necessary to navigators. It is also helpful on land, being used to gauge the height of mountains, as well as for weather predictions.

It is a well-known fact that the pressure

of air decreases before a storm and increases in fair weather. Therefore, when the barometer shows that the air pressure is becoming less (a "falling" barometer), unsettled weather or a storm is indicated. When the air pressure rises (a "rising" barometer), the weather will be fair. A high, steady barometer reading indicates settled weather.

Besides the mercurial barometer, there is a fluidless type known as the *aneroid* barometer. This is a portable device especially useful on land. In the mercurial barometer, the air exerts a pressure on mercury, causing it to register on a graded scale. At sea level the atmosphere will register a pressure on a column of mercury which is about thirty inches high under normal conditions. The aneroid barometer, in which the air exerts a pressure on light, flexible metal, indicates the pressure by a needle on a circular gauge.

Air pressure changes with variations in altitude as well as with changes in weather. The higher the altitude, the less pressure the air exerts. Therefore, the barometer reading decreases as a mountain is ascended. Since 30 is the barometer

IT TELLS THE WEATHER

A barograph like this gives an accurate record of the weather for an entire week. It is a form of barometer.

Courtesy Taylor Instrument Co.

How to Construct a BAROMETER

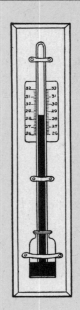

TAKE a glass tube, 34 inches long, 1/8 of an inch in diameter inside, and sealed at one end, and fill it completely with mercury. Then, take a small bottle, one inch in diameter inside and two inches high; next put a little paraffin in it and melt it by holding the bottle over a small flame. The paraffin should cover the bottom of the bottle to a depth of 1/16 of an inch when cool.

Now, place the bottle over the open end of the tube and press it down firmly so that the tube enters the wax and makes an airtight fit. The bottle and tube may then be inverted. Pour a few ounces of mercury into the bottle, and then raise the tube out of the wax, but be careful not to bring the tube above the surface of the mercury in the bottle.

The barometer base is made of wood, about three inches wide, 40 inches long, and about 7/8 of an inch thick. A groove should be chiseled lengthwise to fit the tube, and at the bottom a place should be carved out so that one-half the diameter of the bottle may rest in it. The tube and bottle are then placed on the base. The scale may be made on a strip of cardboard two inches wide.

Mark off six inches, divide each into sixteenths, and number the inch lines from 26 to 32. The scale may be fastened to the base with either glue or tacks, and should be placed either behind or beside the tube. Before fastening the scale, compare the instrument with a standard barometer, and adjust it so that the readings on the scales correspond.

reading at sea level, it is possible to tell the height of any place above sea level by the pressure registered.

The principle of the barometer is based on an experiment performed in 1643 by Torricelli, a pupil of Galileo. Torricelli filled a glass tube, over thirty inches long, with mercury, inverted it in a bowl of mercury, and observed that the column of mercury stood about thirty inches high in the tube. The column was being held up by the fluid in the bowl, which was under the pressure of the atmosphere. From this humble beginning, the modern barometer evolved.

BARON, *bair'on.* In the year 1066, after William the Conqueror subdued England, he rewarded his bravest men with land and called them barons. They were distinguished as greater or lesser barons by the size of their estates. Gradually the lesser barons became dependent on the greater barons, who became known as dukes and earls. Baron has thus become the lowest ranking English title of nobility.

Barons, nevertheless, may sit in the House of Lords in the British Parliament, and are addressed as "My Lord" or "Your Lordship." A baron's wife is called "Madam" or "Your Ladyship." The king often honors distinguished men with the title of baron. That of baronet ranks between the titles baron and knight. A baronet is not permitted to sit in the House of Lords. Instead of "My Lord," he is addressed as "Sir." The title of baron is used in continental Europe as well as in Great Britain.

BARRACUDA, *bair a ku'dah.* Because of its ferocious disposition, the barracuda, which is found in warm ocean waters, is known as "the Tiger of the Sea." Fishermen who like a stiff fight enjoy catching the barracuda. It is claimed that this fish is even more dangerous than the shark; and it is greatly feared by those unprepared for an encounter. The *great* barracuda, from six to eight feet in length, is found off the coast of Florida and around the West Indies; the five-foot *silver* barracuda inhabits California waters, where it is caught for food. Barracuda are related to the gray mullets.

BARRIE, *bair'ie,* James Matthew, Sir (1860-1937). If Sir James M. Barrie had written only the beautiful story of *Peter Pan,* he would be remembered by the world as a great writer. The adventures of Peter, Wendy, Tinker Bell, and the big dog Nana, in Never-Never Land, are known everywhere.

Sir James, however, wrote many other novels and plays that the world cherishes. The majority of them deal with the humble, simple life of his native Scotland. His stories include *Auld Licht Idylls, A Window in Thrums, The Little Minister, Sentimental Tommy, Tommy and Grizel, Margaret Ogilvy,* and *The Little White Bird.*

The numerous plays he wrote offer the same tender qualities as his stories, and several of them have been made into motion pictures. Among these dramatic writings are *The Professor's Love Story, The Admirable Crichton, A Kiss for Cinderella, Alice-sit-by-the-fire, Quality Street, What Every Woman Knows, The Legend of Leonora,* and the dramatization of *Peter Pan.* Based on the World War are his *Old Lady Shows Her Medals, The New Word, A Well-Remembered Voice,* all one-act plays, and *Dear Brutus,* a full-length drama.

Barrie, who was born in Kirriemuir, Scotland, was knighted by King George V in 1913. He was educated at Edinburgh University.

BARRIER REEF, Great. Off the northeast coast of Australia stretches the Great Barrier Reef, the longest in the world. For 1,250 miles it follows the coast line, in some places only a few miles from the shore, and in others more than a hundred miles out. This chain of coral reefs encloses an inland passage for ships, a "canal" set apart from the rough waters of the ocean.

But there are dangers, too, within the

barrier. Navigators must know just where hidden rocks and reefs lurk beneath the surface and be able to avoid shipwreck; and sometimes hurricanes strike terror into sailors' hearts. Pearl oysters abound in the waters of the reef; pearls and mother-of-pearl are, therefore, important products of this region.

BARRY, JOHN (1745-1803). Excluding John Paul Jones, John Barry was probably the most prominent American naval commander during the Revolutionary War. Because of his efforts to make his country strong at sea, he has been called "the father of the American navy." Born in Ireland, he migrated to America when a young man, and soon acquired a fleet of vessels. By the time the Revolutionary War began, he had become wealthy according to the standards of the day.

Having thrown in his lot with the Revolutionists, Barry was offered a commission as captain, and in 1776, when commanding the *Lexington,* he accomplished the first capture of a British ship—the *Edward*. Thereafter, he had defeats as well as successes, and was wounded in one battle. Barry was promoted to the rank of commodore in 1794.

BARTHOL'OMEW'S DAY, SAINT. A feast celebrated August 24 by the Catholic Church, this Saint's day is in honor of Saint Bartholomew, one of the twelve apostles.

Massacre of Saint Bartholomew's Day. On the tragic eve of Saint Bartholomew's Day, in 1572, soldiers of the House of Guise gathered secretly beneath a tower of the royal palace of France to await a signal that plunged France into a night of horror. Under orders from King Charles IX, the soldiers fell upon thousands of unsuspecting men, women, and children of the Protestant faith, and put them to death.

This mass murder was the outgrowth of a long war between the Duke of Guise and the Catholics on one hand, and the House of Condé and the Protestant Huguenots on the other. A treaty of peace was signed in 1570 that only deceived the Huguenots and left them unprepared for treachery. Catharine de Medici, mother of King Charles, persuaded him to order the slaughter, by telling him that Admiral Coligny, the Huguenot chief, was plotting against his life. Catharine afterward forced her son to assume the entire blame, and it is said he died of remorse for his part in the massacre.

BARTON, CLARA (1821-1912). Every American who has received aid in times of disaster venerates the name of Clara Barton, the founder of the American Red Cross. This angel of mercy and kindness was born in Oxford, Mass., and when a young woman she taught school. At the outbreak of the Civil War, she devoted herself to the care of wounded soldiers both on the battlefield and in the hospitals, winning the undying gratitude and devotion of an entire army by her unselfish sacrifice and service.

After giving additional services in the Franco-German War of 1870, Clara Barton returned to America to establish an American branch of the International Red Cross, which had headquarters at Geneva, Switzerland. In 1881 she became its first president, a position she held until 1904. She was responsible for the amendment which provided that the Red Cross would give relief in epidemics and disasters, as well as in time of war. Under her personal direction, the American Red Cross provided relief for sufferers in many major disasters in different parts of the world. See RED CROSS SOCIETIES.

BASE. In chemistry, a base is a compound which will unite with an acid to form a salt. A base always contains some kind of mineral, and when combined with an acid, this mineral replaces the hydrogen present in the acid. The result is something entirely new—a salt. In some cases, however, some of the hydrogen remains in the new compound, so that the salt formed has some acid in it. Lime, known in chemistry as calcium oxide, is one of the more common bases.

BATTER UP!

Courtesy P. Goldsmith Sons, Inc.

BASEBALL. No other sport in America can compare with baseball for excitement, interest, and thrills for players and spectators alike. It is played the country over in lonely hamlets and huge cities, by men and boys, by rich and poor. Professional and amateur games are watched by millions of "fans" every year. Countless other millions follow the fortunes of their teams by radio and through newspapers day by day, studying league standings and records of individual players. Baseball is America's national sport.

Big Leagues of America. Although in America baseball is played by thousands of different groups, the two major leagues of professional players capture the greatest interest. The oldest of these leagues is the National League, composed of these eight teams: the Cincinnati "Reds," the New York "Giants," the Boston "Bees," the Philadelphia "Phillies," the Pittsburgh "Pirates," the Chicago "Cubs," the Saint Louis "Cardinals," and the Brooklyn "Dodgers." Its younger rival, the American League, is also composed of eight teams: the New York "Yankees," the Boston "Red Sox," the Washington "Senators," the Philadelphia "Athletics," the Detroit "Tigers," the Cleveland "Indians," the Chicago "White Sox," and the Saint Louis "Browns."

From April until late September, the teams in each league play one another. Then, at the end of the regular season, the winners from each league, those having the best percentage of games won and lost, meet for the climax of the year, the World Series. The winner of this event, determined by whichever team wins four games in a series of seven, is considered the champion team of the year.

Minor Leagues. Even though the greatest interest is in the major leagues, there are numerous minor professional leagues that play before large crowds throughout the baseball season. These leagues are scattered from coast to coast and from Canada to the Gulf of Mexico. The major leagues usually draw upon these teams for new players. In addition, there are amateur, college, high-school, and grade-school teams and leagues by the thousands, so that American boys cannot grow up without having seen, played, or, at least, heard about baseball.

Rules of the Game. Baseball was unknown before 1842. Originating probably from the English game of "rounders" and other forms of bat-and-ball pastimes, the first set of rules was drawn up in 1845 by the Knickerbocker Club of New York. During the Civil War, the game was played by the soldiers of both Union and Confederate armies; when the war was over, the men took the game back home, thus spreading it throughout the country. In 1871 the National League was formed; the American League became its rival in 1900. These two leagues have since determined the rules of the game, and these rules are followed by everyone who plays.

Until a comparatively recent date, baseball was played only in the United States. Now, however, the game is well known in Canada, and in Japan it has become one of the most popular sports. It is also played to a certain extent in Australia, England, and some countries in continental Europe and Asia. In all countries it is played in the same manner.

The Diamond. The game can be played on any large field, the size of the parks frequently varying. All *infields,* however, have the same dimensions. An infield is shaped like a diamond, with equal sides ninety feet long. At one corner is *home plate,* and at the other three corners are *first base, second base,* and *third base.* Lines extending from home plate to first base and beyond and from home plate to third base and beyond are known as *foul lines;* in the area between these two lines outside the infield is the *outfield,* divided into *right field, center field,* and *left field.* At a distance of sixty feet, six inches from home plate, on a line to second base, is the *pitcher's box.*

Members of the "Nines." There are nine men to a side in baseball: the *catcher,* who stands behind home plate; the *pitcher;* the *first baseman;* the *second baseman;* the *third baseman;* the *shortstop,* who patrols the area between second and third bases; the *left fielder;* the *right fielder;* and the *center fielder.*

The Innings. Nine *innings,* or periods of play, constitute a game, and the purpose of the game is for one team to win by scoring more *runs* than the other. If the runs are even after nine innings, the teams play extra innings to determine the winner. If, at the end of four and a half innings, bad weather stops the game, the winning team is the one having the most runs at the time the game is stopped.

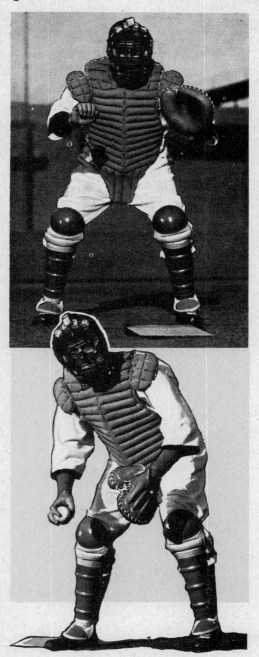

Courtesy Great Western Athletic Goods Co.

BEHIND THE PLATE

Above, the catcher's stance when receiving the pitch. Below, ready to block a runner from third base.

Courtesy Popular Mechanics; Great Western Athletic Goods Co.

HOW HITS ARE MADE

Good batters follow through! Upper left, how the follow-through starts; center, the follow-through completed; right, correct hitting stance. How to bunt and slide are shown in the other pictures.

The Umpires. One or more umpires make the decisions in a baseball game. In most leagues there are at least two umpires for every game, and in important games in the major leagues there are four. One umpire is stationed behind home plate to call *balls* and *strikes*. The others are stationed at the bases to make decisions.

The Players in Action. Let us watch a game in progress to see how it is played. One team is in the field. The pitcher is on his "mound," hoping to prevent the opposing team from making *hits* which might result in runs. Batter No. 1 comes up to the plate. He carries a stick of strong wood, thirty-four inches in length and tapered at one end; this stick is called the *bat*. The pitcher grips the hard, leather-covered, cork-center ball and throws it. It crosses directly above the plate, between the batter's knees and shoulders. Such a pitch is called a *strike*.

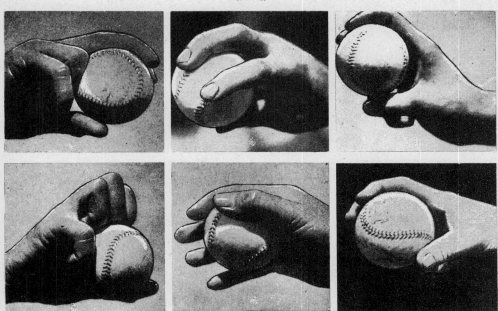

The next pitch is above the batter's shoulders. It is a *ball*. The batter hits the third ball pitched, but it drops to the ground behind the foul lines. It is a *foul ball,* and is strike two. The batter does the same thing with the next pitch, but the "count" remains strike two because only on the first two strikes is a foul considered a strike. The next pitch is below the batter's knees; so it is another ball. The pitcher throws again, and this time the ball goes wide of the plate. That makes the count three balls and two strikes.

If the next pitch is a ball, the batter will take first base without being put out. If it is a strike, or a foul ball that is caught before it touches the ground, he is "out." The pitcher throws again. The batter hits the ball, which bounds along the ground to the shortstop, who fields it and throws to the first baseman. Meanwhile, the batter is running to first base in an attempt to beat the throw. He fails. The play is a *put-out,* and the team at bat has one *out* charged against it.

Another batter comes to the plate. He receives four balls and advances to first

Courtesy A. G. Spalding & Bros. (above); Great Western Athletic Goods Co.

PITCHING POINTERS

Top, left to right, screw ball, fadeaway, fast ball; bottom, knuckle ball, slow ball, curve ball. Lower right, the stance after the follow-through.

base. Batter No. 3 holds his bat high; when the ball is pitched, he does not swing at it but places the bat in the way of the ball. The ball goes only a few feet in front of the plate and is called a *bunt*. As the batter runs toward first base, his teammate on first base runs toward second. The catcher on the other team picks up the ball and throws to first base in time to catch the batter, who is out at first; but the batter has advanced a man to second base and is credited with a *sacrifice hit*.

Batter No. 4, a powerful hitter, takes a heavy swing at the ball and sends it into the outfield. It drops to the ground before one of the outfielders can catch it, and the man on second base runs to third; if it is a long hit, he keeps on and crosses home plate, scoring a *run*. The batter, in the meantime, has run as far as second base on his hit, which is scored as a *double*. The pitcher now throws the ball directly over the plate for batter No. 5, who swings and misses.

The next pitch is directly over the plate for strike two. On the next pitch, the batter again misses for strike three and is out. Since only three outs are allowed, the team at bat is "retired" and takes the field to let the other team come in to bat.

In the half inning described, there were one run, one hit, a base on balls, a sacrifice hit, and a strike-out; and the first man up was put out by the first baseman, assisted by the shortstop. When a batter hits the ball safely so far that he can run around all the bases without being put out, he scores a *home run*.

Running Up a Score. The record of a game is kept in a *box score*. This score gives the name of each player and shows how many times he was at bat, the runs he scored, and the hits, bases on balls, sacrifice hits, stolen bases, put-outs, assists, and errors credited to him. A base on balls and a sacrifice hit do not count as a time at bat.

Because scientific plays are important factors in winning baseball games, managers of teams resort to many devices to score as many runs as possible. For instance, if there are men on first and third bases, the *coach* at first base will give a signal to the man on that base to run to second on the next pitch to the batter. The runner does so; if the catcher throws the ball to second base in an attempt to catch him, the man on third base will run home and score.

If a man runs from one base to another on a pitch when no hit is made and he is not put out, he is credited with a *stolen base*. Another scheme is the *hit-and-run,* attempted when there are one or more men on base. The man on base receives a signal to run as soon as the next ball is pitched. The batter also has received a signal to try to hit the ball regardless of where it crosses the plate; he tries to hit the ball into the area between the runner and the base he has just left. If the batter succeeds, the runner may get to second base or even third base.

Another offensive trick is the *squeeze-play,* resorted to when there is a man on third base and either one or no men out. The man on third receives a signal to start running as soon as the ball is pitched, and the batter bunts the ball. Before the ball can be fielded and thrown, the man on third base is supposed to score a run. It is dangerous, of course, to attempt this play when there are two men out, for the batter may be thrown out at first, in which case the run will not count.

When on the field, players resort to several methods of preventing runs by the opposing team. When there are men on base and a strong hitter is at bat, the batter may be given a base on balls intentionally to prevent his driving in a run, and to make possible an attempt at a *double play* on the next batter, who may be weaker. The double play can be worked in several ways. Most often, however, it is used when there is a man on first base; the batter is made to hit a ball to the second baseman or shortstop, who tags second base or throws to someone who is "covering" the base, forcing the runner out. The ball is then thrown to first base in time to catch the batter. This play must be accomplished swiftly and perfectly.

Pitchers and catchers study the batters they must face through the season, and learn what kind of balls must be thrown to prevent them from hitting too often. With his bare hand the catcher gives signals to the pitcher. Most batters have a habit of hitting to one side of the field; so, whenever a batter with this habit comes to the plate, the team in the field shifts to the side where he usually hits.

Practice Makes Perfect. Baseball players must keep in practice, especially young ones who hope to be stars some day. One of the most important things in fielding is learning how to throw. The ball should be thrown on a line as direct as possible with a snap motion of the arm, rather than a swing. Outfielders must develop their arms to throw far and straight, and infielders must be able to throw fast and straight. Pitchers must learn how to curve and "drop" their pitches by special grips on the ball and by throwing with a twist and snap motion of the wrist. They also must learn control, which is the ability to throw the ball exactly where they want it to go.

In fielding balls that are hit along the ground, a player should hold his feet close together and should "come up with" the ball so that it can be thrown without waste motion. All players must know how to gauge "fly balls" so that they will be under them in time to catch them. In batting, the player should learn how to take an easy swing and meet the ball rather than lunge at it. The left foot of a right-handed hitter should never be drawn back, and the batter should step into the ball.

Heroes of the Diamond. Because of the interest in baseball, good players and teams receive wide publicity. Some of the greatest stars in baseball are "Babe" Ruth, home-run hero of the New York "Yankees"; Ty Cobb, a great base-runner and

Courtesy *Great Western Athletic Goods Co.*

CUTTING OFF HITS
Snappy fielding often changes a likely hit to a put-out. Above, is shown the way first basemen reach for a throw-in. The lower picture shows the proper method to catch a fly ball.

hitter for the Detroit "Tigers"; Honus Wagner, one of the most perfect infielders in the history of baseball; Rogers Hornsby and Frank Frisch, noted for their all-around ability in fielding and hitting; Christy Mathewson, Walter Johnson, Carl Hubbell, and "Dizzy" Dean, famous pitchers; and Lou Gehrig, a star hitter and first baseman, and holder of a record for the greatest number of games played in succession.

Three of the great baseball managers are John J. McGraw, New York "Giants"; Miller Huggins, New York "Yankees"; and Connie Mack, Philadelphia "Athletics."

Softball. A sport that has achieved wide popularity is *softball,* a game similar to baseball but played with a larger and softer ball on a smaller diamond. This sport has become very popular among girls as well as among men and boys. It is also known as *kitten ball* and *indoor baseball.*

A Test of SPEED *and* STAMINA

Courtesy The Athletic Journal

BAS'KET BALL. Today, basket ball is such a popular game in schools and playgrounds and is so widely played all over the country that it is difficult to recognize in it one of the newest of modern sports. Basket ball was invented in 1891 by Dr. James Naismith, who was then an instructor of a gymnasium class at the Y. M. C. A. Training School, Springfield, Mass.

Dr. Naismith devised the game to break up the monotony of wrestling, boxing, and swimming, which were then the only indoor winter sports. He took Rugby football as a model; eliminated kicking and tackling, legalized any form of passing the ball, forbade running with the ball, and

called it basket ball because the manner of scoring was to cage the ball in a peach basket. Later, hoops of heavy wire were substituted as goals.

The game is played by two teams of five men each, the ball being advanced by passing from one player to another or by bouncing (dribbling) the ball on the floor. The aim of each team is to score as many points as possible by tossing the ball into the basket defended by the other team, and to prevent the opposing players from scoring in the basket it is defending.

Each team consists of a *center,* two *forwards,* and two *guards.* The game is divided up into halves in college play, while

Courtesy The Athletic Journal

QUICK THINKING IN HANDLING THE BALL

A good player catches and passes the ball with his hands over the axis. In handling it, he must think fast—an opportunity for a score comes and goes in an instant. Upper left, the player in a position to shoot or pass. Upper right, a one-handed hook shot at the basket. Lower left, a two-handed shot. Lower right, getting ready for a two-handed hook shot.

Courtesy The Athletic Journal

CLOSE GUARDING

These photographs show the methods of guarding the opposing player in a basket-ball game. Upper left, a player tries a one-handed shot while the guard attempts to stop him; upper right, how each man watches his opponent; and, at right, guarding a man to prevent a pass.

most high schools and grade schools divide the game into quarters. At the start of the game, the centers stand within the circle in the center of the floor; the referee throws the ball straight into the air and each center strives to tap it to one of his team mates. Teamwork is essential.

A field goal is a basket scored from play, and counts two points. In case of a "foul," the player fouled receives a free try at the basket from the foul or free-throw line. A successful free throw counts one point. If a player is fouled while making a shot at the basket, he receives two free tosses. If a player makes four fouls, he is disqualified from the game.

In case a player on one team takes more than one step with the ball, steps over the boundary line, or throws the ball over the boundary line, the opposing team receives the ball "out of bounds." The ball cannot be kicked, and opponents must not touch the body of the player having the ball.

Basket ball became an Olympic sport at the games in Berlin in 1936, and was there introduced to the rest of the world.

PRIZES FOR THE ANGLER WHO LIKES A FIGHT

The bass is a good game fish, giving the fisherman a tussle whenever it gets on his line. Left, the large-mouth black bass; right, the calico bass.

BASS. Among the most popular fishes which prey upon other fishes are the different kinds of bass. They excel as game fighters and as food fishes and are probably best known through their small relatives, the sunfish.

The fisherman who has landed a four- or five-pound *small-mouthed black* bass knows well the fighting ability of a fresh-water game fish. The *large-mouthed black* bass live in warmer waters and are not so plucky. In the spring, both of these basses lay their eggs in nests, about 7,000 eggs for each pound in weight of the parent fish. These are guarded by the male parent until the young can shift for themselves. Bass are not so easily reared under artificial conditions as are trout and white-fish.

Rock bass, caught frequently in fresh-water lakes, *warmouth* bass, *crappies* and *calico* bass are other kinds of bass, but are not the equal in quality of the large- and small-mouthed basses.

White bass belong to the same genus as the *striped* bass found in salt water. They rarely exceed eighteen inches in length and two pounds in weight. They are not of the same family as the black bass of fresh water, but belong with the huge *black sea* bass, or *jewfish,* exceeding 300 pounds in weight and well known for its ability as a fighter. Striped bass are salt-water fish which enter fresh water to lay their spawn. They may exceed 100 pounds in weight, and a twelve-pound fish may lay, though it does not protect, 1,280,-000 eggs.

BASSOON'. The bass of the oboe group of wood-wind instruments, the bassoon, is a conical wooden tube eight feet in length, but doubled back upon itself so that the length of the instrument is not more than four feet. Because of a fancied resemblance to a fagot (bundle of sticks) or fagots, the Italians call the instrument the *fagotto,* and it is sometimes called *fagot* in English. The mouthpiece, with a double reed, is attached to a crooked tube leading out from the main tubes, as in the English horn.

When the low notes of the bassoon are played staccato, the effect is highly grotesque. Mendelssohn uses the bassoon to imitate the braying of Bottom in *Midsummer Night's Dream.* Meyerbeer uses it in *Robert le Diable* to accompany the scene in the churchyard where incantations bring the faithless nuns from their graves.

The double bassoon, or contrafagotto, plays still lower notes.

BASS VIOL. The lowest pitched instrument in the orchestra is the bass viol. It is shaped like a violin, and has similar strings, but it is so large it rests on the floor, while its player nearly always stands. It has four long, heavy strings and a range of about two octaves.

BASS'WOOD, or LIN'DEN. Though they break rather easily in severe storms, the basswoods are famous street trees because of their luxuriant foliage. These large, attractive trees are native to Europe and to Eastern North America as far west as Manitoba. The American basswood is superior to other species in that it is free from the attacks of the fungi and insects which are so destructive to many street trees.

The flowers of basswood are famous for

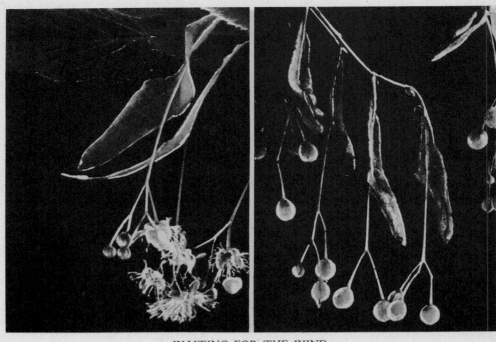

WAITING FOR THE WIND

From the small, greenish flowers of the basswood tree, the fruits, shown at right, develop into nutlike spheres. When it has become ripe, the fruit is carried away by the wind. Wherever it comes to rest, a new plant appears.

their fragrance, and the honey which bees make from the nectar collected from the flowers is even more famous. The flowers are not showy, being greenish yellow. They are borne in few-flowered clusters and develop into nutlike fruits which remain in the cluster until time to be shed. The whole cluster is shed at once, and is carried for some distance by the wind with the assistance of the leaflike wing, which remains attached to the cluster.

The wood of basswood is soft, close-grained, tough, and light brown. It is useful in the manufacture of furniture, cabinets, woodenware, and as paper pulp. The bark of some basswoods is quite fibrous and is used extensively in Northern Europe in the manufacture of mats, ropes, and shoes. The flowers are sometimes used medicinally.

BASTILLE, *bas teel'.* To all Frenchmen, the fourteenth of July is independence day. That day commemorates the fall of the grim old prison known as the Bastille, which was captured in the year 1789 by a mob whose revolt marked the beginning of the French Revolution. The Bastille was built in 1370 by King Charles V, and came to be used almost entirely for political prisoners. It thus became a symbol of the tyrannical government of that period.

On the fateful day in 1789, the mob stormed the gates of the Bastille and finally captured it from the king's guards. The following day the building itself was razed and its key sent to George Washington. Today, the site of the Bastille is marked by a bronze monument dedicated to the independence of the French people.

BAT. The German word for bat, *Fledermaus,* is a very good description of this furry little animal, for it means *flying mouse.* The bat's front legs stretch out to form wings, with which it flits about in jerky, irregular flight.

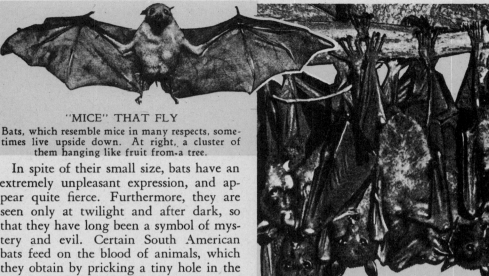

"MICE" THAT FLY

Bats, which resemble mice in many respects, sometimes live upside down. At right, a cluster of them hanging like fruit from a tree.

In spite of their small size, bats have an extremely unpleasant expression, and appear quite fierce. Furthermore, they are seen only at twilight and after dark, so that they have long been a symbol of mystery and evil. Certain South American bats feed on the blood of animals, which they obtain by pricking a tiny hole in the skin with their sharp teeth. Their name of vampire bat therefore seems appropriate. Stories about them have been exaggerated, but they sometimes attack human beings as well as animals. Most European and North American bats eat insects, which they catch in flight or on the ground.

Bats spend the day in dark nooks and crannies, and they remain in these places all winter, sleeping head down. Horseshoe-like growths on the nose, leaflike noses, and a nose resembling a flower are characteristics of various kinds of bats. The expression "blind as a bat" comes from a common though untrue belief that these creatures cannot see. On the contrary, they have small but very keen eyes which serve them well. Bats are mammals of the order Chiroptera.

BATH. For thousands of years man has been taking baths to wash and refresh himself. In ancient Greece the first thing a guest was offered was a bath. Later, the Romans made almost a ritual of the bath. They had huge, beautiful buildings to house pools of hot and cold water, as well as rooms for resting and massaging. Even now the Turks have bathing rooms in connection with their mosques. Public baths are used, in fact, in many parts of the world today.

The Roman baths were, however, the most elaborate ever known. In addition to bathing facilities, they contained beautiful statuary and other works of art, some of which may be seen in museums today. The buildings had four main sections: an undressing room, a cold room, a hot room, and one that was just moderately heated. Bathers went through all these rooms before their bathing was complete and then were given rub-downs with oils and perfumes.

Public bathing in Europe is still no simple matter. Steam rooms, cold rooms, and massages are considered very refreshing and healthful, and are a part of the bath. Sometimes these health baths are taken where unusual natural springs provide hot water, or water with special chemical properties. Such places are called *spas*. People often spend weeks at a time taking treatments of health baths. The best-known European spas are at Aix-la-Chapelle, Baden-Baden, and Karlsbad, in Germany; Spa, in Belgium; and Bagnères, in France.

There are fewer public baths in America because far more private homes are

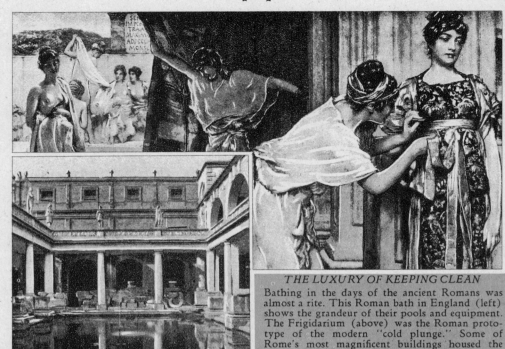

THE LUXURY OF KEEPING CLEAN

Bathing in the days of the ancient Romans was almost a rite. This Roman bath in England (left) shows the grandeur of their pools and equipment. The Frigidarium (above) was the Roman prototype of the modern "cold plunge." Some of Rome's most magnificent buildings housed the public baths.

equipped with bathrooms. Famous spas, however, are found at Hot Springs, Ark., and White Sulphur Springs, W. Va.

Whether baths are healthful depends largely upon the bather himself and the time of day that he bathes. Cold baths, for instance, should be taken in the morning for their bracing, invigorating effect. Since hot baths are weakening, a long rest should be taken after them. Warm baths are restful and may be taken whenever desired. There is a great difference in the effects of baths on different people, and every person should discover for himself the best kind of bath to take.

BATON ROUGE, *bat' on roozh,* LA. This Louisiana city is situated on the Mississippi River eighty miles northwest of New Orleans. It was one of the earliest French settlements in the original Louisiana Territory. Baton Rouge was at times under English and Spanish control, as well as French, before becoming a part of the United States. It became the capital of Louisiana in 1849. But in 1862 the capi-

tal was moved to Shreveport, and in 1864 to New Orleans. Baton Rouge again became the capital in 1882. The city has a commission form of government.

The chief industry of Baton Rouge is oil refining. There are also veneering works, chemical plants, iron and steel mills, coffee companies, and lumber mills. The city is a railroad center and also has an airport. Ocean-going ships sail directly from Baton Rouge to Europe. The city is the home of Louisiana State University and other schools, as well as hospitals and libraries. The population is over 30,000.

BATTERY, ELECTRIC. See ELECTRIC BATTERY.

BATTLE, TRIAL BY, or WAGER OF. During the Middle Ages, a person accused of crime was given a chance to prove his innocence by battling his accuser. Such a performance took the place of our trial by jury. It was believed that if the accused were right, God would protect him and let him win. Thus, he would be judged by the results of the engagement. An accused woman also could have her guilt or innocence decided in a trial by battle by selecting a champion to fight for her. As courts became more enlightened, this custom disappeared.

FLOATING FORTRESS
In America's first line of defense, the 32,300-ton *Tennessee* heads out to sea.

BATTLESHIP. Monarchs of the sea are the huge, armored vessels we call battleships. Bristling with guns and carrying crews of more than 1,000 men, they head the great navies of the world.

They received their name from the old sailing war galleons which were known as *line-of-battle* ships when taking part in naval engagements. Until 1860, battleships were made of wood and moved under sail, or steam and sail combined. After this date, however, *ironclads* appeared, sails were used less, and by the year 1900 large ships weighing thousands of tons were being used by the world's navies.

In 1905 the *dreadnaught* appeared, carrying twelve-inch guns and displacing over 15,000 tons. These ships have been enlarged until now battleships include super dreadnaughts, weighing over 30,000 tons and carrying sixteen-inch guns. There are also large dreadnaughts weighing at least 26,000 tons and firing fourteen-inch guns, and there are small battleships weighing 15,000 tons and carrying smaller guns.

Modern battleships have tall towers and heavily armored, revolving turrets for the guns. Many warships carry airplanes for combat or observation duty. Radio is used for communication. In addition to the huge long-distance guns, battleships also carry anti-aircraft weapons.

When the second World War began in 1939, naval experts watched closely the conflict on the sea. After World War I, many authorities believed that improvements in the airplane and the submarine would make the battleship obsolete. Others insisted that changes in construction and armor-plate would make the large vessels impregnable. Events of the early months of the war showed that, in spite of more efficient defenses, the great warship was by no means invincible. The 29,000-ton British battleship *Royal Oak,* for example, sank only a few minutes after it was hit by a torpedo. However, repeated air raids against British bases showed that large ships could not be destroyed with ease; and the battleship remained valuable for blockade and convoy service.

BAUCIS, *baw' sis,* **and PHILEMON,** *fil' e mon.* According to an old Roman myth, the gods Jupiter and Mercury visited the earth in disguise one evening. In a village they were refused food and rest, although they knocked at many doors. At last, tired and dusty, they stopped at the cottage of an aged couple, Baucis and Philemon, just beyond the village. The travelers asked for food which the old people willingly offered, although they were poor and had little themselves.

Baucis and Philemon were amazed to discover that the milk pitcher was constantly refilled of itself as soon as it became empty. Realizing, then, that their strange guests were not mortal, but divine, they fell to their knees before them. When

A KNIGHT FAITHFUL TO HIS CODE

Chevalier Bayard, "the knight without fear and without reproach," met his death while fighting for France against Milan, in 1524. A stone from a powerful crossbow broke his spine, and, as he finished his last prayers, he asked his friends to allow him to die with his face toward the enemy.

the gods left, they changed the old hut into a beautiful temple and made the old people priest and priestess of it. Years later, when the devoted couple feared that death would separate them, they were both changed into beautiful trees, and stood side by side before the temple that had been their home.

BAUXITE, *bahk' site,* or *bo' zite.* Aluminum, the valuable metal used widely in our homes and industries, is made from bauxite, a mineral resembling coarse rock. Bauxite is of many colors—white, yellow, brown, or red—and is dug out of heavy clay beds. The purest bauxite is found in Arkansas, large deposits occurring also in Ireland. Some of the mineral is found in Alabama and Georgia.

BAYARD, *ba yar',* PIERRE DU TERRAIL, known as CHEVALIER BAYARD (1478-1524).

As a brave and gallant military commander, Chevalier Bayard is remembered by the French people as "the knight without fear and without reproach." He led the armies of three kings, Charles VIII, Louis XII, and Francis I, to notable victories over the Spaniards, Italians, and English, combining courage and chivalry that made him respected and loved by his countrymen.

In 1503 he achieved wide fame for his defense of a bridge at Garigliano, which was being attacked by 200 Spaniards. Twelve years later, Chevalier Bayard was awarded the honor of knighting Francis I, after his triumph at Marignano. He fell on the battlefield of Sesia.

BEACH, REX (1877-   ). As a writer of lively fiction, Rex Beach enjoyed a colorful and successful career. Born in Atwood, Mich., and educated in law, Beach began writing as he grew older, until finally *The Spoilers,* a story of adventure in Alaska, established his reputation as an author. He followed this exciting narrative with *The Barrier, Going Some, The Silver Horde, The Iron Trail, Heart of the Sunset, Flowing Gold, The Goose Woman, The Mating Call, Son of the Gods,* and other stories, and also wrote several plays. A number of his works have made successful motion pictures.

BEACONSFIELD, EARL OF. See DISRAELI, BENJAMIN.

BEAGLE, *be' g'l.* Very much of the fun of autumn hunting is provided by the frisky little beagle hound. Through bushes and across fields he darts after frightened little hares for his master. The beagle is a gentle, friendly little dog, hardly more than a foot high, with a sleek coat of black or brown and white.

BEAN. Among our best-known foods are beans, the seeds of plants known as legumes. Beans have a long and varied history. We all remember the story of Jack-the-Giant-Killer, who was carried by the beanstalk to his struggle against the evil giant. In ancient Greece and Rome, beans were sometimes used in casting votes. For hundreds and hundreds of years these seeds have been eaten as healthful, delicious food. And only recently, soybeans have become valuable in the manufacture of soap, rubber substitutes, and paint.

Probably the navy bean is the best-known species. It is really a kind of kidney bean, the one served under the name "Boston baked beans." This variety is rich in carbohydrates and proteins; it is, therefore, used more than any other single food to feed armies, camps, and other large groups of people for whom nourishing food is needed at low cost.

Other popular varieties are green beans, wax beans, cranberry beans, and lima beans, each of which can be prepared in many appetizing ways.

All beans grow from butterfly-shaped flowers, either on tall vines or on short, squat shrubs. The part of the bean which we eat is the seed, which grows in a pod. It varies greatly in size, color, and shape. The pods of green and wax beans are tender, luscious in flavor and are an important article of food. Cranberry and lima beans, on the other hand, are harvested and used before the seeds are ripe, and the pods or shells are not eaten. Lima beans are grown extensively in California, where they are canned or dried before being marketed.

The bean plant is called an *annual* because it lasts only one season and must be planted each year. Beans grow best in rich, clayey soil, where there is not too much moisture. The plants are very delicate and are easily damaged by frost. Farmers are careful, therefore, to do their planting only after all danger of frost is past.

BEAR. Bears are next-door neighbors to a great many of us, for there is hardly a zoo or traveling circus that does not include one or more of these big, shaggy creatures in its animal population.

Because they are native to so many parts of the globe, bears are familiar sights in the wilds, too. Many are the tales, handed down by pioneers, of thrilling, dangerous, even humorous encounters with these beasts. Resembling a big, clumsy dog, the bear is a likable, peaceable sort of fellow when permitted to go about his own affairs unmolested. He wants to mind his own business, look after his family, and hunt his own meals. His warm coat, strong limbs, and capable jaws fit him to be rather an independent animal citizen without fear of man or beast.

In bodily appearance the bear is deceiving. He looks clumsy because of his loose-skinned bulk supported on short legs, his stump of a tail, and his shambling, flat-footed gait. Actually, he is quite nimble. He runs over rough ground or climbs trees with remarkable speed and agility. Strong claws help him to dig or to cling to a steep tree trunk or to fight. His hearing and sense of smell are acute. He likes

ONE TO PET AND ONE TO FEAR

There is all the difference in the world between these two animals. The koala, at left, is inoffensive and lovable, a living "teddy bear," while the grizzly, at right, is fierce and cunning. The koala is found only in Australia.

to eat honey, fish, fruit, and vegetable matter. All in all, Bruin is equipped by Nature for the rôle that he must play.

Bears usually have dens in rocky caves or crevices or hollow trees. There they pass the winter months in a sort of half sleep, called hibernation. They will not roam far from home during this period and they eat very little, apparently living on fat stored up in their bodies. In the early spring, when berries and tender green shoots bring a fresh supply of food, the bear family begins to stir. The little cubs, usually two in number, are born by this time and will soon require more and more nourishment, and the parent bears must eat heartily to restore their vigor against the coming year.

Spring is the time when bears range far and wide in search of small forest animals, spawning fish, new clover honey, and even lambs or calves from raided farms. This is a dangerous time in the wilds to stand between a bear and his intended dinner or to bother the mother bear and her young.

Kinds of Bears. Family resemblance in bears is so strong that the chief means of distinction between the different kinds are size and natural habitat. Color is not a trustworthy guide to species, as bears of the same kind may differ widely in this respect.

Most individual of the bear types is the *polar* bear, or *ice* bear. It is an exceptionally large animal, some specimens reaching nine feet or more in length. It has creamy white fur and black claws. This coloring enables the bear to hunt among ice floes and on frozen plains with little warning to its prey. Polar bears are strong swimmers. Even in zoos they seem to enjoy nothing so much as a rough-and-tumble swimming match in a pool of icy water. Despite their natural liking for the cold, they adapt themselves well to temperate climates and thrive in captivity.

One of the largest and most feared of the bear family is the *grizzly* of the mountainous region of Western North America. It, too, is a hunter of great cunning and persistence. Grizzlies, once the scourge of

FUR-CLAD MONARCH OF THE NORTH

The polar bear has little to fear in the frigid north. There is no other animal that can best him, and his heavy white coat protects him from the cold.

plains buffalo and deer, now prey upon smaller animals or the stray cattle of Western ranches. When trapped or wounded, they quickly turn upon their enemies and fight with terrific energy. Formerly found from the Black Hills of Dakota to the Pacific and from Alaska to Mexico, grizzlies are now confined to remote reaches of the Western forests and mountains. In color they range from gray to reddish-brown, the former being known as *silvertips*. Some grizzlies weigh over a thousand pounds.

Prized trophy of big-game hunters is the *Kodiak* bear, a member of the Alaskan brown-bear family. It is named from the Alaskan island, Kodiak, where these exceptionally large animals were first seen in

1895. The largest-known bear specimen was a Kodiak which tipped the scales at 2,000 pounds. However, one-ton trophies are rare, even among these giants. The typical Kodiak is yellowish to dark brown in color and weighs about 1,500 pounds.

Black bears are the most widely distributed type in North America, being found in most of the large forest areas north of the Rio Grande River. They are of medium size and, as their name implies, dark in color. Some of them are of a brownish color and are known as *cinnamon* bears. The *Florida* bear and the *Louisiana* bear resemble the black bears. A large brownish-white species of the Hudson Bay region is the *glacier* bear.

Cubs of the *brown* bear of Europe and Northern Asia are quite easily tamed and taught to do tricks. They make clever dancing and performing bears. Other Old World types are the *Himalayan,* the black bear of Japan, the black Malay *sun* bear, and the *sloth* or *honey* bear of India and Ceylon.

Common articles of exchange a few years ago, bearskins are becoming rare and therefore expensive. They are highly valued for furs, robes, and rugs, overcoats and decorations. Bear meat, once obtainable at city markets, is now familiar fare only to hunters. Although bears are not in danger of extinction, their numbers have been greatly reduced by man's advancing civilization.

BEAR, Great. The ancient Greeks, looking up at the heavens, saw a group of seven stars which seemed to them to resemble a great bear. The Latin name for this group, or constellation, of stars, is *Ursa Major,* translated *Great Bear,* and that is their name today. However, in the United States the common name for this group is the Big Dipper, because we think that it looks much more like a dipper than like a bear.

The two stars which form the front, or bowl, of the dipper are called the pointers. A line drawn from the bottom star through the top one will, if continued,

pass near the North, or Pole, Star, making it easy to locate that star. The Pole Star is at the end of the handle of the Little Dipper, another group of seven stars, which looks like an inverted dipper. These two constellations, Great Bear and Little Bear, or Big Dipper and Little Dipper, are always visible in the northern sky.

BEARD, Daniel Carter (1850-1941). A famous pioneer in the boys' organization movement was Dan Beard, who is credited with having inspired England's General Sir Robert Baden-Powell in his creation of the Boy Scouts. Born in Cincinnati, Ohio, he studied art in New York, becoming an illustrator for books and magazines. He started a boys' group known as the Sons of Daniel Boone, which later merged with the Scouts.

In 1919 Beard was made commissioner of the Boy Scouts of America (see Boy Scouts). He was honored by having a mountain in Alaska named for him. Beard is the author of the following books: *Shelters, Shacks and Shanties; Handicraft and Recreation for Girls; What a Girl Can Make and Do,* and *Things Worth Doing and How to Do Them.*

BEAUREGARD, *bo' re gahrd,* Pierre Gustave Toutant (1818-1893). One of the outstanding figures in the Confederate army was General Pierre Beauregard, who issued the order to fire on Fort Sumter, opening skirmish of the Civil War. Later, he was in command during the first Battle of Bull Run and at Shiloh. After assisting in the defense of Charleston and opposing Sherman's march to Atlanta, Beauregard aided Lee in defending Richmond. He surrendered to Sherman in 1865. Following the war, Beauregard was made adjutant-general of Louisiana and became president of the New Orleans, Jackson & Mississippi Railroad.

Beauregard was born in New Orleans. He was graduated at West Point in 1838, served in the Mexican War, and joined the Southern cause when civil war threatened.

FOUR-FOOTED LUMBERJACK
Here we see the hard-working beaver and
some examples of his work. Not only
does he fell trees, as shown by the gnawed
trunk, but he also builds strong, safe
houses in calm water.

BEAVER, *be' vur.* People of fashion in
the nineteenth century paid well for all
the silky beaver fur they could get. They
made it into hats and muffs and warm
collars. So trappers followed the beaver
farther and farther into the wilds beyond
the Mississippi, until they had crossed the
Rockies and had reached the Pacific
Ocean. Settlers followed the trappers to
claim the vast territory which makes up
part of Canada and the United States today. The "course of empire" followed the
beaver trappers westward.

Thus the beaver played an important
part in the settling of North America—
and came near to dying out completely
in the process. Once the source of a great
and profitable trade, this humble, hard-
working little fur bearer is now making
its last stand in a few government reservations in the United States and Canada.

How the Beaver Looks. Nature lovers
are attracted to a study of the beaver because of its industry, engineering skill, and
singular ability to work together with its
kind. It has been likened to the ants and
honeybees among insects and has been
called "the squirrel of the water." One of
the largest of the rodents, or order of
gnawing animals, the beaver is a brown,
furry creature about three feet in length
and from thirty to sixty pounds in weight.
It has a blunt nose, black ears, and small
front feet, like a squirrel's.

The hind feet are large and webbed and
have two claws on the second toe. Most
remarkable is the broad, flat, hairless tail,
covered with tough scales on the upper
surface. This tail is used by the beaver to
steer himself through the water, in which

he builds his home. A slap of this husky paddle on the surface of the water also serves to warn other beavers of approaching danger.

How He Lives and Works. Since the beaver lives on bark and roots and fells trees to make his home and dams, it is but natural that he should have strong, sharp, chisel-like teeth. With them he can ring trees of considerable size and cause them to fall where they will be handy to use. Clay banks, close to forests where trees like aspens and willows are abundant, are ideal beaver-building sites. Although beavers sometimes live alone, they are usually found in well-organized colonies, several families living and working together in complete harmony. Each family has its own house, a substantial two-room structure, called a beaver lodge. This lodge is built of branches and mud as a protection from winter cold and from other animals.

Lodges are built at the water's edge. They are about three feet high and seven feet across, with entrances under the surface. They afford ample room for the beaver pair, their young, and a store of food for the winter months. Beavers do not sleep all winter long, as some animals do; instead, they are active even after the water about the lodges has frozen. Therefore, they must work in the autumn to lay by a goodly supply of bark, twigs, leaves, and roots. Sometimes, when the larder runs low, beavers travel around their home pond or stream, under the ice, in search of something to eat. This is one reason they avoid building where the water runs over a rocky bottom or is so shallow that it may freeze clear to the bottom.

When all else is favorable except the depth of water, the colony will work together to build a dam across the stream, forming a deep, quiet pool. These dams, which sometimes reach hundreds of feet in length and six or more feet in height, are marvels of practical construction, probably the most remarkable of all animal enterprises. They are slowly and carefully built up of brushwood, roots, stones, and mud until they become large and solid enough to withstand even a flood. They are laid with due consideration for the course of the stream, the force of the current, and the suitability of the near-by banks. Constant labor keeps these dams in repair.

In cutting down the trees needed for construction and for food, beavers show amazing intelligence. A pair of them, working in shifts, will fell a sizable tree almost as quickly as a man can with an ax. They gnaw deep, parallel grooves around the trunk and then split out the wood between the grooves, just like accomplished woodsmen. Truly, man pays tribute to this little worker of the wilds when he says that some human being is "as busy as a beaver."

Beaver fur is now rarer and much more expensive than it was in the days when the great fur companies put 150,000 pelts upon the market every year. But, although the boom times of the beaver fur trade have passed into history, the fascinating life of the animal can still be studied in our National Parks. See FUR AND FUR TRADE.

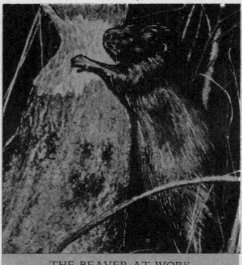

THE BEAVER AT WORK
How he gnaws around a tree

DEATH OF THOMAS A BECKET
To curry favor, King Henry II's knights slew the great archbishop in the Cathedral of Canterbury.

BECKET, Thomas à (1118-1170). A shrine made famous in Chaucer's *Canterbury Tales* was erected in 1172 to one of the foremost personages in English religious history, Thomas à Becket. In 1162, Becket was appointed archbishop by his good friend, King Henry II, and became a champion of the Church, forsaking his former life of luxury. However, a series of quarrels with the king forced him to flee to France.

After a reconciliation, Becket returned to England, but the quarrel was resumed. In a petulant mood, Henry gave utterance to a wish to be rid of the troublesome archbishop. Regarding this as a hint, four barons hurried to the cathedral at Canterbury and murdered Becket while he was at vespers, on December 29, 1170. Two years later, the martyred archbishop was canonized and the splendid shrine was built.

Becket was educated at Oxford and Paris, and studied civil law in Italy. Before his consecration as archbishop, King Henry II appointed him chancellor, and also made him the teacher of his son, Prince Henry.

BED. In geology a bed is a layer of rock. A bed either may be a number of thin layers of rock, or it may be one thick layer. A thin bed of rock is called a seam, and a number of layers taken together are a formation. See GEOLOGY.

BEDE, *beed,* **or BAEDA,** *be' da* (about 672-735). England's earliest historian, "the Father of English History," was Bede, the first great English scholar. His outstanding work was the *Ecclesiastical History of England.* Written in Latin, it was translated a hundred years later by Alfred the Great himself.

Bede was ordained a priest at the age of thirty, and lived and worked in a monastery at Jarrow. He wrote hymns, books on grammar, and Biblical comments. He died while completing a translation of the *Gospel of Saint John* from Latin into English. Bede's work preserves for posterity much of the life of England in Anglo-Saxon times. "The Venerable" was added to his name long after his death.

BEDOUINS, *bed' oo inz.* "Children of the desert" well describes these wandering tribesmen, and that is the meaning of their Arabic name—Bedouins. They are found chiefly in the deserts of Arabia, Syria, Egypt, and North Africa.

Housed in tents or huts, they support themselves by horse trading and robbing and pilfering. Sometimes they raid other tribes of their own people, and frequently they loot defenseless travelers in the desert.

Bedouins live either in families, under a sheik, or in tribes, under an emir. They are entirely ignorant of writing and books, their knowledge being limited to traditions and spoken words. Most Bedouins are undersized and frail in physique, in spite of their active lives

In Bedouin tribes the men wear long shirts, caught with a belt at the waist, and black or red and yellow turbans. The woman wears long pantaloons, a shirt, and a large shawl. See ARABS.

THEY FOLD THEIR TENTS AND STEAL AWAY
Nomadic Bedouins (above) packing up to move on again.

DESERT SHIP AND CAPTAIN
His white camel is this Bedouin's pride.

WORKERS *of the* INSECT WORLD

BEE. No one group of insects has received more popular attention than the bees. This is largely on account of the honeybee, but other forms of bees are almost equally wonderful in their habits and organizations. Bees belong in the great group of insects which includes also wasps and ants, as well as numerous other forms. They have four wings and a body narrowed between the thorax and the abdomen. Jaws are present and are used for various purposes, but not for feeding. There are special mouth parts adapted for gathering nectar from flowers. Bees have both biting, or chewing, and sucking mouth parts.

Kinds of Bees. The honeybee is probably the highest type of insect. Other bees, too, deserve study. The bumblebee is social in habits, like the honeybee, but many bees are solitary, and a few, the guest bees, live alone except for laying their eggs in the nests of others and allowing strange colonies to provide for the young. All types except the guest bees collect nectar and pollen, which they store in their nests for the young, and all bees feed on nectar or other sweet substances.

A structure which is possessed by all bees, but is poorly developed in the guest bees, is a very much enlarged joint in the hind foot. This is usually covered with, or at least surrounded by, many bristly hairs. It serves as an organ for collecting and carrying pollen and is called the pollen basket. It is the most useful structure in distinguishing the bees from the wasps, as they cannot be certainly identified by any other character that is as easily seen.

Solitary Bees may be *miners, wood borers,* or *carpenters,* or they may have other habits. The miners bore into the ground, usually in steep banks, and here make nests which they provide for their young and in which they lay their eggs. The carpenters bore into solid wood and make their nests. In either case there may be many cells, one for each egg. The first cell is provisioned, an egg laid in it, and it is then sealed before the next one is formed. It seems that the last one sealed is always the first one to mature and emerge, thus clearing the way for the one below it.

The mining bees may be as large as the honeybees or even larger, but many of them are small, the smallest of bees belonging to this group. The common carpenter bees are large and resemble the bumblebee, one of them being commonly called the *bald-headed* bumblebee. Another form is quite small.

Solitary bees are much more numerous in species than are the social forms and also exhibit a greater variety of habits. An interesting one not previously mentioned is called the *leaf-cutter* bee. It may be also a carpenter. It makes its nests either in holes it has bored in wood or in other tubelike cavities. These it lines with bits of leaves which it cuts from green plants. The cells are provisioned with pollen and honey, and an egg is laid in each.

As each cell is completed, it is covered with a circular bit of leaf which is cut just a little larger than the hole, so that when it is forced into the hole the edges turn up slightly all around. This forms the base for the next cell. Several pieces of leaves are forced into the hole to act as a stopper over the last cell constructed.

Solitary bees and guest bees have only two forms, the males and the females. The guest bees are often very similar in appearance to the bees whose nests they invade. This is especially true of the kind which infests the nests of common bumblebees.

Social Bees include the honeybee and the bumblebee. Here there are three kinds of individuals, as with ants. The organization of the bumblebee colony is quite different from that of the honeybee. In the first place, the bumblebee colony is not permanent, but breaks up at the end of the summer. The females, or queens, then seek some protected situation where they spend the winter, while the other forms, males and workers, perish. In spring the females start new colonies. The nests may be in old nests of mice or in any suitable place, usually on the ground. Here the eggs are laid, and the first young are tended by the queen. The first eggs develop into workers and, as in the case of the ants, these then take over the work of the colony while the queen continues to produce eggs.

Later in the season the new queens are produced and live in the nest with the old queens until the end of the season. Males are produced at the same time as the queens. Full-grown larvae spin cocoons of silk, and the bees cover these with wax. After the bees have emerged, the cocoons are used for honey storage. The honey has no commercial value, but there are few country boys unfamiliar with it.

The bumblebee is an insect of considerable interest and is of great importance as well, as it is only by its aid that some of the clovers are able to produce seed. The long tongue of the bumblebee enables it to secure the nectar from the flowers of red clover and it is, therefore, a constant visitor to this crop and a means of pollinating the flowers, which is accomplished in no other way so surely. It was necessary to take bumblebees from England to Australia, where they were not native, before red-clover seed could be produced there.

Bumblebees are peacefully inclined and never show any signs of temper until their nests are disturbed, when it is perfectly natural for them to defend themselves to the best of their ability.

About bees, as about ants, there is considerable discussion as to whether they have the power of reasoning or only very highly developed instincts. See ANT.

Honeybee. The honeybee has been cited for centuries as a model of industry. The manner in which the large number of insects composing a colony live and work together for a common purpose, and apparently without conflict among themselves, has always attracted admiration.

The individuals composing a colony, the occupants of one hive, often number many thousands. Since they are the offspring of one mother, a colony of bees may be compared to one large family. The number of individuals in a hive varies greatly at different seasons of the year and under different conditions. The population increases when conditions are favorable and reaches its maximum about midsummer.

When the honeyflow ceases in autumn and frosty nights are the rule, egg laying is greatly reduced and soon stops altogether. Soon there will be no young bees appearing to take the place of the older ones, which are dying every day. The mortality is heavy in late winter and spring, so that the hive population reaches its lowest ebb at that season, and uncared for colonies often die out altogether.

In case of the death of the queen, when

PRIVATE LIFE OF THE BEE

Here we see what goes on inside the beehive: (1) Worker bee building cells. (2) Young bee emerging from cell. (3) Queen bee surrounded by her attendants. (4) Worker attending larvae. shown in successive stages of development. (5) Larva of the next queen of the hive.

there are no eggs or very young larvae in the hive from which to rear another, the colony will die within a few months unless the beekeeper takes care to provide another queen or eggs or larvae from which to rear one.

As already stated, the queen is the mother of the colony and her sole duty is that of reproduction. She has no part in the ordinary activities within the hive. She moves from cell to cell depositing eggs, but gives no personal attention to the offspring which soon hatch from them. The cells in which the eggs are to be placed are first carefully polished by the workers. The queen looks into each cell, apparently to see that it is properly prepared, before she places the egg at the bottom. Early writers stated that the queen bee will lay as many as 300 eggs in one day, which seemed an impossible number for such a creature. It is now known that she often lays as many as 3,000 eggs in one day.

Since it would be impossible for her to consume sufficient food in the ordinary process of digestion to produce such an enormous amount of reproductive matter, the worker bees follow her constantly and feed her with the food which they regurgitate after having partially digested it.

The queen is hatched from an egg which is of the same kind as the thousands which produce workers, but she develops under different conditions. The cell in which she is reared is much larger and much like a peanut in shape. After the egg from which the queen comes is hatched, the young larva is fed upon royal jelly, a creamy-white, jellylike food which is produced by the worker bees. In the larger cell and with the richer food her development is more rapid, and her structure becomes very different from that of

A SWARM OF BEES

Swarming bees sometimes cluster in curious forms. Here, the bees have formed a pendant from a branch.

mature queen takes place in the darkness. During this stage no food is given, and at the end of seven days more (sixteen from the time the egg is laid), the young queen emerges in her adult form.

When the young queen is from five to seven days old, if the weather is fine she leaves the hive for her wedding flight. She meets the drone in the air and one mating is sufficient for life. On returning to the hive, she shortly takes up her duties of egg laying, and is not likely to leave again unless she goes out with a swarm to found a new colony.

Only one queen is permitted to remain in the hive, under ordinary conditions. Occasionally an old queen will be found living in peace with one of her daughters for a short time. Such cases are not frequent and do not continue for long, as the old queen will disappear within a few weeks. The newly emerged virgin queen is very active in hunting out and destroying possible rivals which have not yet left the royal cells.

The drone is the male bee. He is a big, blundering, helpless fellow who has no sting or means of defense. He adds nothing to the store of honey nor does he aid in building the combs or cleaning the hive. He does not even visit the flowers to gather his own food, but depends upon the bounty of his more provident sisters. His sole service lies in mating with the queen to perpetuate the race, and his days are short.

During the warm days of summer, when nectar is plentiful in the fields, thousands of drones may be seen about the apiary, but when autumn comes and the honey-flow stops, or even should there be a dearth of food in midsummer, the drones are driven from the hive to perish through their inability to care for themselves.

The drone is reared in a cell similar in appearance to that in which the worker bee is reared, except that it is larger in size. Both drone cells and worker cells serve for the storage of honey and pollen, when not in use as cradles for the young.

the workers, designed for other purposes.

The egg hatches in three days, and the larva is fed all of the royal jelly it can take for approximately six days. The cell is then sealed over and the transformation from larva to pupa and from pupa to the

CLOSE-UPS OF BEES AND THEIR HOME
The queen bee (upper center) is the most important member of the hive, for she lays the eggs.
The drone (below) is destined to be a mate for the queen. Left, an enlarged view of a worker's
powerful hind leg. Right, a large honeycomb.

The period of the drone's development is longer than that of either the queen or the workers. The egg hatches in three days, the same as the others, but the larva is fed for about seven days, and about fourteen days are spent in the transformation. In all, about twenty-four days elapse from the laying of the egg until the drone appears upon the comb.

Upon the worker bee devolves all the labor of maintaining the community. When she is young, she nurses the larvae and attends the queen. She polishes the cells in preparation for the laying of the eggs and she builds the new combs. As she grows older, she goes to the field and brings home the honey and pollen to provide food for all. She also guards the stores against robbers, and performs the labor of ventilating the hive and of evaporating the moisture from the incoming nectar.

Her lifetime is filled with labor, and her days are numbered by the amount of work which falls to her lot to be done. If, perchance, she emerges from her cell in late autumn, when the harvest is gathered and the work of the year is done, she is likely to live for several months and to have a part in the labors of another season. If, however, she appears in the height of the season when the colony is in a fever of anxious activity, she is likely to wear her life away in from five to seven weeks.

There is great excitement about the hive when a swarm issues. In preparation for swarming, queen cells will be built to provide a head for the colony when the old queen shall leave. It is likely to be when conditions are favorable for establishing a new household that the bees will swarm. The hive will be full of young bees and of hatching eggs and growing brood. The old queen and a large part of the old bees will leave the hive to found the new community. Each bee will fill her honey sac

A BUMBLEBEE NEST

with all the honey she can carry, to provide food for a few days until a new supply may be had from the fields.

Suddenly a great commotion begins, at the moment when the bees decide to start. Thousands of bees will tumble out of the hive as fast as they can, with such a buzzing as one hears at no other time. Soon the air will be filled with the whirling multitude, which fly about for a short time and then settle in a compact cluster on some convenient object. In nine cases in every ten, the swarming bees will soon cluster, but occasionally they fly without hesitation straight away across the fields to some distant home.

When the swarm has quietly settled, the beekeeper brings a hive and puts them into it. If, however, the swarm is unnoticed, they may remain quiet for several hours and even overnight, before leaving for the new home which has been sought out by scouts.

When the bees find the hive, the first ones to enter set up a great buzzing of joy. This is taken up by one after another as the bees file into the new home. Immediately they will begin to cluster in compact festoons hanging from the top of the hive. Wax secretion begins immediately, and within a few hours the new combs will take shape. The tiny wax scales are taken as they appear between the segments of the abdomens of the bees, and are kneaded one upon another into the delicate comb. Each cell has six sides and there is no waste space. The beekeeper uses full

sheets of foundation to insure straight combs of worker cells. Foundation is made of beeswax obtained by melting up old combs. The wax is worked into thin sheets and run through a mill which impresses the exact size and shape of the base of worker cells. If the bees are left to themselves, they will build too large a portion of drone comb. If the drone comb is present in the hive, more drones will be reared than is necessary, and the production of honey reduced in like proportion. With a larger number of workers the colony brings in more honey, while with a smaller number of drones it consumes less in boarding non-productive inmates.

When there is nectar to be had in the fields the worker bees are very active in bringing it to the hive to be ripened into honey. A bee must visit a large number of flowers in order to get a small drop of the sweet liquid. Nectar is very thin, like sweetened water, and a large quantity is required to make a pound of honey. Just what changes take place in the ripening of honey are not fully understood. The bees move the nectar several times from cell to cell within the hive, and apparently some chemical change takes place besides the evaporation of the excess moisture.

The bees work all night long in moving the honey about and fanning their wings to keep up a current of air to carry off the water as it vaporizes. If the hive is small and crowded, a large number of the field bees will cluster on the outside in the evening after they have returned from the fields. However, if there is room and ample ventilation, they are all likely to pass the night within doors, and may perhaps assist in caring for the nectar which they have brought in during the day.

Reaping Sweet Rewards. For the capital and labor involved, beekeeping yields good returns, when undertaken with care and understanding. More than half a million beekeepers in the United States supply the country with honey, one of its favorite confections. See HONEY.

BEECH. Those who live in or have traveled through Southeastern Canada or the eastern part of the United States have probably been attracted by the beautiful silvery-gray bark of beech trees. These trees are so distinctive that they are known practically by every one who lives where they grow and who has any interest in trees. Even though beeches could not be distinguished from other trees in winter by their gray bark, the amateur would have little difficulty in remembering the unusually long, pointed buds which are found on the trees when the leaves are off.

The fruits are borne in small, weakly spined burs and are distinctly three-sided. Throughout a great part of the range of these trees, the fruits are destroyed by insect enemies before they mature, but where this is not the case, the fruits make excellent food for man and beast. The fruit of the beech of Europe is a common food for pigs.

The roots of beech trees do not penetrate the ground to any considerable depth. Instead, they run along just beneath the surface, giving rise frequently to young trees which grow up around the parent plant in dense groves.

Beech wood is excellent for use in furniture, for tool handles, and other uses that require a hard, even-grained wood. It is also a desirable fuel wood and is employed frequently in smoking meats. Its hardness, brittleness, and general close-grained composition make it very durable, and, being resistant to water, it is admirably suited to the making of bowls and for various kinds of underwater construction work.

BEEF. This popular and widely used meat food is the flesh of cattle—cows, steers, and oxen. It is considered the most nutritious of all meats, being one of the chief known sources of protein. There are, of course, many different kinds of beef, taken from different parts of the animal, and these have varying food values. A juicy sirloin steak, for instance, is highest in this respect, with the so-called

FOOD FROM THE BEECH TREE

The fruit of the beech, borne in small, spiny burs, is good to eat. Unfortunately, however, insects destroy many beech trees before they mature.

"round cuts" being second in nutrition.

Most of the beef eaten in the United States and Canada is prepared for the table in the big packing houses in large cities. There the animals are killed painlessly and their flesh is divided into sections. These are sent to the butcher, who cuts the meat to suit his customers. The most desirable cuts are porterhouse, sirloin, prime rib, and round. These fine steaks are from only the very best cattle. Thinner, less desirable animals are slaughtered for canned or corned beef or extract.

Canned and treated beef is cooked before the customer receives it. The meat is packed in sealed cans to keep the contents fresh. Still another way of treating beef is by drying. This meat comes from the best cattle, and is pickled, smoked, and then simply hung up to dry. This is the kind of beef that comes in very thin strips, sometimes called chipped beef.

It is only recently that we have been able to obtain good beef easily. Modern

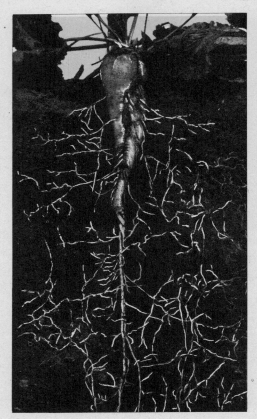

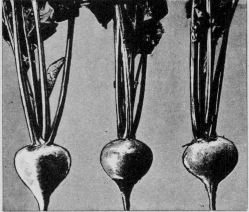

Courtesy U. S. Beet Sugar Association

FOR SUGAR AND PLATTER

At left is a "worm's-eye" view of mature sugar beets ready for harvest. The garden beet, eaten as a vegetable, is shown above.

methods of transporting it in refrigerated cars and storing it in ice boxes provide us with a plentiful supply. Before the day of refrigeration, beef was often eaten after it had begun to decay. Its unpleasant taste was concealed, more or less, with strong spices and other flavors. Today, however, if it is impossible to get the fresh meat itself, appetizing canned and corned beef are always available.

BEELZEBUB, *be el'ze bub.* Mentioned in the New Testament (*Matt.* X, 25) as the name of the chief demon, Beelzebub is really the Hebrew word for *lord of flies.* Beelzebub was the greatest god of the Syro-Phoenician people, and the Philistines built a temple to him at Ekron. The worship of Beelzebub probably had some connection with the innumerable flies which infested the plain of Philistia. In Milton's *Paradise Lost*, Beelzebub is first in rank among the fallen angels who joined Satan in the revolt against the Lord.

BEET. Few summer vegetables are more delicious than the beet, and we are able to eat them the year around by either canning the young roots or storing the fully grown ones in a damp cellar. Beet roots are boiled and served with butter or sauce as a table vegetable, or they may be eaten cold as a salad, and sometimes are pickled in vinegar. The young leaves are used as table greens, but beets have a more important use than this, as they furnish the world with about three-fourths of all its sugar. Sugar beets are grown mainly in Central Europe, but their cultivation is rapidly increasing in the United States, where Colorado is the leading producer. See SUGAR.

The beet plant itself is grown mainly for its root, which is large and juicy and ranges in color from white to a dark red or almost black. The plant develops fully every two years, because during its first year it produces a thickened root, and does not form seeds until the second year. In the garden, however, the plant may be grown as an annual. The beet grows best in a cool, temperate climate having a reasonable amount of moisture.

THE MASTER COMPOSER PLAYS

As Ludwig van Beethoven plays his own compositions, his listeners sit entranced by the magic of his music. He was a master of the symphony.

BEETHOVEN, *ba'toh ven,* LUDWIG VAN (1770-1827). Like Goethe in literature, the German composer Beethoven ranks as one of the outstanding geniuses in the world of music. He was a master of instrumental music, especially of the symphony, despite the fact that he composed many great works while totally deaf.

Born in Bonn, Germany, Beethoven began the study of music at an early age under his father, a singer. When he was eleven he made a concert tour, and two years later was publishing some of his compositions. In 1792 he was sent to Vienna to study under the master Haydn, and there he learned how to compose for the orchestra. In and near that city he taught, conducted orchestras, and performed as a pianist until 1814, when he became deaf. From that time until his death, he devoted himself almost wholly to composing, never yielding to despair.

Beethoven's life was one of sadness. He was never free from financial troubles, for years he could not hear his own glorious music, and his family life was far from happy. Such joyous works as the *Eighth Symphony,* and many lively pieces for the piano, show the triumph of the inner spirit over the disappointments he endured. His *Fifth Symphony,* played often by modern orchestras, and his *Ninth Symphony,* heard seldom because of its difficult structure, are among the most beautiful of all compositions.

Beethoven's major works include one opera, *Fidelio,* symphonies, overtures, sonatas, concertos, and sacred music. Among the favorite melodies more generally known are his *Minuet in G* and the *Sonata in C Sharp Minor,* popularly called the *Moonlight Sonata.*

INSECT WARRIORS
Beetles are equipped for battle.

BEETLE. Among insects the beetles are the most numerous. They are found in practically all parts of the world—some crawling on land, some swimming in water, and some flying in the air. All are good fighters, prepared to defend themselves no matter where they go. Each one carries a coat of armor with him, formed by an outer pair of wings which have become hardened.

The beetle is really fortunate in this respect, for the hardened wings serve to protect his soft back. He has another pair of wings which he can spread when he wishes to make a flying trip. These sheathlike wings gave the beetles their scientific name of *Coleoptera,* which means *sheath-winged*. The common name, beetle, comes from an Anglo-Saxon word meaning *biter*. It refers to the mouth parts, which are suitable for biting and tearing.

The beetle's appetite is one of the most varied in the animal kingdom. He may enjoy tobacco, or he may prefer the delicate flavor of ripe fruit, grain, leaves, and numerous plants. If he lives near the water and likes to swim, he may get his dinner by capturing small fish and other water animals. If he belongs to another of the 180,000 species, he may feed on decayed plants or dead animals. In fact, the list of things that beetles will eat is almost endless.

From Eggs to Adult Beetles. The life history of beetles is similar to that of other insects. From eggs are hatched the larvae, or grubs, which look like thick, clumsy worms. Yet they have jaws, or mandibles, which they can use for biting. The next stage is the pupal, often passed in crude cocoons. The insects emerge from the cocoons as adult beetles. Some of them are flat and round, some long and slender, and others thick and broad. All have large compound eyes and antennae, or feelers, which they use for hearing, smelling, and feeling.

In addition to their coat of armor, beetles have other means of defense. Some of them use their strong jaws; others, when they are pursued, will pretend to be dead and drop to the ground; still others imitate wasps and hornets and so escape attack. One kind of beetle emits an offensive odor to repel its enemies.

The usefulness of beetles in fertilizing flowers, in burying decayed matter, and in devouring certain harmful insects cannot be denied. In general, however, they do more harm than good. To the farmer, especially, they are destructive pests that do great harm to crops.

LIFE STORY OF THE BEETLE

In the upper series of pictures, a grub develops into an adult beetle. Lower left, rhinoceros beetles; and right, a stag beetle.

BEL'FAST, IRELAND. Although most of Ireland is now an independent state, Eire, six counties in the extreme northeast maintain loyalty to Great Britain. Of this Northern Ireland, Belfast is the capital and largest city. It is also the largest city of the island, and the chief manufacturing and shipping center. Belfast is situated in county Antrim, on Belfast Lough at the mouth of the Lagan River, 113 miles north of Dublin.

The city is the center of the Irish linen trade and has most of the spinning mills and power-loom factories of the country.

The building of large steamships is carried on, and brewing, distilling, rope making, and foundry work are among its other industries. Its spacious harbor has been improved and modernized to accommodate the increasing number of ships that clear the port.

The chief schools in Belfast are Queen's College and the religious schools of the Presbyterians and Methodists. The city has a number of modern buildings. The basis of its present wealth was laid in 1777, when the cotton trade became important. The population is over 438,000.

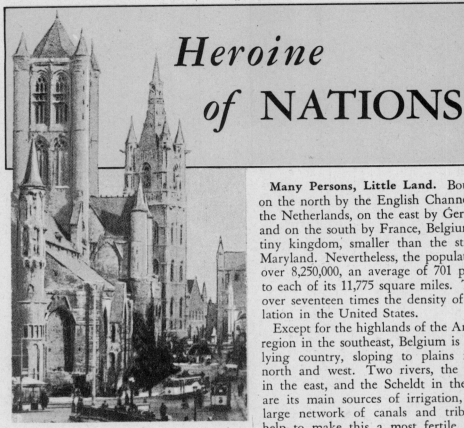

Heroine of NATIONS

BELGIUM, *bel'je um.* Hemmed in between two powerful nations in Europe, tiny Belgium—one of the most densely populated and highly industrialized countries in Europe—was twice in the twentieth century the helpless victim of total war. In both mighty conflicts, the German invaders overran the little kingdom. In historic August, 1914, a desperate Belgium withstood the formidable German army long enough to allow France to mobilize and England to send soldiers over the channel. With the exception of a small section in Flanders, all Belgium was under German military rule during the war.

No match for Germany's mechanized armies in World War II, Belgium surrendered to the invader in 1940, and remained under German domination until freed by the Allies in September, 1944.

Many Persons, Little Land. Bounded on the north by the English Channel and the Netherlands, on the east by Germany, and on the south by France, Belgium is a tiny kingdom, smaller than the state of Maryland. Nevertheless, the population is over 8,250,000, an average of 701 persons to each of its 11,775 square miles. This is over seventeen times the density of population in the United States.

Except for the highlands of the Ardenne region in the southeast, Belgium is a low-lying country, sloping to plains in the north and west. Two rivers, the Meuse in the east, and the Scheldt in the west, are its main sources of irrigation, but a large network of canals and tributaries help to make this a most fertile section of Europe.

Products of the Farms. About forty per cent of Belgium is arable, although much of the north country is too wet for tillage and is under grass. Here, livestock raising and dairy farming are the principal means of livelihood. Pigs, poultry, and rabbits (Belgian hares) are bred on the tiny farms, half of which comprise less than two and a half acres. To the east and south the land is drier, and cattle grazing gives place to sheep herding. The tilled fields in this region are larger and field crops are grown. Oats and wheat are the leading cereals; flax, hops, sugar beets, and chicory are all important as crops. The two staple articles of diet for the peasants are potatoes and rye.

Although these little plots of ground have been tilled for a thousand years, Bel-

BELGIAN BEAUTY
Old windmills and pic-
turesque canals lend quiet
charm to the Belgian
countryside, where farm-
ers till the productive
soil. In ancient Belgian
cities some of the world's
loveliest lace is made.
Ostend (right), on the
North Sea, is a leading
port and popular resort
of west Flanders.

gian soil is the most productive in Europe. Nevertheless, because of the dense population it is necessary to import a large portion of necessary foodstuffs. About one-sixth of the land is covered with forests, and lumbering is an important industry. As in the case of food, however, Belgium must look abroad for most of the building lumber.

From Mine and Factory to World Markets. A portion of Southern Belgium is a continuation of the highly mineralized French Ardenne highlands, and here great industries are located that produce steel, zinc, and cast iron, as well as firearms and machinery of all types. Antwerp

and Brussels are centers for the many diversified industries for which Belgium is justly famous. Gem cutting, especially diamond polishing, has reached a high state of perfection; about 5,000 in this profession are working in Antwerp alone. America absorbs so many diamonds that when a financial crisis puts a check on the purchase of luxuries, more than half the diamond cutters in Belgium are thrown out of work.

The country is a world center for hand-made lace, which is in great demand, although high-priced. In recent years, machine-made lace has been supplanting the hand-made article, but it is not of the

PEASANT BELLES OF SPA
Belgian native costumes are among the most
colorful in Northern Europe.

same quality. Woolen and artificial silk materials are manufactured in Bruges and Liege, while linen, cotton, hemp, and jute are made into almost all known textile wares. Belgium is also world-famous for its glass, pottery, and porcelain wares, a great portion of which is hand-designed. The country imports primarily wheat, breadstuffs, meats, petroleum, and tobacco, but there is such a demand for Belgian manufactures that imports and exports balance.

Brussels is the capital and lies in the heart of the agricultural district of the southwest. Antwerp, fifty miles inland on the Scheldt River, is Belgium's great port and commercial center, and is visited by ships from all over the world.

At Study and Worship. Education is free in Belgium, each commune, or small section, maintaining at least one elementary school. The state and the local province each contribute one-sixth of the cost of upkeep, the commune paying the remaining two-thirds. The state maintains the secondary schools, and each large town has a college. There are four universities:

Louvain University, supported by the Catholic clergy; Brussels University, established with private contributions; and those at Liege and Ghent, supported by the state.

Since the people of Belgium are divided as to language into Flemings and Walloons, one of the two tongues is used in primary schools; students in high schools, colleges, and universities are required to speak both. Although nine tenths of the people are Roman Catholics, there is no restriction on religious worship.

Governing the Kingdom. Belgium's government is an hereditary constitutional monarchy, with the king, Senate, and Chamber of Representatives forming the legislative body. The Senate is composed of members elected by the people, by the councils of the nine provinces, and by the Senate itself. Its members are not paid and it is completely changed after four years. The royal princes automatically become members when they reach the age of eighteen.

Representatives are elected by direct vote for a period of four years. A governor, appointed by the king, rules over each of the nine provinces, which are divided into smaller groups with individual local governments.

Battlefield of Europe. Until the sixteenth century, Belgium had no political individuality, falling into the hands of one aggressive nation after another. Spain gained control during that century, but lost it to Louis XIV of France, who in turn ceded it to Spain at the Treaty of Utrecht, in 1713. Under Napoleon, France annexed Belgium, but was driven out after the overthrow of the empire at Waterloo. The Belgians were united to the Netherlands in 1815 at the Congress of Vienna, but the union lasted only fifteen years, Belgium claiming its independence in 1830. This claim was confirmed a year later by the European powers. Under Leopold II, Belgium gained control over the huge African Congo, which became Belgian Congo after annexation in 1908.

DEVASTATION IN BELGIUM IN WORLD WAR II
International
German tanks proved too strong for successful defense in 1940.

The long and happy reign of Albert I was disrupted by the first World War. Although guaranteed neutrality by Great Britain, France, Prussia, Austria, and Russia, the country was dominated by Germany for four war years. Thousands became unemployed after the factories were pillaged of machinery, which was sent to Germany. However, after the Allied victory in 1918, Belgium was restored to its former status, and enlarged by the former German districts of Malmedy and Eupen.

King Albert died in February, 1934, while mountain climbing near the capital, and his eldest son succeeded him as Leopold III. A year later the queen, the former Princess Astrid of Sweden, was killed in an automobile accident in Switzerland. On May 10, 1940, the Germans once more overran Belgium, and, on May 28 King Leopold surrendered his unhappy country to the invader and became a prisoner of war. He was rescued by the Allies in May, 1945; but, because there was opposition to his return to Belgium, he took asylum in Switzerland, instead. His brother Charles, meanwhile, ruled Belgium as regent.

BELL. The bells that we know today are hollow, metal, cup-shaped instruments with a clapper, or "sounder," inside to make them ring. In very early times, however, they were made from several pieces of metal fastened together, and were rectangular. The reason was that at first no one knew how to cast a bell all in one piece.

What a number of uses a bell has! On Sunday mornings it summons us to worship. We are reassured and guided to safety by the mournful clanging of a bell when sailing in a dense fog. We rejoice when a bell rings out news of victory, and men have marched to war when it called them to arms. A bell tolls at the passing of a loved one. But the tinkling of a bell on a frosty winter night brings to mind happy sleigh rides and Christmas cheer.

The bell signals the arrival of the postman or a neighbor at the door, and it tells us that we are wanted on the telephone. It may rouse us in the morning and warn us of bedtime at night. At sea, time is announced by the ringing of a bell. One bell is for half-past twelve, two

BELLS THAT CALL AND WARN
Beautiful is the mission bell that summons men to worship; bold is the buoy bell, warning of disaster. Below, a giant.

tians, and Israelites had bells. Bells were first used in churches in the fifth century, and towers called campaniles (Italian for bell tower) were constructed.

Bells were small until the thirteenth century, when men learned to cast bronze in larger pieces. In 1400 the Jacqueline of Paris was cast; it weighed about seven tons. Many large bells were cast after that time. Some of the largest and most famous bells are: "Big Ben" in Westminster Tower, London, weight 15 tons, cast in 1856; the Great Bell of Saint Paul's, London, 17 tons, 1881; the Liberty Bell, 1752; Notre Dame, Paris, 17 tons, 1680. Other famous bells are at Cologne, Rouen, Oxford, Bruges, and Vienna; they weigh from 7 to 18 tons.

The largest bell ever made is the Czar Kolokol in Moscow, cast in 1733 and weighing nearly 200 tons. But this giant has never been rung, for it cracked before it left the foundry. The largest bell in use is also in Moscow. It weighs 128 tons. Other great bells are in Burma and in Peiping, China. See LIBERTY BELL.

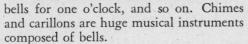

bells for one o'clock, and so on. Chimes and carillons are huge musical instruments composed of bells.

Ever since the early days of Christianity, bells have played an important part in our lives. But even before that, the ancient Chinese, Japanese, Greeks, Romans, Egyp-

THE ORIGINAL "TEDDY BEAR"

One of the queerest of all creatures, the koala of Australia resembles a midget bear, but is actually a cousin to the kangaroo. It is about twenty-four inches long and twelve inches in height, having soft, woolly ashen-gray fur and a button-like tail. The mother carries her young in a pouch, in the same manner as the kangaroo and opossum, and later the young ride on her back. Koalas have long toes and can grasp branches of trees easily, often sleeping back down, like the sloth. These little animals can easily be tamed, but native Australians kill and eat them. They live on shoots and buds of the eucalyptus trees and plant roots.

BELL, ALEXANDER GRAHAM (1847-1922). On March 10, 1876, in the city of Boston, the sound of the human voice was relayed over the electric telephone for the first time, ending three years of work by that benefactor of mankind, Alexander Graham Bell.

Born in Edinburgh, Scotland, Bell began teaching at the early age of sixteen. He continued experimentation with a system of visible speech for the deaf developed by his father, and in 1868 discovered a method whereby those who could not hear could learn to talk. Except for slight improvements, the method is used today.

Bell went to Boston in 1871, becoming a professor at Boston University. Although his reputation was established by the invention of the telephone, Bell by no means rested on his laurels. He invented the photophone, which transmits speech by light rays; the recording discs used on phonographs; an electric probe which finds pieces of metal in the human body; an automatic stabilizer for airplanes, and many other useful articles.

Rich in honors, he lived to see the everyday life of the world altered by the almost universal use of his inventions. See TELEPHONE.

BELLINI, *bel le'ne,* GIOVANNI (about 1426-1516). Called the founder of the Venetian school of painting, Bellini was the teacher of Titian and Giorgione. He was famous as a colorist and helped to create the beautiful golden tone of Venetian paintings. Associated with him were his father, a portraitist, and his older brother, Gentile. Bellini is considered one of the greatest Italian painters of all time. His best-known works include *Peter Martyr, The Crucifixion, The Coronation of the Virgin,* and *The Transfiguration.*

BELSHAZZAR, *bel shaz' ar,* was the last king of Babylonia and the son of Nebuchadnezzar. The miraculous incident of the "handwriting on the wall," which occurred during a lavish feast, is recorded in the book of *Daniel.* It further describes the storming of Babylon by Cyrus the Great of Persia, and Belshazzar's death in 538 B. C.

A Sunday-school hymn, popular years ago, began with these lines:

At the feast of Belshazzar and a
   thousand of his lords,
As they drank from golden vessels,
  · as the Book of Truth records,
In the night, as they reveled in
   the royal palace hall,
They were seized with consternation—
   'Twas the hand upon the wall.

BEN'EDICT XV (1854-1922), GIACOMO DELLA CHIESA. Elected Pope at the outbreak of the World War, Benedict XV succeeded Pius X in 1914. The Holy Father remained impartial throughout the war, and in 1917 made an unsuccessful appeal to the fighting nations to restore peace. Because there were large numbers of the faithful on both sides of the conflict, he faced some of the most difficult problems in the history of the Papacy.

Pope Benedict was born in Pegli, Italy, and completed his training for the priesthood in 1878. From then until May 30, 1914, when he was appointed cardinal, he held many offices in the Catholic Church. He was elected Pope only three months after his appointment. Benedict's rapid rise had been due to his thorough training and his experience in handling negotiations between the Papacy and the European powers.

The Pontiff died of pneumonia in the Vatican on January 22, 1922. It was believed that his death was due in part to his deep sorrow over the plight of wartorn Europe. Shortly afterward the college of cardinals elected, as his successor, Cardinal Achille Ratti, who became Pope Pius XI.

BEN'JAMIN. According to the Bible, Benjamin was the youngest of the twelve sons of Jacob, who founded the twelve tribes of Israel. His mother was Rachel.

When Benjamin was very young, his father journeyed with him and his many brothers to Hebron, in the kingdom of Canaan, on the eastern shore of the Mediterranean Sea. There they lived for many years, and Benjamin founded the tribe of Benjamites. Finally, after a bitter war among the tribes, the kingdom of the Israelites was divided, and Benjamin and his followers united with Judah.

BEOWULF, *ba'o woolf.* In the British Museum, in London, there is a piece of manuscript nearly a thousand years old. It is *Beowulf,* the earliest epic poem written in England. *Beowulf* belongs to the Anglo-Saxon period of English literature, and would be impossible to read without a dictionary. It may be found in translations, however, and well repays reading.

The hero, Beowulf, is one of the most attractive characters in the legends of the past. He is our childhood ideal of a brave and noble warrior—one who slays monsters and dragons and thinks nothing of his own safety. As the story goes, he sailed from England to Denmark with fourteen companions to save King Hrothgar from Grendel, a fierce monster who broke into the palace every night and carried away the king's men. After everyone had left the banquet hall one night, Beowulf fought with Grendel and wounded him mortally. The monster escaped, however, and went to a far-away sea to die.

Later, Grendel's mother, as fierce as her son, came to the palace and carried off one of the nobles. Beowulf gave chase and slew the mother in a vicious fight. In his old age, Beowulf died of wounds received in a terrible struggle with a fiery dragon, which he killed.

BERBER, *bur'bur.* In North Africa lives an ancient race of dark-haired, brown-skinned people called Berbers. Retaining many age-old customs and superstitions, the men of some of these tribes still wear silver nose rings and carry long swords or curved daggers. The Berbers are not warlike unless molested, preferring to till the soil and tend their herds of sheep or goats. They frequently live in tents, or, in colder regions, build crude houses of stone or brick.

Racially, the Berbers are divided into the Shilluhs, who inhabit Morocco; the

Kabyles, of Algeria; and the Tuaregs, who occupy the vast desert regions. Intermarriage between the Berbers and the Arabs has produced the race called Moors.

BE'RING, Vitus Jonassen (1681-1741). Although a Dane by birth, Vitus Bering joined the Russian navy when he was a young man, and served Peter the Great in the wars against Sweden. Later, the czar commissioned him to explore the North Pacific. Consequently, in 1728 Bering started out from Kamchatka, a peninsula in Northeastern Siberia. On this voyage he discovered the sea and the strait which now bear his name. Having satisfied himself that Asia and North America are not connected, he returned to Saint Petersburg. In 1741 he started out on another voyage of exploration, sailing again from Kamchatka. He never returned from that voyage, for his ship was wrecked on a barren island. That bit of land was named Bering Island in his honor.

BERING SEA and STRAIT. The narrow channel which separates Asia from North America and connects the North Pacific with the Arctic Ocean was named Bering for its discoverer (see Bering, Vitus). The strait was fully explored by Captain Cook in 1778. A thick fog or haze usually enshrouds this region, and during the long winters the water in the strait is always frozen.

The strait varies in depth from 175 to 180 feet. At its narrowest point, between Alaska and Siberia, it is about fifty-six miles wide.

Bering Sea. The stretch of ocean south of Bering Strait is known as Bering Sea. It, too, was named for Vitus Bering. This sea lies between the western coast of Alaska and the eastern coast of Siberia. Its area is 886,000 square miles. In the northeastern portion the water is quite shallow, but some places in the southwestern portion reach a depth of 12,000 feet. Like the strait, Bering Sea is frozen during the winter and is overhung with fog most of the year. Consequently there is little navigation, but the sea has seal fisheries.

Heart of the Reich

BERLIN, GERMANY. Successively capital of the Prussian kingdom, the German Empire, the German Republic, the third Reich (under the Nazis), and, after World War II, the Allied Control Commission for Germany, Berlin has a history reaching back to the Middle Ages. For centuries the home of the Hohenzollern rulers, it became, under Bismarck, the political center of the continent. This position was lost following Germany's defeat in World War I and never wholly regained. It has always been the center of culture and trade for the Germans. After World War II, the Americans, British, Russians, and French governed Berlin in separate zones.

Berlin's population in 1939 of 4,332,000 made it the largest city on the European continent and the fourth largest in the world; London, New York, and Tokyo alone had more inhabitants than Berlin.

Berlin lies near the heart of the European continent. Located on a plain in Eastern Germany, it is 700 miles from the great capitals of Europe. The Spree River flows through the city, and a system of connecting canals provides for uninterrupted transportation by boat to the North and the Baltic seas. Hamburg, Germany's greatest commercial port, is 180 miles to the northwest.

From Village to Metropolis. The seven-hundredth anniversary of the founding of Berlin was celebrated in 1937. In 1237 it was a small and poor village. The place grew very slowly for several centuries, and in 1688, as the capital of the province of Brandenburg, it had only 20,000 inhabitants. However, beginning in 1701, as the capital of the new kingdom of Prussia, Berlin enjoyed a modest growth under Frederick I and Frederick the Great. During the Napoleonic wars, the city suffered from repeated French invasions, and the population declined. Napoleon carried away the beautiful golden chariot and horses from atop the gate to the city, but this treasure was returned after the French defeat at Waterloo.

Not until after 1871, when it became the capital of the new German Empire, did Berlin enjoy marked progress. By 1910 it had outdistanced Vienna in population. Under Hitler, the city began rebuilding; age-old districts gave way to new subways and modern government buildings, and modern streets replaced cobble-stone lanes. A large area of the city was damaged by bombing in World War II. The following paragraphs describe it as it was in 1939.

A World City. Named for its border of trees, Unter den Linden has long been the most famous avenue in Berlin. The Great Elector, Frederick William, planted a double line of lindens over 250 years ago; they were replaced in recent years with younger trees following the construction of a subway. At the end of the avenue stands the Brandenburg Gate, which was erected in 1789 and is a copy of the Pro-

AVIATION HUB OF THE NORTH

Tempelhof in Berlin is one of the busiest airports in Europe. In time of peace, Germany maintains regular service from Tempelhof to continental and Asiatic points, and to the Americas.

pylaea in Athens. The chariot and horses atop the gate are a symbol of victory and progress.

The most famous of the older buildings is the former royal palace, now a museum. It was built by Frederick the Great and last occupied by William II. It contains over 600 great rooms with inlaid floors of rare beauty, many works of art, and perhaps the most beautiful throne room in Europe. Opposite the palace are the old and new museums and the National Gallery. Near by is the Armory, containing a rare collection of trappings used by knights of the Middle Ages. Many of these buildings were damaged in World War II.

The huge building that houses the Air Ministry is perhaps the finest government building; the Parliament building is an impressive example of classic architecture adapted to modern needs. Olympic City, built for the Olympic games of 1936, consists of three stadiums and several theaters and halls, the largest stadium seating 110,000 people. The House of German Broadcasting, an odd, circular-shaped building containing broadcast studios, and

the Berlin Radio Tower were built somewhat later.

In the heart of Berlin is the Tiergarten (Animal Garden), formerly a hunting preserve of the royal family, but today the home of the zoo and aquarium. The world's first planetarium is also found there. The largest park is called Green Forest. It is so huge that children can walk there for hours as in a wooded countryside. The most revered monument in the city is the War Memorial to the two million Germans who died in the first World War. Before Germany's defeat in World War II, it was attended constantly by a guard of honor.

Near the memorial stands a great equestrian statue of Frederick the Great. In front of the Parliament building rises a colossal figure of Prince Bismarck, and across the square the slender, golden Victory column, with an eagle at the top, commemorates the victory over France in 1870.

Berlin is the home of the finest educational institutions in Germany. Foremost among them is the University of Berlin, famous for its graduate departments in medicine and philosophy. The Technical College, the Royal School of Agriculture, the Royal School of Music, the Royal Academy of Arts, the Military Academy, and the Artillery and Engineering School are all well-known professional schools. Illiteracy is practically unknown in Berlin.

Commerce and Industry. From over thirty railway stations, streamlined or express trains ran to every part of Europe. The first streamliner in the world made its initial trip between Berlin and Hamburg in 1930. Templehof was one of the most complete airports in the world, and from there one reached any point on the continent in a single day. There were also regular air routes to Africa, South America, and Asia. The local city transportation system consisted of both elevated and subway trains that ran first- and second-class cars.

The German factory system centered around Berlin. Steel, clothing, electrical machinery, and beer were among the leading products, although practically every commodity in general use was made there. The city had the largest publishing house in Europe.

Dirt and Crime Outlawed. Berlin was easily the cleanest city in Europe and one of the best managed. The Federal government had always intervened in local affairs of the city. This was especially true under the old empire that ended in 1918. Under the German Republic, from 1919 to 1933, there was corruption in city affairs, but after 1933 the mayor and the city assembly were little more than the mouthpiece of the Nazi officials.

The Nazi regime was very strict, but efficient. It was unlawful even to drop a piece of paper on the street. Crime largely disappeared, and traffic regulations were enforced. Open markets were conducted in the streets, the farmers bringing their products to the squares at daybreak and selling them in especially provided stalls. By night, however, everything had to be removed, because the streets were then scrubbed thoroughly with torrents of water from fire hoses. See GERMANY.

MOTORIZED INFANTRY ON PARADE IN BERLIN   *Inter-Continent*
A demonstration of soldiers in armored cars, before the outbreak of war in 1939.

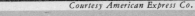

Courtesy American Express Co.

ATLANTIC PLAYGROUND
A view of the sun-drenched harbor of Hamilton, capital of the island group. The town, picturesquely situated on the landlocked bay, is a favorite resort for tourists.

BERMU'DA ISLANDS. Famous as a vacation center, Bermuda is located in the Atlantic Ocean about 580 miles east of North Carolina. The 300 tiny coral islands form a bouquet of color and charm, covering an area of not more than twenty square miles. Although the Bermudas are the farthest north of the coral islands, they are washed on all sides by the warm waters of the Gulf Stream, and their climate is always mild.

Since no pleasure cars are allowed on the islands, bicycles are a common sight. Bananas, onions, lily bulbs, and sweet potatoes are grown commercially.

The islands were originally discovered in 1522 by a Spaniard named Juan Bermudez. They were first settled, however, in 1609, under the leadership of an Englishman named Sir George Somers, and are now a crown colony of Great Britain. Because of their vital position, halfway between British interests in the West Indies and in Canada, the British government maintains both a naval base and a military station on the islands. In 1940 the United States leased territory in the Bermudas for naval and air bases. Only 16,000 of the 30,000 inhabitants are white people. Hamilton, with a population of 3,000, is the capital and most important city.

PERMANENT RECORD
More effective than anything else in capturing and convicting criminals are fingerprints, the tell-tale "calling cards" of every person. They cannot be changed, even by surgery. These show the five types under which all fingerprints are classified.

BERTILLON, *bair te yoN',* **SYSTEM.** Criminals seeking to escape the law have had to move more cautiously than they did before Dr. Alphonse Bertillon invented a means of identification. There was a time when they could dye their hair, alter their faces, and grow beards, thus evading capture by the police. But times have changed.

Dr. Bertillon invented his system in 1879 in Paris. His plan was to measure portions of the heads, bodies, and limbs of criminals. The parts measured were thought never to be alike in any two persons and never to change in adults. In the Bertillon system, records of these measurements are kept, as well as general descriptions of the criminals and an account of any scars or deformities.

In 1885, Bertillon published his method. Criminal identification was long based on it, but fingerprinting and photographs have largely replaced the original system. Now, the first time a criminal is arrested, the police make a complete record of him.

BERYLLIUM, *beh ril'i um,* **or GLUCINUM,** *gloo si' num.* Among the rarest of the elements is beryllium, a steel-white metal first isolated in 1828. Lighter than aluminum, it has been found to add considerable strength to alloys made with that metal. But it is so expensive that it cannot be put to this valuable purpose commercially. It is now used chiefly in the manufacture of X-ray tubes, since it permits relatively free passage of the Roentgen rays. Beryllium is one of the elements in glittering emeralds and aquamarines.

BESSEMER, Henry, Sir (1813-1898). One of the world's great inventors, Henry Bessemer is best known for his development of the practical process for making steel which bears his name. He was born in Charlton, England. At an early age he worked in his father's type foundry, and it was there that he first became interested in metals.

During the Crimean War, he decided that there was need for better iron in cannon; so he carried on numerous experiments. These experiments led to the Bessemer process of making steel, which revolutionized the industry. In this process molten iron is hardened by decarbonization with a blast of air. In 1879 Bessemer was knighted by Queen Victoria in recognition of his contribution to science. See STEEL.

BE'TEL, or BE'TLE. If one were so lucky as to journey to beautiful Bali, or to any of the South Sea Islands or the Orient, one of his first thoughts would be that in this part of the world there were no tooth brushes. For the inhabitants of these countries are betel-nut chewers, and their friendly smiles reveal rows of blackened, decayed teeth in red, drooling gums.

The tree that bears the nuts responsible for this habit is the graceful betel palm. It grows to be forty feet in height, and is found in profusion in many parts of Asia and the East Indies. The betel nut itself is the size of a small hen's egg. It grows inside a fibrous shell similar to that of a peanut.

Since betel-nut chewing is so popular a pastime, great attention is given to the preparation of the fruit. First the shells are removed; the nuts are then boiled in water, cut into slices, and dried in the sun. The slices are wrapped in leaves of the betel vine, a creeping plant of the pepper family; a small amount of flavoring matter, such as shell lime or cardamom, is added. The betel nut has a very spicy taste and is enjoyed by millions of people. In spite of its bad effects upon the teeth and gums, betel-nut chewers credit it with medicinal properties to which it has no claim.

BETH'LEHEM. Near Jerusalem, in Palestine, is a little town known throughout the Christian world. It is Bethlehem, the birthplace of Christ. But Bethlehem was a famous town even before the birth of Christ, for there David was born, and there Rachel and Ruth lived. Today it is called Beit Lahm and is the home of three convents, one for Roman Catholics, one for Greeks, and one for Armenians. A grotto under the Church of the Nativity is known as the place where Jesus was born, and thousands of travelers from all over the world journey to see it every year. The chief trade of the present village is in crosses, beads, and relics. The population is about 7,000.

BIBLE. No other book has ever been read by so many people as the Bible. A person may travel to such far-away places as Africa, India, Japan, China, Persia, and Arabia, and he will find people of all colors and races using the Bible, or parts of it, as their guide to religion. He will find them reading it in many languages, for it has been translated into more than 400 different languages and dialects.

Although we think of the Bible as one book, it is really a collection of sixty-six books. The name, in fact, comes to us from the Greek word for *books*. These books of the Bible are divided into the Old Testament and the New Testament. The Old Testament tells the story of the Jews before the time of Christ; the new Testament deals with the life and teachings of Christ.

The Old Testament. The Old Testament contains these thirty-nine books:

Genesis	Song of Solomon
Exodus	Isaiah
Leviticus	Jeremiah
Numbers	Lamentations
Deuteronomy	Ezekiel
Joshua	Daniel
Judges	Hosea
Ruth	Joel
I and II Samuel	Amos
I and II Kings	Obadiah
I and II Chronicles	Jonah
Ezra	Micah
Nehemiah	Nahum
Esther	Habakkuk
Job	Zephaniah
Psalms	Haggai
Proverbs	Zechariah
Ecclesiastes	Malachi

The first five books of the Old Testament, *Genesis, Exodus, Leviticus, Numbers,* and *Deuteronomy,* are known as *books of the law.* The next twelve,

TAKING THE BIBLE TO THE PEOPLE

A wandering preacher reading the Bible to village folk gathered in an English public square, four hundred years ago. During the Middle Ages, few people could read. So the preachers tramped from place to place with the Holy Book, and, standing before a cross, read it aloud.

Joshua, Judges, Ruth, I and II Samuel, I and II Kings, I and II Chronicles, Ezra, Nehemiah, and *Esther*, are historical. *Job, Psalms, Proverbs, Ecclesiastes, Song of Solomon,* and *Lamentations* are poetry. The last sixteen books are prophecies.

The New Testament. The New Testament contains twenty-seven books, which appear in this order:

Matthew	II Thessalonians
Mark	I Timothy
Luke	II Timothy
John	Titus
The Acts	Philemon
Romans	To the Hebrews
I Corinthians	Epistle of James
II Corinthians	I Peter
Galatians	II Peter
Ephesians	I John
Philippians	II John
Colossians	III John
I Thessalonians	Jude
Revelation	

The books of the New Testament can also be divided into groups. The first five are the story of Christ and His followers. They tell of His birth, life, and crucifixion. They also tell how His devoted followers, shunning worldly riches and braving persecution by the Romans, took

His teachings to parts of the world other than Jerusalem and founded a new church. After these five books came the Epistles, many of them written by Paul. The final book of the Bible gives a vision of a new earth and heaven.

The Apocrypha. A number of sacred books not accepted by Protestants as parts of the Bible are called the Apocrypha. They are accepted only by the Roman Catholic Church.

Versions of the Bible. There have been many versions of the Bible, but the first one that we know very much about was produced in Greek, perhaps three centuries before the birth of Christ. This version is called the *Septuagint*. It was used by the Jews and also by the early Christian Church.

Originally, the books of the New Testament were written in Greek, although some persons believe that the gospel of *Saint Matthew* was written in Hebrew. The oldest versions of the New Testament which are still in existence were written in the fourth and sixth centuries, but none of these is divided into chapters and verses as our modern Bible is. It is not known when these divisions first appeared or who first made them.

Although the Bible has been translated into hundreds of languages, the English and German versions are best known for their beauty and accuracy. The first printed version of the New Testament in English was translated by William Tyndale and appeared in Germany in 1525. This translation was the basis for several other versions that came later. It was also the forerunner of the King James version, the one used today in most parts of the English-speaking world. Previous to this work, however, an edition called Cranmer's Bible appeared in England in 1540. A version of the Old Testament, published in 1609-10, is the one recognized today by the Roman Catholic Church.

During the reign of James I of England, Hugh Broughton, a Hebrew scholar, told the king a new translation of the Bible was desirable. The king accepted the suggestion in 1604, and forty-seven scholars were selected to work on the translation. These translators were divided into six groups, who met in Westminster, Oxford, Cambridge, and London. The revision was begun in 1607 and was published in 1611 as the King James version.

This version was used without change for many years and was acclaimed by scholars as the finest ever made. In 1870, however, a group of churchmen in Canterbury, England, recommended that the Bible be revised further. American and British authorities worked together on this revision. The New Testament was completed in 1881, the Old Testament in 1884. An American revised version was printed in 1901.

The Bible as Literature. Besides being the religious guide for nearly one-third the world, the Bible, especially the English version, is known as the most beautiful book in literature. Many modern novels and plays are based on stories and incidents from the Bible; and most of our forms of literature—the short story, the drama, poetry, the epic, and the fable—are found in its pages. Great music also has sprung from the Bible. The composer Handel used several passages from *Isaiah* for his great choral work, *The Messiah.* The *Psalms* also have been set to music that has been sung and played for years.

The great essayist Macaulay once wrote, "If everything else in our language should perish, the English Bible alone would suffice to show the whole extent of its beauty and power." His opinion has been echoed by many other writers. Following this article are several of the great Bible stories that have always been favorites with readers of the Good Book.

PROPHETS, PRIESTS, AND KINGS, SAINTS AND SINNERS, BOOKS AND PLACES, APPEARING IN THESE VOLUMES

Abraham	Ecclesiastes	Hosea	Judea	Philip
Apostles	Eden	Isaac	Judges, Book of	Philistines
Ararat	Egypt	Isaiah	Leviticus	Proverbs
Babel, Tower of	Elijah	Jacob	Luke, Saint	Psalms, Book of
Babylon	Elisha	James, Saint	Magdalene, Mary	Red Sea
Beelzebub	Esau	Jehovah	Mark, Saint	Ruth, Book of
Bethlehem	Esther	Jeremiah	Mary, the Virgin	Sadducees
Cain	Exodus	Jericho	Matthew, Saint	Samaria
Calvary	Ezekiel	Jerusalem	Moses	Samson
Canaanites	Ezra	Jesus Christ	Nazareth	Samuel
Chronicles, Book of	Gabriel	Job	Nebuchadnezzar	Sanhedrin
Cities of Refuge	Galilee	John the Baptist	Nehemiah	Saul
Corinthians	Galilee, Sea of	John, Saint	Noah	Sinai
David	Genesis	Jonah	Numbers, Book of	Solomon
Dead Sea	Gethsemane	Jonathan	Palestine	Tabernacle
Deborah	Gilead	Jordan	Passover	Thessalonians
Decalogue	Goliath	Joseph	Paul, Saint	Timothy
Delilah	Gospels	Joshua	Pentecost	Titus
Deluge	Herod	Judah	Peter	Tyre
Deuteronomy	Hittites	Judas	Pharisees	Vulgate

JERUSALEM

ABRAHAM AND ISAAC

In the land of Ur of the Chaldees, which lay between two great rivers of Mesopotamia, lived a good and rich man named Abram. He was happy there with his wife Sarah, his large staff of servants, and herds of cattle and sheep; and he thought he was to spend the rest of his life in the fruitful valley. But one day God called Abram and told him to go to a land called Canaan, many miles away on the eastern shore of the Mediterranean Sea. Abram, a God-fearing man, obeyed and left his home for the new land.

Abram settled in Canaan. Then God again called him and told him that he was to become the father of a chosen people who were to inhabit all the new country and be ruled by their own kings. Abram was to be called Abraham, which means *father of many*. To Abraham's great delight, God also promised him a son, for he and Sarah had no children. When the son was born to them, they were so happy that they named the child Isaac, meaning *laughing*. To show his great joy and thankfulness, Abraham offered sacrifices of burnt lambs to God, which was then the custom.

One day God decided to test Abraham. "Take thy son Isaac, whom thou lovest," He commanded, "and go to the land of Moriah. Thou must offer him there as a burnt offering, upon a mountain which I will tell thee of." Abraham was sad to have to sacrifice his only son, but he did not rebel or complain. Obediently the next morning he saddled his ass, gathered wood for fire, and departed with his son Isaac and two servants. When the little group reached the land of Moriah three days later, Abraham saw the mountain where he was to offer his sacrifice. He told the servants to wait while he and his son worshiped.

Abraham and Isaac then went on toward the summit. Isaac did not know why they were going up the mountain. "Father," he said, "here is fire and wood, but where is the lamb for the offering?" "My son," Abraham replied, "God will provide the lamb."

When they reached the top, Abraham built the altar and prepared the fire. Then he placed Isaac on the wood. But just as he was about to offer him as a sacrifice, he heard a voice calling, "Abraham, Abraham." "Here am I," Abraham answered. "Lay not thine hand upon the lad, for now I know thou fearest God," the voice said. Abraham knew then that God was only testing him, for he saw a ram caught in a thicket, and he sacrificed it instead of his son. Then the father and son walked down the mountain and went home. Abraham received even more blessings than

REBEKAH AND THE SERVANT
He asks for water at the well.

before, for his willingness to give up his dearest possession for God.

After many years Sarah died, and Abraham grew old. Isaac came into manhood, and Abraham decided that Isaac should have a wife. Because most of the people living in Canaan worshiped idols, Abraham wanted his son to marry a woman from Mesopotamia, where his kinsmen still lived and worshiped the true God. So Abraham sent his oldest and most trusted servant with ten camels and valuable gifts to his old homeland to find a wife for Isaac.

At the end of a long journey the servant came to a city in Mesopotamia and found a well outside the gate. It was late in the day, and a group of women were gathered about the well, drawing water. The servant stopped, rested his camels, and prayed to God to show him a wife for Isaac. The old servant's prayers were answered, and he was told that the woman who should respond in a kindly tone when he asked for water should be Isaac's wife. Then he noticed a beautiful, dark-eyed girl at the well. He approached her, saying, "Let me, I pray, drink a little water out of thy pitcher."

"Drink," she answered kindly, "and I will draw water for the camels also." She gave the servant a drink from her pitcher and brought water for the camels. He gave her a gold earring and bracelets.

The girl, whose name was Rebekah, told the servant that she was the daughter of Bethuel and that he should come to their house with the camels to rest. The servant was happy when he heard these tidings, for he knew that her father was a kinsman of Abraham. Rebekah ran home and told her mother and father and brother of the servant, and showed them the gifts.

Her brother, Laban, ran to the well and invited the servant to the house. The old servant accepted; but, before he would eat or drink, he told the family he had come from Abraham to find a wife for Isaac and that he wished Rebekah to return with him to Canaan. Bethuel and Laban listened and gave their consent, for they felt it was God's will. The happy servant, when he heard these words, gave to Rebekah, her mother, and her brother the costly jewels and brilliant garments which he had brought. The next day the old servant began his journey home, accompanied by Rebekah and her nurse.

Isaac, in the meanwhile, had remained at home. He was lonely, since his mother was dead and Abraham was old. One evening he went to walk in the fields alone and saw a caravan of camels in the distance. Walking to meet the caravan, he found the old servant with a bride for him. When the beautiful Rebekah saw Isaac, she covered her face with a veil, as was the custom of the time, and descended from her camel. Isaac was pleased with Rebekah and welcomed her to his home and made her his wife.

Abraham, too, was pleased. He gave all his herds and flocks to the happy couple and was comforted in his old age. After a while Abraham died, and Isaac and Rebekah sorrowfully buried him in a cave that had been set aside as a tomb for the family.

JACOB RECEIVES ISAAC'S BLESSING

Disguising himself as his brother Esau, he obtains the farewell blessing from his father.

THE TWO BROTHERS

Some years after Abraham died, Isaac and Rebekah became the parents of twin sons, Jacob and Esau. Unlike most twins, the two boys were very different. Esau, the elder, was strong and hairy and became a great hunter, known throughout Canaan for his ability to use the bow and arrow. But Jacob was not so strong as Esau, and remained at home to look after his father's flocks. Because he was the eldest son, Esau was his father's favorite. He also had the right to inherit his father's property. This privilege was called the birthright.

Returning from hunting one day, Esau was very hungry. He wanted something to eat more than he wanted anything else in the world. When he came into the house, he found that Jacob had cooked some pottage, a tasty dish of vegetables. "Give me, I pray, the pottage to eat, for I am very faint," he said to his brother.

Jacob, jealous of Esau's birthright, replied, "I will give thee the pottage, but thou must first sell me this day thy birthright." Ordinarily, the eldest son in a family would have done nothing of the sort, but Esau was thinking only of his hunger. So he accepted Jacob's terms and sold his birthright for a bowl of pottage.

Now Isaac, the father, was growing old and had become nearly blind. He was unable to tell his sons apart, even though they were so different in appearance. Being very fond of venison, or deer meat, he said one day to Esau, "Take thy bow and kill a deer, that I may taste again the venison that I love." Because he felt that he had not long to live, he told Esau that upon his return he would give him his farewell blessing. It was customary for the father, shortly before his death, to bestow a blessing upon the eldest son.

Rebekah overheard this request and was greatly displeased that Esau should be favored over Jacob, her favorite. As soon as Esau had left, she told Jacob to bring two young goats from the field. Jacob obeyed, and Rebekah cooked the meat and seasoned it to taste like the venison which Isaac liked so well. She told Jacob to dress in Esau's clothes. Then she put the skins of the goats on his arms and neck so that he would seem hairy like his brother. Jacob, however, was afraid that a curse would be placed upon him for deceiving his father. But when he told Rebekah of his fear, she replied, "Upon me be the curse, my son; only obey my voice."

Jacob then took the meat to his father. The aged man felt the hair on his son's arms and legs and thought him to be Esau, even though the voice was Jacob's. After he had eaten the meat, he drew his son to him and smelled of his garments, strong with the odor of the fields and the woods. Not knowing that this was Jacob, he bestowed the prized farewell blessing.

Esau, meanwhile, had shot a deer. Upon his return home, he placed a fine piece of venison before his father. Of course, he did not know that Jacob had already received the blessing that was meant for him. When Esau asked for the blessing, Isaac did not understand. "Who are thou?" he cried. "I am thy first born," Esau replied. Isaac knew then that Jacob had stolen the blessing intended for his brother. Esau was disappointed and angry at being cheated. He swore that he would kill Jacob. Esau asked his father to bless him, also, but Isaac could not take back the solemn words which he had bestowed upon Jacob.

When Rebekah learned that Esau had threatened to kill her favorite, she advised Jacob to leave Canaan and go to the home of her brother, Laban, in Mesopotamia, whence she had come and where Abraham had first lived. Jacob did as she told him and set out for Mesopotamia. When he arrived, he was received with open arms and was invited to live with his uncle. So Jacob made his home with Laban.

Before long, he fell deeply in love with the younger of Laban's two daughters, Rachel, and wished to marry her. Laban promised that he would consent to the wedding if Jacob would serve him for seven years. Jacob agreed, and for seven years he served his uncle. At the end of that time Jacob asked for Rachel's hand, but Laban said he could only consent if Jacob would serve him for another seven years. Jacob did so. He and Rachel then married, had sons, and prospered.

After living in exile for twenty years, Jacob decided to return to Canaan. He was eager to see his family again and to make friends with his brother, whom he had not seen in all that time. So Jacob set out with his family, his servants, and his flocks and journeyed to Canaan. As he approached the home of Esau, he halted and sent messengers ahead to ask forgiveness; for he feared that Esau might still carry out his threat to kill him. Despite their pleas, the messengers were unsuccessful and returned to Jacob with the news that his brother would meet him with a force of four hundred men. Then Jacob prayed to God to save him.

The next day, having sent other messengers ahead with gifts of goats and camels, he ran out to meet Esau alone and knelt down before him. Seeing his brother before him, Esau's wrath suddenly disappeared, and the brothers embraced and wept for joy at seeing each other again. When Jacob told him that the herds he had sent were for him, Esau answered, "I have enough, my brother; keep that thou hast unto thyself." But Jacob, wanting to prove to his brother that he no longer was greedy and selfish, insisted that Esau keep the gifts. The two brothers parted friends.

Esau went to his own home, and Jacob journeyed on to Hebron, a city in Canaan. There his father, Isaac, was still alive. Jacob lived in Canaan for many years, grew even more prosperous, and reared twelve sons who became the founders of the Twelve Tribes of Israel.

THE ISRAELITES DELIVERED FROM BONDAGE

During the time of the patriarch Jacob, a great famine fell upon the land of Canaan. No grain or grass grew, and it became necessary for Jacob and all his people to seek more fertile fields. The children of Israel, as they were called, went to Egypt. At that time Egypt was ruled by a kind and just Pharaoh, who welcomed the Israelites. For a time the Israelites were happy; they grew prosperous, increased in numbers, and became a power throughout the new land. But Jacob died, and his body was taken back to Canaan to rest with his forefathers.

Not all the Pharaohs were kind, however. After some years there came to the throne of Egypt a king who was harsh and cruel. He made slaves of the Israelites. "Behold," he said, "the people of the Children of Israel are more and mightier than we. We must keep them from multiplying, or they will join our enemies and fight against us." He ordered that all boys born to the Israelites be killed at birth, but no one would do so wicked a thing. Then he commanded

THE BLOOD SIGN
No harm befell a house marked with lamb's blood.

that all Israelite boys should be thrown in the river at birth.

The Story of Moses

Many of the Israelitish women hid their babies so that the Egyptians would not throw them into the river. One of these women, named Jochebed, had a beautiful son whom she was determined to save from such a fate. When he was three months old, she took him down to the river bank where reeds and bulrushes grew very thick. There she made a little ark, or boat, of bulrushes and covered it with pitch. In it she placed her little son, and told her daughter, Miriam, to watch over him in the rushes.

A few days later, Pharaoh's daughter, with her handmaidens, came down to the river to bathe. She saw the little boat and told one of her servants to bring it to her. As she opened it, the baby began to cry, and Pharaoh's daughter took pity on him. She discovered that he was one of the Hebrew children. Miriam, seeing that the princess had taken a liking to the infant, ran up to her. "May I not go and call one of the Hebrew women to nurse the child for thee?" she asked. "Go," said the princess; so Miriam went to her own mother. Jochebed appeared before the princess and was told to take the child and nurse him and that the princess would pay the expenses. Pharaoh's daughter named the child Moses, which means *drawn out;* when he grew older, she adopted him and reared him in the royal palace.

Moses was brought up as a member of the king's family. He received all the advantages of the princess' wealth and became a favorite at her court. But even though he was living in the palace, he never forgot that his own people were slaves. Every day he saw them making bricks and toiling in the cities and fields of the Egyptians. He saw them whipped and beaten by their cruel taskmasters, and decided to do something to help them.

One day, while out walking, he saw a particularly cruel Egyptian beating a Hebrew unmercifully. Moses became so enraged that he struck and killed the Egyptian. The Pharaoh soon heard of the matter, and Moses was forced to flee from the country to save his life. He went to the land of Midian in Arabia, where he became a shepherd for a priest named Jethro. He fell in love with one of the seven daughters of the priest and married her.

While Moses was living the peaceful life of a shepherd, things were growing worse in Egypt. The old Pharaoh died; but the new one was even more harsh and wicked than the old one, and the children of Israel were under worse taskmasters than before. God heard their cries and decided to help them. He selected Moses to lead them out of Egypt.

One day, when Moses was tending his sheep, God came to him in the form of a burning bush and told him to take his people back to Canaan where they had come from many years before. Moses, a modest man, protested, saying that he was afraid he was not strong enough for the task. God, however, promised to watch over him and to send Moses' brother, Aaron, to help him. It was to be Aaron's duty to tell the people that Moses was to lead them.

Moses left Jethro's home and met Aaron on Mount Horeb. From there they went to Egypt. First they had to win the trust of the chief men of the Israelites. When they had done this, they had to gain the confidence of their own people, who at first did not trust them. When they had at last succeeded in these tasks, they went to Pharaoh and asked him to permit the Israelites to go into the wilderness for three days to worship God.

Not only did Pharaoh refuse; he became very angry at such a request and set about to punish the Hebrews even further. At the time, the Israelites were making bricks out of clay and straw. Pharaoh now ordered that the slaves were to gather all the straw themselves and yet make just as many bricks as they had made before. This, of course, was almost

THE CRUEL PHARAOH'S OWN SON IS STRICKEN

Not even the first-born of the Egyptian ruler was spared by the God of the Israelites in the last but most terrible plague.

impossible. When the Israelites could not make the required number of bricks, the Egyptians beat and whipped them. In this state of affairs, it was difficult for Moses to fulfill his duty.

The Israelites' Escape

Moses again appealed to God and was told that his people would surely be freed. Then God inflicted terrible plagues upon the Egyptians, as a punishment for Pharaoh's refusal to let the Israelites go. First came the plague of blood, caused when Aaron struck the water in the river with his stick. All the waters in the land ran crimson with blood. The Egyptians had no water to drink, and all the fish died. The curse lasted seven days, but still Pharaoh refused to grant Moses' request.

Then came the plague of frogs, which Aaron brought about by stretching his rod over the waters. The frogs swarmed over the land. Pharaoh became fearful and asked Moses and Aaron to have God remove the affliction. "First, thou must promise to let my people go," Moses told Pharaoh. "I will let thy people go," the king said, "that they may do sacrifice unto the Lord." The curse was removed, and all the frogs died; but the next day Pharaoh refused to keep his promise.

Eight other plagues came before the final one, and through them all, the Children of Israel were protected by God. After the plague of the frogs, all Egyptians and their animals were covered with slimy, creepy things; then swarms of flies flew into all their houses. Another curse was the death of all the Egyptians' cattle and sheep. After this came plagues of boils, pestilence, hail and fire, locusts, and darkness. But even these plagues were not sufficient to make Pharaoh relent, and it became necessary for God to afflict Egypt with one last terrible plague that would force Pharaoh to let the Israelites go. This affliction was to be the death of the eldest son in every Egyptian household, including the king's; but no Israelite home was to be touched.

The night before this most severe of all curses, every man among the Children of Israel was ordered to kill a lamb, dip a plant in its blood, and make three marks of blood on the outside of his house. Then the lambs were to be roasted, and the people were to feast while the angel of death struck down the children of the Egyptians.

All this came about. The wails of the Egyptians went up throughout the land, even in the house of Pharaoh himself, but none of the Hebrews was harmed. It is from this occurrence that the Feast of the Passover has come down to modern times, celebrated by Jews once a year.

Pharaoh could not bear the affliction. He called Moses and Aaron to him and told them to take the Children of Israel out of the country. The next morning the Israelites started to leave the land of Egypt and the bonds of slavery. Led by Moses, they set out for the Promised Land by way of the Red Sea, for the only other way was through the land of the Philistines, a fierce, warlike people. Their only guide was a cloud which always went before them, becoming a pillar of fire to give them light at night.

Even after the terrible curse inflicted on the Egyptians, the cruel and treacherous Pharaoh wanted to bring the Hebrews back. He assembled a great army of men in chariots and on horses and went after the Hebrews. He sighted them on the shores of the Red Sea. The Israelites, seeing the Egyptians, became frightened. They went to Moses and cried, "Because there were no graves in Egypt, must we be carried here to die in the wilderness?" Moses calmed his people and told them that the Lord would not desert them.

At this moment, the cloud which had guided them moved from its place in front and that night came between them and Pharaoh's army. The side toward the Egyptians grew dark, so that the soldiers were lost, but on the Israelites' side there was light. God commanded His people to move forward. As they did so, Moses lifted his rod and stretched it toward the Red Sea. A strong wind from the east sprang up and blew all night, and in the morning there was a dry path across the sea.

The Egyptians, seeing that the Israelites had escaped, tried to follow. But, in their haste, the wheels of the chariots fell off, so that they could not go fast. When they started to cross on the path which separated the waters, Moses reached out his rod and waved it over the sea; the waters that had been piled up on each side of the path came together again and drowned the entire Egyptian army.

When they saw how they had been saved, the Hebrews prayed to God, thanking Him for their deliverance. Then they proceeded on their way to the Promised Land.

THE ISRAELITES ENTER THE PROMISED LAND

Even though the land of Canaan was not very far from Egypt, it took the Children of Israel forty years to reach the Promised Land. Their leader, Moses, grew very old and died before the Israelites reached the River Jordan. The Israelites, however, were not without a leader, for God had chosen Joshua, the son of Nun, to take Moses' place, and it was Joshua who completed the mighty task that Moses had begun many years before.

God had declared that the Israelites were to inhabit the city of Jericho in Canaan. When they neared the boundary of the country, Joshua sent ahead two men to look over the city and the surrounding country. These men crossed the Jordan and entered Jericho. They went to the home of a woman named Rahab, who sheltered them.

The king, hearing of the two spies, sent soldiers to find them. When the soldiers came to Rahab's house, she took the two men to the roof and there hid them under some stalks of flax drying in the sun. After the king's soldiers left, Rahab went back to the roof and told the spies that she knew the Children of Israel would conquer the city; but she begged that she might be spared from harm. The spies agreed to her request and told her to hang a scarlet thread in her window, so that the Israelites would know which house was hers.

As was the custom in ancient days, Jericho was surrounded by a high wall to protect her from enemies. Rahab's house was very close to the wall; so, when the two spies were ready to return to the Israelites' camp, they had only to let down a rope from a window and over the wall; then they dropped to the ground beyond the wall. While the king's soldiers searched for them, they hid in the mountains for three days before going back to their camp and reporting to Joshua.

Joshua made his plans for the capture of the city. Then he led his people to the banks of the Jordan and camped there for three days. The Israelites started across the river on the fourth day. The priests led the throng, carrying the sacred Ark of the Covenant. When they stepped into the river, the waters separated. The priests remained in the middle of the river until all the Israelites had passed to the other side. When all had safely crossed, the waters came together again. At last the tribes of Israel were in the land of Canaan.

God had promised that they would capture the city in seven days. There was, however, no battle outside the walls, as was sometimes the case when a city was attacked. Instead, the soldiers merely marched around the city once a day for six days. Marching with them were priests carrying the Covenant, and other priests who blew rams' horns. On the seventh day the soldiers and priests marched around the city six times. Then, the seventh time, the priests blew a loud blast on their trumpets and the people gave a great shout. At this, the walls of Jericho

JOSHUA AT JERICHO

The leader of the Israelites sees his army enter the great city of the Promised Land, after wandering forty years.

fell, and the Israelites rushed forward to take possession. As had been promised, no one was harmed in the house of Rahab where the scarlet thread hung in the window.

After Jericho was captured, the Israelites took over the entire land of Canaan. They tilled the soil and tended their flocks as they had done before they became slaves in Egypt. With the help of God they also made their own laws and, after a time, came to be ruled by men called judges, who were chosen by God.

RUTH AND NAOMI
The Reward of Loyalty

Many years after the Israelites conquered Jericho and inhabited the land of Canaan, there was a famine so severe that many people were forced to leave the country. One of the men who left his home was Elimelech. With his wife, Naomi, and his two sons, he went to the land of Moab, a country which lay far beyond the Jordan River. There the family was happy and prosperous for a time. But soon Elimelech died, and Naomi and her sons, who had married Moab women, stayed in the country and tilled the fields. Ten years after Elimelech died, Naomi lost her two sons and was left alone with her daughters-in-law, Orpah and Ruth.

Naomi was sad in the land of Moab and longed to return to Bethlehem where her family lived. So one day she set out for Bethlehem with Orpah and Ruth.

Now, the two daughters-in-law had never been outside their own country, and Naomi knew that they would be frightened and lonely in a strange land. She told them of the hardships they would face, and begged them to go back to their own people, where they were known and where they might find comfort in their grief. Orpah finally consented to return, but Ruth would not listen to her mother-in-law's plea. Instead, she answered, "Entreat me not to leave thee, or to return from following after thee; for whither thou goest, I will go; and where thou lodgest, I will lodge; thy people shall be my people, and thy God my God."

Naomi could not be harsh with Ruth after this beautiful reply; so the two sorrowful women went on and finally reached the city of Bethlehem. There, Naomi was welcomed by her old friends and relatives, but she asked them not to call her Naomi. Instead, she told them to call her Mara, which means *bitter*. When they asked for a reason, she told them that the Lord had treated her bitterly and had taken away her husband and two sons.

Naomi and Ruth were very poor. They had no money and no food, so Ruth said she would go out into the fields and pick up the barley which the reapers had left behind when they harvested. She went to the fields of a man named Boaz, who was a rich relative of Elimelech. One day he came into the field and saw the strange young woman working hard at gathering the grain. Asking who she was, he was told that she refused to desert her grief-stricken mother-in-law. Boaz was very kind to Ruth and ate with her during the daytime, and told the reapers to let some grain fall purposely for Ruth. As the harvest went on, Ruth continued to gather the grain, and she and Naomi were able to live comfortably.

Before long, Boaz fell in love with Ruth; and when the threshing season was over, he asked her to be his wife. Naomi, happy that Ruth should have met one of her relatives, gave her consent. So Ruth and Boaz were married. After a time a son was born to them, and Naomi became his nurse. The child was named Obed. Many years later he became the grandfather of David, who was one of the great kings of Israel.

SAMUEL ANOINTS SAUL
The last of the judges creates the first king of the Jews.

SAMUEL
The Last of the Judges

For a long time the Children of Israel were ruled by men called judges. These men were really the high priests of the tabernacle, but their power was so great that they became the leaders of the entire country. One of these judges, named Eli, was a good man, but he had two wicked sons. Eli was very unhappy because he thought that one day they would become judges after he died, and he knew that God would be displeased. He longed for someone good and just to succeed him.

One day a woman came into the tabernacle to pray. She was weeping and spoke so softly that Eli could hardly understand her. She finally told him that the blessing of having a child of her own had been denied her, and that she and her husband,

Elkanah, wanted a son more than anything else in the world. Eli told Hannah, for that was her name, to trust in God, that He would answer her prayers. Hannah returned to her home and prayed again. She vowed that, if God should give her a son, she would place him in the service of the Lord. After a time her prayers were answered, and a son was born to her. Elkanah and Hannah gave thanks to the Lord and named the little boy Samuel.

Not forgetting her vow, Hannah took Samuel to the tabernacle and showed him to Eli. "I am the woman who prayed here," she told him, "and this child is the blessing I asked for. Therefore, I have given him back to the Lord, and he shall belong to the Lord as long as he lives." Eli took the child and promised to bring him up in the service of God. Hannah visited her son often and brought him a new coat at every visit.

Eli was very happy to have Samuel with him, because the boy was eager to learn and obeyed all his commands. One night Samuel heard a voice saying, "Samuel, Samuel." He awakened and ran into the room where Eli was sleeping, saying, "Here am I." He thought it was the high priest who had called. But Eli said, "I did not call." Young Samuel went back to his room puzzled, because he knew no one else who could have called him. He went back to sleep, and in a little while he was awakened again by the voice calling, "Samuel."

Again he answered, "Here am I," and again he ran to Eli's room to find out what he wanted. But the high priest had not called this time either; so Samuel returned to his bed. Then for the third time he heard the voice, and this time he said to the high priest, "Here am I, for thou didst call me." Eli then knew that it was the voice of God that Samuel had heard.

"Go, lie down," he told the boy, "and if He call thee, say 'Speak, Lord, for Thy servant heareth.'" Samuel returned to his bed; and when the voice called for the fourth time, he answered as the high priest had ordered. Samuel was very sad when the voice said that Eli and his sons were going to be punished. It was revealed to him that the sons were wicked and that Eli had not kept them from their evil ways as a strong father should have done.

The next morning Samuel unhappily went about his work in the tabernacle. He did not want to tell the old high priest what God had revealed to him. But Eli called him and said, "Samuel, my son, what is the thing that the Lord hath said unto thee? I pray thee hide it not from me." Even though Samuel was a good boy and did not want to hurt the man who had treated him kindly, he could not refuse; so he told Eli of the punishment that God would give to him and his sons.

Eli sadly nodded his head and said, "It is the Lord! Let Him do what seemeth Him good."

For a little while nothing happened. At that time the Israelites were engaged in a war with the fierce Philistines, who lived in a neighboring country. First one side would win a battle, then the other. But one day the Israelites lost a great battle. When the soldiers returned, the people asked why they had been defeated, and were told that it was because the Ark of the Covenant, which contained the precious Tablets of the Law, had not been with them. The chiefs of the army then decided they would do battle with the Philistines again and that this time the Ark would be carried out to the field of battle.

Now, ordinarily, the Ark was never taken out of the tabernacle unless God advised it. This time, however, the people did not pray to God, and the sons of Eli removed the Ark from the tabernacle and took it to the battlefield. Everyone cheered when the Ark was brought out. The Philistines heard the shout but could not understand it. They asked what the shout was for; but when they were told about the Ark, they were not disheartened. That day the Philistines defeated the Israelites in another great battle. The two sons of Eli were killed, but the greatest calamity of all was the capture of the Ark by the enemy.

Eli, old and blind, heard the cry of despair that went up when it was learned that the Ark was lost. He could endure the news of the death of his sons, but the capture of the Ark, which he was pledged to protect, was too great a shock. He fell from his seat, when he heard the news, and was killed.

Samuel was stricken with grief when he found Eli dead and heard that the Ark had been captured; but he knew that it was the fulfillment of the message he had received from God. He then became judge over all the people. After seven months the Israelites regained the Ark,

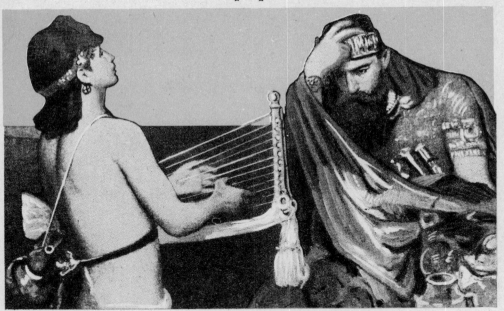

YOUNG DAVID PLAYS HIS HARP FOR SAUL
The king of the Israelites is comforted by the young shepherd's music.

and Samuel was happy. He offered sacrifices to God; and God, in turn, blessed the people and Samuel. But the boy who had been called by God was not to be the ruler of his people quite all his life. When Samuel became very old, the people demanded a king. Samuel was not unhappy, for he was old and tired, and was content to do what the people wished, and what God willed. So, before he died, he anointed the first king of Israel, who was named Saul.

DAVID AND JONATHAN
A Story of Friendship

Saul, the first king of Israel, was a strange man. One day he might be happy and cheerful, but the next day he might be glum and silent. Whenever he was in one of his gloomy moods, he would call musicians and poets to his throne to entertain him; and after they had played or sung to him, he would feel better.

One time, however, his servants were unable to find anyone who could help the king. Saul remained angry for many days and brooded for hours at a time

without saying a word. One of his attendants, eager to please the king, finally suggested that he had heard about a skilled harpist; so messengers were sent to bring this musician to the court. The messengers brought back a strong, manly youth of sixteen, with red hair and a handsome face. He was David, a tender of sheep. Saul was greatly pleased with the youth and received much comfort from the sweet songs the boy played upon his harp.

David stayed at the court and became a great favorite of the king and his attendants. But this pleasant existence was not to last long. After a time the Israelites were threatened by a neighboring warlike people, the Philistines, and Saul proceeded to form an army to defend his country. David went back to his father's house and again became a shepherd. Three of his brothers, however, joined the Israelite army.

One day Jesse, David's father, sent the boy to the camp with food. While there, David heard the soldiers talking about a giant in the Philistine camp named Goliath, who was bigger and stronger than anyone in the Israelite army. They told how the giant had issued a challenge for someone from the Israelite army to meet him in single combat; but no one was brave enough to do battle with him. David, however, was not afraid and asked to be sent against the giant. "Thou art but a youth," said King Saul. David, however, insisted that he be allowed to fight Goliath.

Finally Saul consented. He offered the youth a helmet and a coat of mail, but David refused these things. He took with him only a slingshot and five smooth, round stones. When Goliath saw who was coming out to meet him, he was very much amused. David, not heeding the taunts of the giant, calmly placed a stone in the sling and aimed at the huge Philistine's forehead. He let go the sling, and the stone struck Goliath squarely in the middle of the forehead, killing him instantly. The Philistines fled when they saw their huge soldier killed by a youth without armor.

David became a great hero and general, and everyone praised him for his bravery. But Saul, who had at first liked the youth when he played the harp and sang for him, began to brood and to wonder about him. He became suspicious that David would seek to take away his kingdom. He was especially angry when Jonathan, his son and heir, became David's best friend. Jonathan, however, gave no thought to his father's anger. Instead, he gave David his royal robe, sword, girdle, and bow; and his "soul was knit with the soul of David, and he loved him as his own soul." The two were always together, and the people grew accustomed to seeing the two strong, brave youths in the market place or leading the army. Saul's jealousy of David increased, however, and soon David feared that he would have to flee for his life. Jonathan tried to make his father feel more kindly toward David and thought that he had succeeded.

David was supposed to attend a certain feast, but feared a plot to kill him; so he told Jonathan that he would not attend. Moreover, he told Jonathan that if Saul should ask where he was, he should answer that he had gone to Bethlehem. "Thou wilt know from his manner of receiving this news whether my life is still in danger," David told Jonathan. Then they agreed on a signal. The day after the feast, David would hide near the stone of Ezel. Jonathan would go into a nearby field and shoot three arrows. Then he would send a boy to find the arrows, saying to him, "Behold, the arrows are on this side of thee," or "Behold, the arrows are beyond thee." If the words "beyond thee" were shouted, David would know that Saul still intended to kill him.

When the feast occurred, David was absent, and Saul asked Jonathan where he was. Jonathan replied that David had gone to Bethlehem. Saul then flew into a rage and warned his son that as long as David was alive his right to the throne was in danger. Jonathan knew then that his father meant to kill his friend. In great sorrow, he went to the field and shot the arrows. David heard the words "beyond thee" and knew that his life was in danger. The two friends wept and said farewell and David fled into the hills.

Some time later, Saul formed an army to pursue David, who had intrenched himself and his followers on a sand hill. Jonathan braved his father's wrath and saw his friend again when Saul's forces had surrounded the hill. Jonathan told David that he should have no fear, that the name of the next king of Israel would be David and not Jonathan. This was the last time the devoted friends ever saw each other, and their final meeting was one of tears and sorrow. In the battle David defeated Saul, but he forgave the king for seeking his life. Later, Jonathan was killed in a battle against the Philistines. When David heard of his friend's death, he composed this beautiful passage:

DAVID WITH HIS SLING

"The beauty of Israel is slain upon thy high places: how are the mighty fallen!

How are the mighty fallen in the midst of the battle! O Jonathan, thou wast slain in thine high places.

"I am distressed for thee, my brother Jonathan: very pleasant hast thou been unto me: thy love to me was wonderful, passing the love of women.

"How are the mighty fallen, and the weapons of war perished!"

It so happened that in the same battle, which the Israelites lost, Saul killed himself by falling on his sword. When David heard this, he was as stricken with sorrow as he was when he heard of his friend's death. Later, he was crowned king, fulfilling Jonathan's promise, and he became one of the greatest of Israel's rulers.

STORIES OF DANIEL

In Babylon on the Euphrates River, far to the east of Israel, dwelt the great and powerful King Nebuchadnezzar. His armies conquered all the lands around, and finally conquered Israel, too. When he captured the city of Jerusalem, he carried away large numbers of Jews, whom he placed in captivity in Babylon. As in Egypt many years before, the Children of Israel were set to work building palaces and temples.

Now, even though Nebuchadnezzar had conquered Israel, he admired the Jews in many ways and ordered that a group of Jewish youths be selected and given special training for service in his own vast and splendid palace in Babylon. He commanded that only handsome, strong, and intelligent boys be chosen.

One of the boys chosen for this select group was Daniel. Even though he was to live in a country where the people worshiped idols, he vowed that he would never forget the teachings of his Hebrew forefathers. Daniel was taken to Babylon with the other chosen youths and went to live in the palace.

Nebuchadnezzar ordered that all the boys should eat the same meat, and drink the same wine that he did. But Daniel thought that it would be sinful to do so because the Babylonians also used meat and wine in sacrifices to their idols. He asked the chief officer to let him and three companions eat other kinds of food, but the officer refused, even though he was fond of Daniel.

The officer placed the four boys under the charge of the royal cook, who was told to feed them meat and wine. Now, the reason Nebuchadnezzar wished the chosen youths to eat meat and drink wine was that he believed such a diet would make them healthy. He had decreed that at the end of three years the boys should be brought before him.

Finally Daniel, in order that he and his three companions might not have to eat the sinful food, proposed a test to the cook.

"Try us," he said, "and give us only vegetables to eat and water to drink for ten days. At the end of that time, compare our faces with those of the young people who have eaten of the king's food; and if we do not look so well as they, then give us whatsoever thou thinkest best." The cook agreed, and the four youths were given only vegetables and water, while the others ate meat and drank wine.

At the end of ten days the faces of Daniel and the other three boys were fatter and clearer than those of the rest of the group. So these four boys continued to eat as they pleased. At the end of three years, when they were called before the king, they were found to be healthier, more handsome, and wiser than all the rest.

The King's Dream

One day Nebuchadnezzar sent for some of his wise men. He told them that the night before, he had had a disturbing dream but had forgotten what it was. He wanted them to tell him of the dream and also to interpret it. When the wise men protested that no one in the world could bring back a forgotten dream, Nebuchad-

KING NEBUCHADNEZZAR BOWS BEFORE DANIEL

DANIEL READS THE HANDWRITING ON THE WALL
The prophet foretells the unhappy fate of Belshazzar's wicked reign.

nezzar grew very angry. He swore that he would kill all the wise men of Babylon if they could not do as he asked. Now Daniel had grown up to be one of the wise men of Babylon; and when he heard of the king's threat, he went to him and asked for more time. He promised Nebuchadnezzar that after a few days he would be able to tell the dream· and reveal its meaning. The king agreed, and Daniel went home to pray to God. His prayers were answered and the dream was re-vealed to him. He returned to the palace and told the king:

"Thou sawest in thy dream, O King, a great image. The form of it was terrible, and it shone with exceeding brightness as it stood before thee. Its head was made of fine gold, its breast and arms were of silver, the rest of its body was of brass; its legs were of iron, and its feet were part of iron and part of clay. As thou beheld it, there came a stone cut out of a mountain, that struck the image upon its feet and broke them to pieces. Then the image fell, and the iron, the brass, the silver, the gold, and the clay were broken up together by the stone, into pieces as small as the dust which is left on the threshing floor; and the wind blew them away, no one could tell where. Afterward the stone that had broken the image became a great mountain and filled the whole earth."

Nebuchadnezzar was greatly pleased, for he remembered that this was indeed the dream. Then the king asked Daniel to explain the dream to him. The wise man replied that the dream was a warning of things to come; that all the different metals, the gold, the silver, the brass, and the iron signified different kingdoms. The gold, he said, was Nebuchadnezzar himself because he was the greatest king of all. Other kingdoms would follow but all would be destroyed; and a new kingdom of the Lord, as strong as the rock in the dream, would take their place and would never be torn down.

When Nebuchadnezzar heard these things, he knelt before Daniel and said, "Your God is a God of gods, and a Lord of kings, and a revealer of secrets, seeing thou couldest reveal this secret." He rewarded Daniel with many gifts and placed him at the head of all the wise men in the land.

The Handwriting on the Wall

While Nebuchadnezzar reigned, Babylon became powerful and strong and ruled over many lands. When he died, his son, Belshazzar, came to the throne. But Belshazzar was not so great a king as his father had been, and other nations began to make war on the Babylonians. Daniel was still living in Babylon when Belshazzar ruled, and was one of the wise men of the time.

One night Belshazzar gave a grand feast for a thousand of his nobles. Choice meats and tasty sweets from all over the country were brought in, and wine was served in the gold and silver vessels which the Babylonians had taken from the temple in Jerusalem many years before. When the feast was at its height, a man's hand suddenly appeared and began to write strange, unknown words on the wall. The king and all his nobles grew fearful, for they had never before seen such writing, and soon they were terrified.

When the hand stopped writing and disappeared, the king called in his wise men and said, "Whoever shall read this writing and tell what it means shall be clothed in scarlet and have a chain of gold about his neck and shall be the third ruler in the kingdom." But the Babylonian wise men were unable to read the mysterious words.

When the queen heard of the strange hand and the words which no one could read, she went to the king and said, "Be not troubled, O King. There is a man in thy kingdom who has the wisdom and understanding of the gods and who was made chief of all the wise men by thy father, Nebuchadnezzar. Let this man, Daniel, be called; he will tell thee what the writing means."

So Daniel was brought to read the writing, and the king offered him the costly gifts if he should tell what the words meant. "Keep thy gifts to thyself," Daniel replied, "and give thy rewards to another. I will read and interpret the writing for the king."

Before he started to read, however, Daniel rebuked the king for his worship of idols and for all the pomp and glory of the kingdom. "Thou hast not humbled thine heart," he said, "but hast been proud and sinful. Behold the golden vessels of the temple of God, which thou and thy lords have filled with wine."

Then he told the king that the hand which had appeared was sent by God, and he read the words, which were, "Mene, Mene, Tekel, Upharsin," meaning "God hath numbered thy kingdom, and finished it. Thou art weighed in the balance and art found wanting. Thy kingdom is divided and given to the Medes and Persians."

When Belshazzar heard this, he gave Daniel the clothes of scarlet and placed a chain of gold around his neck and made him the third ruler of the kingdom. And that same night, Babylon was attacked by the Medes and the Persians, and Belshazzar was killed. As the hand had written on the wall, the great kingdom of the Babylonians was divided between the Medes and the Persians.

Daniel in the Lions' Den

When Babylon was captured by the Medes and the Persians, Darius the Mede became king. He chose one hundred twenty princes to rule over the land, and they, in turn, were governed by three presidents. One of these presidents was Daniel, who became the favorite of the king. In fact, Darius placed Daniel at the head of Babylon as the chief president, because of his wisdom. The other presidents and princes were jealous and plotted to have Daniel killed, so that they would have his power. They tried to find out evil things about him; but because Daniel was a good and kind man, they were unable to tell Darius anything that would cause him to be angry with Daniel.

The people of Babylon still worshiped idols, but Daniel remained true to the God of his forefathers and prayed in his room three times a day. The jealous presidents and princes decided to use this information against him. So they went before Darius.

"King Darius, live forever," they said. "All the presidents of the kingdom, the governors, and the princes, the counsellors, and the captains have consulted together to make a royal law, that whoever shall pray to any God or man except thee for thirty days shall be cast into the den of lions. Now, O King, put this law into writing and sign it so that it cannot be changed; for the laws of the Medes and the Persians never change." Darius saw no objection to the law; so he had it written, and signed it.

Although Daniel heard about the law, he did not waver in his worship of God.

DANIEL AND THE LIONS
God protects the prophet from harm while he is imprisoned in the dungeon.

He continued to pray in his home, with the windows open so that everyone could see. His enemies waited until he knelt down to pray; as soon as he did so, they hastened to Darius and told him that Daniel had disobeyed the law he had just signed.

Darius admired Daniel and was greatly troubled that he should have signed a law that would injure the chief wise man of his kingdom. But he had to carry out the law, for not even he could change it. Daniel was seized, and as he was placed in the lions' den, Darius came to him and said, "Thy God, whom thou servest continually, he will deliver thee." Then Darius sealed the door of the den and sorrowfully went back to his palace, where he fasted and remained awake all night.

In the meantime, Daniel was surrounded by the fierce beasts. But he prayed to God, and his prayers were answered. Early the next morning, Darius hastened to the den to see how his trusted adviser had fared. "O Daniel," he called before he unlocked the door, "is thy God whom thou servest continually able to deliver thee from the lions?" Then, joyfully, he heard the voice of Daniel answer him in these words: "O King, live forever. My God hath sent His angel, and hath shut the lions' mouths, so that they have not harmed me. For I am innocent before him, and I have done thee no hurt." The king then unlocked the door to the den and released Daniel.

Knowing of the plot to have Daniel killed, Darius then ordered that all the presidents and princes who had plotted against him should themselves be thrown into the den. The order was carried out, and all the evildoers were killed by the lions.

Darius made a new law that everyone in the land should honor Daniel's God, and the faithful wise man received even more honors than he had before. When Darius died and Cyrus the Persian came to the throne, Daniel was given the highest posts in the country, for the new ruler admired him as much as Darius had. Cyrus was kind to all the Jews who were captives in Babylon. In the first year of his reign, he permitted them to return to Jerusalem to rebuild their temple, which had been destroyed many years before. He also returned all the gold and silver vessels and ornaments which Nebuchadnezzar had taken when he conquered the Children of Israel.

BIBLIOTHÈQUE NATIONALE, *be ble o tek' nah syo nal'.* This "national library" of the French people is the largest library on the continent of Europe. Since 1536, a copy of every book printed in France has been placed in its archives. Thus it corresponds to the Library of Congress in Washington, D. C., which contains a copy of every book carrying an American copyright.

The Bibliothèque Nationale is in Paris. Someone has estimated that it would take one person over 7,000 years to read all the books in it, if one book a day were read. Besides its more than 2,600,000 printed volumes and maps, it has hundreds of thousands of manuscripts, engravings, coins, and medals. Originally, the library was the private collection of writings of the French kings. The present building was completed in 1875.

THE BICYCLE'S GRANDFATHER
More than 100 years ago, men rode the "hobby horse" the first bicycle.

BICYCLE, *bi'sik'l.* This light, two-wheeled vehicle of "the gay 90's" bridged the gap, in personal transportation, between the horse and motorized equipment. It was small, easily handled and stored, could carry many times its own weight, and multiplied the rider's speed and travel range many times. Moreover, it was cheap, and a great deal of fun.

"A Bicycle Built for Two," or tandem, really carried many a couple into matrimony—bicycle picnics were the memorable events of vacation time—and the sturdy member of the "Century" club who could wheel his hundred miles in a day cut a dashing figure in his social circle.

Not many years ago, it was believed that the bicycle would become as scarce

FORBEARS OF THE MODERN "BIKE"

From the hobbyhorse of 1818 (above), to the wabbly high-wheeler of the 70's (right), bicycles gained in favor because they carried folks far and fast, with little effort. Below, a parade of fashionable riders rolls down Riverside Drive in New York City. "Scorchers" who went too fast were subject to arrest.

Left, early lever-operated bicycle. Right, half ride, half run.

IN THE NINETIES
The "tandem" of days gone by.

in the United States as the horse and
buggy. Yet, today, thousands of boys and
girls, and men and women, too, ride
bicycles for pleasure and exercise. It is
not unusual to see groups of a dozen or
more holiday makers pedaling down a
city street. Many stands and shops rent
bicycles by the hour or day to adult
riders; while boys and girls usually prefer
to have their own. In the summer, special trains carry big-city cyclists and their
mounts to pleasant reaches of the countryside every week end.

It was in the last decade of the nineteenth century, however, that bicycle riding reached its height. Then, there were
bicycles built for two, three, four, and
sometimes as many as five or six persons.
But, with the coming of the automobile,
their popularity waned, and it was not until many years later that bicycling became
an important pastime again.

In Europe, the custom of riding bicycles never disappeared. In any large
European capital, thousands of people
may be seen riding them to and from
work. In fact, there are more bicycles

in Europe than there are automobiles, a
situation that is just the reverse in the
United States. Economical operation
makes the "velo" the average Berliner's
or Parisian's most practical means of
rapid transportation.

Bicycles today have been greatly improved over the old models. Coaster
brakes, ball bearings, pneumatic tires,
spring seats, and electric lamps have combined to make bicycling safer and more
comfortable. Some bicycles are equipped
with gears, permitting the rider to pedal
quite easily when going up a hill. A good
bicycle can be purchased for $25 or less.
Formerly, they cost and weighed much
more.

Although two-wheeled vehicles were
known as long ago as the time of the

A MODERN TRIO
A healthful way to travel to school.

Egyptians, it was not until 1816 that a
bicycle similar to the one we know today
was invented. This first bicycle, invented
by Baron von Drais, a German, was a
queer-looking affair. It had two wheels
connected by a bar. The rider straddled
the bar and moved by kicking the ground
first with his left foot and then with his
right, sometimes attaining a speed of ten
miles an hour. The only way in which
he could go faster was to coast downhill.

This machine was known as the *drai-
sine,* and was followed by the *curricule,*
which was also called the *hobby horse* or

dandy horse. It had pedals on the front wheel. The *velocipede* was the next improvement; it looked very much like our modern bicycle, except that the frame and wheels were made of wood and it was rather clumsy to operate. After the velocipede was introduced into the United States, in 1866, it became popular almost immediately.

Soon, strange devices with huge front wheels and tiny rear wheels made their appearance. It took nerve and daring to

ing vehicle. Six-day races are held in several cities during the winter every year. In these exciting contests, two men form a team, and they alternate with one another in the race, one sleeping and eating while

**BIGHORN
CHAMPION
MOUNTAIN
CLIMBER**

This is the bighorn, or Rocky Mountain sheep, agile denizen of the crags and peaks of the West. He is one of the most difficult of all animals to capture or shoot.

ride one of these, for the rider was perched far above the ground, and the machine was not very stable. Next to make its appearance, about 1885, was the *safety* bicycle, in which both wheels are of equal diameter and pedal power turns the rear wheel by means of a chain and sprockets. In 1880, John B. Dunlop of Ireland fitted rubber hose to the wheels of his son's bicycle, beginning the development of the pneumatic tire which means so much to the modern automobile. When the automobile came into use, small motors were attached to some bicycles, marking the beginning of the motorcycle.

Besides being widely used for pleasure and business, the bicycle serves as a rac-

the other rides. The purpose of the long and strenuous grind is to "lap" the other teams, or lead them by one full length of the oval course. The pair scoring the most "laps" at the end of the six days wins the race. Amateur riders have shorter contests.

Modern streamlining for trains, airplanes, automobiles, and boats is said to have developed from the crouched position assumed by cyclists to cut down wind resistance.

BIG'HORN. Dizzy heights of mountain crags, which no hunter can hope to reach afoot, hold no terrors for the bighorn, elusive wild sheep of the Rockies. This hardy game animal, which is also known as the Rocky Mountain sheep, has large, curved horns, about three and one-half feet long. Its wool is grayish brown over the body, lighter on the face, with a white patch on the rump and a black line along the spine. Its protective coloring is so effective that hunters must aid keen eyesight with powerful binoculars to sight bighorn as they graze, usually in groups of twenty or thirty, against the rocky background of their usual range. A close shot is a rarity.

BILL OF RIGHTS. After the United States Constitution had been ratified, some of the states insisted that it failed to guarantee certain rights of the people, such as freedom of speech, freedom of the press, and trial by jury. Therefore, at the first session of Congress in 1789, the first ten amendments to the Constitution were proposed, covering such rights, and all were ratified by 1791. These amendments have since been called the Bill of Rights of the Constitution.

Similarly, bills of rights have also been inserted into the constitutions of most of the individual states, enumerating rights of the people that may not be violated, and limiting the rights of the state legislatures.

England also has a Bill of Rights. It is an act of Parliament, passed in 1689 and stating the fundamentals of liberty which are vitally associated with the British form of government. Since the Revolution in 1789 there have been several bills of rights in the history of France.

In general, a bill of rights is a manifesto listing the fundamental rights which should naturally belong to a free people.

BINOCULAR, *bi nok'u lar,* **INSTRUMENT.** Used to magnify objects that are small or far away, a binocular instrument may be in the form of a microscope, telescope, or field glass, having two lenses and tubes so that both eyes can be used. See Microscope.

BIOG'RAPHY. Some of the most interesting stories in the world are biographies—personal histories of individual lives. Biography shows us the world through another's eyes; it tells the things we like to know about successful and brave men; about beautiful and charming women; or even about people who have been failures. There are many types of biographies.

The Life of Washington, by Irving, presents the heroic soul and magnetic personality of the first President; in his immortal *David Copperfield,* Dickens draws heavily upon the trying experiences of his own unhappy childhood, thus offering an autobiography—the life story of a person written by himself. In *David Copperfield,* the autobiography appears as fiction. In the various books of the Old Testament, the spiritually charged lives of the patriarchs unfold dramatically in what is biography in its most simple form. Boswell's intimate *Life of Dr. Samuel Johnson* is a famous example of a biography in which the daily acts and sayings of a great man are faithfully recorded by a humble friend.

Biographies have undergone a change of style since the ancient Greeks and Romans wrote of their heroes and gods. They were content merely to tell of the events in the life of an individual. The Greek author Plutarch, however, in his *Parallel Lives,* compared Roman and Greek men, thus laying the foundation for later improvement in the scope of biographies.

During the Middle Ages, writers confined their biographies chiefly to saints and martyrs, but in 1774, in his *Life and Letters of Gray,* Mason introduced personal and intimate facts from the pen of the subject himself. To Samuel Johnson, however, is accredited the modern trend in biography. His *Life of Savage,* published in 1744, although incomplete, marks the change to a critical and intimate style.

One of the most famous early American works is the *Autobiography* of Benjamin Franklin. Popular biographies of more recent date include: *Napoleon* and *Bismarck,* by Emil Ludwig; Lytton Strachey's *Queen Victoria;* Carl Sandburg's *Abra-*

ham Lincoln; and W. E. Woodward's *George Washington* and *Meet General Grant.* There are many collections of biographical narratives, among which are the *English Dictionary of National Biography, Cyclopedia of American Biography,* and *Dictionary of American Biography.*

BIOLOGY, *by ol'o ji.* The greatest mystery in the world is life—that strange spark which distinguishes living things from non-living things. It baffles and fascinates man now as much as it ever did, and today he devotes his broadest field of scientific work, biology, to its investigation.

Because we ourselves are living and dependent upon living things to keep ourselves alive, the study of life is of vital importance. Anything which will make life happier for us is worth while, and the problems which have been and are being solved by biologists have made, and will continue to make, living a pleasanter experience for us.

An Age-old Problem. Of course, men have tried to learn about life since the dawn of history, but the science of biology really begins with Aristotle, the immortal Greek thinker whose teachings still dominate the philosophy of Western civilization. In the third century before Christ, he founded the science of natural history, and this is accepted as the forerunner of modern biology. He believed that we should go directly to Nature herself to gain an understanding of the mysteries of life. But for centuries men considered themselves superior to the natural world and refused to go to the bottom of things. So it was hundreds of years before people began to follow Aristotle's example. It was thought arrogant to believe anything except the views of some supposed authority, or to make any attempt to test the truth of his statements.

One of the first men to break away from the accepted form of reasoning was Vesalius, a Belgian anatomist who lived from 1514 to 1564. He refused to believe what had been written about the structure of the human body until he could see for himself. Vesalius set a splendid example of studying through observation, but it remained for William Harvey, an Englishman (1578-1657), to open up the vast field of experimentation. It was Harvey who first discovered the circulation of the blood, and thus created such a stir that biologists definitely took up the dual method of observation *and* experimentation.

Biology Becomes Systematized. Of course these pioneers made mistakes; often they reached conclusions based on evidence which they misinterpreted. But with the invention of the microscope, their investigations became far more accurate, and their conclusions more dependable. Before very long, however, data accumulated so rapidly that scientists became hopelessly bogged in a welter of varying terms and phrases. The science of biology owes whatever precision and exactness it may claim to the Swedish botanist who called himself Linnaeus (1707-1778). He devised the Latin system of terminology which is the basis of the system used today, and brought order out of confusion.

Then biology began to branch out. There developed the belief that great problems of life could be solved by comparing the anatomies of different living things. Cuvier (1769-1832), a French naturalist, founded a school which followed this line of thought with great success, and added much to the knowledge of the organization of animals. About the same time, another Frenchman, Bichat (1771-1802), laid the basis of our knowledge of animal tissues—foundation stone of much of present-day observation.

Bichat and Cuvier studied living structures pretty much as they were, with little regard for what they had been or might become. It remained for von Baer, a Russian scientist who lived from 1792 to 1876, to introduce this line of reasoning with his work in embryology. Embryology takes up the study of the embryo—the undeveloped organism which is the start of every living object.

While these advances were being made, studies were going on in other fields. The Swiss physiologist, Haller (1708-1777), added to the work started by Harvey, and he was followed in the nineteenth century by Johannes Müller, a German (1801-1858). Their work soon brought physiology into its own as a distinct field of work under the great general heading of biology.

Biology and Evolution. In 1859, when he published *The Origin of Species,* Charles Robert Darwin (1809-1882) startled the world with the theory of evolution. His work was based on that of three men who preceded him: Erasmus Darwin (1731-1802), his grandfather; and two French scientists, Count Georges Buffon (1707-1788) and Jean Baptiste Lamarck (1744-1829). Charles Darwin presented the theory so systematically, and backed it up with such a mass of evidence, it was accepted by many prominent scientists of his own generation, and has dominated biological thought ever since his time. In brief, this theory is that living things, both plants and animals, have developed from earlier forms, now extinct. A good deal of argument has prevailed as to the causes of evolution; the scientific world quite generally accepts the basic idea.

Life from Living Things. One long-standing superstition still clung—the idea that life could come from non-living matter. This meant that certain scientists believed that bad meat produced flies, a conclusion obviously based on nothing more than the fact that there are flies on bad meat. Though occasionally refuted by doubting investigators, that notion lasted from the days of Aristotle to the time of the great French chemist, Louis Pasteur (1822-1895), who definitely proved that the living bacteria found in spoiled food did not spring to life spontaneously.

From there Pasteur went on to methods of treating disease. He laid the foundation for other scientists, and out of their combined work have come our methods of detecting and controlling disease-making organisms—the field called bacteriology.

A Hundred Sciences in One. Because biology is the science of living things, it includes, in a broad sense, every bit of knowledge that has to do with material life. The plumber, for instance, may be regarded as a biologist, since, when he puts plumbing in a house, he does it in such a way that human life will be protected. So is the housewife a biologist, in the sense that the meals she prepares, if they are wholesome for human consumption, will prolong life. And when we plant seeds, and fertilize and cultivate the ground, we are applying our knowledge of plant and animal life, or biology. Perhaps the most important of all practical biologists is the farmer.

But the scientist finds this too unwieldy, and so divides biology into many fields for other specialists, such as physicists and chemists and engineers. Heating a house, for instance, concerns life very directly. But it is generally considered a part of the abstract science of physics, as applied by the engineer.

But still directly under the heading of biology are *zoölogy,* the study of animals; *botany,* the study of plants; *anatomy, comparative* anatomy, *embryology, physiology,* and *bacteriology,* which are mentioned earlier in the article; *psychology,* the science of human and animal behavior; all branches of *medicine,* and several others. On the border line are such subjects as *biological chemistry* and *biological physics* and *human geography.*

Because of this great breadth of biology, no one person can understand it all. So we begin its study with the great field, and then concentrate on one of the myriad branches. We try to learn how living things move, feel, eat, reproduce, and fight for existence; and how they adapt themselves to their environments. And, if we are thoughtful, we look for evidence of what life itself is.

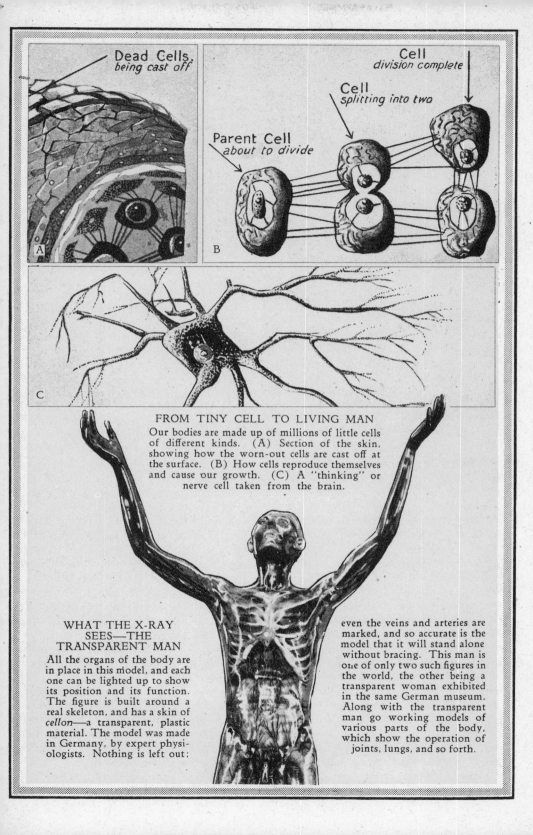

Dead Cells, being cast off

A

Cell division complete

Cell splitting into two

Parent Cell about to divide

B

C

FROM TINY CELL TO LIVING MAN

Our bodies are made up of millions of little cells of different kinds. (A) Section of the skin, showing how the worn-out cells are cast off at the surface. (B) How cells reproduce themselves and cause our growth. (C) A "thinking" or nerve cell taken from the brain.

WHAT THE X-RAY SEES—THE TRANSPARENT MAN

All the organs of the body are in place in this model, and each one can be lighted up to show its position and its function. The figure is built around a real skeleton, and has a skin of *cellon*—a transparent, plastic material. The model was made in Germany, by expert physiologists. Nothing is left out: even the veins and arteries are marked, and so accurate is the model that it will stand alone without bracing. This man is one of only two such figures in the world, the other being a transparent woman exhibited in the same German museum. Along with the transparent man go working models of various parts of the body, which show the operation of joints, lungs, and so forth.

A LOVELY FRIEND
". . . and sheen of Birches, on a hill."

BIRCH, *burch.* Two centuries ago, when America was still an English colony, the original Americans, the Indians, glided silently over the streams of the Northland in their graceful, white birch-bark canoes. Elsewhere, Indian boats were merely hollowed logs, called dugouts. These were heavy and hard to manage. But where the birch tree grew, the boats were so light a single man could carry one across portages between waterways.

Yet they were strong enough to carry heavy loads on the water. To the northern American Indians, their canoes were as important as automobiles are to us, and they owed these necessities to the flourishing birch, whose tough, light bark can be peeled from the tree almost like the skin of an orange.

Nowadays, birch bark is used largely for little trinkets and souvenirs, but the trees themselves are prized for the gleaming whiteness of their trunks and their graceful branches, which provide bright contrast in a stand of darker trees. Otherwise, the chief value of the birch is the lumber it furnishes. Birchwood furniture is very popular, and makes an enduring cabinet wood. Birch logs are also a very delightful firewood.

The birch is of the same botanical family as the alder, the hazel, and the ironwood, and there are nine different kinds, or species, in the United States and Canada. First and best known of these is the *canoe,* or *paper,* birch. This has the striking coat of white, thin bark, and bears oval leaves with fuzzy undersides. It is found throughout the north.

Then there is the *American white* birch, which lacks the pure glossiness of the paper birch, and whose leaves are more definitely pointed. The *yellow* birch is, of course, known by its color, and by the fact that it grows much taller than the others, sometimes reaching a height of more than 100 feet. For this reason, the yellow birch is particularly valuable for its lumber. The *sweet,* or *black,* birch does not look like a birch at all, but has a black trunk. It gives a peculiar oil, tasting like wintergreen, and it produces birch beer. This tree grows as far south as Florida, but does not appear in the West.

Another birch with a fragrant bark is the *red,* or *river,* birch. This red-twigged, fast-growing tree is found all over the eastern half of the United States, living in river bottoms. A purely decorative birch is the European white birch, which is set out in lawns and makes an effective, rather delicate addition to the landscape.

Birches, however, are not limited to America. They are found in the colder regions of Europe and Asia, in several different forms. They show definite family resemblances to the American species, having the same yellowish green leaves in the early summer, and the pure yellow later on. The leaves are generally somewhat the same shape—the oval of an egg —in all the different species.

Nature's Plumed People

BIRDS. Few creatures of the animal kingdom are as attractive as birds. Their beauty of form and color, their graceful motion in flight, their gift of song, and their interesting habits amaze and delight all lovers of Nature. From earliest time, birds have attracted man's attention. Literature abounds in reference to them, from the cackling of geese that saved Rome and the flights from which the ancient oracles read their auspices, to the flocks of migrants that told Columbus of land ahead, and to the lovable songsters that have inspired our modern poets.

Every season of the year, birds enliven our interest. In the spring the bluebirds and the robins come back from the south. We marvel at their nests and methods of caring for their young, and in the summer we see them gathering in clans for the annual southward trek. Then, in the fall, we watch the ducks and geese fly high overhead, winging their way to warmer climates, and in the winter we praise the plucky sparrows and pigeons who forage in the snow to find food. Life would be dreary, indeed, without birds.

Birds' Part in Man's Life. Birds are more than just a source of wonder to man. They play a big part in his life in a number of ways. On the farm, swallows and nighthawks devour insects that would injure crops; hawks and owls eat mice and other rodent destroyers of the field, and vultures and gulls feed on refuse. Some birds are nuisances, such as the seed-eating martins, crows, and sparrows; while others, like eagles and hawks, kill poultry and young livestock. Still others eat fruit. But birds all have an important part in the life on the farm, and if some do cause injury, useful birds more than make up for it by the good they do.

Such birds as chickens, ducks, geese, turkey, quail, grouse, and pheasants are valued as food. Hunting wild birds for sport is healthful recreation; and if good and full use is made of all birds so killed, and if the sport is carried on under humane regulations, it is a proper form of recreation. No one needs to be told the value of birds as pets. Canaries, love

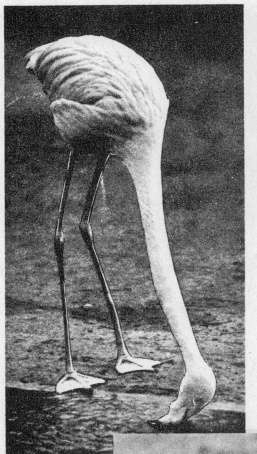

birds, parrots, and other winged creatures in cages bring cheer to the home, and the whole family can enjoy the fun of taming the robins and other birds that nest near the house.

Their Place in Nature. It seems strange to think of birds as cousins to snakes and lizards, yet they have the same ancestors. Birds, however, are more highly developed than all other animals except mammals. The first bird was a huge creature that had claws, toothed jaws, and a long, lizard-like tail. But modern birds have lost their teeth, and their

THREE KINDS
OF BIRDS

Each built for a particular mode of life. The flamingo (above), a wading bird, uses his long neck to reach food when he is standing in deep water. This swimmer, a duck (upper right), has waterproof feathers. A hook-beaked bird of prey—the peregrine falcon (lower right).

FITTED FOR THEIR JOBS

Here are two specialists of the bird world. The woodpecker (above) is a climber, so he has sharp claws to cling to trees. Reed warblers (right) are perching birds, equipped to grip small twigs and reeds.

tails are different from those of lizards. They have adapted themselves to life on the ground, in the air, and on the water. Some birds, like ostriches and emus, have lost the use of their wings and can live only on the ground. Other species, like penguins, can move more easily through the water than on land.

General Description. Birds have a much higher body temperature than mammals, ranging up to 112 and 114 degrees Fahrenheit. Their circulation also is more rapid. Their feathers are marvelous creations. Light, but strong, they cover the body, furnish the wings with the power to move, and make a rudder of the tail. The feet have a horny covering, and some, like the hawks and owls, are large, strong, and equipped with sharp talons for tearing their prey. Others, like the swallows,

have weak feet. Their bills are developed to suit the type of life they lead.

Although most birds use their wings for flying, they have other uses. Penguins use them as oars when in water and sometimes as forefeet on land. And birds use their wings to protect their young and eggs. Like the wagging of a dog's tail, the wings of a bird will flap to show its feelings. Some birds also tuck their heads under their wings when they sleep.

The plumage of a bird is of all colors and shapes. Some develop enormous crests, others very long tails, or plumes. The color of the plumage ranges from black, white, and gray to the most brilliant hues imaginable. This coloring is not by accident. Birds which nest on the ground have colors that blend with the landscape to foil their enemies. The gor-

BOTH READY FOR INSTANT ESCAPE—BY DIFFERENT MEANS
A runner and a scratcher. The ostrich (above) cannot fly, and so uses his long legs for running. The scratcher is a turkey (right), who can "take off" on short notice.

geous tanagers, toucans, and parrots are in less danger, and so are more gaily colored. The drab birds are beautiful singers and call their mates that way, while the colorful birds rely on their plumage, rather than song, to attract their mates.

All the senses possessed by human beings are found in birds. Even though they have no external ears, they can hear very well and can distinguish between sounds. They have very keen sight, but their senses of smell, taste, and touch are not so well developed.

Habits of the Birds. Birds are found almost everywhere, but it is in the woody and open places that we find most of them. They can adapt themselves to different situations when necessary, but usually they like to live in places best suited for feeding and mating. In many of their actions, they resemble mankind, but, of course, we cannot say that they have the same emotions and feelings that we do. They do, however, express fear, pleasure, and surprise, and some of them seem to have a sense of humor, as well as the physical feelings of hunger and thirst.

Do birds talk to one another? There is little doubt that birds have a way of communicating with one another through various kinds of notes. For instance, if you should learn the call of a robin, and whistle it in a park, it is probable that robins will gather around you. Young birds can utter calls of alarm and hunger, and older birds can warn their young by notes. Crows and jays might be said to have a large vocabulary, and they, like the starlings, can be very noisy. Yet some birds can hardly make a sound.

Among North American birds, the thrushes are the best singers, and wrens and thrashers are almost as good. The mocking bird, who imitates other birds,

A BEAK FOR EVERY PURPOSE

(1) Raven's beak, for killing small animals. (2) Parrot's beak, for cracking nuts. (3) Fish-catching beak of a heron. (4) Bone-crushing beak of a falcon. (5) The strange weapon on a hornbill's beak. (6) Beak of a South American fruit eater—the toucan. (7) Powerful flesh-tearing beak of a curassow. (8) Beak of a deep-sea fisherman, the pelican.

has a greater repertoire than the others. Morning and evening are the best times to hear birds sing and call, and most birds sing their best during the spring.

How do birds fly? Their wings correspond to the arms of a man, and when they are extended they present a wide surface for resistance to the air. The wing bones are light but strong, and in many cases are hollow. Large breast muscles work the wings. Birds keep their balance by means of a system of semicircular canals in the head which are filled with a fluid influencing the nerves. Human beings have a similar organ in the head.

There are four methods of flight. The first is the steady and continuous wing beat which is used by most birds. A second way is a rapid fluttering, such as is used by the humming bird when he flaps his wings 214 times a second! The humming bird can fly backward as well as forward. A third variation is motion of the wings followed by a glide, as done by swifts and swallows. The fourth method is the soaring of birds such as gulls and hawks, which can stay aloft a long time without a single wing beat.

Birds can fly fast, their speeds ranging from 30 to 200 miles per hour. Even more remarkable is their endurance. They can fly long distances without stopping, and even such small birds as the warbler will cover the 800 miles across the Gulf of Mexico in a single flight.

Probably the most mysterious thing about birds is why they migrate. This is the regular movement of birds from their breeding range to their winter homes and back again. It is supposed to have had its beginning in the Glacial Period, thousands of years ago, when the northern part of North America was covered with ice. There was no food in the desolate icy wastes, and the birds flew to regions of plenty. The migratory habit is now considered an inherited instinct.

In the United States, the principal months for the southward movement are August, September, and October, and for the northern migration, March, April, and May. Some birds migrate by day, like the swallows and hawks; and others at night, like the thrushes and wood warblers. Some do not migrate at all; others move only 100 miles or so. Still others go from the Northern to the Southern states; while a number travel all the way from the United States and Canada to South America. The longest migratory flight is that of the Arctic tern, which travels from the Arctic Circle to the Antarctic Circle and back each year, a total distance of some 22,000 miles.

There are several routes of migration through the United States. The most important of these is by way of the Mississippi Valley, thence down through Mexico across the Gulf of Mexico or by way of the West Indies. The Pacific coast and Atlantic coast are other highways.

In migration, birds often fly only a few hundred feet above the surface of the earth, although geese have been known to fly at an altitude of more than five miles above sea level. They find their way by instinct, which is amazing in some cases, for the same birds often will return to the same tree and yard, year after year. Homing pigeons have this sense developed to a high degree. One might think that birds would prefer to remain in the south rather than travel back and forth. But, if this were done, there would not be enough food for all.

Some people claim to be able to tell whether there is going to be a hard winter or an early spring by the flights of birds. It is true that weather has a great effect on bird migration, but they are affected by the temperature of the place they are leaving, rather than that of the place where they are going.

Most birds mate every year, but some birds, like hawks and eagles, pair for life. The house wren sometimes has two or three different mates in the same season. The mating season is usually in late winter, and there is always great excitement in a bird colony at this time.

LIFE BEGINS IN A CUCKOO'S NEST—THE BATTLE FOR SURVIVAL

The biggest of those three eggs (upper left) will hatch into the rowdy who throws his smaller brothers out of the nest, one after the other (upper right and lower left). At the age of two days he rules the roost alone (lower right).

Nests of birds vary from a few straws or rubbish on the ground, or a few chips in a hole, to the tiny exquisite, lichen-covered cradle of the humming bird, the flask-shaped mud nest of the cliff swallow, and the immense stick nest of the eagle that is sometimes ten feet high and six feet in diameter. Nesting in the Central states takes place chiefly in May and June. Most birds use a nest only once, but species like certain hawks and owls return to the same nest year after year.

All birds are born from eggs which vary from the tiny beanlike product of the humming bird to the giant eggs of the ostrich. Eggs that are white are usually laid in closed and protected nests, while spotted eggs are placed in open ones. The usual number is from one to six. If the young birds, like those of swallows and hawks, are born with few or no feathers, helpless and with eyes closed, they need to be fed by the parents for some time. Those of quails, grouse, gulls, and ducks, however, are hatched fully feathered and are able to run about or swim almost as soon as they are dry from the shell. Most parent birds guard their young with watchful care, and often attempt to lure their enemies away.

Aluminum bands (above) fixed to the legs of migrating geese (right) and other birds, tell us where they come from, and how far they fly.

must record what he sees immediately and not trust to memory.

In the notebook should be recorded the kind of bird, the weather, distance covered, whether the birds occurred in flocks or singly, their songs, call notes, flight, actions, food, mating, nesting, and anything else that can be written about them.

Spring is the best season for studying the birds, and winter is the poorest, although one should make trips in all sorts of weather and seasons to see them.

One method of bird study that has given

One of the strangest things about birds is the way they eat. They always seem to be hungry. They will eat much more than their weight every day. The reason is that they are very active and warm-blooded and need a huge amount of food to keep their body heat at the proper level. Nature has given birds good digestive organs for this need. It is well that birds do eat so much, for they help to keep in check the hosts of insects that menace humanity. Birds, however, very rarely store any food, as do the squirrels. They eat when they find food, and when the supply gives out, they go somewhere else.

The Study of Birds. Many worthwhile hours may be spent studying birds, for they are among the most interesting and fascinating of all animals. To study them, one should learn their names and how to identify them. This can be done through illustrated books. Then a trip should be taken to a nearby woods, a park, or a field. With field glasses, birds can be observed from a distance, and if you have a camera, you can get some very beautiful and unusual pictures. A notebook is necessary, for the student of birds

man much information about the life history and migration of birds is banding. A small aluminum band bearing a serial number and directions for returning the record is fastened around the leg of a nesting bird or one trapped for the purpose. The movements of such a bird are thus traced when it is captured again.

Another way of studying birds is to collect them, but no bird should ever be killed unless it is put to some good use. It is well to remember that the collection of birds and eggs requires state and Federal permits.

Protecting Birds. There are three enemies of birds—wild animals, domestic animals, and man. It is hard to exercise any control over wild enemies, except by killing off the weasels and foxes and the hawks and owls that prey upon them. But such slaughter is not always wise, because sometimes these animals do much good in other ways. The cat is the worst of the domestic animals that are enemies of birds. Every year the number of birds killed by cats is tremendous. Care should be taken to prevent these animals from causing too

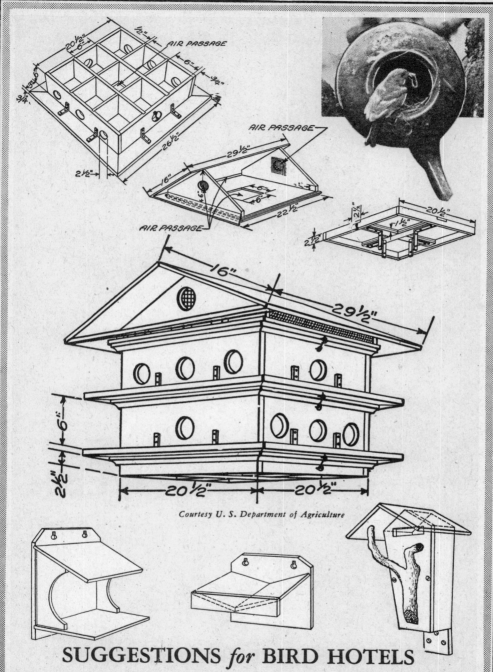

AIR PASSAGE

AIR PASSAGE

AIR PASSAGE

Courtesy U. S. Department of Agriculture

SUGGESTIONS *for* BIRD HOTELS

Martins like company, so houses for them must be large and roomy, big enough for many birds. Here is a model of a martin house that is sure to attract a colony of the purple-feathered creatures. Upper left, the martin house with the roof removed, showing necessary air passages; upper center, measurements for the top story; right, foundation for the bird hotel, and center, the complete house. Upper right, a teakettle is a quaint nesting place for a robin. The lower diagrams show details of attractive robin houses which should measure about six inches in width, eight inches deep, and eight inches high.

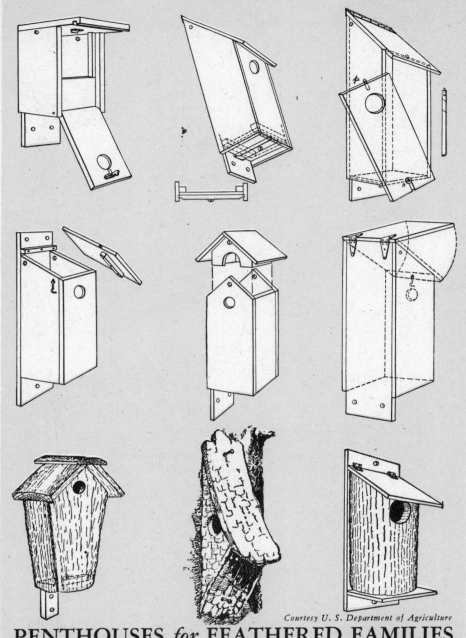

Courtesy U. S. Department of Agriculture

PENTHOUSES *for* FEATHERED FAMILIES

Bluebirds, robins, nuthatches, wrens, and finches like dwellings just big enough for one family. These models are of the type permitting a person to observe the lives and habits of birds. They range in size from four inches wide, four inches deep, and six inches high for wrens, to 6x8x10 for robins. Upper left, a house with hinged front held by a catch; upper center, removable bottom released by cleat; upper right, swinging front; middle left and center, dwellings with removable tops; middle right, hinged top; and below, models of rustic houses with the bark left on the wood.

serious damage to our bird population.

Next to the cat, man is the worst enemy of birds. What with shooting for food, for sport, for fun, and for other reasons, it is a wonder there are as many birds left in the world as there are. It is estimated that waterfowl and shore birds are not over one-tenth as numerous as they were a century or so ago. Some birds are extinct altogether. Laws, however, are now being passed by the Federal and state governments, and shooting is restricted to certain weeks of the year.

One of the most effective means of protecting birds is the setting aside of tracts of land where birds are absolutely protected. Some states, like Pennsylvania and Minnesota, have a large number of such reservations, and their effect on bird life is very great. There are about seventy bird reservations under jurisdiction of the Federal government, scattered throughout the United States.

Descriptions of birds included in these volumes and other information will be found under the following headings:

Albatross	Cuckoo	Indigo Bird	Partridge	Starling
Auk	Curlew	Jay	Peacock	Stilt
Baltimore Oriole	Darter	Junco	Pelican	Stork
Birds of Paradise	Dickcissel	Kingfishers	Penguin	Swallow
Bittern	Dipper	Kinglet	Petrel	Swan
Blackbird	Diver	Kite	Pheasant	Swift
Bluebird	Dove	Lark	Pigeon	Tailor Bird
Bobolink	Duck	Linnet	Pipit	Tanager
Brown Thrasher	Eagle	Lyre Bird	Plover	Tern
Bullfinch	Egret	Macaw	Ptarmigan	Thrush
Buzzard	Emu	Magpie	Puffin	Titmouse
Canada Goose	Falconry	Marsh Hawk	Quail	Toucan
Canary	Finch	Martin	Quetzal	Turkey
Canvasback	Fish Hawk	Meadow Lark	Rail	Turkey Buzzard
Cardinal Bird	Flamingo	Merganser	Raven	Turnstone
Carrier Pigeon	Flicker	Mockingbird	Redstart	Turtle Dove
Cassowary	Flycatcher	Mound Bird	Rhea	Vireo
Catbird	Frigate Bird	Nest	Road Runner	Vulture
Chaffinch	Gannet	Nighthawk	Robin	Wagtail
Chat	Goldfinch	Night Heron	Rook	Warbler
Cockatoo	Goose	Nightingale	Ruff	Waxwing
Condor	Grebe	Nutcracker	Sanderling	Weaver Bird
Coot	Grosbeak	Nuthatch	Sandpiper	Whippoorwill
Cormorant	Grouse	Oriole	Scissorbill	Widgeon
Cowbird	Guinea Fowl	Ostrich	Shoveler	Woodcock
Crane	Gulls	Ovenbird	Shrike	Woodpecker
Creeper	Hawk	Owl	Snipe	Wood Pewee
Crossbill	Heron	Oyster Catcher	Sparrow	Wren
Crow	Humming Bird	Parrakeet	Sparrow Hawk	Wryneck
Crow Blackbird	Ibis	Parrot	Spoonbill	Yellowlegs

BEAUTY ON THE WING
The bird of paradise, whose dazzling green and gold plumage makes him the most brilliant creature of tropic jungles.

BIRDS' NESTS. See NEST.

BIRDS OF PARADISE. In sheer brilliance of plumage, the male bird of paradise, with his bright yellow head, his green throat, and his lovely golden plumes, is unsurpassed. Related to the crow, the birds of paradise are confined entirely to the Australian and New Guinea regions. There are many species. The *great* bird of paradise is the largest, and is found only in the Aru Islands. It has beautiful, elongated tail feathers, and may be easily caught in the mating season, while displaying this plumage to the female during the course of a frenzied nuptial dance. Of duller hue, the female is usually somewhat smaller and less attractive than her mate.

The *king* bird of paradise is conspicuous because of the coiled tail, with its effective spiral of feathers, while the *twelve-wired* is so named for its dozen wirelike feathers, which curve forward from its short tail. The *lesser* bird of paradise is small, being about the size of a sparrow, and lacks the gorgeous color of the other species. Because the birds are so easily caught, efforts are being made to limit their slaughter and sale by the natives. It is unlawful to bring the plumage of birds of paradise into the United States.

BIRDS OF PREY. Owls, eagles, and other feathered flesh eaters are called birds of prey because their chief diet consists of other animals. They have strong, sharp beaks and claws, and are vigorous flyers. They pursue and seize their weak prey on land, water, or in the air, often carrying it away to hidden eyries for their young. Falcons, hawks, and vultures are also birds of prey and the scourge of farmers in the wilder sections of the country. The principal birds of prey are described under separate headings in these volumes.

BIR'MINGHAM, ALA. Situated in one of the richest coal and iron regions in the country, Birmingham has become a leading industrial center of the South and the largest city in Alabama. It lies in the long, narrow Jones Valley, about 100 miles northwest of Montgomery, the state capital, and is protected by mountains to the northwest and southeast, on the slopes of which are the residential sections. Most of the better homes overlook the city proper, which is always enveloped in a smoky haze from the great factories and industrial plants of this "Pittsburgh of the South." It is the county seat of Jefferson County.

A canal connects Birmingham with the navigable Warrior River, sixteen miles distant, affording a direct water route to the Gulf of Mexico. On all sides are the minerals that contribute to its prosperity. It is in the heart of three great coal fields —the Warrior, Coosa, and Cahaba—constituting an extension of the bituminous

FLYING FLESH EATERS

Hooked beaks for tearing flesh and powerful talons for carrying their prey are the weapons of these strong birds. Among them are the eagle (above), the owl (left center), the falcon (right), and the hawk.

beds of Pennsylvania. The Red Mountains bordering Birmingham are composed largely of hematite, an iron ore. In addition, there are vast deposits of limestone, which complete the trio of resources necessary to the manufacture of steel.

Dolomite, marble, bauxite, sand, gravel, quartz, and millstone also are mined, close to the city. Pig iron and steel are the leading products of Birmingham's industries. Other revenue producers are lumber, machinery, cement, brick, cotton goods, chemicals, explosives, and rubber tires. The annual industrial output amounts to about $650,000,000.

This leading industrial center has built schools which are as fine as any in the South. The two institutions of higher education are Howard College, a coeducational Baptist school, and Birmingham-Southern College, a Methodist institution, also coeducational.

Birmingham's city limits were extended in 1910 to include a number of northern suburbs. Its population, 178,270 in 1920, increased forty-five per cent to 259,678 by 1930, and to 267,583 by 1940. The population of Greater Birmingham, which includes the suburbs of the city, now exceeds 400,000; about one third of the people are Negroes.

BIRMINGHAM, ENGLAND. Metal is King in Birmingham. Located in the heart of the British industrial district, this city is also near the geographical center of England. Here, gold, silver, and bronze wares are made, as well as enormous quantities of steel and plated goods, needles, pins, screws, and nails. The city leads in the manufacture of British firearms, has a mint for copper coins, and only Croydon surpasses it in the production of British automobiles.

Birmingham's industrial dominance is accounted for by the nearness of great coal and iron deposits and its location midway between London and Liverpool. The city has been criticized for deplorable conditions existing among the working classes; however, far-reaching improvements have been effected in housing and living conditions.

There are many schools of higher education in the city, including Mason University and several technical colleges. An art institute of renown, with an art school in connection with it, is open to the public. Birmingham's population of over 1,040,000 gives it second place among English cities.

BIRTH′STONES. According to ancient custom, each month of the year is represented by a certain precious or semi-precious stone. If you were born in April, for instance, your birthstone would be the diamond—the jewel associated with that month.

The idea is thought to have originated with the twelve-stone breastplate worn by the high priest of Israel, mentioned in the Bible (*Exodus* XVIII). In any case, the practice of wearing one's birthstone became popular in Poland in the eighteenth century, and from there the custom spread. The superstitious believe that wearing the stone of one's birth month brings good luck.

Modern jewelers have revived the birthstone idea as a sentiment. Listed below are the months and their stones, as chosen by the American National Retail Jewelers' Association:

January	Garnet
February	Amethyst
March	Bloodstone or aquamarine
April	Diamond
May	Emerald
June	Pearl or moonstone
July	Ruby
August	Moonstone or peridot
September	Sapphire
October	Opal or tourmaline
November	Topaz
December	Turquoise or lapis lazuli

BISH′OP. In some Christian churches there are officials known as bishops, who supervise, or oversee, a number of parishes. In fact, the word comes from a Greek word meaning *overseer*. The Anglican, Roman Catholic, and Greek Churches believe that the office of bishop has been handed down from the twelve apostles of Jesus, but most Protestant denominations do not accept this belief.

In the Roman Catholic Church, the bishops are appointed by the Pope, and in the Anglican Church they are appointed indirectly by the crown. The bishops of the Protestant Episcopal and Methodist Episcopal churches, however, are elected by a general conference or convention of church representatives.

THE "IRON CHANCELLOR"
Bismarck, ruthless builder of an empire.

A bishop superintends church affairs in a certain specified district called a *diocese*. Bishops in the Methodist Episcopal Church are exceptions to this rule, for they have no dioceses, but move about from place to place. The duties of a bishop are, in general, to supervise the clergy, to administer the churches under him, to manage church property and various church institutions, to ordain ministers, and to call and preside at conventions of church representatives of the diocese.

Besides the denominations already mentioned, others having bishops are the Reformed Episcopal Church, the African Methodist Episcopal Church, the United Brethren in Christ, and the Evangelical Association.

BISMARCK, *biz'mark,* N. D. Named for the famous Chancellor of the German Empire, Bismarck, a city of over 15,500, has been the capital of North Dakota since the division of the Dakota Territory in 1889. It is situated on the Missouri River in the south-central section of the state, in the heart of a great dairy, fruit, and wheat belt.

Bismarck was founded in 1873, and for six years thereafter was the western terminus of the Northern Pacific Railroad, when construction was suspended because of a financial panic. From 1883 to 1889 it was the capital of the Dakota Territory.

Flour and grain mills are located there, as well as several assembly plants for agricultural machinery. It is the military post and the United States Indian agency of the state, and has an Indian school for girls. The North Dakota State Penitentiary and Fort Lincoln Military Reservations are situated near by.

BISMARCK - SCHÖNHAUSEN, *biz' mark shern' how zen,* OTTO EDUARD LEOPOLD VON, Prince (1815-1898). "Iron Chancellor" and creator of an empire, Prince Otto von Bismarck, foremost German statesman and diplomat, guided Prussia, and then all Germany, to political dominance in Europe. Even the World War could only change, but not destroy, the realm he forged through blood and iron.

Bismarck was born in Brandenburg province of a noble Prussian family, and represented the ruling class, called Junkers. After studying law and languages, he joined the army. Turning soon to politics, he held several minor offices before becoming a member of the Prussian lawmaking body, the Diet. In 1851 he was appointed Prussian representative to the German Federation at Frankfort. Here he applied his genius to forcing Prussia into a position of leadership among the German states. Especially did he hope to eliminate the rival state of Austria, for Bismarck planned a Germany which would leave the Hapsburgs out.

In 1859 Bismarck left the Diet to become Ambassador to Russia, and a few years later he was appointed president of the Prussian cabinet. At last he was close to realizing his dream of a united nation. Seizing as an excuse a dispute between Austria and Prussia over the Danish territory of Schleswig-Holstein, which they had conquered in 1864, Bismarck hurled Prussia's powerful military machine against Austria, and overwhelmed that country within seven weeks. Austrian influence in Germany was thus destroyed, and in 1867 Bismarck founded a North German Federation, with the king of Prussia at its head and himself as prime minister.

The new power of Prussia soon led to disputes with France. Bismarck welcomed a war with the French because he saw in it the opportunity to unite all Germany under the Prussian crown. Again German military might could not be withstood, and, after the capture of Napoleon III and the complete rout of the French by General Moltke, the German Empire was established at Versailles in 1871. His dream a reality, Bismarck became Imperial Chancellor, and was awarded the title of Prince by the grateful new emperor, William I.

For nineteen years Prince Bismarck remained the dominant political figure in Europe. In 1879-1881 he formed the Triple Alliance of Germany, Austria, and Italy, which endured until the World War. The young William II, however, "dropped the pilot" in 1890 by forcing his resignation. With the iron hand gone from the helm, Germany soon took the route that led to the World War and defeat. See FRANCO-GERMAN WAR; GERMANY.

BIS'MUTH. Grayish white in color, but tinted slightly with red, bismuth is a brittle metal, so brittle that it can easily be broken into a powder. Another peculiarity of the metal is that it melts at a very low temperature. In fact, if it is properly mixed with other metals, the resulting compound will melt over the flame of a candle. Although it is sometimes found in a native state, most of it is obtained from ore having other metals. Bismuth is commercially valuable in making pewter, printers' types, medicines, paints, and cosmetics.

BI'SON. See BUFFALO.

HIS CRY FILLS THE SWAMPS
This is a bittern, the wading bird which lives in marshes and utters a weird, booming call in the spring.

BIT'TERN. Of all the marsh birds found in America, the American bittern has probably the most interesting habits. This solitary bird will stand so very still among the rushes, with its long neck and bill pointing straight upward, that it can hardly be seen by the sharpest eyes. It feeds on such food as frogs, salamanders, insects, mice, and fishes.

The booming spring call of the bittern is its strangest characteristic, and has been compared to the working of an old wooden pump handle, *pump-er-lunk, pump-er-lunk.* Another note is like that of driving a stake into the mud, and so the bird has come by the common names of *stake driver, thunder pumper, bog-bull,* etc. Those who have been fortunate enough to watch the bittern giving its call say that it goes through the queerest spasms and twistings, acting as if it were sick at its stomach, until finally all at once the notes boom out.

There is no truth in the statement that the call is given with the bill in mud or water. Altogether, a person interested in birds will find few species so well worth study as this one, which most people know nothing about, though they may hear it every year of their lives.

This bird varies in length from twenty-three to thirty-four inches, and its bill is fully three inches long. It is colored brown and buff, with many streaks and speckles. The underparts are lighter, and each feather has a brown stripe. The legs are a dull yellowish green; the eye is yellow. During the winter the bittern lives from Virginia and California southward, but in early spring it moves into the Northern states, and to Central Canada for the nesting season.

BIT'TERROOT. When Lewis and Clark made their historic expedition through the valley of the Missouri River in the first decade of the nineteenth century, they found a plant whose starchy roots, though bitter, could be cooked and eaten. Named the bitterroot, it was later adopted as the state flower of Montana. A single rose-colored flower, opening only in sunshine, is borne on the flower stalk, which is surrounded by succulent green leaves. The root itself is long and tapering. While cooking, the plant has an odor similar to tobacco, and therefore is sometimes called *tobacco root.* It is also found in Canada.

BITU'MEN. Soft coal, the kind many persons burn in their furnaces to heat their homes, is called bituminous coal. It receives its name from *bitumen.* This is not the name for any definite substance, but for a kind of substance that burns easily. Asphalt is bitumen in solid form; naphtha is a typical fluid bitumen, and even natural gas is sometimes so classed. All such substances are composed chiefly of compounds of hydrogen and carbon. Some are used in making cellars, roofs, walls, and arches water-tight, others are burned to provide light as well as heat. The ancient Babylonians are believed to have used a bituminous mineral as a cement. See ASPHALT; COAL.

BIZET, *be za',* GEORGES (1838-1875). This French composer never knew that his melodious opera, *Carmen,* would be the delight of music lovers for many years after his death. When it was first produced in Paris, in 1875, it was a failure, and its composer died broken-hearted. *Carmen* is still performed by all the grand-opera companies of today, and the leading rôle has been played by Emma Calvé, Mary Garden, and other prima donnas of first rank. Bizet received his musical education at the Conservatory of Music in Paris, and in Italy, and was a promising student, receiving many prizes. His compositions, however, were not appreciated in his own day.

BLACK. Most of us consider black to be the darkest of all colors. It is more scientific to say that black represents the absence of color. It has been shown that when all the colors of the rainbow are combined, we see them as white. The color of any object is the color of the light wave which is "bounced off" or reflected from it. Thus, when an object is white it must be true that all the colors have been reflected from it. In the same way, when no color is reflected, the object appears black. Such an object is said to absorb all colors, and hence is really not colored, as there is no color reflected. We never see really true black because there is no object which fails to reflect in some degree, or which absorbs all color rays. See COLOR.

BLACK, HUGO LA FAYETTE (1886-   ). In 1937, on the retirement of Associate Justice Willis Van Devanter, President Roosevelt appointed Senator Hugo Black of Alabama to fill the vacancy. The President felt that the Supreme Court was too conservative, and this appointment gave him the support of an outstanding liberal.

Hugo L. Black was born in Harlan, Ala. He was educated for the law at the University of Alabama, where he received his LL.B. in 1906. He practiced law in Ashland and Birmingham, and served as prosecuting attorney for Jefferson County in 1915-17. In 1926 he was elected to the Senate seat formerly held by Oscar Underwood. In the Senate, Black allied himself with the progressive elements, and as chairman of the committee investigating ocean and air-mail contracts (1934) and in an investigation of lobbyists for the utilities, he showed that he was an able inquisitor. As Associate Justice, he consistently upheld the liberal point of view.

BLACKBERRY. The prickly, fruit-bearing blackberry plant is commonly called a bramble and belongs to that same thorny family as the raspberry and dewberry. Its seedy but delicious fruits are jet black when ripe and make excellent jams, jellies, and wines, not to mention pie! The blossoms are pink or white and the berry is hard and red until ripe. Thriving in a wide variety of temperate climates, the shrub is often used as a very effective hedge. Luther Burbank created a "white blackberry" by crossing the blackberry and a bramble having light-colored fruit.

BLACKBIRD. Strange as it may seem, blackbirds belong to the same large family as do the bright-colored orioles, the black and white bobolinks, and the brown-streaked meadowlarks. The blackbirds proper include, in North America, the *red-winged* blackbird, the *rusty* blackbird, the *yellow-headed* blackbird, the *Brewer* blackbird, and the *tricolored* blackbird. The red-winged blackbird is the best known of the species. The male is a shiny

black except for wing patches of red bordered with yellowish buff. The female is grayish or blackish with darker streaks and has no bright colors. The birds are about nine and one-half inches long. They hang their nests in reeds, tufts of grass, cattails, or bushes growing from very wet soil or in water. Although they do considerable damage to grain fields, they also do a great deal of good by destroying injurious insects and weed seeds.

The rusty blackbirds are a shiny black all over and are about the same size as the red-wings. They nest in bushes a few feet above the ground.

Two western species are the yellow-headed and the Brewer blackbirds. The entire head, neck, and throat of the male yellow-head is a rich yellow, with the rest of the body black and some wing mark-

THIS BLACKBIRD IS HELPFUL
He is eating a destructive worm. But sometimes the bird himself will eat seeds and damage crops. He is a relative of the larks.

ings paler. The Brewer is similar to the rusty blackbird except that the head of the male is a glossy purple black in color.

A Pacific-coast species is the tricolored blackbird, generally bluish black in color, with a dark-red wing patch bordered with white. Like the other blackbirds, it lives in marshes.

BLACK-EYED SUSAN. A wild, yellow daisy, the black-eyed Susan is the state flower of Maryland. The black cone-shaped center of the flower head is surrounded by golden rays, and the heads are often three to four inches across. The height of the stalk is usually about two feet. It grows wild in most parts of the United States and is also an attractive garden flower.

GOLDEN GAIETY IN THE MEADOW
Black-eyed Susan, delightful American weed

BLACK'FISH, or TAUTOG, *tau tog'.* The most common American name for these dark-colored fish is the Indian word *tautog,* meaning *sheep's head.* These plump fish are found on the Atlantic coast of America. They are caught up to two feet in length and from two to twelve pounds in weight. The flesh is palatable.

BLACK'FOOT. According to legend, the Blackfoot Indians received their name because the dark ashes of prairie fires clung to their moccasins. More properly called Siksika, these peaceful tribes are found today in Montana and in Alberta, Canada, and number about 5,000. Most of these ancient red men live on reservations. They are divided into three tribes, the Blackfoot proper, the Piegan, and the Blood.

BLACK FOREST. A favorite tourist resort and an excellent source of fine lumber, the Black Forest follows the storied Rhine through Baden to Württemberg in Southwest Germany, and is really a chain of wooded mountains topped by the 4,900-foot Feldberg peak. The lower slopes are covered with fine oak and beech trees, while higher up only great firs are found.

BLACKFISH
INDIANS CALL HIM "TAUTOG"
Meaning "sheep's head." It's a blackfish.

The lumber industry is important, and toys, clocks, and numerous wood articles are manufactured. There is also some iron mining. Plentiful lakes and abundant snow in winter, together with the quaint old-fashioned people and villages, make the region popular as a vacation center. The Black Forest area is about 100 miles long and fifteen miles wide.

BLACK HAWK (1767-1838). On a bluff near Oregon, Ill., stands a colossal stone figure of a tall, magnificent Indian chief—the white man's tribute to a brave defeated foe. The figure is that of Black Hawk, who led the Sac and Fox tribes in their last stand to retain possession of their happy hunting grounds.

In 1804 the Sacs and Foxes agreed to cede to the United States lands extending for about 800 miles along the eastern bank of the Mississippi River. When Black Hawk became chief of the tribes, he refused to recognize the agreement, saying that the Indians had been bribed to make it while they were drunk.

Black Hawk served with the British for a short time during the War of 1812, and in 1823, when most of the Sacs and Foxes moved to their new reservation beyond the Mississippi, their chief and part of the tribe refused to leave their old hunting grounds. The Black Hawk War followed, and it was in this conflict that Abraham Lincoln served as a captain in the Illinois militia. The Indians were defeated and

THE TRAGIC END OF THE BLACK HAWK WAR

The Battle of Bad Axe, in which the heroic but misguided Indian chief, Black Hawk, was defeated. His hopes of regaining lands east of the Mississippi ended with this encounter.

Black Hawk and two of his sons became captives. They were later released and allowed to join their people on a reservation near Fort Des Moines.

BLACK HOLE OF CALCUTTA, The. On a stifling summer night in India, in 1756, the rebellious Hindu potentate Siraj-ud-daula seized the British city of Calcutta and jammed 146 European prisoners into a tiny, ill-ventilated guard room at Fort William. Next morning all but twenty-three of the captive whites had died a horrible death by suffocation.

That little guard room was the "Black Hole of Calcutta," scene of one of the most hideous incidents in the history of British rule in India. Its site is marked with a black marble slab and a fitting monument to the courage of the British defenders of Fort William. The city remained in the hands of the native rebels until the following year, when it was recaptured by the celebrated "Clive of India" and Admiral Watson.

BLACK SEA. Known at one time as a "Russian lake," the Black Sea is today open to the ships of all nations. In the town of Balaklava, situated on that sea, occurred the memorable "Charge of the Light Brigade" during the Crimean War.

The sea lies between Europe and Asia in Southern Russia, and is separated from the Sea of Azov by the Crimean peninsula. The Black Sea is the *Pontus Euxinus* of the ancients, who probably so-named it because its turbulent waters seemed to turn black when lashed by the winds. This great inland ocean is 750 miles long, 380 miles wide, and in some places nearly a mile and a half deep. It covers 165,000 square miles, an area greater than that of the five Great Lakes.

The Bosporus, the Sea of Marmora, and the Dardanelles connect it with the Mediterranean, but navigation is difficult at times because of the violence of the storms. The sea is almost wholly frozen over during the winter.

BLACK'STONE, Sir William (1723-1780). Many modern legal textbooks are based upon one of the most famous books on law ever written, *The Commentaries on the Laws of England,* by Sir William Blackstone. For two centuries this work has been regarded as the lawyer's bible.

After Blackstone was admitted to the bar, in 1746, he became a teacher of law at Oxford University, where his lectures attracted great attention. His *Commentaries* are copies of the lectures that he delivered upon the law and constitution of England. They were published in 1765, after he had resigned from the university.

After the American Revolution, Blackstone's works became almost the only American interpretation of English common law. Thus, although the greatest English jurist, Sir William influenced the United States more than he did Britain.

BLANC, Mont. See Mont Blanc; Switzerland.

BLANK VERSE. In reading the great literary masterpieces of the world, we often find beautiful poetry that has no rhyme. This is called blank verse, a type of writing that has been used by poets ever since the sixteenth century. Shakespeare used blank verse in his plays; Longfellow's *Evangeline* is a well-known example of rhymeless poetry; Walt Whitman, Carl Sandburg, Amy Lowell, and other famous American poets have employed it. An extreme form of this type of poetry, called *free verse,* has been used by some modern poets.

There follows an example of blank verse taken from Shakespeare's *King Richard II:*

This royal throne of kings, this sceptred isle,
This earth of majesty, this seat of Mars,
This other Eden, demi-paradise,
This fortress built by Nature for herself
Against infection and the hand of war,
This happy breed of men, this little world,
This precious stone set in the silver sea,
Which serves it in the office of a wall
Or as a moat defensive to a house,
Against the envy of less happier lands,
This blessed plot, this earth, this realm, this
England.

BLARNEY CASTLE
An Irish legend challenges the visitor.

BLARNEY STONE. A tradition of Eire attracts many visitors to Blarney Castle, near the city of Cork. It is the time-honored custom of kissing the famous Blarney Stone.

In order to press his lips against this stone, the pilgrim must enlist the aid of attendants, who hold him and lower him, head first, from the top of the wall. Performing this rite is traditionally believed to impart the gift of eloquence.

According to legend, the original owner of the castle saved it from would-be attackers by addressing them in clever, flattering speeches. His persuasive powers were attributed to the Blarney Stone, and so succeeding generations have sought it out as a mystic source of silver-tongued oratory. Smooth speech is still often called *blarney.*

BLAST FURNACE. Iron ore, the substance from which iron is manufactured, contains many impurities. In order to remove these impurities and reduce the iron ore to metal, the ore must be passed through a blast furnace. See Steel.

Iron ore, coke, and limestone are dumped or *charged* into the furnace; and fire, intensified by a blast of pre-heated air, is applied to the charge. The impurities are driven off as gases, or float to the top of the molten mass in a form called *slag*. The liquid iron is then drawn off at the bottom of the furnace.

BLASTING. A thunderous report, and the ground trembles underfoot; a hail of shattered rock, and reek of burning powder fills the quaking air—another blast has been touched off.

Before the days of explosives, rock was broken up in quarries by hammering, with chisels and wedges, and by the expansive force of heat. These methods not only required a great deal of labor, but also were extremely slow. The use of gunpowder introduced a new and powerful agent for quarrying. It did not take long to discover that explosives, if used correctly, could do as much work in an instant as a man or even a machine could do in many days. As soon as this was understood, explosives were applied to new kinds of work, and special kinds of explosives were made for definite uses.

Explosives, principally dynamite, are now used in the building of roads, in clearing farms of trees and stumps, in combating fires in cities and forests, in removing obstructions from water, and in mining operations. Some of the explosives frequently used besides dynamite are picric acid, T.N.T. (trinitrotoluol), pyrotol, and siliceous earth saturated with nitroglycerine. In ordinary operations, holes from one to six inches in diameter are bored into the rock by means of a steel-pointed drill. The explosive is then placed in the hole, and the rest of the space is filled up or *tamped* with broken stone, clay, or sand. A long powder fuse is lit, or an arrangement of electric wires, permitting a spark to jump between two wires close together, is used to ignite the charge.

In larger operations, mines or shafts of considerable width are excavated with machinery and take the place of the holes. These shafts are sunk to various depths, sometimes more than sixty feet, terminating in chambers used for the powder charges. Electricity is always used to fire explosives when several charges must be set off at the same time. Frequently, more than twenty tons of gunpowder have been fired in one blast.

One of the greatest of blasting operations was the removal of the reefs known as Hell Gate, in the East River, near New York. An entrance shaft was sunk on the Long Island shore, from which the reef projected. From this shaft nearly twenty tunnels were bored in all directions, extending from 200 to 240 feet. When the tons of dynamite and powder were exploded, millions of tons of rock were dislodged.

The most notable blasting operation of the present century was at the Culebra Cut (now Gaillard Cut) on the Panama Canal, in October, 1913. With forty tons of dynamite placed in 1,000 holes, Gamboa Dyke was blown up, and the waters of two oceans rushed in to complete the waterway across the isthmus. President Wilson, in Washington, more than 2,000 miles distant, pressed an electric button which set off the explosion. See GUN-POWDER; DYNAMITE.

BLEACH'ING. It is believed that bleaching, or whitening fabrics in the sun, was first practiced a long time ago—probably in ancient Egypt. Fabrics were spread in the sun and were wet again and again until they became white. So women today who hang their washing to whiten in the sun are using an old method of bleaching.

In the Middle Ages, the Dutch developed a very good method of bleaching, but one which required six months for bleaching linen. In this process, cloth was dipped in lye and soaked in buttermilk; then it was washed and spread on the grass to dry. Because of the great skill of the Dutch in bleaching, the better grades of linens came to be called *hollands*. The finest fabrics were bleached on the best plots of grass and were called *lawns*.

Today, cloth is bleached chemically in factories. Methods differ in many respects,

MARLBOROUGH'S CHARGE IN THE BATTLE OF BLENHEIM
The fighting English Duke leads his forces to victory over the French and Bavarians.

but in every case the cloth is bleached in chemical solutions which dissolve the natural color of the fibers and fabrics and leave them snowy white.

BLEEDING HEART. Drooping, heart-shaped blossoms give the bleeding heart its name. The plant is a great favorite among gardeners, for its lovely red color adds much to the charm of any garden. The bleeding heart originally grew only in Japan and China, but was introduced into Europe about 1846. It is now widely grown in America.

BLENHEIM, *blen' im*. In 1704, during the War of the Spanish Succession, the decisive Battle of Blenheim was fought near the small Bavarian village of that name on the Danube River. There the combined forces of Germany and England, under Prince Eugene and the Duke of Marlborough, overwhelmed the French and Bavarians, and saved Europe from the domination of Louis XIV of France. See Succession Wars.

BLENNERHASSET, *blen ur has' et,* Harman (1765-1831). A wealthy English-

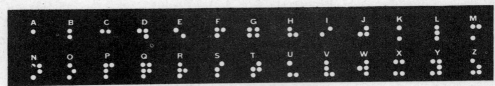

READING—WITH FINGERS FOR EYES
In the Braille alphabet for the blind, raised dots form letters.

man, Harman Blennerhasset emigrated to America in 1797. For a number of years he lived a quiet, leisurely life in his mansion on an island in the Ohio River. But in 1805 Aaron Burr visited him with plans to establish an empire in the Southwest. Blennerhasset was enthusiastic about the plans and advanced money to train men and to buy supplies. He really believed that his dream of a great empire would come true, but the scheme was discovered. He himself was tried for treason, and although he was cleared of the charge, he lost all his property. In 1831 he died in England, a poor and disillusioned man.

BLIND'FISH. As the name tells us, blindfish are sightless fish. They are found in the water of great caves, such as the famous Mammoth Cave in Kentucky. They grow to be four or five inches long. Although these fish are now blind, there are indications that they had eyes a long, long time ago. Light passes right through the colorless bodies of these fish. On the head and body are small "feelers" which are used as organs of touch.

BLIND'NESS. Blindness is a deficiency, or lacking, in the sense of sight, and may be temporary or permanent. It is caused by a disease or defect of the eye, the nerve of the eye, or the brain. Old age is often the cause of blindness, as the fluid of the eye may dry up. Babies are sometimes born sightless because of poorly formed eyes, or become so through an infection which sets in a few days after birth.

Helping the Blind to Help Themselves. Until the latter part of the eighteenth century, the education and instruction of the blind were sadly neglected. The first school for the blind was founded in Paris in 1784, and others were soon established throughout Europe. Finally, the New England School for the Blind was founded in Massachusetts in 1829. The name was later changed to the Perkins Institution and Massachusetts School for the Blind. The fine work done there became known all over the United States, and today every state makes some provision for the education of the blind.

One of the first and best-known pupils

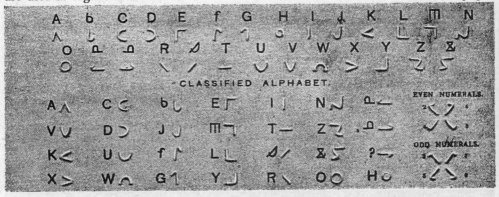

ANOTHER KIND OF LETTERING FOR THE BLIND—THE MOON SYSTEM
This alphabet consists of simplified characters, embossed on paper.

FOUR-FOOTED "EYES"

No stumbling over this high curb! (upper left). Prize "Seeing Eye" dog (upper right). Signaling an obstruction (lower left). A dog takes his master traveling (lower right).
The joy of a "Talking Book" (below).

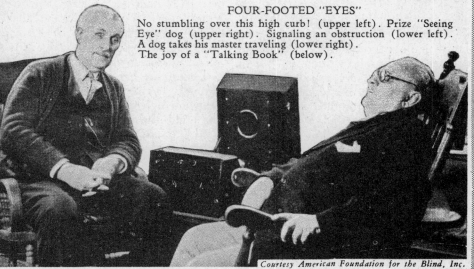

of the Perkins Institution was a little girl by the name of Laura Bridgman. She was deaf and dumb as well as blind. Through the work of Dr. Howe, the superintendent of the school, she was taught arithmetic, geography, and other subjects that a little girl learns in school. Eventually, she devoted her life to the teaching of the blind. The education of Laura Bridgman proved what could be done for blind people, even those who suffered the additional handicap of being deaf and dumb. Another illustration of this marvelous training is the career of Helen Keller, who became one of the outstanding women of her age.

Today, blind children receive an education very much like that given to a normal person. They study reading, writing, arithmetic, and music; and in addition to these regular school subjects, they are taught sewing, knitting, crocheting, broommaking, and other trades. Many of the blind have very keen hearing and are successful piano tuners.

Reading Through Touch. Since the blind must rely on their sense of touch for most of their knowledge, special books are necessary to teach them to read. The most widely used system is one known as Braille. Raised dots represent the letters of the alphabet, a different number and arrangement being used for the different letters. The blind read by running their fingers over these dots. Many important works are written in Braille, but the books are very expensive. Most of the blind are forced to depend upon the public libraries for their reading material. To give the blind a greater opportunity for reading, the government allows all Braille books to be carried through the mails without charge.

Dog Guides for the Blind. Near Morristown, N. J., there is a remarkable training school called the Seeing Eye. Its origin may be traced to the efforts of Mrs. Harrison Eustis, who began training German shepherd dogs at Vevey, Switzerland, in 1923. The Swiss government commissioned

her to train the dogs for patrol work in the Swiss Army and the customs service. Mrs. Eustis later investigated the German schools that trained dogs to guide blind soldiers, and in 1927 she began publishing a magazine called *The Seeing Eye*.

This venture aroused wide interest. A young American who had been blinded in a basket-ball game went to Vevey at the invitation of Mrs. Eustis, and devoted considerable time there to workouts with a trained dog. On his return to the United States he lectured on the value of dogs as guides, laying the groundwork for the founding of the Seeing Eye.

Today, many blind people go there, and after a course of four weeks' instruction are able to rely upon one of the trained dogs to lead them through all kinds of traffic. The dogs are taught to obey and to answer verbal commands, as well as signals given to them by the tightening of the leash. They are also trained to disobey commands that to them seem dangerous. For example, if a dog is commanded to turn to the right but sees that there is a hole in the ground or something that might trip his master, he will disobey the command and avoid the danger.

Consideration for the Blind. Much has been done to brighten the lives of the blind. All the education that the blind receive helps them to sense more fully the beauty in the world. It is well for us to remember that these people cannot enjoy the beauties about them except through the kindness and help of their fellowmen. It is, therefore, our duty to aid the blind whenever we can.

BLIZ'ZARD. Any person who has ever experienced a blizzard knows how destructive these winter storms can be. Persons and animals exposed to them can easily lose all sense of direction and die of cold and exhaustion. In the grip of a blizzard, light and telephone lines are torn down, airplanes crash, and boats are tossed about like chips. Blizzards are clouds of snow and ice particles driven onward by

NATURE'S SYMPHONY—OF SOUND AND COLOR

Here are some of the birds most common in our woods and fields. (1) Blackbird. (2) Barn Owl. (3) Goldfinch. (4) Swallow. (5) Magpie. (6) Yellowhammer. (7) Starling. (8) House Martin. (9) Skylark. (10) Song Thrush. (11) Wren.

furious gales. They occur in the United States mostly in the North-Central and Western states. In typical storms the wind may blow at the rate of fifty or sixty miles an hour, while the temperature will sometimes fall twenty to fifty degrees below zero.

The needle-like snow particles which accompany the wind have a biting, penetrating effect, and neither man nor beast can long withstand them. The icy blast is so painful that it arouses a kind of frenzy, and many of those who have died in blizzards have completely lost their senses before they perished. The blizzard of 1888 was one of the worst that was ever experienced in the West. In that storm, about 250 field laborers succumbed while seeking shelter from the storm.

BLOCKADE'. One of the most effective ways of defeating an enemy during a war is to close its ports and prevent ships from bringing in ammunition, supplies, food, or other goods. This is called a blockade. It was the British and French blockades of each other's countries in the Napoleonic wars that led to the War of 1812, because of England's searching of American ships carrying goods to France (see CONTINENTAL SYSTEM). During that war, Britain declared a blockade of the Atlantic coast, but did not have enough ships to enforce it. Such blockades are called "paper" blockades, because they exist on paper only.

Under international law, only nations at war have the right of blockade, and they must first notify neutral nations. Also, there must be an armed force sufficiently strong to carry out an attempted blockade. If a neutral ship should try to go through the blockade and discharge its cargo, the ship and goods may be seized by the blockading country.

In the American Civil War, the Union Navy maintained a blockade of Southern ports. It was, perhaps, the most extensive blockade in history, but it could not prevent the Confederate blockade runners from taking out over a million bales of cotton and bringing in much needed food, munitions, and other supplies. See CONFEDERATE STATES OF AMERICA.

In both the first and the second World War, the Allies maintained an effective economic blockade of Germany. Germany countered with submarine warfare, which, although it took its toll of Allied and neutral shipping, proved less effective.

BLOCK AND TACKLE. Hoisting huge loads weighing hundreds or thousands of pounds would be an almost impossible task were it not for the block and tackle. This ingenious arrangement of ropes and pulleys is fairly simple. The *block* is a grooved pulley enclosed in a shell which may be attached to some firm object by a hook or bolt. When a rope connected to the load is run through the pulley and pulled, it lessens the weight of the load. With two pulleys and several grooves for the ropes, the weight is decreased even more.

The force of the lifting power is doubled by a single block, and tremendously increased with the addition of strands in the block and tackle. The *movable block* is attached to the object to be lifted, while the *fixed block* is connected with solid support. Some types of block and tackle are quite unusual in design, being small and made of chain, but powerful enough to lift several tons with very little strain.

BLOCK'HOUSE. Many years ago, before the great city of Chicago was even a village, a stockade called Fort Dearborn was located on the flat shore of Lake Michigan. Here was garrisoned a small detachment of troops, and here a tiny band of settlers made their homes. Indian battles were frequent in those days, and when an attack was forthcoming, the white men and their families huddled behind the stalwart wooden walls of the fort for protection.

At the northeast and southwest corners of the stockade were heavy, solid-looking structures known as blockhouses. Narrow slits in the walls gave the settlers and soldiers a vantage point for surveying the

INVADERS BEWARE!
A blockhouse, "fort" of the pioneers.

surrounding land for some distance, and a protected place to fire at the red-skinned warriors. Ladders inside permitted the men to reach these perches, which were so important in protecting the fort.

These blockhouses were similar to others on many stockades and forts on the frontier. They were usually perfectly square, and sometimes they had two stories, with an overhanging second floor all around. There were more holes for guns cut in the floors of these upper stories, so that if attackers came close to the house, perhaps to break in, the defenders upstairs could fire straight down on the intruders.

Numerous blockhouses were built by the early settlers in America, as a protection against Indians. They were actually small forts, and not homes at all, and they saved many lives during the pioneer days. Blockhouses were last used in warfare in South Africa, in the Boer War.

BLONDEL, *bloN del'*. This famous French minstrel of medieval times was the trusted servant and music teacher of King Richard the Lion-hearted. One of the romantic figures of legend and story, he appears in Scott's *The Talisman.*

While Richard was returning from the Third Crusade, in 1191, he was captured by the Duke of Austria and placed in prison. None of his friends knew where he was. One day, according to a well-known story, he was sitting in his cell in Durrenstein Castle when he heard Blondel, who had come to search for him, singing a favorite ballad. The king sang the tune back to the minstrel, thus identifying himself, and Blondel soon secured his beloved master's freedom.

BLOOD, *blud*. Such familiar expressions as "blood is thicker than water," "a person of gentle blood," and "he gave his blood for his country" indicate the importance of this vital body fluid. Blood sustains life by circulating through a wonderful system of arteries and veins. It is composed of red and white corpuscles, or cells, and of *plasma,* a fluid which is about nine-tenths water.

The tiny corpuscles in the blood do an enormous amount of work. Red corpuscles carry oxygen and nourishment to all parts of the body. These cells also contain a red substance called *hemoglobin,* which gives the blood its color. The "whites" are known as "fighters," for under certain conditions they become a defense army to protect the body from invaders in the form of bacteria. They kill the bacteria and neutralize the poisons or toxins that the bacteria form.

Another interesting substance found in the blood is called *fibrinogen.* When a person is bleeding from a severe cut, the fibrinogen stops the bleeding.

Blood Pressure. The heart pumps blood through the arteries. Under normal conditions the blood flows easily, for the walls of the arteries are elastic and stretch with every heart beat. When people grow older, the walls of the arteries sometimes thicken and lose their elasticity. Then the heart must work harder to pump the blood. The increased pressure, which is not normal, is called high blood pressure. People suffering from this condition should be careful not to take strenuous exercise, because added strain is put on the heart.

Blood Transfusion. When blood from one person is transferred to the veins of

A FRIENDLY DOG, WITH SAD FACE

A prize bloodhound, peerless canine tracker.

another the operation is called a transfusion. Transfusions are frequently given to people who have lost a great deal of blood or who suffer from certain illnesses. The person who gives his blood is called the donor. Whole blood may be drawn from the donor and immediately injected into the sick person's veins, or freed from fibrin and transferred from a receptacle. There are four types of blood; and since different types do not mix, the donor must have the same type as the person receiving whole blood. However, transfusions of plasma—blood liquid with the red corpuscles removed—may be made regardless of types. See ARTERIES; HEART; VEINS.

BLOOD'HOUND. Fierce by reputation, but gentle by nature, the bloodhound probably received its name for its natural ability to follow the blood scent of wounded animals. It is now employed primarily in tracking criminals, especially escaped convicts who take to open country. Besides possessing a keen sense of smell, the bloodhound is characterized by long, flopping ears, wrinkled forehead, black nose, long muzzle, and domelike skull. The dog is of medium height, black or tan in color, and its general ex-

pression is one of extreme melancholy. A very old breed, the bloodhound can be traced to the time of William the Conqueror. When introduced into the New World, this dog was often used to trace fugitive slaves.

BLOOD MONEY. A custom still heard of among the Arabs is the paying of blood money by a manslayer to the nearest relative of the murdered person. Formerly, the practice of paying these fines was common in many countries. For the most brutal murder, such as killing a sleeping person, the criminal was turned over to the slain man's relatives for vengeance.

BLOOD'Y ASSI'ZES. After the suppression of a rebellion against King James II in 1685, led by James Monmouth, his nephew, about 300 Englishmen were sentenced to death in a term of court later called the *Bloody Assizes*. A great number were whipped, sentenced, and fined, and about 1,000 were sent to America as slaves. The court was held in Winchester and was presided over by Chief Justice George Jeffries, later appointed Lord Chancellor.

BLOW'PIPE. One of the easiest methods of obtaining pure metal from the impure is by the use of a blowpipe. When air is blown horizontally into a gas flame through this instrument, two flames are made to appear. By placing copper, lead, or other metal in the interior of the inner blue flame, all oxide is removed and the pure metal is left. This is called the *reducing* flame, and is capable of creating the change since it contains no oxygen.

If, however, the metal is held at the point of greatest heat, the tip of the inner blue flame, it will soon be changed to the oxide of the metal; hence the name *oxidizing* flame.

The blowpipe is usually about seven inches long, and is about one-half inch in diameter at one end, tapering to a very small opening at the other end. In order that the person using the blowpipe may see the flame he is producing, the pipe is often bent at right angles about two inches from the smaller end.

BLÜCHER, *blük'ur,* GEBHARD LEBERECHT VON, Prince of Wahlstadt (1742-1819). Already a famous soldier, General von Blücher further distinguished himself at the Battle of Waterloo in 1815. It was he who turned the tide of battle against Napoleon by arriving with his troops at the decisive moment. At the age of seventy he had been made commander in chief of the Prussian forces fighting the French, and he showed great heroism in the battles of Lützen and Bautzen.

In 1814 Blücher commanded the Prussian army which invaded France and entered Paris. At the renewal of war, a year later, he led his army into the Netherlands, where he was defeated by Napoleon at Ligny. Two days later, however, he had his revenge at Waterloo, when he joined forces with the Duke of Wellington. Shortly thereafter, he again made a triumphal entry into Paris.

BLUE. Blue skies mean happiness, and the blues mean depression! Blue, like red and yellow, is a primary color; from blends of those three colors come all the other hues—violet, orange, brown, green, and all the rest. Nature is lavish in her use of blue; we find it in the blue of the sky, the lakes, and the sea. The most brilliant blues in the mineral world are the sapphire and turquoise. Our principal source of blue for dyes is indigo. We have given very different meanings to the word blue, just as the color blue has different tones. *True blue* means honest, loyal; *to feel blue* is to be melancholy. The color blue usually suggests cool beauty.

It is interesting to note that the blue of the sky is caused through the reflection of sunlight by dust particles in the air. That blue which looks so deep and solid on a clear, sunny day is really only colorless atmosphere.

BLUE'BELL. Bells that never tinkle, unless in fairy ears, are the bluebells of early spring. These nodding, bell-shaped flowers are among the first to bloom every year. The name is applied to several kinds of bell-like flowers — the Virginia cowslip, the bellflower, and the harebell that is Scotland's beloved "bonnie bluebell."

BLUE'BIRD. Listen for the first cheery notes of the bluebird, and you will know that spring has arrived. This well-loved song bird belongs to the thrush family, and ranges throughout North America westward to the Rocky Mountains and northward into Southern Canada. In winter the bluebird withdraws to the Southern states, but moves north again early in the spring along with the robin. Then its soft, sweet call thrills those of us who listen for it. The poet E. E. Rexford has expressed our feelings when he says:

Winged lute that we call a bluebird, you
   blend in a silver strain
The sound of the laughing waters, the
   patter of spring's sweet rain,
The voice of the winds, the sunshine,
   and fragrance of blossoming things:
Ah! you are an April poem, that God
   has dowered with wings!

The bluebird has confidence in us, and likes best to build its nest close to our homes, in some hollow limb in the orchard or pasture or in the "bluebird box" which we provide. The English sparrow is doing all it can to drive out the bluebird and we must help our friend to fight this intruder. A box five or six inches square, with a hole one inch and a half in diameter near the top of one side, will be very satisfactory. It should be fastened in some open place to a pole or on a sunny tree trunk, seven to nine feet above the ground, and must be ready early in the spring. The bluebird's nest is a loose affair of grasses, and from four to six or sometimes seven bluish-white eggs are laid. There are two or three broods.

The bluebird is so well known as hardly to need describing. It is about seven inches long, sky blue above, with a brownish-red breast and white underparts. The

GAME FIGHTER, GOOD TO EAT—A BLUEFISH

female is duller in color than the male. Young bluebirds have spotted breasts at first, showing their relation to the thrushes. The food of the bluebird consists of insects and wild fruit.

BLUE BONNET. During the midsummer flowering season, Texas prairies are turned into solid masses of blue by this species of wild lupine. On account of this remarkable and beautiful display, the blue bonnet has been selected by the Texas legislature as the state flower. The individual flowers are interesting; they resemble the flowers of the sweet peas, to which they are closely related. The blue bonnet is usually found on sandy soils.

BLUE'FISH. The common bluefish of the Atlantic and the California bluefish of the Pacific belong to entirely different families. Both are excellent food fishes.

Few fishes are more destructive to other fishes than are the common bluefish. The fact that they move in large schools makes it particularly dangerous for smaller or less powerful fish to stay near them. They are especially fond of menhaden. It is estimated that a bluefish weighing six pounds destroys at least ten other fish every day. Their appetites make them popular with those who fish with hook and line, for they bite readily. When once hooked, they make an excellent fight for freedom, and when landed make one of the best of food fishes.

Bluefish do not keep so well in market as some other sea fish, but when fresh they are a very popular food. They rarely exceed three feet in length or fifteen pounds in weight. Bluefish are not always common in a given locality, sometimes disappearing for years and then reappearing for a time, but may be found in the Atlantic and Indian oceans and the Mediterranean Sea. They seem to prefer a water temperature of 40°F. or above.

BLUE GRASS. Kentucky is "the Blue Grass State," famous for its race horses and for the blue grass that furnishes excellent pasturage for them. By early June the meadows of Kentucky are thick with this grass, and if it is kept clipped after the spring growth, it will remain green all summer. It is a favorite grass for lawns, too, as far north as Canada, and thrives best on clay soil with a limestone bed.

BLUE JAY. See JAY.

BLUE LAWS. Back in colonial days, this name was given to the Puritan laws of Connecticut, as related by the Rev. Samuel Peters, who was expelled from Connecticut to England, and afterward ridiculed the ways of the colonists. Many of these laws are now believed to have been invented by the exiled clergyman himself. Some of the blue laws he reported were:

"No woman shall kiss her child on the sabbath or fasting day.

"No one shall run on the sabbath day, or walk in his garden, except reverently to and from meeting.

"No one to cross a river on Sunday but an authorized clergyman."

Today there are laws respecting violation of the peace of the Sabbath, prohibiting amusements, and restricting the sale of liquor and cigarettes. Those who object to such restrictions call them blue laws.

BLUEPRINT. You can make pictures of interesting leaf forms and patterns with blueprint paper, just as architects and engineers make blueprints of their plans. Place the leaf over a piece of blueprint paper and expose it to the light. After a short

HOW YOU CAN MAKE A BLUEPRINT OF A FLOWER

You need only blueprint paper, clothespins, and a piece of glass. Clamp the flower between paper and glass, expose it to light and you have a perfect floral pattern.

time, the plant should be removed and the blueprint paper washed in pure water. The print of the pattern or leaf will appear white on the blue paper.

Blueprint paper is prepared by brushing a piece of paper with a solution of oxalic acid and iron. Then the paper is treated with a solution of potassium ferrocyanide. When this paper is exposed to sunlight or electric light and then washed in water, it turns blue. The parts of the paper that have been covered by the leaf pattern or by lines of the architect's plan will remain white. Blueprints are really photographic pictures.

BLUE RIDGE. Famed in song and story as the "Blue Ridge Mountains of Virginia," this rugged range is not Virginia's alone. It is the easternmost ridge of the Appalachian Mountains, stretching from West Point, N. Y., to the northern borders of Georgia and Alabama. The southern end of the range is crossed by the Black Mountains, South Mountains, and Nantahalas.

"BLUE SKY" LAWS. Every year thousands of persons invest their money in stocks and other securities that have no more value behind them than a patch of "blue sky." To prevent this sort of fraud,

the United States government and most of the states have adopted laws forbidding the sale of worthless securities and the use of untrue statements and empty promises of great profits. These measures are called "blue sky" laws. Before the Federal Securities Act of 1933 was passed by Congress, the Post Office Department estimated that more than $100,000,000 was invested every year in dishonest securities, and some financial experts believe the figure was even higher. This amount has decreased, but many people are still being defrauded by salesmen of fake stocks and bonds.

In the states, "blue sky" laws vary. Some of them require dealers in stocks and bonds to secure a license from the state and to file complete information concerning the securities they place on the market. The laws usually require that permission must be granted by the state before these securities can be sold. The state governments, however, do not place their approval on the stocks as investments, and even highly speculative securities are allowed to be sold if the company does not make false promises and misrepresentations.

Under the Federal act, information con-

BAD-TEMPERED PIG—A WILD BOAR
This savage cousin of the domestic hog is fierce enough for royal favor.

cerning the stocks or bonds must be registered with the Securities Exchange Commission, and action similar to that taken by many states is in the hands of this body.

BLUN'DERBUSS. An odd-looking gun with funnel-shaped mouth, the blunderbuss was a weapon of the days when gunpowder was new. It was useless for accurate shooting from a distance, but deadly at close range, for the bullets would spray over a wide circle from its flaring muzzle. Several bullets could be loaded into it. Because of its clumsiness and waste of effort in firing at its target, its name is applied today to persons who are generally awkward and inefficient.

BO'A. Coiling its powerful body around its victim, a serpent of the boa genus of South America can crush the bones of an animal as large as a deer or sheep, then swallow it whole. The throat and neck of this enormous snake is elastic and stretches wide enough to take in a meal larger than itself. After such a feast, the boa lies motionless, as if asleep, sometimes for several weeks.

The largest boas of the New World are found in the forests of Brazil and Guiana. They may reach a length of thirty feet, and are among the largest snakes in the world. In the tropical forests of the Old World are the pythons, a related group that also kill by strangling and crushing (see PYTHON).

The boa constrictor, also found in South America, is the snake commonly thought of when the term boa is used. This serpent is light brown above, with dark brown crossbars, and its underparts are yellow with black spots. The boa constrictor is seldom longer than twelve feet. It can capture animals as large as dogs or sheep, but has not the strength of the larger boas. There are other species in Central America and Mexico.

BOAR, *bore.* Once a sport of kings, and still a popular and dangerous sport in India, Ceylon, and Burma, is "pig-sticking"— hunting the wild boar. Much larger than its cousin, the domestic pig, the boar is swift, strong, and ferocious, and often when at bay it will turn upon the hunter to gash him with its curving tusks. Hunters on foot used to fight the boar with spears in Northern Europe and the British Isles. Today, the hunters in Asia usually ride horses. The boar is covered with short hair and stiff bristles, which form a ridge along its back. It feeds at night on plants.

Grain Dealer *to the World*

BOARD OF TRADE. In a great hall within a Chicago skyscraper, men gathered in small groups are shouting excitedly to each other, with arms flung high and fingers moving as if signaling; messengers dash in and out of the clusters of men, telegraph keys and tickers click unheard in the tumult, clerks chalk figures up on a huge blackboard, confusion and din seem general.

But it is not confusion to the men there on the floor. It is order. This is the trading floor of the Chicago Board of Trade, the principal grain-trading center of the United States. Men known as brokers meet there to buy or sell wheat, corn, oats, rye, cotton, and other farm products for their customers. Each grain has its own trading "pit"; yet the grain itself may never be seen in that pit, where the flying fingers are signaling bids and offers to buy or sell; the brokers themselves seldom if ever handle the grain.

In the Beginning. In any great city there are brokers whose business it is to handle orders for grain for their customers, receiving commissions or fees for their services. The stock exchange grew out of the daily luncheon meetings of brokers at a London coffeehouse. The board of trade grew out of similar meetings of grain traders. They needed a convenient place for trading; they needed an organization to make rules to govern their business, in order to end abuses and corrupt practices that dishonest dealers might attempt. So they formed an association, agreed to abide by its rules, and called it the board of trade.

How Prices Are Made. Many believe that traders on the board are merely gamblers who manipulate prices of farm products and hold the farmer at their mercy. Speculation undoubtedly has its effect on prices. So does government control. And so does war, bringing scarcity of man power, scarcity of grain, and sometimes artificial price-fixing by government. But the one great influence which determines prices at the leading world grain market, in Liverpool, at the leading American market, in Chicago, and likewise at markets around the earth, is the law of supply and demand. With scarcity, prices rise; with abundant crops, prices fall.

A Pool of Information. The price of wheat grown in Kansas is not governed merely by the abundance of the harvest in that state. Conditions the world around affect it. Thus the board of trade becomes a

At the same time, the latest price is recorded on blackboards on the exchange floor.

If a bushel of wheat should be worth more in Boston one morning than the sum of the Chicago price and the transportation costs from Chicago to Boston, the telegraph would promptly tend to equalize the value. Traders would buy the low-priced wheat

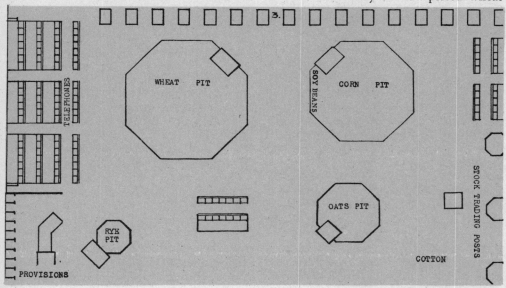

Courtesy the Chicago Board of Trade

HOW "LIGHTNING" TRADING CAN BE ORDERLY
Board of Trade Exchange Floor plan speeds business through careful arrangement.

pool of information into which reports flow from every growing and consuming center in the world. The farmer himself cannot keep in touch with crop prospects in Argentina, nor predict the amount of wheat Germany must import in any year; he cannot estimate the chances of war, nor tell from day to day how much grain is stored in elevators in Manitoba and in Europe.

It is the everyday business of a board of trade to know world conditions. Facts and opinions on the supply and demand of grain, provisions, and cotton are registered every minute during trading hours at the Chicago Board of Trade. As price changes are made on the trading floor, the news is carried simultaneously by tickers and private wires to more than 600 American cities.

in Chicago and contract to sell equal quantities in the higher-priced market in Boston. This process is called *arbitraging,* and tends to equalize grain prices all over the world.

Grain Is Graded by Standards. There are different grades of grain, just as there are variations in quality of food and clothing. These grades are standardized; what is accepted as "No. 1 Hard" (the best quality of wheat) in one part of the world is so rated everywhere. At the Chicago Board of Trade there are "cash grain" tables laden with small paper bags, each containing a sample from a carload of grain which has been inspected, graded, and certified by inspectors of the state of Illinois.

Trading by Signals. Any person who wishes to buy or sell grain on a board of trade must do so through a member of the board. He gives his order to a firm of brokers; the order is sent quickly to the firm's trader in the pit, and the latter executes the order. There, in the turmoil of the pit, a vast volume of business is conducted through a very simple process. There may be so much noise that the voice of a neighbor in the pit is drowned out; yet contracts to buy and sell thousands of bushels of grain are made and the traders may never exchange a word while doing it.

Through a system of signals, or sign language, the traders make themselves understood. The unit of trade in grain is 5,000 bushels, indicated by each finger held vertically. Two fingers, for example, mean 10,000 bushels; four fingers 20,000 bushels. The open hand extended toward another trader means an offer to sell; the back of the hand means a buyer's bid. Price signals are indicated by the fingers held horizontally: a closed hand means an even cent; one finger extended means one-eighth cent, and so on.

For instance, wheat having sold at 90 cents, a trader catches the eye of someone opposite in the pit who has 10,000 bushels to sell, and signals that he will take the "10" wheat at 90. The seller, in reply, holds up his right hand with the index finger extended horizontally, indicating that he wants one-eighth cent more than the price quoted, or 90 and one-eighth cents a bushel. The buyer motions acceptance and signals back "one-eighth."

The seller and buyer then note on their cards "Sold 10 at one-eighth, Jones"; and "Bought 10 at one-eighth, Smith," respectively, the number of bushels bought or sold always meaning so many thousands. The good faith of the parties is the binding force of the contract, for the traders do not compare rates until they leave the pit.

Speculators Gamble. Thousands of men "buy" grain in large quantities with no intention of having it delivered to them, and "sell" grain they never actually possessed. They simply gamble on the rise and fall of prices. For example, Mr. A one morn-

ing finds wheat quoted at $1. He knows that discouraging crop reports are abroad, and believes the price will rise. To describe the case rather bluntly, this man goes to his broker and "bets" that wheat will advance. He may "buy" 10,000 bushels—worth today $10,000—and deposit with the broker enough money to protect him against a fall in price. If he pays one-third of the value of his purchase, a rather high margin, the broker advances the other two-thirds, charging interest on the loan and a commission for handling the deal.

Should the price drop to a point where the speculator's margin will not cover his loss, he loses his entire deposit unless he is able at once to increase his margin. If the commodity rises in value, he may order his "holdings" sold at any moment the board is in session, and secure his profits.

It may be, to reverse the transaction, that a dollar seems too high a price for wheat. Reports show a vast crop maturing on hand —more than enough to meet world needs. The speculator therefore "sells" any desired quantity at $1, and if, fortunately for him, the price falls, he "buys" at a lower price the wheat he has already "sold" and promised for delivery in a future month. Thus he reaps a profit. On the contrary, if he has guessed wrong and the market does not "sag," he loses.

Cornering the Market. There have been instances when vast capital has been employed to "corner" the market; that is, to secure the entire available supply of grain and hold it. When the supply on the market becomes scarce, brokers must purchase from the man or group of men who have the "corner"; and since there are no competitors, they must pay whatever price is set for the grain. Sometimes great fortunes have thus been made within a few days, but more frequently the conspirators have attempted too ambitious a program and have been ruined. The most memorable attempted wheat corners on the Chicago Board of Trade occurred in May, 1867, when the price of wheat was forced to $2.85; in September, 1888, when wheat sold as high as $2.00; and in May, 1898, when it went to $1.85.

At the conclusion of a trading day, all parties who have made purchases or sales must make complete reports at the central office, or clearing house. If a trade shows a net gain, the trader is paid; if he has lost, he must at once pay what he owes.

If a trader is "long" on a deal, he is a buyer, expecting to realize a profit on an advance in price. If he expects a lower trend, he sells "short." This is known as dealing in "futures." A "bull" is a trader who buys in the belief a rising market is approaching. A "bear" is one who expects a falling market; he sells "short," hoping, bearlike, to "squeeze" the optimistic one and extract a profit.

Rules of the Board. All boards of trade have stringent regulations to prevent fraudulent practices. The smallest fraud on the part of any member, however prominent he may be, is punished by immediate suspension, and his trial is conducted like one held in a court of law. The rules also provide for strict penalties in case goods are not delivered at the time stated in each contract.

The Chicago Board of Trade. Wheat traders occupy the largest pit at the Chicago Board of Trade. There is a corn pit, in which soybeans are also sold; an oats pit, and a rye pit. The exchange floor has a section where cotton is traded, a place for the trading of lard, and securities-exchange posts. On the sides of the large trading room are cash-grain tables and batteries of telephone and telegraph operators and tickers to provide the immense communications service.

In the room are hosts of messengers, brokers' representatives, and clerks, and several employes who mark the latest price quotations on huge blackboards as fast as reports come over the wire. Employment is directly given to 30,000 persons, and indirectly to 100,000 persons, by reason of the Board of Trade. There are more than 1,500 members on the Chicago Board. A "seat" costs several thousand dollars, the actual price depending upon business conditions.

Radio broadcasts of current prices are made six times daily from the Chicago Board of Trade, and at the end of each trading day, the closing prices are listed in newspapers. In that way farmers can decide when to sell their grain to the country "elevators" or storehouses. The work of telephone operators is an important link in the lightning-like speed of the Board's quotations and the various transactions.

Orders from world points arriving at office headquarters of member firms are telephoned directly to the exchange floor. There they are transmitted by messenger or signal to pit brokers. When an order is executed, confirmation flashes back over the same quick route. So highly geared is the service over these privately leased wires that it is possible for an order to leave Kansas City, Minneapolis, or some other point, be carried out by a Board of Trade member, and be confirmed back to the point of origin within fifteen seconds.

Canadian Boards. In Canada a board of trade is a chartered association of business men similar in purpose to what in the United States is usually known as a *chamber of commerce*. See CHAMBER OF COMMERCE; STOCK EXCHANGE.

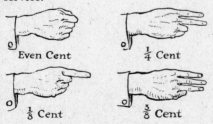
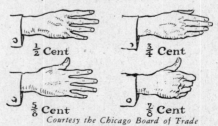

Even Cent   ¼ Cent   ½ Cent   ¾ Cent

⅛ Cent   ⅜ Cent   ⅝ Cent   ⅞ Cent

Courtesy the Chicago Board of Trade

Fortunes in the flip of a finger—Chicago Board of Trade price signals.

Man answers the Call of the Sea

BOAT, *bote*. From the earliest times when primitive man first ventured to ride a floating log downstream, boats have played an important rôle in the history of mankind. Boats antedate history. It might be said that civilization began with water transportation. Certainly civilization has followed the world's waterways and water routes.

Had man, basically a land animal, not overcome his inherent fear of water, we would today be living primitive lives with little hope of progress. Perhaps it was intense hunger, greed, or danger, perhaps curiosity, which forced early man to conquer natural water barriers.

Primitive Boats. "Probably in a thousand different places, at a thousand different times, a thousand savage men found that by sitting astride floating logs they could ride the surface of the water," writes Hawthorne Daniel in *Ships of the Seven Seas.*

After early man found he could ride a log, he learned that, by lashing two or more logs together with roots or reeds, a crude raft could be made. Then he could transport himself and his possessions by water. He learned how to use a pole to control the direction of his craft, and then how to make and use paddles with which to propel it.

Later men, using fire and their crude stone tools, hollowed out logs. Thus, the seaworthy, sturdy *dugout* came into use. Dugouts, even today, are used by peoples in various parts of the world; some of these hollowed logs are sufficiently large to carry twenty people.

Another early craft was the *coracle,* which was a long, woven reed basket covered with hides. The coracle seen today in Wales and on parts of the Irish coast has been changed only in its covering, which is now canvas. The *kufa,* a type of coracle, is a large, round, willow-reed basket, covered inside and out with asphalt, which is obtained from springs near the Tigris and Euphrates rivers. Today, on these same rivers, these craft may be seen just as they were 4,000 years ago.

The Eskimo, for his *kayak,* has a framework of driftwood, bound together with cords cut from reindeer or walrus hide. Over this frame are tightly stretched hides that have been carefully sewn together, so they will be waterproof. Around the opening on the top, which is large enough to admit only his body, he sews a flap with a drawstring. The Eskimo crawls into this opening, pulls the drawstring tight about his waist, and knows that though he turns topside over, no water will get into his boat. The paddle, too, is made of hide stretched over wood or whalebone. Of similar construction to the kayak, which is only for one, is the *umiak,* or woman's boat. This boat has an open top, and can carry heavy loads and as many as twelve people.

The American Indian, in the making of his *canoe,* used the same principles of boat making: his canoe was a light framework over which was stretched the best material available, which in his case was birch bark. Modern canoe builders use treated canvas. Canoes, because of their light weight and

delicate structure, are easily capsized and punctured on jagged rocks. The *punt* and *dory,* with their flat bottoms, are difficult to tip, carry heavy loads, and hence are favored for fishing and for sport.

There are many types of *outrigger* canoes. But they all have one thing in common, an outrigger. This is a pole of light wood, such as bamboo, floating a few feet outboard, and held rigid and parallel to the hull by one or more cross-bars. On larger boats, several poles may make up each outrigger. Usually there is only one, but sometimes an outrigger is attached to either side of the canoe. The outrigger is really a balance bar and keeps the canoe from upsetting.

BOATS
UNCHANGED
FOR
CENTURIES

An occasional ducking doesn't bother the natives of Tajikistan, who ride "goatskin ferries" (right). The inflated skins require skillful handling. The ancient kufa (below) is a basket covered with asphalt, and ranks among the oldest of water craft. Old 4,000 years ago, this type of boat is still common in the Near East.

QUEER CRAFT OF FAR WATERS

Here are primitive craft of three peoples. Above, the Eskimo in his kayak of waterproof hides. Left, a South American Indian canoe, shaded against the tropic sun. Below, a Japanese vegetable market puts to "sea" in a hand-power barge.

The Oar and the First Sail. When man first enlisted the aid of wind in propelling his craft is not known; probably the first sail was a hide held in the wind. The development of sails progressed slowly. The earliest known ships with sail were those of ancient Egypt. We know from Egyptian paintings that their craft had hulls modeled after the breasts of swimming birds, and that to the mast in the middle of the ship was attached a square sail. But these boats could sail only with the wind, and it was not until about 300 B. C. that the sail arrangement was developed to permit sailing in any direction.

The Phoenicians were the first real sea-going people in history. Although it is they who gave us our alphabet, they left no important records of their contribution to the advancement and improvement of shipbuilding. Because they had a real love for the sea, Phoenician sailors helped to man the fleets of other nations. We know they sailed to England (Cornwall) for tin. It is thought that the Phoenicians

SHIPS OF THE ANCIENT WORLD

(A) Three thousand years ago, Egyptian barks like this plied the Nile. (B) A Phoenician bireme—launched thirty centuries before Christ. (C) A Greek merchant ship of 500 B. C. (D) A trireme—ornate pleasure ship of Nero's Rome.

Barge, Ewing Galloway. Chinese junk, Cunard-White Star, Ltd.

THE KINDLY WIND FILLS SAILS OF EVERY FORM AND COLOR

The patchwork sail on a hard-working Adriatic barge (above, left). The stout matting sails of a Yangtze junk look like down quilts. Below, Sulu sails are blazoned with bold designs.

invented the *bireme* and the *trireme*. These were long, wood craft propelled by oars; the bireme had two banks or tiers of rowers, one above the other; the trireme had three.

It was the Greeks, however, who developed the trireme, and that name was given to all ships of this type, even though they had five, or more, banks of oars. Their war boats were rowed, but the trading vessels used both sails and oars. The ingenious, careful planning of the Greeks utilized every inch of space in the triremes, without sacrificing the freedom of move-

ment and efficiency of the rowers. Hundreds of slaves, compelled to man the oars, were chained to crowded benches and forced to pull at the heavy oars, keeping pace with the relentless stroke for hours on end. "Galley slave" was no figure of speech in those days, but a sentence of unceasing physical overexertion and brutal whip lashes across naked backs.

Rome, finally taking to the sea, was challenged and defeated by the Carthaginians. But with that persevering, indomitable spirit which made her "Queen of Land and Sea," she refused to accept

DREADNAUGHTS OF OLD

(1) Viking ship of the seventh century. (2) England's finest in the thirteenth century. (3) Carved prow, vessel of the English navy under Charles I. (4) Stern of an eighteenth-century French ship. (5) British "three-decker" man-o'-war, 1640. (6) Proudest of English ships—H.M.S. *Victory*.

Courtesy American Express Co.

TRICKY—BUT USEFUL
This Arabian *hurjia* is made of palm leaves. It has a double bottom, but it leaks anyway. Right, a native's wicker fishing boat high in the Andes, on Lake Titicaca.

defeat. She eventually drove the Carthaginians from the sea and established her own supremacy. Roman ships plied the Atlantic, and we know they voyaged to England and there established colonies. Perhaps these Roman ships in northern waters, far from the Mediterranean home ports, influenced the Vikings.

The Norse used both sail and oars and rows of shields, as did the Phoenicians, as protection from the enemy. The single sail, narrower at the top, was made of flax, sometimes even of velvet, and was ornamented with patterns of rich color. Gilded heads of serpents or dragons formed the prow; some craft were decorated above the water line. Truly, the Viking ship, with its long, sweeping lines of strength and grace, was a thing of beauty. The Norse crew were picked men; as navigators they knew no peers. From the Northland they sailed to Iceland, and to Greenland; and, beyond doubt, to North America, several hundred years before Columbus.

The Scandinavian, English, and Dutch vessels of later days were modeled after those of the Vikings. From their day to the close of the Middle Ages, there were no radical changes, only development in water-craft design. During this period, the steering oar gradually disappeared from the side of the ship and returned as the rudder slung at the stern. The *carack,* a three-masted, high-sided vessel, was probably the first real ship—not merely a big boat.

Sailing Vessels. With the gradual passing of slavery, the galley type of craft was eclipsed by the sailing vessel While Venice was challenging Genoa for the control of the Mediterranean, Spain, Portugal, and England were improving their vessels. Probably modeled after the Italian ships were the *caravels* of Portugal and Spain. They were of light draft, and had two or three masts, high sterns, and high overhanging bows. As the Viking vessels were models for the English and Dutch, so the caravel influenced ship construction in the Mediterranean. The three ships of Columbus' little fleet were of the caravel type, as were the ships of Vasco da Gama, Americus Vespucius, the Cabots, Magel-

Left, courtesy American Can Co. Right, courtesy Popular Mechanics, Inc.

WHEN SAIL RULED THE TRADES

Left, a salmon packet in full sail. Right, a clipper—fastest sailing ship of all time.

lan, Drake, and other maritime explorers.

The sixteenth century saw many developments in shipbuilding. Three important types may be mentioned. The *galleon* was a craft whose length was three times its beam (width); it was low in the waist (center part), and had a high quarterdeck and a square forecastle. The *galleass* had lower sides, stern, and bow than the galleon, and was longer in proportion to beam. The *pinnace,* which later was called a *sloop,* was a small boat, and served a mother ship.

In the seventeenth century, the *frigate* first was launched by the English. Out of the improvements made by American shipwrights on French models, there developed the designs of the first Yankee frigates, the privateers. Then came the *packets,* which had full-bodied, able hulls, and slant spars, sails, and rigging. The packets were supplanted by the *clippers,* the fastest sailing ships on the sea. American ship designers and builders, realizing that speed offered the only hope of escape

from British men-of-war, designed these craft to "clip" over the water at the swiftest pace yet known. These craft, the *Baltimores,* or *Chesapeakes,* as they were sometimes called, had a displacement of 75 to 200 tons. Some were rigged as *schooners,* some as *brigantines,* some were *brigs* with square sails.

In 1869, the *Sir Launcelot,* which was probably the finest type of clipper, made the passage home from China, a distance of over 14,000 miles, in eighty-nine days. The framework was iron, and the ship was 197 feet long and 33 feet wide. It carried 46,000 square feet of sail. But the picturesque beauty of the clipper, with sails spread to the breeze, gradually gave way to the power and speed of steam.

Steam Rules the Sea. The eighteenth century saw many experiments with steam as an aid to navigation. Robert Fulton, though not the first to understand the possibilities of steam, was the first to make a really practical steamboat. The Atlantic was first crossed by steam power in 1819.

Courtesy Southern Pacific Railroad

QUEENS OF RIVER AND SEA

A Mississippi River "stern-wheeler," pride of the Father of Waters; and (left) the *Queen Mary*, a palatial Atlantic liner.

slow but sure, were consistently made. The *screw propeller* replaced paddle wheels; *turbines* supplanted the cylinder-type engines; then the turbine was superseded by the more efficient internal-combustion *Diesel engine,* using oil instead of coal. Not only are the large ocean liners equipped with Diesel motors, but these engines are also used on many commercial craft, such as *oilers, tankers, tugs,* and *freighters.* For a detailed treatment of the modern ships of the sea, consult the article SHIP.

Boats are "Home" to Millions. In many parts of the world, the population practically lives on the sea. The rivers of South China are so crowded with small craft and houseboats that they form an almost solid raft. These boats house permanently thousands of people. On them, children are born, live, and die without knowing other homes. In Canton and in British Hong Kong, the picture is the same, and is duplicated in other rivers of China. Living quarters aboard these boats

The boat that made the passage, like all the first ocean-going steamers, carried sail, and was propelled by *paddle wheels.*

Despite the shipping world's scorn for these "clumsy tubs of steamboats," which frequently broke down, improvements,

SPEED AND THRILLS WITH RACING HULLS

A stiff breeze fills white sails as racing sloops maneuver. Below, the outboard speedster rides its wake at fifty miles per hour.

are often miserable, but are perhaps better than most of those ashore in the crowded cities.

The Dutch, British, and Scandinavians are great sea folk. Thousands live on barges along the Dutch canals. London, although far inland, is one of the greatest of commercial ports, thanks to the numerous barges that reach the city by way of the Thames River. American waters also supply homes for thousands engaged in commerce and fishing. Those who can afford the luxury of private yachts spend weeks or months at a time cruising in these floating palaces of the sea.

For further reading on the fascinating subject of life on the water, see the following articles:

Canoe and Canoeing   Rowing
Gondola   Sailboat and Sailing
Motor Boat   Yacht and Yachting

NAMED FOR HIS SONG
The bobolink, noisy cousin of the blackbird.

BOB'OLINK, REED'BIRD, or RICE-BIRD. This bird leads a double life. In the meadows and orchards of the Northern states and Southern Canada, its bubbling, rollicking song is one of the best-loved sounds of spring and early summer. Then the male is gaily dressed in black, buff, and white, but later, when the nesting period is over, he changes to the dull, yellowish streaked plumage of the female. In late summer the bobolinks move southward, becoming known as reedbirds in the Middle States, where they are shot in numbers for food, during a short season. A little farther on in the Carolinas and Georgia, they fall upon the ricefields and there are unpopular as ricebirds, because of the damage they do each year.

They winter in South America, but again on the return trip in the spring, do some harm pulling rice in the newly planted fields. It is hard to believe that the same bird can lead two such different lives. Their northern welcome is well expressed by the poet, Thomas Hill, as follows:

> Bobolink that in the meadow,
> Or beneath the orchard's shadow,
> Keepest up a constant rattle
> Joyous as my children's prattle,
> Welcome to the North again.

The bobolink's nest is constructed of dry grasses and weed stems on the ground in northern meadows, and is cleverly hidden. There are from four to seven eggs, grayish white spotted with brown. The bobolink is a favorite subject for the poets. Those who are not familiar with William Cullen Bryant's beautiful poem *Robert of Lincoln* have a treat in store if they will seek it. The poem gives the whole story of this interesting bird.

BOEOTIA, *be o' shi ah.* In the days of ancient Greece, the people usually thought of themselves not as Grecians but as citizens of one of the great cities; for example, they might be Athenians or Spartans. When the Boeotians, a foreign people, invaded the central part of Greece about 1124 B.C., and conquered the Pelasgians and Phoenicians living there, they formed the Boeotian League of independent cities, headed by Thebes.

Boeotia was the region between Attica and Phocis, a level land around the basin forming Lake Copaïs. The Boeotians sided with the Persians during the Persian invasion of Greece in 480 B.C. They were bitter enemies of Athens in the Peloponnesian War, although they had formerly been associated with Athens in the Athenian League.

About the time that Alexander the Great was beginning to dream of conquests, the Boeotian League, under the leadership of Epaminondas and Pelopidas, reached its greatest power, and fought bitterly against the young conqueror. The Boeotian League endured in some form or another until the second century B.C., when it was broken up by the Romans.

The Boeotians cared little for culture, being dull and lacking in imagination. To the south of their country are the Helicon Mountains, where the Greeks went to worship the Muses, patron goddesses of the arts and sciences.

BOER, *boor.* In South Africa are many people descended from hardy Dutch settlers, who founded a colony there in 1652. They are called Boers, from the Dutch word for farmer.

BOER WAR. See SOUTH AFRICAN WAR.

BOG. There are 79,000,000 acres of bog in the United States—an area larger than the British Isles! Wet, soggy ground from which water cannot drain is called bog, marsh, or swamp, in America; in Europe a bog is usually considered a swamp where peat develops.

Wherever surface water cannot run off readily, evaporate quickly, or drain into deeper earth, a bog results. Perhaps it was originally a shallow lake that became filled with soil and vegetation. Rotting in the wet earth, the vegetation became peat, and, under proper conditions, coal.

Swamps cover one twenty-fourth of the area of the United States. As bogs they are waste land; yet, if they were drained, they might be very fertile soil for farming; and if peat were needed to fill a scarcity of other fuel, it is estimated that thirteen billion tons of dried fuel could be recovered from these swamps. Its heat value would be less than that of an equal tonnage of coal, however, for peat is bulkier and contains more moisture.

The most extensive marshes are found in the north temperate zone, large areas occurring in Ireland, England, Holland, North Germany, Canada, and the United States. In the tropics, heat evaporates the moisture and limits the number of swamps, but they have developed in places of heavy rainfall where heat and moisture produce a heavy mantle of vegetation which not only prevents rapid run-off, but also checks evaporation.

Swamps are the breeding places of mosquitoes which carry the germs of malaria and fever, and for this reason it is very desirable that they be drained. See DRAINAGE; MARSH; PEAT.

BOG OAK. Trunks and branches of oak are often found buried in bogs, and the wood, called bog oak, is frequently of great value. The years spent in the damp earth so preserve this oak that the grain of the wood is as beautiful as it was originally. Of shiny black color, like ebony, the bog oak is frequently used for decorative furniture and small ornaments, such as brooches or earrings.

BOHEMIA. An independent kingdom in the Middle Ages, later a crownland of Austria, and after the World War a province of Czechoslovakia, Bohemia today is a part of a German protectorate.

The Boii, a tribe of uncertain origin, settled in this fertile farming country at the beginning of its history. The Germans drove them out about 12 B.C. During the next thousand years, Bohemia was first a part of the Moravian kingdom and then fell under German rule. From 1278 to 1305, the Bohemian kings gained great power, ruling from the Adriatic Sea to the Elbe, and later kings of Bohemia were the emperors of Germany. The little country managed to keep its independence in the turbulent fifteenth century, but in 1526 the Hapsburg kings became its rulers, and until the downfall of the Hapsburgs in the first World War, Bohemia was part of the Austro-Hungarian Monarchy.

For more than a hundred years, the Czechs, who were the strongest element in the mixed people of Bohemia, tried to inspire a national sentiment in the land, and when Austria-Hungary became embroiled in World War I on the side of Germany, the Czechs knew their opportunity had come. Many of their soldiers deserted and joined the enemies of the Austrian emperor, and when the Hapsburg Monarchy collapsed, in 1918, the Czechs of Bohemia joined the Moravians, Ruthenians, Slovaks, and Silesians to form the Republic of Czechoslovakia.

Bohemia was then over 20,101 square miles in area. Its population was more than 7,000,000. Prague (Praha), the largest city, was the capital of the republic. The flourishing province of small farms, busy manufacturing plants, and valuable mines fell prey to the aggression of Adolf Hitler. In 1938 he annexed the Sudeten area along the German border, and in 1939 he partitioned Czechoslovakia; Bohemia and Moravia were a German protectorate until the defeat of Germany in 1945. See CZECHOSLOVAKIA.

BOIL'ER. The steam you see rising from the kettle on the kitchen stove is the power that drives giant locomotives, that turns the propellers of swift ocean liners, that runs machinery in factories, and heats offices and homes.

But it is the boiler that harnesses steam's mighty power. A boiler is a strong vessel of iron, steel, or copper in which water is heated until it develops steam under pressure, and the term usually includes the furnace for burning the fuel, as well as the parts for controlling the fire and providing safety.

Hot steam is used to heat homes and skyscrapers by its circulation through pipes and radiators. Steam under pressure expands rapidly when given an opportunity; thus, when released into the pipes it immediately shoots up through them— even to the top of a seventy-story tower.

Boilers vary in design according to the purpose in view. Those on railway locomotives move with the engine and are in a horizontal position. Others are stationary and may be in an upright position. In some boilers, the water is heated in pipes which are surrounded by the fire; in others, the fire and hot gases pass through pipes which are surrounded by water.

Regardless of their type, all boilers have the same general characteristics: (1) a large surface area must be exposed to the heat; (2) heat must be used without waste; (3) they must be able to withstand great pressure; (4) they must not corrode or weaken. See STEAM ENGINE.

BOIL'ING POINT. When a kettle of water is placed on a hot stove, the water will soon begin to bubble vigorously, indicating that it has reached its *boiling point.* No matter how much longer the kettle is left on the stove, the water will not reach a higher temperature, but will gradually evaporate, in the form of steam. The boiling point is influenced by atmospheric pressure. At sea level, standard of measurement for this pressure, water boils at 212° on the Fahrenheit thermometer (on which the freezing point is 32°), and at 100°

on the centigrade thermometer (on which the freezing point is 0°).

By an increase of pressure on the water in the form of a cover or lid on the vessel containing the liquid, the boiling point is raised, and foods may be cooked more quickly. This principle is applied in the pressure cooker, in which a high temperature is reached without boiling. In the high mountains, where atmospheric pressure is lowered, the boiling point is much lower than at sea level, and a cover must be put on the container to raise it to a point where foods can be cooked properly. Because impurities in water raise the boiling point, foods cooked in salty water receive a higher degree of heat than in clear water.

Some liquids have a higher boiling point than water, while others boil at a lower temperature. Mercury, for instance, boils at 662° Fahrenheit, and ether at 96°.

BOISE, *boi'ze,* IDA. It is said that a French-Canadian trapper, on seeing the beautiful foliage on the site of what is now Boise, capital of Idaho, cried, "Les bois! Les bois!" (the woods, the woods). From this French term the city has taken its name.

Boise was founded in 1863, when Major Lugenbeel of the United States Army began the construction of Camp Boise. Surrounded by the peaks of the Boise range and located on the Boise River, the city is the trade center of the territory, being one of the largest wool markets in the world. From an artesian well flows hot water which is used extensively for heating buildings, while the river is the source of irrigation and manufacturing power. The city's most rapid growth took place between 1900 and 1910, following extensive irrigation projects in Southern Idaho. The largest city in the state, Boise has a population of about 26,130.

BOLEYN, *bull'en,* ANNE (1507?-1536). The daughter of a noble, Anne Boleyn became the second of the six wives of King Henry VIII of England. It was while Anne was lady of honor to Queen Catherine that Henry fell in love with her. Unable to obtain permission from the Pope to divorce Catherine, the king broke away from the Church, had a divorce declared legal, and married Anne in January, 1533. In September of that year Elizabeth was born, destined to become one of England's greatest rulers.

Henry, however, tired of his new queen and fell in love with her lady of honor, Jane Seymour. He therefore accused Anne of infidelity and treason. At her trial Anne was found guilty and was sentenced to death. She was beheaded on May 19, 1536, only three years after her marriage. A few days later the fickle Henry married Jane Seymour.

BOL'IVAR, SIMON (1783-1830). As the people of the United States revere the name of George Washington as "the Father of his Country," so do many South Americans honor the memory of Simon Bolivar. He. has been called "the South American Washington," because of his leadership in the revolts of several South American countries against the authority of Spain.

Bolivar was born in Caracas, Venezuela, and studied law in Madrid, Spain. Returning to South America in 1809, he immediately became active as a leader of revolutionary parties. In 1819 he became president of Greater Colombia, and four years later he was made dictator of Peru. He wrote the constitution for Bolivia, but his popularity waned when his enemies accused him of attempting to become dictator of all the countries he had aided. Today, he is honored by Venezuela, Colombia, Panama, Ecuador, Bolivia, and Peru as their liberator. Bolivia is named for him.

BOLIVIA, *bo liv'i ah*. Shut off from the sea by neighboring South American republics is Bolivia, one of the most sparsely populated nations in the world. Only 3,500,000 persons live in this potentially rich land of 506,792 square miles, an average density of approximately six to the square mile.

Courtesy Thomas Cook and Sons

WORK OF A LOST CIVILIZATION
Bolivia has many of these pre-Inca idols.

A Rugged Land of Varied Climate. Lying in the west-central part of South America, Bolivia is bounded by Brazil, Argentina, Paraguay, Chile, and Peru. In the western part of the nation are the Andes Mountains, where most of the mineral deposits lie and the majority of the cities and villages are located. Between two parallel ranges of the mountains is the Bolivian plateau, at a height of 12,000 to 13,000 feet above sea level. Here also is Lake Titicaca, the highest navigable body of water in the world.

A plain descends gradually east from the mountains to an area of lowlands. These lowlands have a semi-tropical climate, a contrast to the mountainous region, where the temperature becomes quite cold. The center of the country is tem-

SOUTH AMERICAN "CAMEL"
The haughty llama, hardy beast of
burden of the Bolivian Indian.

Courtesy American Express Co.

perate. Rain falls in great quantities in December, January, and February over most of the country.

Although Bolivia is a comparatively large country, there is only one main railroad to serve it. This road runs from Cuzco, Peru, to Antofagasta, Chile, on the Pacific coast, through the Bolivian cities of La Paz and Oruro. Pack animals are the principal means of transportation, since roads are few and poor. Navigable rivers cross the eastern and central part of the land, the largest being the Bermejo, the Pilcomayo, the Bene Itenez, and the Marmore.

A Rich Land, Poor People. More than half the population of Bolivia consists of illiterate Indians. These are the Aymaras, descendants of the ancient Incas, and the Quichuas. Almost all of the tilling of the soil in the region of the plains is done by the Aymaras. With primitive tools and ancient methods, they grow sugar, cotton, wheat, rice, maize, tobacco, and coffee,

but their fertile soil has yet to yield the crops of which it is capable.

The Quichuas are the domestic servants and miners of Bolivia, and to them falls the task of digging out the rich deposits of gold, silver, lead, tin, and antimony, and working the oil and rubber fields. Bolivia is second to Brazil, in South America, in the export of rubber, and is next to the Malay Peninsula in the production of tin. It also leads in antimony production.

The white people, mostly of Spanish descent, hold all the leading professional and commercial positions, while the mestizos, people of mixed white and Indian blood, are the small tradesmen. Spanish is the national language, although the Indians still speak their native tongues. Sucre, a town of 32,000 persons, is the capital; but La Paz, with a population of 320,000, is the largest city and the real seat of government.

The Republic Today. In form, the government of Bolivia is similar to that of the

United States. The President and Vice-President are elected for four years. Seven Ministers correspond to the Cabinet of the United States. There are two legislative branches: a Senate composed of sixteen members, and a Chamber of seventy Deputies, elected for four years. The country is divided into eight departments composed of provinces and cantons.

Education is supposed to be compulsory, and a system of schools exists, but the laws requiring attendance are not enforced. It is estimated that only 35 out of 100 Bolivians can read and write. There are only two universities having more than one department, those at La Paz and Sucre.

Roman Catholicism is the state religion, but other religious bodies enjoy freedom of worship.

From Spanish Colony to Republic. The country was first discovered by white men in 1538, when the Spaniards under Pizarro conquered the Incas who were in control of that part of the continent. Until 1825, when the people secured their independence under Simon Bolivar, for whom the republic was named, the land was ruled by the cruel Spaniards, who enslaved the Indians and forced all the inhabitants to obey harsh laws.

The republic, however, did not bring much peace to the people. Revolutions occurred during its early history, and, in 1898, there was a civil war that lasted six months. In 1938 Paraguay and Bolivia ended a long-standing dispute over the Gran Chaco, territory lying between the countries. Bolivia kept its oil fields and secured a corridor to the Paraguay.

SCOURGE OF COTTON—THE BOLL WEEVIL
About fourteen times life-size, this view clearly shows the pest's boll-puncturing snout.

BOLL WEEVIL, *bole wee'v'l.* The chief enemy of the cotton plant is an insect known as the boll weevil. It was found in Mexico about 1862, although no one knows just how it got there. By 1892 it had spread to Texas. At that time experts warned the government that the spread of the insect could be stopped only if a certain area were marked off where no cotton was to be planted; for they knew that the boll weevil spreads only through the cotton boll. But the advice was not heeded, and the boll weevil continued to spread wherever cotton was grown.

The weevil is about a quarter of an inch long, a snout accounting for half the length. It damages cotton by puncturing a hole in the boll. In this hole the female deposits her eggs. The larvae hatch within a few days and begin eating. The larvae cut up the cotton fiber so that it loses practically all its value. The average life of a weevil is five days.

With radio addresses and pamphlets on the latest and best methods of fighting the pest, the government helps the farmer destroy the weevil. The Department of Agriculture recommends that, in the fall, old stalks and fallen bolls be removed from the field and burned. The field should then be plowed and, by proper planting and fertilizing, should be prepared for an early crop. Also, at a cost of five dollars an acre, the farmer can spray the crop in an effort to hold the pest in check, but it is an open question whether the method is worth the expense. However, even the most effective methods do not eliminate the weevil; they only check its spread.

BOLOGNA, bo lo'nyah, ITALY. At the foot of the Apennines, eighty miles north of Florence, lies the famous old city of Bologna. It is the home of the oldest university in Italy, the University of Bologna, founded more than seven centuries ago. There are also many magnificent churches and cathedrals, built a long time ago. Bologna is today a railway and industrial center. The principal manufactured products are macaroni, leather, machinery, silk, glass, and, of course, the well-known Bologna sausage.

Bologna was originally an Etruscan city, named Felsina. After almost a thousand years it passed into the hands of the Romans under the name of Bononia, until finally, under Charlemagne, it became a free city in the year 800. It came under Papal control early in the sixteenth century because of feuds between the Italian nobles. There followed several struggles to throw off the power of the Pope, culminating in Austrian control, which lasted until 1849.

In 1860 Bologna became part of the new kingdom of Italy. Now capital of the province of Bologna, it has a population of about 270,000. Although it is a modern city, ancient Roman ruins are still visible in places.

BOMB, bom, or bum. The great exploding shells that killed and destroyed during the World Wars were formerly called bombs. In modern speech the word refers to explosives hurled by soldiers or terrorists, to shells dropped by airplanes, or to depth charges fired from ships of war.

A bomb usually consists of a metal ball or shell containing nitroglycerine or other explosive substance. It may be set off by a timed fuse, by impact, or by a clockwork mechanism.

BOMBAY', INDIA. The "gateway to India," Bombay is the capital of Bombay presidency, or province, on the western coast of India. The city is on an island that extends into the Arabian Sea. This island, eleven miles long and three miles wide, is joined to the mainland on the north by causeways.

At the southern end of the island, on the side toward the mainland, is Bombay's greatest treasure—her harbor. It is considered one of the finest natural harbors in the world. The traveler approaching from the south is treated to a view that he will long remember. Passing among numerous islands, he sees on the one side the beautiful and imposing buildings of the city of Bombay; and on the other side, the shore of the mainland sloping toward mountainous heights in the east.

Because the island city is nearer to Europe than is her rival, Calcutta, on the opposite coast of India, Bombay has outdistanced Calcutta in foreign trade. In the spacious harbor with its modern docks, shipyards, and piers, steamships that ply the European route are always to be seen. The most important exports are cotton and manufactured cotton products. Other industries are tanning and dyeing and the making of pottery, brass utensils, and carved wood objects.

In Bombay are found many fine buildings, including banks, the University of Bombay, a museum, courts of justice, hospitals, and a library. The imposing Victoria Station is the western terminal of all important Indian railways.

Bombay is the second largest city in British India, with a population of about 1,490,000. This population is made up of all races, creeds, and nationalities—Europeans, Parsees, Arabs, Japanese, Afghans, Tibetans, and many others. The language most generally understood is Bombay Bāt, a mixture of Hindustani and several other languages.

Along the coast the average temperature is 79°, and the yearly rainfall is about seventy-five inches. Cooling sea breezes and sufficient rain prevent too excessive heat, thereby contributing greatly to the activity and industry of the people.

BONAPARTE, *bo'na pahrt.* This is the surname of a family whose most famous member was Napoleon I, Emperor of France. The family bore the Italian name *Buonaparte* until Napoleon rose to power in France. At that time the name was changed to *Bonaparte.* Because other members of this family achieved prominence, it is interesting to study the careers of the more important ones.

Carlo, or Charles, Bonaparte (1746-1785). After studying law in Pisa, Italy, Napoleon's father, Carlo Bonaparte, married Letizia Ramolino in 1764, and set up his household in Ajaccio, the capital of Corsica. When he saw the futility of struggling for Corsican independence, he transferred his loyalty to France. Later he journeyed to Paris and there secured free admission to a military school for his second son, Napoleon.

Jerome Bonaparte (1784-1860). Napoleon's youngest brother, Jerome, began his career in the French navy. After a trip to the West Indies, he spent some time in America. There he married Elizabeth Patterson, an American girl. But Napoleon, then emperor, forced his brother to give up his American wife and return to France to become king of Westphalia. Jerome ruled unwisely and extravagantly for six years until Napoleon's defeat at Leipzig. After the Battle of Waterloo and the fall of the empire, Jerome traveled widely in Europe. Then, under Napoleon III, he was a marshal of France and president of the Senate.

Joseph Bonaparte (1768-1844). The eldest brother of Napoleon I, Joseph was indebted to his brother for all the success that ever came to him. After a military career, he was made king of Naples in 1806. Two years later, in 1808, Napoleon sent him from Naples to Madrid to become king of Spain. Unpopular in Spain, Joseph fled for his life in 1813. Later he lived in the United States under the title Count of Survilliers. Eventually he returned to Italy, where he resided until his death in 1844.

Louis Bonaparte (1778-1846). Another brother of Napoleon I, Louis also had a military career, attaining high rank in the French army. He married Hortense, daughter of the Empress Josephine by her first marriage. He was king of Holland from 1806 to 1810. He attempted to rule justly and wisely but was continually dominated by Napoleon and finally abdicated. Louis fled to Bohemia and finally to Rome, dying in exile at Leghorn. His son, Charles Louis, became Napoleon III in the second French empire.

Lucien Bonaparte (1775-1840). Born at Ajaccio, Corsica, Napoleon's next younger brother, Lucien, migrated to Marseilles in 1793 and there distinguished himself as an orator and politician. As president of the Council of Five Hundred, Lucien aided in the overthrow of the Directory and in the establishment of the great Corsican. He rose in power with his more famous brother, only to be sent to Spain as a mere ambassador after losing the royal favor. Lucien eventually settled in Rome, however, devoting himself to study and writing. In Rome the Pope made him Prince of Canino. He came to the aid of the emperor only shortly before the Battle of Waterloo. The fall of the empire sent him again to Rome, where he lived until his death.

Charles Joseph Bonaparte (1851-1921). Grandson of Jerome, king of Westphalia, Charles Joseph was born in Baltimore. He was educated at Harvard University and became a lawyer in 1874. He was Secretary of the Navy in 1905-1906 and Attorney-General until 1909, under President Theodore Roosevelt. See NAPOLEON.

BOND. Anything that binds is a bond. Just as a rope holding two pieces of wood together is a bond, so is the promise of an individual, a business firm, or a government to pay money. Bonds are of different types. There is the *bail* bond, which is the promise of a person to forfeit his own or someone else's money or property if he does not appear in court for trial. Then there is the *indemnity* bond, which pledges a special firm, called a *surety company,* to pay a municipality, society, organization, or another company money if its financial officer should steal funds.

The most common form of bond is the *investment,* or *loan,* bond. It is a note issued by the Federal government, a city, a state, or a private corporation to raise money. Funds from the sale of bonds may be used for improvements such as roads, bridges, buildings, street-car lines, railroads, schools, hospitals, waterworks, sewage-disposal plants, and in fact, for anything that costs more money than the taxing body or company has on hand. Or the funds may be sold to reduce debts or to finance the reorganization of a business.

When a person buys a United States government bond, he is relying upon the faith of the government to pay him back. When he purchases a state or city bond or one issued by some other local taxing body, he is paid back through the taxes of that body. When he buys a bond of a private corporation, he may have either a mortgage on the company's business or a promise from the company that it must fulfill before it meets any other obligations.

In *mortgage* bonds the company pledges its resources as a guarantee. Interest is paid at stated intervals, and the bonds are paid back in full after a number of years. If interest payments are not made or if the entire worth of the bonds (the principal) is not paid upon the day promised, the owners of these bonds may foreclose on the company to recover their money from the sale of the pledged property.

Debenture bonds are merely promises to pay. The owner of such a bond does not have a mortgage on the company's property. If the company cannot pay the interest or the principal on these bonds, the owners are reimbursed before other creditors when the company clears up its affairs. Mortgage bonds usually run for a longer time than debenture bonds and pay less.

On each bond there are coupons telling the dates on which interest is to be paid and how much the interest is to be. When the day comes for the payment of interest, the owner of a bond clips the coupon for that date and takes it to a bank, where he is paid. The bank then collects the money from the company which issued the bond.

Some bonds are *registerable.* This means that the owner may, if he so desires, register his name with the company, and the principal will be paid only to him. If the owner dies or someone buys the bond from him, the secretary of the company is notified, and the money is paid to the person registered. When both principal and interest are registerable, the interest is paid also to the person recorded on the books of the company. Some bonds are *registered;* that is, the company keeps a record of the owner's name whether requested to or not. Interest on a registered bond is sometimes paid by check rather than by coupon.

Usually, the more reliable the corporation or taxing body, the lower will be the interest rate; United States government bonds pay a low interest because investors have a great deal of faith in the government. During the first and second World Wars, however, when the nation needed vast sums of money, the United States floated special issues of government bonds in low denominations and at high interest rates to attract purchasers. The Liberty Bonds of World War I were negotiable, and varied in value. The War Savings Bonds and Victory Bonds of World War II, however, were not negotiable; they had a par value ranging from $25 up and matured in ten years.

BONE. The solid framework, or skeleton, of the body is composed of bones. These bones support the soft tissues; protect vital organs, like the heart, from injury; provide a place of attachment for the muscles; and, by the formation of joints, make movements possible.

"THE HORSE FAIR"
Famed example of Rosa Bonheur's surpassing skill in depicting the animals she knew so well.

Bones are hard on the outside and covered by a protecting membrane called the *periosteum*. The life of the bone depends upon the soundness of the periosteum, which carries blood vessels supplying the inner part of the bone with the nourishment that it needs. If the periosteum is destroyed, the inner parts of the bone cannot do their work, and the bone becomes diseased. The inner part of the bone is much softer than the outer, and is filled with marrow, a fatty tissue.

Bones are made up of two kinds of matter, mineral and animal. In adults the mineral content of bones is greater than it is in children. For this reason the bones of adults are more brittle and more easily broken than the bones of children. Because a child's bones are flexible, however, they are easily bent and may become misshapen if attention is not paid to proper posture.

Bones are classified according to their size and shape. In the human body there are *long* bones, such as those in the arms and legs; *short* bones, such as those in the wrist and ankle; *flat* bones, such as those in the shoulder blade; *irregular* bones, such as those of the vertebrae or backbone; and *mixed* bones, such as the ribs (see the article SKELETON).

Bones are sometimes attacked by bacteria, particularly the pus-producing ones and those of tuberculosis. Rickets and scurvy are diseases of the bones due to improper food. In rickets, a disease of children, the bones fail to ossify (harden) properly. As a result, when the child begins to walk, his bones become deformed, sometimes permanently. In scurvy the periosteum is affected, and the teeth often fall out. Both of these diseases can be corrected if a proper diet is followed before the disease is too far advanced.

In ancient times the bones of animals were fashioned into arrowheads and fish-hooks. Today, bones are used in many manufactured products, the most important of which is probably fertilizer. Other products are soap, glue, boneblack, buttons, and gelatin.

BONHEUR, *bo nur'*, MARIE ROSA (1822-1899). One woman who succeeded in winning recognition of her remarkable talent was Rosa Bonheur. She was a French painter of animals and farm life. When still in her 'teens, she astonished art critics

AFLAME AND SINKING—BUT VICTORIOUS!

The gallant American frigate *Bon Homme Richard* is abandoned after the defeat of the British man-o'-war *Serapis* in a famous sea battle of 1779.

with two excellent pictures, *Goats and Sheep* and *Two Rabbits*. In 1865 her fame had become so widespread that she was decorated with the Cross of the Legion of Honor by Empress Eugénie. Rosa Bonheur was the first woman to receive this decoration. The Luxembourg Museum in Paris now exhibits her *Plowing in Nivernais;* the Metropolitan Museum of Art in New York City possesses the famous painting, *The Horse Fair.*

BON HOMME RICHARD, *bo nom' re shahr'.* During the Revolutionary War, France furnished the United States with a small fleet commanded by John Paul Jones in the flagship *Bon Homme Richard.* (This name, meaning *the good man Richard,* was the French form of Benjamin Franklin's pen name, Richard Saunders.) On September 23, 1779, this fleet encountered two British convoys leading a fleet of forty-one merchant ships off the coast of Scotland. In the struggle that followed, the main battle was between the *Bon Homme Richard*

and the *Serapis,* a powerful ship of forty guns.

The bloody three-hour engagement ended in a hand-to-hand fight on deck, and victory for the ship of John Paul Jones. However, this vessel was so badly damaged, it sank two days later. The crew had already been safely transferred to the captive *Serapis.* American prestige on the high sea dates from the victory of the *Bon Homme Richard.* See JONES, JOHN PAUL.

BON'IFACE. Nine Popes were known by the name of Boniface. **Boniface I** (418-422) was appointed by the Emperor Honorius, and together they brought Illyria under the Church. **Boniface II** (530-532) was a German, though born in Rome, and was the first Pope to use the title "Universal Bishop of Christendom." **Boniface III** (died 607) reigned nine months. **Boniface IV** (608-615) is remembered for converting the Pantheon at Rome into a Catholic church. **Boniface V** (619-625) was instrumental in Christianizing England. **Boni-**

face VI (died 896) enjoyed a reign of only fifteen days. **Boniface VII** (983-985) was an antipope and a rival of Benedict VI. **Boniface VIII** (1294-1303) had been a great scholar as Benedetto Gaetani. He attempted to make the Papacy supreme in the spiritual world and claimed precedence over all temporal rulers. His greatest struggle was with King Philip IV of France, whose agents finally seized the Pope, confined him, and then freed him just before he died. **Boniface IX** (1389-1404) was Pope in Rome at the same time as the antipope, Benedict XIII, reigned in Avignon. His attempts to heal the great schism in the Church were

not successful. He was a native of Naples.

BONNEVILLE DAM. Situated on the Columbia River between the states of Washington and Oregon, is the great Bonneville Dam. It is named after the French-born explorer, Benjamin Bonneville, who spent five years in the vast Rocky Mountain region in 1831-1836. To cost $80,886,000 when completed, the huge dam is a unit in a Federal plan to furnish low-cost electricity and irrigation to an extensive valley region. Bonneville Dam will be 170 feet in height and 250 feet long. See articles on COLUMBIA RIVER; GRAND COULÉE DAM; IRRIGATION.

THE SCROLL OF THE PENTATEUCH

Most ancient book in the world is this 3,400-year-old scroll containing the first five books of Moses. It was written twelve years after the Israelites entered Palestine.

BOOK. In books is stored all the knowledge of mankind. Books hold for us in their countless pages the accumulated learning of all the centuries, so that we are able to pass on to others what little we may learn ourselves.

There are all sorts of books: scientific books that reveal the underlying causes of things, books of geography and travel that tell us of the wonders of the earth, and historical volumes that lead us back along the pathways man has trod since the dawn of civilization. There are books of biography that tell us of the lives of those who have lived greatly and well in times past; collections of inspiring poetry and literature that awaken in us the best desires of our natures; philosophical and religious books that comfort and assure us amid life's trials and struggles.

ANCIENT BOOKMAKING I
First step in making books in the Middle Ages was
to make the paper.

Some books, both classic and modern, are for our pleasure and enjoyment in moments when we seek relaxation and entertainment. A person who has the habit of reading is never alone, for he can find thousands of people, real and imaginary, as his companions, and any number of interesting places to go and things to do by opening the pages of a book.

The Story of Bookmaking. We are so used to books that we can hardly imagine a world without them. Yet books as we know them today are not very old when we compare their history to the art of writing, which has existed thousands of years. Until the middle of the fifteenth century, when Gutenberg was credited with perfecting the printing process, man had preserved his writings in a number of ways.

The early Egyptians carved inscriptions on stone walls. The Assyrians made wedge-shaped marks on clay tablets which they hardened by baking in the sun. Wax-coated tablets of wood or soft metal were inscribed with a pointed tool, called a stylus, by the Greeks and Romans. Holes punched in the sides of the tablets permitted cord or metal rings to hold several tablets together, making a form of book.

Writing on papyrus was a way of preserving the thoughts and history of early peoples, particularly the Egyptians, Greeks, and Romans. For pens, reeds were dipped in gum water colored with soot. Later, parchment, made from the skins of sheep, took the place of papyrus, and it was found to last for centuries. Pieces of parchment or papyrus were glued together to form a long sheet that was rolled up to form a scroll.

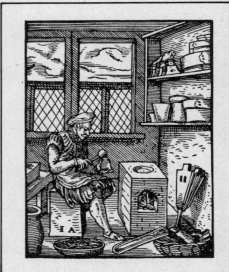

ANCIENT BOOKMAKING II
The typecaster, or typefounder, cast the type for
the primitive press.

The name of *volumen* was given to the scroll, and it is from it that we derived the word *volume* to refer to books.

About the time of the ninth century, paper made from plant fibers began to be used. Although it was brownish in color, thick and rough, records written on it were readable. Books came into being, the product of monks who laboriously copied old manuscripts in order that the Scriptural writings and Greek and Latin literature might be preserved. These books were heavy and cumbersome and could not easily be carried around. In addition, they were so expensive that few people could afford them. At that time, however, so few persons could read that there was not a great demand for books.

This situation changed after printing was perfected. Although the first printed books were expensive, it was not long before they began to circulate among the common people. These earliest printed books were devoted mainly to editions of the Bible and other religious works and to translations of Greek and Roman classics. They were beautifully decorated and bound, but they

ANCIENT BOOKMAKING IV
Final step in the manufacture of the book was binding it in exquisite covers.

ANCIENT BOOKMAKING III
Printing the book was a hard, tedious process, but the work was beautiful.

did not have the name of the publisher, the date, or a title page. They continued to be large, and the paper was not of very good quality.

As the demand for books increased, however, better paper was used, the size became smaller, and printing became an art. Printers throughout Europe vied with one another to see who could put out the most attractive and praiseworthy books. Many of these books have come down to us as masterpieces of the printer's art.

As the years wore on, further changes took place. High-speed presses eliminated the slow and painstaking decorations, and

books began to be circulated in the millions instead of hundreds. Book writing increased as more and more people learned how to read and demanded knowledge. India paper came into use at this time. This paper, which is strong and opaque but extremely thin, could be used to print the entire output of such authors as Shakespeare, in one volume.

Although book publishing progressed swiftly in Europe in the eighteenth century, it was many years before it became widespread in America. Benjamin Franklin aided in bringing the art to the attention of the new nation, but there was little activity until the nineteenth century. Printing and publishing of books, however, has taken amazing strides since the beginning of the twentieth century. In recent years, American publishers have produced approximately 10,000 titles annually. In addition to works of fiction, scientific, biographical, and practical books also have been eagerly read by the public. "Best sellers," those books that enjoy the widest sale, sometimes run to over a million copies of first printings.

LEARNING'S WALLS AND ROOF
Bindings shelter the world's culture.

BOOK'BINDING. The very earliest writings were not bound in covers as are our books today. Even after papyrus came into use, it was not at first necessary to make bindings because the writing was done on long strips of papyrus that were afterward rolled up and put away for future use. But when sheets of papyrus and parchment came into use, something had to be done to keep them together and in the right order.

Thin wooden boards were first used in bookbinding. These boards not only held the pages together but kept them flat. Later it was found desirable to cover the boards with leather, velvet, vellum, parchment, or white pigskin; and many of these bindings were elaborately decorated with gold or jewels or ivory. After the invention of printing, when the pages of books were made smaller, pasteboard instead of boards was used to stiffen bindings.

For a long time bookbinding was done almost entirely by monks in the monasteries. Because the work was done by hand, books

were too costly for the average person to buy. However, the introduction of bookbinding machinery and the use of cloth for covers in the nineteenth century reduced the cost and placed the books within the reach of almost everybody.

Today, machinery does practically all our bookbinding, with the exception of some expensive hand binding on rare editions. All stages, from folding the sheets to fastening on the cover, are taken care of by machines. Buckram, a coarse linen fabric treated with glue, and paper boards are now the materials commonly employed in covering books.

The craft of bookbinding is a very interesting and worth-while art for anyone. For highly skilled craftsmen binders, it is also very profitable. Books on the subject can be obtained from libraries, or a great deal can be learned by taking apart and putting together again the binding of an old book. Bookbinding offers an opportunity to develop both manual skill and artistic ability, for a binding should be both durable and attractive, and in keeping with the contents of the book.

BOOK'KEEPING. Anyone who owns a business or who wants to keep a record of his personal finances should know something about bookkeeping. By recording the amount of money taken in and the sums spent, he is able to tell at all times just what he has on hand. For instance, if each week a boy recorded in a ledger or notebook how much money he received as allowance and how much he earned, and then listed the sums spent for such things as moving pictures, candy, a pitcher's glove, or tennis balls, he would have a simple system of bookkeeping, showing him just how much he spent and how much he had at all times.

Small businesses usually keep a record of the day's trade, the amount of cash taken in and spent, and an account of all debts and assets. Larger businesses require more complicated systems of bookkeeping; men carefully trained in accounting are placed in charge of such records.

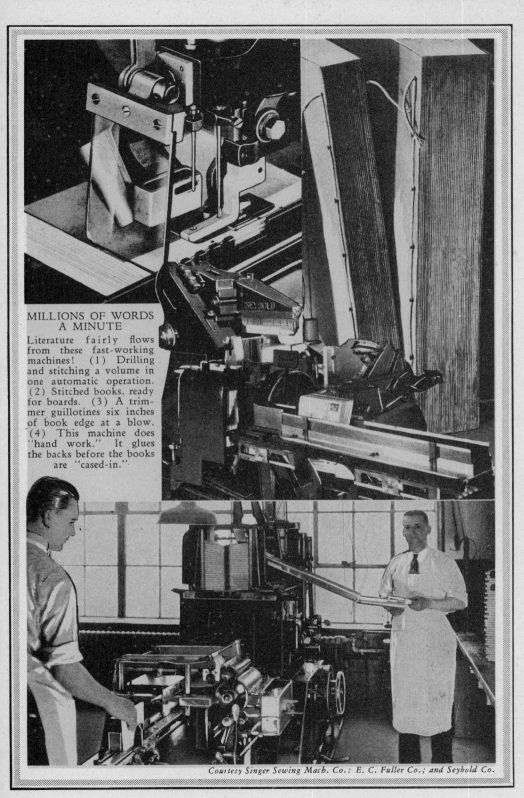

MILLIONS OF WORDS A MINUTE

Literature fairly flows from these fast-working machines! (1) Drilling and stitching a volume in one automatic operation. (2) Stitched books, ready for boards. (3) A trimmer guillotines six inches of book edge at a blow. (4) This machine does "hand work." It glues the backs before the books are "cased-in."

Courtesy Singer Sewing Mach. Co.; E. C. Fuller Co.; and Seybold Co.

MACHINE CRAFTSMEN

Top, rounding and backing books at high speed. Center, making covers, at twenty per minute! Below, stamping on elaborate gold-leaf book titles and decoration, and the final pressing to make books hold their shape.

Courtesy
Ludlow Typograph Co.;
and E. C. Fuller Co.

AN ADVENTUROUS PIONEER

Daniel Boone, hunter, soldier and Indian fighter, saved many settlers from death at the hands of the Red Men, when the wilderness of Kentucky and Tennessee was an American frontier.

BOOM'ERANG. Simple in appearance yet amazing in action is the boomerang, a weapon used by the aborigines of Australia. There are two kinds of boomerang—the returning and the non-returning. The non-returning type is a weapon used in war; the more popular returning type is now used chiefly as a toy.

The boomerang is made from wood bent at an angle sometimes as high as 120°. A curve of about 90° is, however, the most common, except for the non-returning type, which is much straighter. The boomerang is usually from two to four feet long, flat on one side and convex, or rounded, on the other. In the hands of an expert it can be made to loop away and even bounce on the ground before flying back to the thrower. The proper twist, when it is thrown, determines where the weapon will go and what it will do.

BOONE, DANIEL (1734-1820). A fearless pioneer and crafty woodsman, Daniel Boone helped to blaze the westward trail in America. His explorations encouraged a stream of settlers to Tennessee and Kentucky before the Revolutionary War, and his fearlessness aided the settlers against the Indians when the war came.

Daniel Boone showed his love of outdoor life during his boyhood days along the North Carolina frontier, where he had moved with his parents from Pennsylvania. When still a young man, he penetrated Eastern Tennessee; near Boone's Creek, in that part of the state, there is standing today a tree with an inscription to the effect that Boone "cilled a bar" there in 1760. Some time later, he and five companions pushed westward into Kentucky. He was captured by Indians and later lived alone in the wilderness for weeks. Eventually, he took his family and numerous other settlers to the Kentucky River, where he built a fort called Boonesboro, now designated by markers.

The Revolutionary War broke out in the same year that Boone settled in Kentucky, and he was active on the side of the American colonies. Again he was taken by the Indians and, while a captive, heard them plotting to attack Boonesboro. Boone managed to escape. After four days in the wilderness, during which he ate only one meal, he reached the settlement in time to warn the town and to aid in repulsing the Indians.

Like many other pioneers, Boone cared little for the laws of civilization. When Kentucky became a state, he lost his land because of improper title registry. Undismayed, he moved his family to Missouri, then Spanish territory. He neglected the law again; and when the territory became American through the Louisiana Purchase, he lost his land again. Congress, however, returned the land to him because of his services in pioneering. He died at the age of eighty-seven.

In honor of Daniel Boone, the Daughters of the American Revolution in North Carolina, Virginia, Tennessee, and Kentucky marked a trail through their states in 1915. It was in these four states that Boone pioneered in his early days.

BOOTH. The Booths were a family of actors well known both in the United States and in England during the nineteenth century.

Junius Brutus Booth (1796-1852). Born in England, Junius Brutus Booth was a Shakespearean actor in London before he came to America in 1821. He was the father of Edwin Thomas and John Wilkes Booth, both of whom achieved prominence, but for entirely different reasons.

Edwin Thomas Booth (1833-1893). One of the greatest Shakespearean actors of all time, Edwin Booth was born in Bel Air, Md. He far surpassed his father, Junius, in talent. Making his first stage appearance at the age of sixteen, he was considered a finished actor while he was still a young man. He is remembered chiefly for his rôles in the great tragedies *Othello, Hamlet,* and *King Richard III.* His dignity, grace, and cultured voice enabled him to give distinction to any part he played.

John Wilkes Booth (1839-1865). The younger brother of Edwin, John Wilkes Booth was also an actor. During the war between the states, he fought with the Confederate army. In 1865 he became a party to a conspiracy to assassinate President Lincoln. On the evening of April 14, 1865, he shot the President at Ford's Theater in Washington, and escaped in spite of a broken leg. Discovered two days later, he refused to surrender and was shot. It is believed that he inherited from his father a touch of insanity, which accounts for his rash actions.

BOOTH, the name of a family of religious and social workers.

William Booth (1829-1912). Founder of the Salvation Army and religious worker of world-wide renown, William Booth was born in Nottingham, England. At an early age he became a preacher, then an evangelist; in 1864 his evangelistic work took him to London. Here he started a small mission band which developed into the Salvation Army in 1878, and was its first general.

General Booth was particularly successful as an organizer and was also a writer. His best-known work is *In Darkest England*. In 1855 he married Catherine Mumford, who became his co-worker and also acted as an independent reformer among women and children.

Booth soon extended his field to include the United States and also India and Aus-

SHOES "ON THE HOOF"
The hides of cattle furnish leather for shoes, made
on high-speed machines (right).

tralia. Everywhere he was recognized with distinction as a leader in reform and in social betterment. His children carried on his great work after him; the oldest son, William Bramwell, became general of the Salvation Army upon his father's death in 1912. Another son, Ballington, was an active leader in Australia, but in 1896 he severed his connection with the Salvation Army, came to the United States, and formed the Volunteers of America.

Ballington Booth (1859-1940) gained his greatest recognition for his work with the Volunteers of America. He married Maud Charlesworth in 1886. He wrote *From Ocean to Ocean.*

Evangeline Cory Booth. Like other members of her family, Evangeline Booth assisted her father in the work of the Salvation Army. For her services during the first World War, when she directed the Army's many activities in the war zone, she received the Distinguished Service Medal. After serving five years as field commissioner in London, she was appointed Army commissioner in Canada. Five years later she assumed charge of the organization's work in the United States. There she re-

mained until 1934, when she became commander. She retired in 1939.

Frederick Saint George de Latour Booth-Tucker (1853-1929) was born in India. He is remembered for his ability as an organizer with the Salvation Army. He resigned from the India Civil Service in the Punjab, to join the Salvation Army, where he became very active. In 1888, when he married Emma Ross Booth, one of General William Booth's seven children, he adopted the name Booth-Tucker.

During his career he was foreign secretary at Army headquarters in London, held joint command of the United States with his wife, and later was special commissioner to India. He resigned from his last command in 1927 and died two years later.

BOOTS AND SHOES. Many thousands of years ago, after man first wore clothing, he also found it necessary to protect his feet, and from the crude animal-hide sandals of those early days he evolved leather footwear of many designs and shapes. The most common type of footwear in use today is the shoe, composed of a hard-leather sole and soft-leather or fabric uppers which reach to the ankle or slightly above. Boots are higher, covering the calf or reaching sometimes above the knee. In England, however, a boot may mean any shoe reaching as far as the ankle.

Different types of shoes are used for various purposes. Rubber-soled and soft-soled shoes are used for sport; moccasins for recreation; cleated shoes for baseball, football, soccer, and golf; hobnailed shoes for lumber workers; and soft, fabric shoes for house or bedroom slippers. In Holland, wooden shoes are still worn to some extent; sandals are common in several Asiatic and African lands and elsewhere.

Man's Early Shoes. When man first covered his feet, he used the skin of animals, fastening the skins to his soles by means of thongs. Sometimes he packed grass into these crude shoes to keep his feet from freezing. In Egypt, where the weather was warm, open sandals were worn by the nobles. Many were made from woven or interlaced palm leaves and papyrus. Some were of leather. The majority of people, however, went barefoot.

The Greeks bestowed much care on their footwear. They wore sandals strapped around the instep and ankle, and shoes fitted to the foot. As in Egypt, many persons continued to go barefoot, and shoes were seldom worn inside a building or house. In Rome, both men and women wore sandals and slippers. Indoors they wore slippers that were very much like those we know today. Boots were laced up the front or bound around the ankle with straps.

During the Middle Ages, shoes became very elaborate and extravagant. Long, pointed shoes, sometimes called *poulaines,* were the fashion. It was a mark of honor to have shoes with long, pointed toes; in fact, some were so long that they could be doubled back to the knee. Shoes were later made with thick soles, and short people wore shoes with soles several inches thick to make them look taller. Heels came to be a part of the boots worn by horsemen, and

in the eighteenth century both men and women wore high heels on their shoes. For a long time there was no difference between a shoe for the right foot and one for the left. But in England, toward the end of the eighteenth century, a different last was devised for each foot.

From Home Cobbler to Factory. In the earliest colonial times, each householder was his own cobbler, making shoes as best he knew how. Some of these shoes were modeled after the Indian moccasins, but most of them were copied from the styles brought over from Europe. As time went on, men who became skilled at cobbling did all the shoemaking for the community. A cobbler visited the home of each customer and made shoes on the premises. After a time, shops were set up, and customers went to the cobbler to have their shoes made. As business increased, a cobbler would find it necessary to employ people to help him; and so a factory system began.

Although some factories were set up in New England long before the war between the states, it was not until that conflict created a demand for strong, durable shoes in huge quantities that shoe factories as we know them today came into being. With the invention of the McKay sewing machine at that time, many shoe factories sprang up, and machine-made shoes have been the rule rather than the exception ever since. The shoe industry, however, no longer is confined to New England. New York, New Jersey, Chicago, and Saint Louis are important centers for this industry.

The Modern Shoe in the Making. Shoemaking today is a very specialized craft. If we were to visit a shoe factory, we should find one group of men doing nothing but cutting pieces of leather from patterns, either by machine or by hand. In another department the uppers are sewed together, each bit of sewing being a separate undertaking. In a third department the soles are made and fastened to the uppers by machines. In yet another department heels are pressed into place and fastened to the shoes. Finally the shoes are polished, and the laces or buttons are put in. They are then ready for shipment.

Today, shoes are manufactured in nearly all countries, but the United States, Czechoslovakia, and Great Britain normally make the greatest number. The yearly production of shoes in the United States alone is over 400,000,000 pairs.

BORAH, WILLIAM EDGAR (1865-1940). During his 33 years of service in the United States Senate, William E. Borah of Idaho was one of the most courageous and independent members of Congress. He was an authority on the Federal Constitution and a persistent advocate of non-intervention in the affairs of Europe. To progressive causes, both social and economic, he gave whole-hearted support.

Borah was born in Illinois. After his graduation from Southern Illinois Academy, he began the study of law in a private office in Lyons, Kan., and also attended the University of Kansas. In 1901 he began to practice law in Boise, Idaho.

He entered the Senate in 1907 and was serving his sixth consecutive term when he died. Nominally a Republican, Senator Borah always reserved the right to break with party nominees. He supported President Roosevelt on many issues, but opposed the plan to enlarge the Supreme Court and repeal of the arms embargo. The Senator was chairman of the Foreign Relations Committee from 1924 to 1933. He represented the minority on the committee thereafter, exercising great influence.

BO′RAX. This is the common name for a very useful substance known also as sodium borate. It is a white, crystalline salt found chiefly in several dry regions of Tibet, Chile, and the United States. Most of the borax used in the United States and Canada comes from Death Valley or the Mojave Desert in Southern California.

Uses. Melted borax has the very useful property of being able to dissolve the oxides of the metals, and, as the various oxides produce characteristic colors, this property makes it valuable for enameling. Fully one-third of the borax used in the United

States is employed in the manufacture of enamel ware, such as bath tubs, kitchen sinks, and kitchen utensils.

In the soldering of metals, a little powdered borax is often put on the parts to be united. The borax is melted by the soldering iron and dissolves the oxidized metal, cleaning it so that the solder adheres and makes a tight joint.

Borax is a valuable flux material (a flux is a substance which unites with another substance that melts at a high temperature, the mixture melting at a low temperature). It is also used as a cleansing agent, as a preservative, as a mild disinfectant, and in the manufacture of glass. It is useful in softening hard water, by precipitating the calcium in the water and preventing it from acting on the soap and causing a scum instead of allowing the soap to lather.

BORE. This name is applied to high waves frequently formed by tides near the mouth of a large river or in an inlet of the sea. These tidal waves usually occur only in those estuaries that are wide where they meet the sea, but which are narrow inland. As the tide reaches the narrow shores, the water of the river or inlet is piled up, often to such an extent that boats are unable to make headway against it. Large bores are common in the Canadian Bay of Fundy, where they often reach a height of forty feet. They also occur at the mouth of the Amazon, the Severn, and the Tsientang rivers. See TIDES.

BORGIA, *bor′ja*. During the fifteenth and sixteenth centuries, one of the most prominent families of Italy was the Borgia family. Originally from Spain, they became powerful in Italy, often using unscrupulous methods.

Cesare Borgia (1478-1507) was one of the cruelest and most treacherous of the power-seeking nobles of his time. He was the son of Rodrigo Borgia, who became Pope Alexander VI in 1492. With the backing of his father and a remarkable skill at avoiding punishment for his murders, he seized control of Central Italy. When his father died, however, he was driven from

THE DANCE OF A DUCHESS

Pope Alexander VI, surrounded by his cardinals, is entertained by his beautiful daughter, Lucretia Borgia.

Italy and was killed in Spain while aiding the king of Navarre in a campaign. Despite his faults, Cesare was a brave soldier and ruled the people he conquered with shrewdness and justice. He also was a patron of the arts.

Lucretia Borgia (1480-1519) was a sister of Cesare. She was a beautiful and intelligent woman and married several times. Although she has been accused of a number of murders by poisoning, the charges have never been proved. As the wife of the Duke of Ferrara, she was a patron of art and learning.

BORGLUM, *bawr' glum*, GUTZON (1871-1941). One of America's outstanding sculptors, Gutzon Borglum is best known today for his work on Mount Rushmore, in South Dakota. There, in granite rock on the side of the mountain, he carved four colossal heads of Washington, Jefferson, Lincoln, and Theodore Roosevelt. More than fifty feet high, these figures will endure for ages.

Born in Idaho, Borglum was educated in Nebraska and Kansas, and studied art in San Francisco and Paris. He began to attract notice in 1902, when some of his work was exhibited in Paris and London. Although the Mount Rushmore work was his largest undertaking, he also designed the Confederate Memorial to be carved out of Stone Mountain near Atlanta, Ga. Some of his other noteworthy accomplishments are *The Mares of Diomedes,* in the Metropolitan Museum, New York; a group of statues in the Cathedral of Saint John the Divine, in New York; a bas-relief in the Pan-American building, Washington, D. C.; and a large head of Lincoln in the Capitol, Washington, D. C.

BOR'ING MACHINES. Digging a hole in soft earth or sand is usually an easy task. It can be accomplished with a spade, or, if necessary, with the bare hands. But drilling a hole in hard substances, such as rock, metal, or wood, calls for special tools known as boring machines.

There are several types of these machines. The simplest, one that we use in our car-

SCULPTURE FOR THE AGES
Built to the scale of men 465 feet high, the
Mount Rushmore Memorial, by Gutzon Borglum
(left), is visible for miles. The sculptor's son
completed it after Borglum's death.

penter shops and workrooms, is the brace
and bit, which is composed of a spiral
augur rotated by a crank. This tool, efficient though it is in drilling holes through
wood, is not strong enough to cut through
metal or rock.

Drilling machines, or presses, of various
types are used for the drilling of metal. The
drilling machine ordinarily used in repair
shops drills only one hole at a time, but
drilling machines used in factories where
articles are produced in quantities will drill
as many as a hundred holes at one time.

A power rock drill has a chisel-shaped
cutting edge which is driven with a rapid
back-and-forth motion by sharp blows; the
drill automatically revolves a short distance.
These blows may be struck by steam, compressed air, or electrical power. When there
is only a small amount of drilling to be
done, it may not be possible to use a power
machine, and a hand drill is used. Such a
drill may be simply an ordinary bar of steel
with a sharp cutting edge. It is struck with
a hammer.

When it is necessary to drill rock, a hollow drill is used. It consists of a hollow
steel tube with a cutting edge of points

WHEN BORNEO WAS OPENED TO THE WHITE MAN
England gained a foothold in savage Borneo, in 1842, when James Brooke, who later became Rajah Brooke, made his first treaty with the Rajah of Borneo.

studded with diamonds. Such a drill is called a diamond drill. Because diamonds are harder than any other material, they can cut through hard rock effectively. As a diamond drill revolves, it cuts out of the solid rock a core which may be brought up for examination. This type of drill is power-driven.

BOR′NEO. Wild-animal paradise and land of the proverbial Head Hunter, the great island of Borneo is located in the East Indies, southwest of the Philippines. The South China Sea, the Java Sea, and the Strait of Macassar surround Borneo. With an area of more than 290,000 square miles, the island is larger than Texas. It is crossed almost in the middle by the equator.

The Netherlands, or Holland, rules over two-thirds of the island; North Borneo is a British possession; Sarawak, ruled by a sultan, is controlled by Great Britain; and Brunei, once independent, now has British overlords. The population of the British portion is 790,000. The rest of the island, belonging to the Netherlands, has a population about 2,200,000, mostly natives, including some of the most savage tribes.

Being a mountainous island, Borneo has

rich but nearly untouched mineral deposits, including gold, quicksilver, copper, sulphur, tin, petroleum, and an inferior yellow diamond. The numerous rivers are mostly navigable. The great humidity and heat make the lowlands unhealthful, but the ground is fertile, producing tobacco, spices, sugar cane, and tropical fruits. The country abounds in a variety of wild monkeys, orang-utans, tiger cats, and wild birds, including the great falcon. A small buffalo is the chief beast of burden, for horses are so rare that only the wealthy European inhabitants can afford them.

Most of the natives are practically wild Mohammedan Malays and Bugis in the south, and uncivilized Sulus in the north. The Dyaks occupy the interior, and include the Ibans and Kayans, who cut off and preserve the heads of enemies. Trading and seafaring are the chief occupations along the coasts, and mining, in the mountains, is carried on largely by the numerous Chinese immigrants. There are not over 5,000 white people on the entire island. See DYAKS.

BO'RON. A hard, gray substance, boron is an element found in combinations like borax and sassolite. It was discovered in 1808. See BORAX.

BOS'PORUS. Separating the continent of Europe from Asia Minor is the narrow strait called the Bosporus. It connects the Black Sea and the Sea of Marmora. For centuries it was a check against invading hordes from the East. The proud old city of Constantinople, or Istanbul, as it is now called, stands on the north bank. The Bosporus is a life line for the ships of several nations and a commercial route of prime importance. It is only about eighteen miles long and less than three miles across in its widest part.

The Treaty of Berlin in 1878 confirmed an earlier agreement of 1841 allowing no warships to pass through the strait without the consent of Turkey; merchant ships, however, could pass as they pleased. Following Turkish defeat in 1918, the strait was declared demilitarized and open to all ships. However, in 1936 the Convention of Montreux was signed, by which Turkey gained the right to remilitarize the territory surrounding the Bosporus and the Dardanelles.

In ancient times Darius of Persia is said to have constructed a great bridge of boats across the Bosporus on his Scythian expedition. At one time, the name was applied to the Cimmerian Bosporus, the narrow channel connecting the Black Sea and the Sea of Azov.

ONCE A HOME OF TYRANNY
Boston's Old Statehouse, whence British governors misruled in colonial days.

BOS'TON, MASS. Oliver Wendell Holmes, one of the great American poets, once called the city of Boston "the hub of the solar system." His phrase seemed to find agreeable response from the people of America, and since then Boston has been known as "The Hub." It is true that much of the historical and cultural life of the United States has revolved about this Massachusetts city. Geographers probably know Boston as the capital of the state, the largest city in New England, and the ninth largest in the United States; but the average American knows it better for its traditions and historic setting.

Courtesy Thomas Cook and Sons
BOSTON'S GOLDEN DOME
The Statehouse, on historic Beacon Hill.

The first college in America and now one of the greatest—Harvard—was established in a Boston suburb; the great writers of America—Longfellow, Lowell, Holmes, Hawthorne, Emerson, Parkman, Henry James, and many others—lived and wrote in or near Boston; literature, music, painting, and all the other arts have flourished there; men who helped to carve the nation's history—Paul Revere, John Adams, Samuel Adams, John Hancock—had their homes in Boston. Yes, Boston truly is "The Hub."

The City on the Bay. A beautiful harbor, formed by an indentation of Massachusetts Bay, forms the setting of Boston. The Mystic River, bounding the city on the north, and the Charles River empty into the harbor. Located about 230 miles northeast of New York, Boston proper has an area of almost fifty square miles and a population in 1940 of 770,816. Including the many suburbs, the population was over 2,350,514.

The site of the city was once an 800-acre peninsula abounding in inlets and marshes. A tongue of low land, often covered by the tide, connected the peninsula and the mainland. During the nineteenth century the size of the peninsula was increased to over 1,800 acres by the filling in of the inlets and marshes. The "Back Bay" district, once an inner harbor formed by the mouth of the Charles River, became what is now the city's most exclusive residential district.

One of the most confusing things to a stranger in Boston is the old business section in the northern part of the city. It is closely built and has many narrow, winding streets. It has been said, truthfully or otherwise, that these streets follow the original wandering paths to the water's edge. The principal street in the business section is Washington; it is so narrow that the street itself is often used by shoppers crowded off the sidewalks.

A fashionable residential section extends west to Brookline, which has the reputation of being the richest town in the United States. East Boston lies to the north and east. Charlestown, where are located the Bunker Hill Monument and the Boston Navy Yard, is north of the Charles River. Cambridge, the seat of Harvard University, is across the Charles to the west. Street-car lines, subways, and elevated railways connect the principal parts of the city.

Where History Was Made. With so much tradition behind it, Boston obviously must have many historic buildings, interesting for the part they played in the struggle for American independence. The Old State House on Washington Street was built in 1748. In this building James Otis gave his speech opposing the writs of assistance, search warrants used by the British to collect import duties; here, too, the people first heard the Declaration of Independence.

Another famous building is Christ Church, better known as Old North Church from the story of *Paul Revere's Ride*. It is said that from the belfry, signal lanterns were hung, "one if by land and two if by sea," to inform Paul Revere of the coming of the British. Other historic buildings are King's Chapel, attended by the king's officers during colonial times; Old South Meeting House, the scene of many important meetings of the colonists;

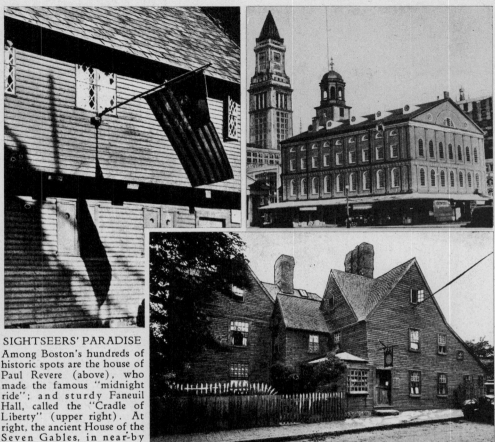

SIGHTSEERS' PARADISE
Among Boston's hundreds of historic spots are the house of Paul Revere (above), who made the famous "midnight ride"; and sturdy Faneuil Hall, called the "Cradle of Liberty" (upper right). At right, the ancient House of the Seven Gables, in near-by Salem.

and Faneuil Hall, known as "the Cradle of Liberty," but first built as a market house.

Boston also has several cemeteries of historic interest. Among these are King's Chapel Burying Ground, Copp's Hill Burying Ground, and the Old Granary Burying Ground. All contain many quaint old gravestones, marking the graves of the most prominent people of colonial days.

History. Although Captain John Smith sailed into Boston Harbor in 1614, the real history of Boston did not begin until 1630, when a band of colonists under John Winthrop moved over from Charlestown. Because some of the settlers had formerly lived in the town of Boston in England, the new settlement was officially given the name Boston. In 1632 Boston became the capital of Massachusetts Bay Colony, thereafter developing rapidly into a religious and educational center. By the time of the Revolutionary War the population had increased to 20,000 and the city had become the center of colonial opposition to England. Before the war broke out in earnest, the city had experienced the Boston Tea Party, the Boston Massacre, and the battles of Lexington and Bunker Hill.

Boston's advance was rapid following the war. Shipping was the most important industry until the Civil War. The citizens of Boston supported the anti-slavery side in the war, furnishing men for the Union army and navy. The city has experienced several fires during its

THE BRITISH MAILED FIST IN COLONIAL BOSTON
An engraving of the "Boston Massacre" by the Revolutionary hero, Paul Revere.

history, the most severe being in 1872; however, instead of retarding the town's development, the fires aided it, for the burnt districts were always rapidly rebuilt and improved. Boston has not spared old historic buildings which were in the way of improvements designed to make the city more beautiful.

Boston Today. Of the many parks in Boston, the most interesting is Boston Common. It is America's oldest public park and contains many beautiful and historic monuments. The Public Garden lies south of the Common. At one entrance is a colossal equestrian statue of Washington. Between the Public Garden and the Back Bay district runs Commonwealth Avenue, 240 feet wide, down the center

of which is a parkway of trees, walks, and statuary. There are also about 11,500 acres of parks outside Boston proper.

Boston has a number of beautiful modern buildings, the result of the city's improvement plans. Among them are administrative buildings, railroad terminals, office buildings, churches, and theaters. The most prominent is the Statehouse, noted for its immense gilded dome; it is now used as the capitol building.

Of libraries, schools, and hospitals, Boston probably has more than her share for a city of this size. The public library, of magnificent architecture and decoration, has Shakespearean and music collections which are unsurpassed. There are five or six well-known colleges and universities

THE BOSTON TEA PARTY—A MASQUERADE IN EARNEST
Dressed up as Indians, these angry colonists dumped cargoes of tea from three British ships.

in and about the city, Harvard and Massachusetts Institute of Technology being the most prominent. There are also other types of educational institutions, including the finest school for the blind in the United States, the Perkins Institution and Massachusetts School for the Blind.

Being the largest coast city in New England, Boston is the center of the financial and commercial activity of that section of the country. It is also one of the largest American ports in amount of foreign trade, ranking first in the Western Hemisphere as a fish port and second only to London as a wool port.

Important exports are meat and other food products, leather, cotton and woolen goods, and iron and steel products; imports are wool, hides, sugar, drugs, fish, and rubber. Leading manufactures in addition to the exports are refined sugar, boots and shoes, clothing, and pianos; other important industries are shipbuilding, printing, and publishing. New steamship docks, air terminals, and railroad stations have given Boston ample provision for transportation and trade. The South railroad station, covering thirteen acres, is one of the largest in the world.

One of the strangest facts about Boston is that although its traditions are so truly American, thirty per cent of its population is foreign-born. Canadians and Irish make up about forty per cent of the foreign population, other nationalities including English, Scotch, German, Italian and Russian-Jew.

BOSTON MAS'SACRE. The historic Boston Massacre occurred on March 5, 1770, when a group of English soldiers fired into a gathering of citizens in Boston. Three persons were killed and seven were injured. The cause of the trouble was the opposition of the colonists to the Townshend Act, which levied heavy taxes on lead, glass, paper, paint, and tea. The shooting was done by soldiers sent to force the colonists to pay the duty.

The soldiers were tried for murder and were acquitted, largely through the efforts of their attorneys, John Adams and Josiah Quincy. The trial, however, resulted in the removal of the hated troops.

BOSTON TEA PARTY. As a protest against the tax placed on tea shipped to the colonies, a group of Boston citizens in 1773 decided to destroy a shipment of tea. Accordingly, on the night of December 16, they disguised themselves as Indians, boarded the ships of the British East India Company in Boston Harbor, and threw 342 chests of tea overboard. The event became known as the Boston Tea Party. The deed was committed so quietly and efficiently that there is little doubt that it was carefully planned.

BOSWELL, *boz' wel,* JAMES (1740-1795). Down to London on a holiday went the young Scottish student, James Boswell, in 1762. There he luckily met Samuel Johnson, literary light of the metropolis. Boswell admired the older man tremendously and the two became great friends. In the course of their frequent conversations, Boswell set down the observations which later served as source material for his *Life of Samuel Johnson,* one of the best biographies ever written. Published in 1791, it presents a graphic picture of a great personality.

Boswell's acquaintance with Johnson greatly altered his intended career; he never seriously practiced law, but devoted his life to Johnson and to literature.

BOTAN'IC GARDEN. Nature's fairylands, the marvelous botanic gardens which grow near some of our great cities, are beautiful preserves where plants are grown for scientific observation.

Usually, the plants are arranged in groups or families and placed in settings suggestive of their native habits. There are rock gardens, aquatic gardens, rose gardens, wildflower preserves, etc. An arboretum is a botanical garden in which trees and shrubs are the chief displays.

The truly beautiful things of the world are not always best known to those who go about in search of the strange and the wonderful. Every year thousands of tourists visit Boston, Mass., and are thrilled by its quaint historic landmarks. But, with scarcely an exception, they leave without having seen what is, at times, one of the most beautiful sights in the world—the Arnold Arboretum, at Harvard.

The love which Americans bear for lilacs is attested in yards and gardens throughout the land. And the lilac blossoms which shed their Oriental perfume over the Wisconsin lawn in late May are so like those that bloom a trifle earlier on the abandoned farms in New England— in color, size, and scent—that it is easy to believe the western bush has descended from the eastern, through slips passed on from farm to farm across the intervening distance.

Imagine then, a mass of lilacs—bush after bush of them—each bush bearing clusters that are larger and more fragrant than any most of us have ever seen. And imagine each bush to have its own distinctive color of flower, and a distinctive size and shape for both the individual blossom and the cluster. Picture not merely white lilacs and *lilac* lilacs, but also lilacs of a blue as vivid as the bachelor's button or the larkspur, but richer and more exotic; and some with a deep and full rose tone. What the imagination can picture is but a fraction of what the eye can see at the Arnold Arboretum in lilac time. Or, in cherry-blossom time, the Arboretum is for the visitor a succession of fragrant blooms of every shade of pink. A bit earlier, it is a fairyland of azaleas.

Moreover, just as each lilac bush bears a placard which shows the country of its origin (and perhaps a personal name), so each cherry tree displays its place of birth. Thus we learn that some of the trees have come from Japan, and some from the faraway interior provinces of China, where there are no railroads and travel is so difficult that it takes months to reach them. For the business of the Arnold Arboretum is to gather, from far and near, a collection of all the trees and shrubs which will grow in the severe winters of the North, so that botanists may study them and horticulturists and plant breeders may enrich our American flora.

The Arnold Arboretum is a good example of a botanic garden which specializes in plants of a particular type or filling a particular need. Other famous gardens are the *Jardin des Plantes* (Garden of Plants) in Paris, France, one of the oldest of existing gardens and one having the greatest number of specimens; Kew Gardens in London, and the municipal gardens at Bologna, Leyden, and Upsala.

In the United States, there are the botanic gardens at Brooklyn (including a children's garden and a greenhouse); the Morton Arboretum, near Chicago; California Botanic Garden, Los Angeles; Letchrock Park Aboretum, Portage, N. Y.; United States Botanical Garden, Washington, D. C.; Missouri Botanical Garden, Saint Louis; and the New York Botanical Garden, Bronx Park, New York City.

If none of the greater gardens are near, even the smaller conservatories of city parks are worth seeing. See CONSERVATORY.

THE STUDY
of BUD and BLOSSOM

BOTANY. Man is so dependent upon plants for food, medicine, shelter—and even the oxygen he breathes—that it is natural he should devote intensive study to this great kingdom of living things. Botany, the study of plant life, is a science that covers every form of plant existence, from tiny, one-celled algae to the towering redwoods of California. It describes the thousands of living things included in this form of life, identifies them by their parts and habits, tells how they live and reproduce, records their distribution, and designates the place they hold in relation to each other and to life in general. So vast is this study that many other sciences, such as chemistry, economics, geology, and medicine, all are influenced by its findings.

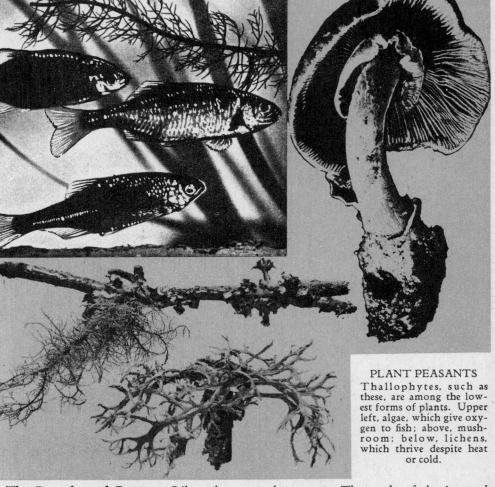

PLANT PEASANTS

Thallophytes, such as these, are among the lowest forms of plants. Upper left, algae, which give oxygen to fish; above, mushroom; below, lichens, which thrive despite heat or cold.

The Branches of Botany. Like other broad sciences, botany is divided into several branches. *Taxonomy* has to do with the divisions and classifications of plants (see *Divisions of the Plant World,* below). The practical importance of taxonomy is obvious, for without accepted standards of classifying, there might be as many plant groups as there were botanists. A second branch, *morphology,* is concerned with the development of plants from the standpoint of the structure of their organs.

Anatomy, a third branch of botany, is closely related to morphology, as it deals with the structure of the tissues that make up the organs. The study of the internal structure of the tissues themselves—the behavior and relationships of the cells—is *cytology.* Closely related to both anatomy and morphology is *plant physiology,* which is concerned with the functions of plant organs—how they work.

These latter branches — morphology, anatomy, cytology, and physiology—all provide the botanist with material for classifying the great hosts of the plant kingdom. These are the basic divisions necessary to an understanding of how higher plants developed from primitive forms. But the botanist may go still further. He

MIDDLE-CLASS PLANTS
Ferns are included in the group known as pteridophytes, which have stems, roots, and leaves, but cannot produce seeds. These are various types of ferns.

may want to study the relations of plants to each other, and to observe their reactions to their surroundings. This phase of botany is *ecology.*

Other fields of the subject may be mentioned. There is the study of fossil plants, or *paleontology;* there is the study of plant diseases, or *plant pathology;* and *economic botany,* which has to do with the relation of science to agriculture, horticulture, and forestry.

Divisions of the Plant World. Until we know how the plant kingdom is divided, we can have no clear understanding of our multitude of plant forms—the flowers, the trees, the grasses, and so on, down to the simplest types. Our plant world is divided into four major groups, or *phyla* (plural of *phylum*). It is believed that the members of the first phylum were the earliest plants to develop, and that from this division all the higher plants de-

veloped, in orderly succession. This theory is called *organic evolution.* The four phyla are listed below.

Thallophytes. The thallophytes have neither leaves, stems, nor roots. Each consists of a simple structure called a *thallus,* from the Greek for young shoot. We divide thallophytes into three groups:

(1) Bacteria and blue-green algae, the simplest of plants, each consisting of a single cell. (The study of bacteria is in itself a separate science, *bacteriology.*)

(2) Green algae, brown algae, and red algae, which are seaweeds.

(3) Fungi, which include molds, mildews, certain blights, wilts, and rots; yeasts; ergot; lichens; smuts and rusts; toadstools, mushrooms, etc.

Bryophytes. In the bryophytes, which have rootlike, stemlike, and leaflike parts, we see the beginnings of that specialization in which each part of a plant has its

ARISTOCRATIC CONIFERS

Cone-bearing trees like the spruce and fir in a botanical class by themselves.

particular work. We divide bryophytes into two divisions, liverworts and mosses. Liverworts were the first many-celled plants to adjust themselves to life on the land. Mosses are the descendants of the liverworts. These are prostrate plants, growing low on ground or rock.

Pteridophytes. This group includes ferns, horsetails, or scouring rushes, and ground pine, or club moss. These plants have a more complex organization, which permits them to grow up into air and increase their share of sunlight. They have roots, stems, and leaves, and barely fall short of the ability to produce seeds.

Spermatophytes. These are the seed-bearing plants, the highest in organization and the ones with which we are most familiar. They are found everywhere upon the earth, in Arctic and tropic, in swamp and desert, on land and in water. They are the plants that furnish mankind with so many of the things necessary for existence. The spermatophytes, through their seeds, can retain life without activity, and in situations not favoring growth, they sometimes live for years. They also have great ability to store food. We divide them into two groups:

(1) *Gymnosperms,* or naked-seed spermatophytes, chief of which are the pines and other cone bearers.

(2) *Angiosperms,* or enclosed-seed plants, among which are most of our familiar plants and practically all those which are important for food, clothing, and shelter.

The angiosperms, in turn, have two great divisions—*monocotyledons* (plants with one seed leaf) and *dicotyledons* (plants with two seed leaves). These groups are further divided into *orders, families, genera,* and *species.*

Strange Dominions of the Plant Kingdom. The study of the various branches of botany has answered many questions which have puzzled man for centuries. One of these is: What is the difference between a weed and a flower? Actually, there is no real difference. Some plants that we know as weeds are quite beautiful, but because they are of no use to us commercially, or because they are pests in our grain fields and gardens, we call them weeds. The daisy is a good example. In the florist's shop, it is sold as the charming *marguerite,* but in the corn or wheat field it is the *whiteweed* which crowds out

when we realize that a plant has no brain, yet it is only one of the many marvelous devices of Nature for caring for living things.

Parasites are another group of unusual plants about which botany tells us. These are plants that live off other plants, taking food from their hosts and giving them

EVERYDAY PLANT CITIZENS

Angiosperms, which have closed seed cases, are the most common of all plants. Above, and left, seed pods; center, poppy flower; right, winged maple seeds.

other plants that are cultivated for food.

One of the strange things that botany has shown us is the existence of "meat eaters" among the plants. These are insect-eating plants, like Venus's flytrap and the pitcher plant. The pitcher plant catches wayward insects through funnel-shaped leaves. The insects crawl in, are drowned in the water within the leaves and digested by the plants. Venus's flytrap has hinged leaves which snap together whenever an insect touches one of the three hairs on either side of the hinge. An automatic trap seems almost impossible to believe

nothing in return. Mildews, yeast, and mushrooms are all parasites. Mistletoe, which we use to decorate our homes at Christmas time, is a half parasite, since it lives off trees in the southern part of the United States; but it has green leaves. A true parasite never has leaves.

There are also strange differences among plants placed by botanists in the same family. The apple and the rose seem to have many points of difference, yet they are in the same family. And the potato surely seems far removed from the petunia, but they too, have a family rela-

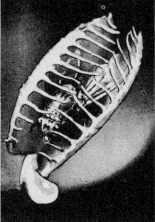
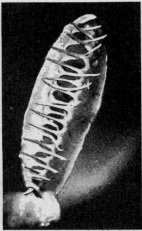

Courtesy Popular Mechanics

ONE FEEDS ON FLESH—THE OTHER ON PLANTS

Above, Venus's flytrap snaring an insect. The victim is entrapped by hairs on the hinged leaves, which snap together and imprison him. Left, mistletoe, a parasite that grows on trees, symbol of romance at Yuletide.

tionship. The cranberry and the trailing arbutus are both grouped together, and so are the lily and the asparagus.

Plants, like animals, must struggle to maintain their existence. Nature helps them by giving them organs especially adapted to providing them with moisture and air, while insects and wind help to spread their seeds; but man and other animals make this struggle the harder. Forests are a very good example. If the cutting down of trees were not held in check, these plants would disappear, and nothing

Nature could do would bring them back. By and large, however, the forces that destroy plants and the forces that help them live balance each other, and plant life remains fairly constant. Our study of these forces provides object lessons for us in our own struggle for existence.

A Familiar Science. When men lived in caves and rude houses, there was no real study of plant life. Our ancestors probably paid little attention to the green things that grew about them. Trees furnished shelter and food. Plants and berries were good to eat, but the primitive man took these things for granted. He did not feel that it was any more necessary for him to care for and study plants than it was for him to guide the river that flowed into the sea.

But as living conditions improved, and man came to know more about the world, he began to look at plants with greater interest. He considered them seriously when he was searching for something to help him fight sickness and death. As he gradually discarded his superstitions and beliefs that such things as feathers, cat's claws, and snake fangs would cure him, he

BROTHERS AND SISTERS

It is difficult to see the family resemblance between the fragrant petunia (upper left), the poisonous nightshade (upper right), and the familiar potato (center). But they are all members of the same family. The lovely wild rose (lower left) and the delicious apple also are in the same botanical family. There are many other strange relationships among the plants, about which we would know nothing were it not for the study of botany.

Strange Members of the Same Families

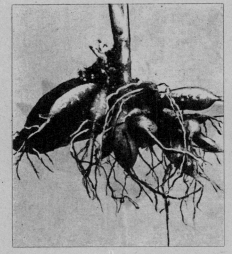

HOW SOME PLANTS MULTIPLY

Each of the tubers of the dahlia (left) and the garlic (right) will produce a new plant if planted separately.

wondered if plants might have healing virtues. He began a systematic study of them, and found that some were very helpful, while others were useless. The American Indians were well versed in the use of plants as medicines and food, and gave white men valuable information concerning plant life.

During the time of the Greeks and Romans, philosophers studied plants and made some remarkable discoveries concerning them. In the writings of Aristotle, we find many references to plants which are used by botanists today. But botany as a science did not develop until the eighteenth century. At this time, Linnaeus (Karl von Linné), of Sweden, made a thorough study of plant and animal life, and classified plants for future botanists. With the invention of the microscope, a great impetus was given botany, and Charles Darwin's discoveries and theories of natural selection further helped.

The list below includes most of the general articles connected with botany, but many of these have special lists, to which the reader is referred. For further study of botany, these articles will prove helpful.

Air Plants	Cross-Fertilization	Grafting	Pollen
Algae	Cycads	Grains	Protoplasm
Aquatic Plants	Deciduous Trees	Grasses	Pteridophytes
Bacteria and	Diatom	Gymnosperms	Puffball
Bacteriology	Diffusion	Herbs	Roots
Biology	Diseases of Plants	Leaves	Rusts
Botanic Garden	Dyeing	Leguminous Plants	Sap
Breeding	Ecology	Lichens	Seeds
Bud	Evergreen	Mildews	Spice
Bulb	Fermentation	Mold	Spore
Carnivorous Plants	Ferns	Mosses	Spurge Family
Cell	Fertilization of Plants	Nature Study	Stems
Cellulose	Fiber	Nut	Tree
Chlorophyll	Flowers	Osmosis	Vegetables
Citrus	Fruits	Parasite	Weeds
Composite Family	Fungi	Phanerogamous Plants	Yeast
Coniferae	Germination	Plant	

MASTERPIECE OF A DEVOUT PAINTER—THE BOTTICELLI "MAGNIFICAT"

BOTTICELLI, *bot te chel'le,* Sandro (properly Alessandro di Filipepi) (1444-1510). One of the finest painters of the Italian Renaissance was Botticelli, who belonged to that famous group known as the Florentine school. As a young artist he was trained by the goldsmith Botticelli. Some authorities say that he assumed the name of his master. Others say the name Botticelli, meaning *little barrel,* was given him by an older brother.

In later years he studied under Fra Filippo Lippi, who taught him how to wield a brush with expression and imagination. Botticelli was very religious, and his Madonnas, the most famous of his works, show his zeal for the Church. Many of his paintings are hung in the Pitti Palace, Florence; the Gardner Museum, Boston; and the Metropolitan Museum, New York. The Sistine Chapel in the Vatican, Rome, contains several fine frescoes by him. Other famous works by Botticelli include *The Triumph of Spring, Birth of Venus, The Nativity,* and *The Adoration of the Magi.*

BOTTLE. Like soldiers standing rigidly at attention, bottles line the shelves of stores, pantries, and medicine chests, waiting to serve the needs of mankind. These leak-proof vessels, distinguished from most containers because they hold liquids, are usually made of glass. In special instances, they are also made of metal, stone, pottery, rubber, plastics, and, in the wilds, of animal skins.

Bottles are absolutely essential for the storage and transport of thousands of materials with certain liquid or gaseous content. This need has been recognized and met in various fashions since the beginning of history. Medicines, toilet preparations, carbonated beverages, distilled water, milk, and acids needed in the home and in industry are stored and transported in bottles. Without them, man's use of liquids would be limited, indeed.

Because there are so many filled bottles in constant circulation, it would seem that thousands and thousands of persons would be needed to clean, fill, and seal them all. It is true that many people are employed in this work, but modern automatic machines greatly increase the speed and simplicity of the process. For instance, in a milk-bottling plant, there are machines which wash, sterilize, fill, and cap bottles all within the space of a minute or so.

The bottles travel on a special conveyor to the machine; they are washed automatically and sterilized, and, as they move under faucets from an overhead vat, exactly the right amount of milk is run into them. Still moving along on the conveyor, they come under an automatic capping machine which puts the paper covers on them. Then they are carried to a depot where they are put into the containers and placed on the milk truck. Not a hand touches the bottle from the time it is put into the mechanized system until it is ready for the consumer.

The first bottles were probably made by sewing up a goat's skin and using one of the legs as the neck of the bottle. In some parts of the world, such as Southern Europe, West and Central Asia, and parts of Africa, water and wine are still stored in this manner. Ancient, too, are bottles of glass; fragments remain of earliest Egyptian types. During the Middle Ages, leather bottles were in common use in Europe. But as science and invention progressed, the need for bottles became more urgent, and it was found advisable to make most bottles from glass.

Before Michael Owens, an American, invented a machine for making glass bottles, they were blown by human breath. The glass blower was a true craftsman, handing his skill down to his sons. With practiced skill, he would gather the molten glass in a glowing "gob" on the end of a tube, and then blow through it. The glass would form a pear-shaped bubble. While this glass was still hot, he would swing it into a mold, and by blowing still more, make the glass take the form of the mold.

Today, however, bottles are made much more safely, quickly, and precisely, by machines which suck the molten glass into a form, then blow the bottle into the shape of the mold with compressed air. This process has resulted in low-cost bottles which speed distribution of products of the farm, the factory, and the laboratory, at reduced prices.

Every visit to a drug store is an object lesson as to how varied bottles can be— in shape, size, and color. Some are tall and exquisitely thin, others are square, stout, and stubby. Still others are triangular or round, or fashioned like a miniature mosque, with dome and minaret. Many are colored, to suit the fancy of the dispenser and attract the eye of the buyer. Attractively labeled, they present a gleaming display of the bottle's importance in man's organized living.

BOULDER, *bole'dur.* Any more or less rounded, detached mass of rock, larger than a cobblestone, is considered a boulder. Many boulders have been transported great distances by glaciers, or lesser distances by streams; and some have been worn by waves without much transportation. At the brink of Yellowstone Canyon is a huge glacial boulder, apart from all other rocks, unlike any formation in the vicinity, rounded and scarred from its journey. Boulders such as this could not have reached their present resting places save by the tremendous force of glacial action. In some cases, boulders are developed by the weathering away of the surrounding parts of the ledges of rock of which they were originally a part.

provision for an irrigation canal was passed by Congress. The plans and specifications were prepared and construction was started during Herbert Hoover's administration; the dam, first known as Hoover Dam, was completed in 1936.

The dam itself is 727 feet high, 1,180 feet across the top, and 650 feet at the bottom. During construction the river water was directed to four tunnels, two on each side of the river channel, driven through the

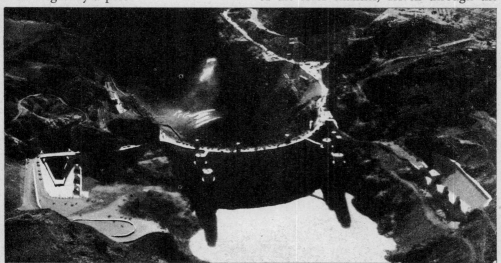

Courtesy Santa Fe Railway

A MIGHTY WORK OF MODERN ENGINEERING—BOULDER DAM
A raging torrent has been made a lake—a desert transformed into fertility.

BOULDER DAM. Located between the walls of the Black Canyon on the Colorado River, where it forms the natural boundary between the states of Arizona and Nevada, is Boulder Dam.

Harnessing the Colorado River in order to provide water for farming and domestic use, generate power, and control floods, long has been a problem of the seven states in its river basin. Dropping 8,000 feet in its 1,700-mile course, the Colorado River menaces California's Imperial Valley with flood. Because the river waters touch several states, the question presented many problems.

Finally, a bill authorizing the building of a dam, erection of a power plant, and

solid rock of the canyon walls, opening above the dam site, and discharging below it. Each of these tunnels was more than 3,000 feet long, and fifty-six feet in diameter.

The construction of Boulder Dam is one of the greatest engineering projects of modern times; it formed Lake Mead—the largest body of water ever created by man. This artificial lake or reservoir is 115 miles long, with an area of approximately 146,500 acres. The water in the reservoir would cover the entire state of New York to a depth of one foot.

Water for the domestic use of Los Angeles and other cities and available irrigation for over two million acres of land have been made possible by Boulder Dam.

Just below the dam, half on the Nevada side, half on the Arizona side, is the U-shaped power plant—a steel and reinforced concrete structure 1,650 feet long. It will ultimately have a rated capacity of 1,835,000 horse power from seventeen huge generators. This is about one eighth the total now available for generating electricity in the United States; Niagara, for example, has a rated capacity of 452,500.

The cost of the project is $165,000,000. An average of 3,500 men were employed, most of whom, with the government force, were housed in the new town of Boulder City, which promises to become a popular resort city.

BOURBON, *boor'bon*. For nearly 400 years, Europe felt the power and tyranny of the Bourbons, one of the strongest and most arrogant royal familes ever to rule in the Old World. From this proud dynasty came kings for France, Spain, and Naples, as well as queens, dukes, and duchesses for other countries.

The story of the Bourbons begins in the early tenth century, when Adhemar became lord of the ancient Bourbonnais, province of France. His children gained land, money, and power, rising to a high position among the nobles of the country. In the year 1272, Beatrix, the daughter of a Bourbon, married Robert, of the royal French line of Capets. Their son, Louis, the first Duke of Bourbon, had two sons who established the first main branches of the line. The Dukes of Bourbon constituted the elder branch which ended in 1527, when the Constable of Bourbon was killed.

Henry of Navarre was the first Bourbon to sit on the throne of France. A descendant of the younger line of Bourbons, he ruled as Henry IV. He was followed by Louis XIII. Then came Louis XIV, whose court was the most brilliant in Europe in the seventeenth century, and after him came Louis XV. The French Revolution occurred under another Bourbon, Louis XVI, and the family reign was broken for a

time with his execution in 1793. His son, Louis XVII, never reigned, but Louis XVIII, brother of the unfortunate Louis XVI, restored the Bourbon dynasty in 1815 after Napoleon was defeated at Waterloo.

After his death, in 1824, Charles X, another brother, ascended the throne, ruling until 1830, when he was forced to abdicate. Louis Philippe, of the Orleans line, descended from Louis XIII, ruled until 1848, when another revolution brought the monarchy to an end in France.

In 1700, Louis XIV placed his grandson, Philip, Duke of Anjou, on the throne of Spain as Philip V, founding the Bourbon line in that country. His descendants ruled until 1931, when revolution forced Alfonso XIII into permanent exile.

The Bourbons started still another dynasty in Naples in 1735, when a son of Philip V of Spain became King Charles III of Sicily and Naples. Except for brief intervals during the Napoleonic era, the family ruled over this little kingdom until all the Italian states were united into one kingdom under the House of Savoy in 1860. See FRANCE; SPAIN.

BOW, *bo*. From earliest times until gunpowder came into use, the bow was man's deadliest weapon for hunting or warfare. Today, we find it still used for these purposes in primitive lands, while civilized people preserve its popularity in sport (see ARCHERY).

Bows were first made of bone or wood and were fairly small. The armies of the Egyptians and Assyrians placed great trust in their bowmen, and the Greeks and Persians used bows with great skill in their wars. But the bow as a weapon in warfare did not decide the issues of battle until the fourteenth century, when the Hundred Years' War began between England and France.

At Crécy, on August 26, 1346, a small English army repulsed large, heavily armed French forces with the *longbow,* a six-foot weapon made of wood from the English yew tree. So powerful was this bow that its three-foot arrows pierced the

THE SHADOW OF THE GUILLOTINE FALLS ON THE ROYAL HOUSE OF BOURBON

Louis XVI and Marie Antoinette, one-time king and queen of France, in prison after attempting to flee the country, during the Revolution of 1791. The fury of the revolutionists led to the trial and execution of these unfortunate rulers, who were charged with conspiring with foreign governments.

armor of the French. At the end of the
day, when the bodies of French warriors
lay strewn about the field, it was known
that English yeomen and the English longbow were far superior to mounted knights
in suits of heavy metal. Again, at Poitiers
in 1356, and at Agincourt in 1415, the English longbow repulsed the French.

Another deadly weapon of the Middle
Ages was the *crossbow,* which shot arrows
from a horizontal position by the release
of a trigger. The string of the bow was
pulled back by a ratchet or windlass to give
it greater power. Crossbows were made
of iron, wood, bone, metal, and tendons.
They were often large, weighing as much
as twelve pounds. They could fire bolts,
stones, or other missiles with accuracy and
a tremendous amount of force. Military
crossbows had an effective range of over
300 yards. They were outlawed by the
Church for their cruelty, but hunters and
armies of Europe persisted in using them.
The most highly valued were bows of the
famous Toledo tempered steel, made in
Spain.

Powerful though the longbow and crossbow were, gunpowder sealed their doom.
Throughout Europe the bow became used
less and less, and even in lands of the savages, the rifle came to replace the bow.

BOWLING. In New York City there is
a street named Bowling Green, bringing
memories of the days when the early
Dutch settlers on the grassy lawns of New
Amsterdam had played *skittles,* or *nine-
pins.* This was a game which had been
popular for centuries in Holland and Germany. On the other side of the English
Channel was played the game *lawn bowls.*
From these old games developed our modern *bowling.*

The game today is played indoors and
with ten pins. The first bowling courts,
which were of clay, appeared about the
middle of the nineteenth century. Today
the game is played on wooden *alleys,* indoors. These regulation alleys, made of
hard, smooth, polished wood, are forty-one
or forty-two inches wide and sixty feet

SMALL BUT SHADY
Leaves and seeds of the box-elder, a maple.

from the *foul* line to the first pin. Back of
the foul line is a *runway* of at least fifteen
feet, and back of the pins is a two and one-
half foot *pit.* On each side of the alley are
gutters to catch the ball if it is inaccurately
rolled.

The *pins,* each fifteen inches high, are
bottle-shaped, and must weigh not less
than three pounds, two ounces each. The
ball which the bowler throws must not
weigh more than sixteen and one-half
pounds, nor have a circumference greater
than twenty-seven inches. Two holes, into
which thumb and forefinger are inserted
for a firm grip, are in each ball.

Any number may play the game, the
object being to knock down as many pins

possible. The pins are set up in tri-
ngle formation with the apex toward the
ul line. A game consists of ten *frames,*
ch player rolling two balls, or one
ame. A *strike* occurs when the player
nocks down all the pins with his first
ll; a *spare* occurs when they are all
wn with the second ball rolled.

The player making a strike adds ten to
e number of points scored on his next
ame. Should he roll three strikes in suc-
ssion, he scores thirty in the first frame.
he player making a spare adds ten to the
umber of pins bowled over next.

There are many variations of the ten-pin
ame, such as *head pin, duck pin, candle
n,* etc. Other variations of bowling are
ayed with fewer pins.

BOX-EL'DER. The box-elder, or ash-
aved maple, as it is sometimes called, is
mmon over a large area in the United
ates. Its fruit, which ripens early in the
ummer, looks like the "wings" of the
aple tree. Its rapid, spreading growth
akes it a hedge favorite. Because its wood
soft and brittle, easily broken, the tree is
ot among the most desirable shade trees.
ommercially, the wood is used for boxes,
ates, and fence posts.

BOXER REBELLION. Some think the
rm *Boxer* a nickname humorously
ined by foreigners, for members of Chi-
se secret societies formed at the end of
e nineteenth century which were called
"ists of Harmony." Others say that
oxer is the incorrect translation of the
hinese name of a Nationalist group.

With the rapid growth of foreign com-
ercial and territorial expansion, these
cieties, which at the first were patriotic
ganizations opposing Western customs,
adually became more antagonistic. The
ar of exploitation, and the increasing de-
ands by foreign powers for further con-
ssions to greedy nations, caused ex-
tremists to demand a "closed door" pol-
y. They took for their slogan, "Destroy
e foreign devils."

The climax came in June, 1900, when
e German minister was slain in Peking.

Missionaries, native Christians, and diplo-
mats of the city were besieged in the British
legation, where they had fled for safety.
Hundreds of foreigners were killed and
property of inestimable value was damaged or destroyed during the two months'
rebellion which followed. The foreign nations—United States, Great Britain, France,
Germany, and Russia—which had life and
property interests in China, organized an
army, and on August 14 recaptured the
city.

China apologized, and was forced to pay
a large indemnity. The United States, in
1908, during the Presidency of Theodore
Roosevelt, returned one-half its share with
the request the funds be used to educate
Chinese students in America.

BOXING. This sport has been described
as a game of "give and take," but its most
important element is self-defense from an
opponent's blows. Boxers were among the
contesting athletes in the early Olympic
Games of Greece, and boxing is one of the
few sports which people of nearly every
race and clime enjoy. Since it teaches fair
play, self-confidence, and courage, it is
taught in schools and clubs throughout the
United States and other parts of the world.
Probably no other sport calls into play as
much alertness, co-ordination, and quick
thinking as does boxing.

Padded fingerless gloves of varying
thickness are worn by the boxers. A match
usually lasts a specified number of rounds,
each round ranging in length from a minute to three minutes, with a one-minute
intermission between rounds. If a contest-
ant is knocked down, he is allowed ten seconds to get up. If he fails to do so, his
opponent is the victor. Many matches are
decided by points depending on how many
blows each boxer has struck on his opponent's body. Judges decide which boxer is
the winner.

The principal blows in boxing are the
hook, the *straight jab,* and the *uppercut.*
Hooks are delivered at a fairly close range,
the elbow being bent at right angles. The
straight jab is a quick blow struck at full

THRILLS OF THE PRIZE RING
Powerful attack, skillful defense, and plenty of fast action are sure to bring boxing fans to their feet. Cheers are for the champion, his glove raised in victory.

arm's distance, the elbow being straight at the end of the blow. The uppercut is delivered from beneath. It is a short, upward-swinging blow, delivered at close quarters, and is usually meant for the jaw. At all times, the wrist is held rigid. Forms of defense are the *block, slip, parry, counter blow,* and *clinch.*

Boxers are classed by weight, the following numbers being the maximum limit: flyweight, 112 pounds; bantamweight, 118 pounds; featherweight, 126 pounds; light-weight, 135 pounds; welter-weight, 147 pounds; middleweight, 160 pounds; light heavyweight, 175 pounds; heavyweight, over 175 pounds.

Professional boxing in which the participants receive money for their services is prize fighting. See PRIZE FIGHTING.

BOX TREE. The stubby, slow-growi evergreen box tree grows in Englar Southern Europe, and some parts of As There are more than thirty species. T tree is usually a scrub, reaching heights twelve to fifteen feet. Its small, oval lea are glossy green, and the tree is grow good deal for ornamental shrubbery a garden hedge.

Its very heavy and hard yellow wood take a handsome polish. It is used exte sively in wood carving and turning, and the construction of wood cuts, or engra ings, slide rules, flutes, and other woo wind musical instruments.

BOYCOTTING, *boi' ḳot ing.* When a group of persons with common intere refrain from dealing with an individual another group, in order to discipline t fender, they make use of the *boycott*. This rm means simply *to have nothing to do ith*. A labor union sometimes boycotts a rporation believed to be unfair to union or. Reform organizations really endorse boycott when they urge people to refuse buy sweatshop products, or not to pat-nize shops that ill-treat their employes. The word owes its origin to a Captain arles Boycott who lived in Ireland in 81. He so angered the tenants on the ate of his employer that they persuaded e other people of the county "to have thing to do with Captain Boycott." In urse of time, the name of this offender came the name of the punishment meted persons considered unfair.

BOYLE'S LAW. If the volume of gas in y given space is under a pressure of one und per square inch, the pressure will be ubled to two pounds per square inch if e space is reduced half, provided the tem-rature remains the same. This is an illus-tion of Boyle's law in physics, which tes that the volume of gas at a constant nperature varies inversely as the pressure

exerted upon it increases. The principle was developed in 1662 by the English chemist, Robert Boyle. It is known in France as Mariotte's law.

BOYNE, BATTLE OF THE. The crushing victory of King William III of England over the dethroned James II in the Battle of the Boyne (1690) made the English supreme in Ireland for two centuries. Aided by Dutch and Huguenot soldiers, King William defeated the Irish army of James so decisively that the former king fled to France, thus ending the rule of Catholic kings in England. The battle was named for the Boyne River, in Eastern Ireland.

BOYS' AND GIRLS' 4-H CLUBS. A four-leafed clover, with an H on each leaf, representing Head, Heart, Hands, and Health, is the emblem of the 4-H Clubs for girls and boys, organizations for youth de-

FOUR-H CLUB WORK BRINGS RESULTS
This handsome pig (left) has just won a 4-H con-test. So have the boys (above) with their dairy equipment.

velopment in agriculture and home economics.

In the latter part of the nineteenth century, some county school superintendents in Midwestern rural communities organized several clubs of this type, and were aided by the agricultural colleges. These clubs were formed as a check on the growing migration of young people from country to cities. However, it was not until 1908, when the United States Department of Agriculture became interested and provided funds, that the work started in earnest.

Now, the clubs are headed by state agents, specialists, county leaders, home demonstration agents, and others. More than a million farm boys and girls are members, and more than five million have graduated to adult responsibilities.

ing, and home management, and efforts a conservation of game, soil, forests, and othe natural resources, are some of the lines o activity, and accurate records are kept o all work done. Four-H work also feature exhibits, contests, dramatic and musica performances, and field meets to demon strate the progress made. Interest in th phase of the organization is growing rap idly. The money required for many of th things 4-H Clubs do is earned by the men bers, and demonstrates the value of the club training. It is estimated that the tot membership earns about $25,000,000 a yea

Primarily for the teaching of newer an better methods in agriculture and hom economics, the clubs also have for a purpos the development of initiative, leadership and executive training. They encourag the strengthening of farm communitie

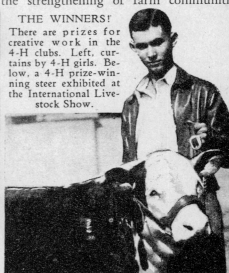

THE WINNERS!
There are prizes for creative work in the 4-H clubs. Left, curtains by 4-H girls. Below, a 4-H prize-winning steer exhibited at the International Livestock Show.

Four-H members represent every state and territory of the United States, and make up the largest group of its kind in the world. The average age of members is ten to fourteen years. Membership, which is voluntary, is based on the promise that the boy or girl will learn more about agriculture or home economics than he or she knew before, and give practical demonstrations of their increased knowledge. Demonstration is particularly emphasized. The club motto is "To Make the Best Better."

Cattle and poultry raising, gardening, corn growing, canning, cooking, dressmak-

both socially and financially. They stre better co-operation between rural familie In this way, leaders of the organizatio hope to teach its members and the natio at large the importance of good farming and to strengthen the country under th leadership of rising generations.

Information about 4-H Clubs may be s cured from the Office of Co-operative E tension Work, Department of Agricultur Washington, D. C.

All photos courtesy of the Boy Scouts of America

KNIGHTS of the Modern Age

BOY SCOUTS OF AMERICA. "Do a good turn daily" is a slogan of over 2,000,000 youths in more than seventy countries, members of the Boy Scouts. No other movement of its kind has ever met with the extreme popularity enjoyed by this international organization. Started in England by General Sir Robert Baden-Powell in a trial experimental camp in 1907, the Boy Scout movement was founded in 1908. It spread to the United States in 1909 and was incorporated in 1910. Today there are over 1,866,000 Boy Scouts in America; they belong to about 57,000 troops and packs.

The aims and purposes of the Boy Scouts are to develop character and citizenship through proper leadership, making it possible for the boy to indulge in Scouting activities as a game. Each Scout learns first aid, lifesaving, signaling, tracking, cooking, woodcraft, nature study, and many handicrafts. Because the Scout creed is one of service, such groups as the Red Cross, fire departments, and the police receive the aid of Scouts in times of emergency.

The Boy Scouts of America was granted a charter by Congress in 1916 as a non-military, non-political, and non-class organization. No restrictions are made as to race, religion, or class. The entire movement hinges on the twelve Scout Laws, taken from the code of the knights, as stated in the official *Handbook for Boys*. These laws are:

1. *A Scout is trustworthy.* A Scout's honor is to be trusted. If he violates his honor by telling a lie, or by cheating, or by not doing exactly a given task, when trusted on his honor, he may be directed to hand over his Scout Badge.

2. *A Scout is loyal.* He is loyal to all to whom loyalty is due—his Scout leader, his home, and parents and country.

3. *A Scout is helpful.* He must be prepared at any time to save life, help injured persons, and share the home duties. He must do at least one "Good Turn" to somebody every day.

4. *A Scout is friendly.* He is a friend to all and a brother to every other Scout.

5. *A Scout is courteous.* He is polite to all, especially to women, children, old people, and the weak and helpless. He must not take pay for being helpful or courteous.

6. *A Scout is kind.* He is a friend to animals. He will not kill or hurt any living creature needlessly, but will strive to save and protect all harmless life.

7. *A scout is obedient.* He obeys his parents, Scoutmaster, Patrol Leader, and all other duly constituted authorities.

8. *A Scout is cheerful.* He smiles when-

SCOUTS BELIEVE IN BUILDING CHARACTER

Scouting combines learning with sports and camping. Here are some of the other activities. Above, a Leader explains the flag-signaling system used in the army and navy. Left, this Boy Scout is at home in his canoe because he has been taught how to handle it with skill and safety. Below, a group of Scouts work out a budget problem on paper.

MARCHING FOR FUN—And Health

These Scouts are "hoofing it" to a summer camping spot, carrying all their equipment with them. The flag is their troop insignia. They will make camp, cook dinner, and spend the night in "pup" tents like that below. At the right is the badge of a First Class Scout.

BOY SCOUTS OF AMERICA

BE PREPARED

ever he can. His obedience to orders is prompt and cheery. He never shirks nor grumbles at hardships.

9. *A Scout is thrifty.* He does not wantonly destroy property. He works faithfully, wastes nothing, and makes the best use of his opportunities. He saves his money so that he may pay his own way, be generous to those in need, and helpful to worthy objects. He may work for pay, but must not receive tips for courtesies or "Good Turns."

10. *A Scout is brave.* He has the courage to face danger in spite of fear, and to stand up for the right against the coaxings of friends or the jeers or threats of enemies, and defeat does not down him.

11. *A Scout is clean.* He keeps clean in body and thought, stands for clean speech, clean sport, clean habits, and travels with a clean crowd.

12. *A Scout is reverent.* He is reverent toward God. He is faithful in his religious duties, and respects the convictions of others in matters of custom and religion.

Each Scout must also take this oath: "On my honor I will do my best: 1. To do my duty to God and my country, and to obey the Scout Law. 2. To help other people at all times. 3. To keep myself physically strong, mentally awake, and morally straight." The Scout motto is "Be Prepared."

Scouts are organized into patrols and troops. A patrol is made up of no more than eight boys, and a troop consists of no more than four patrols. A boy leader heads each patrol, and an American citizen, at least twenty-one years old, called a Scoutmaster, heads each troop.

The Scout wears a regulation uniform, consisting of a broad-brimmed hat, khaki shirt, belt, breeches or shorts, stockings, and tan shoes. In addition, around his neck he wears a neckerchief, of some color determined by his troop. On his hat he wears his metal badge, which changes as he advances in Scout work. On the right sleeve is sewed a medallion indicating his patrol, and on the left sleeve is his troop number.

According to the official *Handbook for Boys,* any boy of twelve or over may join the Scouts. First he becomes a Tenderfoot, the lowest class, by meeting the following requirements:

1. Know the Scout Oath, Law, Motto, Sign, and Salute and the significance of the Badge and Uniform.

2. Know the composition and history of the Flag of the United States of America and the customary forms of respect due to it.

3. Tie nine kinds of knots.

After a month as a Tenderfoot, the boy may take his test to become a Second Class Scout. The requirements are:

1. Have at least a month's service as a Tenderfoot and know how and when to wear the Scout uniform.

2. Show what to do and tell what and what not to do in case of a variety of accidents and ailments.

3. Know elementary signaling.

4. Track half a mile in twenty-five minutes or describe the contents of a store window, after having observed four windows for one minute each.

5. Go a mile in twelve minutes at Scout's Pace—fifty steps running and fifty walking, alternately; or stride and stake out a four-acre tract of land.

6. Use a knife and hatchet properly.

7. Build a fire in the open, using not more than two matches, and to care for and put it out.

8. Cook a quarter of a pound of meat and two potatoes in the open without the use of utensils.

9. Earn and deposit a dollar in a bank, or earn and raise a farm animal, or earn and contribute a dollar or its equivalent to the family budget or to welfare work in the community.

10. Know the sixteen principal points of the compass.

11. Demonstrate practice of five Rules of Safety at home, in school, on the street, or some other place.

12. Furnish evidence of having put into practice the principles of the Scout Oath

FROM WOODCRAFT TO SEAMANSHIP

Many new groups have grown from the Scout movement. Biggest is that of the Sea Scouts, here shown (above) learning correct life-saving practice, and (right) manning an old-time sailing ship. The insignia is the badge of the Sea Scouts. Sea Scout Patrols are organized from the older members of regular Scout Troops. Their program is essentially for able, manly boys and provides the variety and adventure that they normally crave. Another organization is built around the Cubs, a complete program for younger boys.

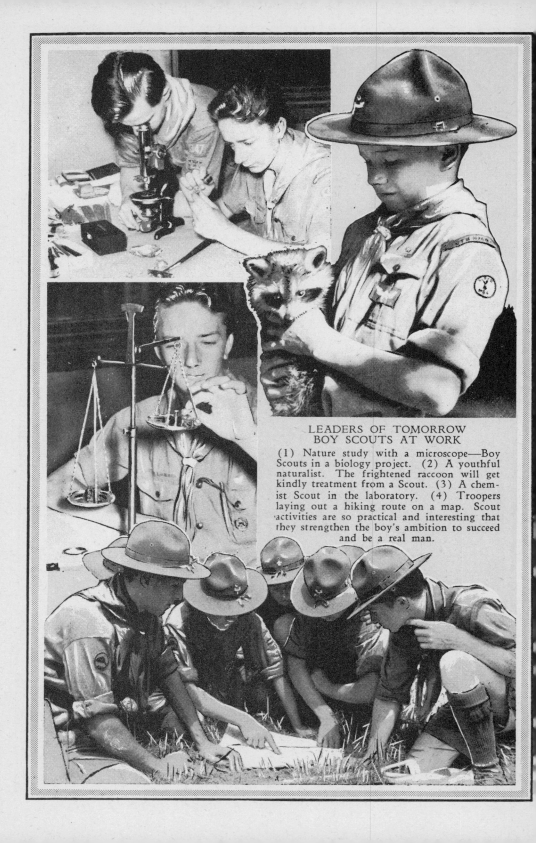

LEADERS OF TOMORROW
BOY SCOUTS AT WORK

(1) Nature study with a microscope—Boy Scouts in a biology project. (2) A youthful naturalist. The frightened raccoon will get kindly treatment from a Scout. (3) A chemist Scout in the laboratory. (4) Troopers laying out a hiking route on a map. Scout activities are so practical and interesting that they strengthen the boy's ambition to succeed and be a real man.

and Law in daily life, wherever he may be.

The boy may become a First Class Scout after he passes the following requirements:

1. Two months' service as a Second Class Scout and ability to distinguish ranks and positions of other scouts by their badges and insignia.

2. Swim fifty yards.

3. Earn and deposit at least two dollars in the bank, etc. (See *Second Class Requirements.*)

4. Send and receive a message by semaphore, code, or sign language.

5. Make a round trip to a point at least seven miles away on foot or in a boat, and give an account of the journey.

6. Tell what first aid is and give demonstrations of it for various types of accidents and injuries.

7. Prepare several kinds of food in the open.

8. Read a map correctly and, from notes, draw a rough sketch map.

9. Use an ax for felling light timber or make an article of carpentry or demonstrate repair of a damaged tree.

10. Judge distance, size, height, weight, and number within twenty-five per cent.

11. Describe fully ten species of plants or six species of wild animals or birds, and find the North Star and name and describe three constellations.

12. Furnish evidence that he has put the principles of the Scout Oath and Law into practice in his daily life.

A Scout may advance even higher in the organization through the merit-badge system. A badge is given for knowledge and proficiency in each of 101 subjects, all of outdoor, vocational, or educational value. The Second Class Scout may qualify for five badges out of a selected list of forty, and the First Class Scout may obtain as many as he can. If a boy has been a First Class Scout for three months, has obtained five merit badges, and has been active in scout work and lived up to the Oath and Law, he may advance to Star Scout.

Following another three-month period, he may become a Life Scout, after qualifying for ten merit badges, five of which are designated. The highest rank in the organization is that of Eagle Scout; the boy must be a Life Scout for six months and obtain twenty-one merit badges, twelve designated, to obtain this outstanding position. Bronze, silver, or gold palms are given for extra merit badges earned. No matter how high in the organization a Scout advances, there is always a further goal for him to attain.

Some of the outstanding Boy Scouts of the United States have taken part in various exciting and dangerous expeditions. One was with Byrd on his first Antarctic trip; another was with MacGregor in Greenland; a third went on one of Martin Johnson's African journeys.

The Boy Scouts are organized under a national council and an executive board. The President of the United States automatically becomes honorary president of the Scouts when he assumes his office. All members of the board and council are outstanding men.

For Scouts fifteen years of age and over there is Senior Scouting. This includes Explorer Scouting, advanced Scouting on land, and Sea Scouting, a nautical program with Sea activities. Rover Scouting is available for boys of seventeen and up. The Cub Program was developed in 1930 for boys nine, ten and eleven years of age. Their activities lead directly into those of the older group. Provision is also made for the many boys living in rural sections. These boys may become Lone Scouts and do Scout work by themselves or in groups of farm patrols.

For information concerning the Boy Scouts, write to headquarters at 2 Park Avenue, New York City, N. Y.

INDIAN CUNNING BESTS A BRAVE BRITON

The dying General Braddock, wounded and forced to retreat after his attack against Fort Duquesne, where his forces were ambushed and defeated by the Indians.

BRAD'DOCK, EDWARD (1695-1755). A British general, Braddock sailed to America in 1754 as commander of the British troops during the French and Indian War. A year later he went to Hampton, Va., and met the Virginia troops near there for an expedition against Fort Duquesne, a French post.

He reached Frederick, Md., on April 24, and was forced to wait for supply wagons organized by Franklin. There George Washington joined him, Washington becoming aide-de-camp to Braddock. Refusing to heed the warning of the young experienced soldier, Braddock set out from Fort Cumberland with an army of about 1,200 men. On July 9 an advance division under Gates was startled by war whoops, which the soldiers heard for the first time, and which caused them to retreat in disorder. The Virginians, familiar with Indian fighting, sheltered themselves behind rocks and trees; but Braddock, scorning Washington's advice, kept his army drawn up in platoons, firing blindly into the forest.

Nevertheless, Braddock's bravery was conspicuous, and several horses were shot from under him before he at last fell, mortally wounded. Washington was forced to lead to safety the remaining men, less than half the original force..

BRAD'FORD, WILLIAM (1590-1657). Among the passengers on the *Mayflower* in 1620 was William Bradford, destined to be second governor and chief historian of Plymouth Colony. He was born in Yorkshire, England. At an early age he joined the Separatist Church and was imprisoned for a short time, later emigrating to Holland with friends. He was one of the leaders of the 102 persons who sailed for the New World in October, 1620. After the death of John Carver, Bradford became governor of the little colony, and with the exception of a five-year period, held the office until his death.

He was a just but firm man, and it was his guidance that brought prosperity to the colony. He was the author of *The History of Plymouth Plantation,* from which all present accounts of the period are taken. This work disappeared during the Revolutionary War, but was found again in 1855 in an English library. The original is now in the state archives of Massachusetts.

BRAGG, BRAXTON (1817-1876). During the war between the states, Braxton Bragg, a soldier and engineer, served with the Confederate army. Born in North Carolina, Bragg attended West Point, graduating in 1837. Following service in the wars against the Seminole Indians and the Mexican War, he was promoted to the rank of lieutenant colonel in the United States Army, but resigned in 1856 to take up farming in Louisiana.

At the beginning of the Civil War he commanded the Confederate forces at Pensacola as a brigadier general. He later was made a major general and then a general.

Bragg took part in the Battle of Shiloh and replaced General Beauregard in the West. Following defeats at Perryville, Murfreesboro, and Chattanooga, and a victory at Chickamauga, he asked to be relieved of his command. Jefferson Davis, President' of the Confederacy, then appointed him military adviser. After the war he was engaged in civil engineering.

BRAH'MA. The general name for the Supreme Being in the Hindu religion, Brahma has more than one meaning, depending upon the grammatical form used. It is really the name of an idea. In one grammatical form, it is the term for the Universal Power—the spirit of which the Hindus believe their souls to be a part. Brahma is not an individual deity in the usual sense. With another different grammatical ending, the word refers to a god represented by an idol. He is one of the three powerful Hindu gods which form the Triad. The other two gods are Vishnu and Siva.

Brahma is the god of Fate and controls life and death—as the agent of the universal power. This god is represented by an idol, a red or golden colored figure with four heads and as many arms. He is not worshiped by the common people, and there is only one temple sacred to him.

HERE LIVES A STRANGE GOD
A shrine to the Brahman deity Vishnu at Barwa-Sagar. The structure is of great antiquity.

BRAH'MANISM. Two great sects of India form one of the world's important religions. This religion is Brahmanism, so-called because the priests are known as Brahmans. One sect is made up of followers of the god Vishnu, the preserver; the other is composed of followers of the god Siva, the destroyer and reproducer. The more highly educated members of the religion regard the god they choose, usually Siva, merely as a symbol, through whom

HINDU SYMBOL
This is Siva, the four-armed creator and destroyer, one of the divine triad of Brahmanism.

they attempt to gain purity of the soul. But low-caste Hindus often worship, with degrading ceremonies and rites, this same deity in another of his many forms, that of a female.

Brahmanism was founded on ancient religious writings called Vedas. The oldest literature provides for the worship of natural objects, such as the sun and the sky. Later, animal sacrifices were included. Natural objects were reduced to symbols in later Vedic writings; and in the fifth to the first centuries B. C., the religion began to be divided. The higher thinkers recognized only one god; but the masses accepted three, Vishnu, Siva, and Brahma.

Brahma, however, practically disappeared, only one temple remaining in his honor today. The priests, or Brahmans, interpreted and explained the sacred writings. It was the Brahmans who developed the Sanskrit literature and became the poets, lawgivers, scientists, statesmen, and administrators of India.

A Brahman must pass through four states. In the first he studies the Vedas. He may take alms and is exempt from taxes and corporal punishment, but he may not eat meat nor eggs, or touch leather and some animals. After he marries, he enters the second state and is expected to have a son and to train him for the holy calling.

The third state is a retirement from the world for solitary meditation. The fourth state is a cruel one of self-denial. These last two states, however, are very seldom reached and are regarded as ideals of Brahmanism, rather than as realities.

BRAHMS, JOHANNES (1833-1897). Many students of music consider "the three B's," Bach, Beethoven, and Brahms, as the greatest composers of all time. Regardless of whether this opinion is justified, it is certain that Brahms must be ranked among the masters of music.

Courtesy C. G. Conn, Ltd.

JOHANNES BRAHMS

Born in Germany, Brahms received his earliest musical training from his father, who played the double bass in an orchestra in Hamburg. At the age of twenty, Brahms played several of his compositions for Robert Schumann, a leading composer. In a few years he was recognized as a promising composer and later was acclaimed throughout Europe for his symphonies, concertos, songs, and other works. His *German Requiem* is the work which first gained him recognition. Although the claim once was made that it was difficult to understand Brahms' music, his compositions are now more and more in demand by the public. Few symphony orchestras today pass a season without playing Brahms.

BRAILLE. See BLINDNESS.

BRAIN. Because of his wonderful brain, man has become the ruler of the world. He is not the largest of the animals, nor the strongest; but he has the best brain and consequently can think the best.

The brain and the spinal column make up what is known as the central nervous system. The brain is merely an enlarged extension of the spinal cord. Membranes form a protective lining between the bony skull and the brain.

Parts of the Brain. The brain itself has three parts: the *cerebrum,* or large brain; the *cerebellum,* or small brain; and the *medulla oblongata,* or spinal bulb.

The cerebrum, sometimes referred to as the forebrain, is the largest part of the brain. It is divided lengthwise into two parts called *hemispheres* and consists of a number of folds which greatly increase its surface area. The cerebrum governs man's thoughts and all his voluntary actions. In addition, it contains the centers, or areas, which enable him to see, hear, taste, and smell. If one of these centers is injured, man loses his ability to perform the action controlled by that particular center.

The cerebellum is much smaller than the cerebrum. It is located in the back of the head, below the cerebrum. It regulates the muscular movements of the body. When this portion of the brain is injured, a person has difficulty in walking or even standing. His muscles do not receive the proper instructions from the cerebellum. The cerebellum has nothing to do with conscious life. For this reason, an injury to it does not affect one's ability to hear, see, etc.

The medulla oblongata is really the upper part of the spinal cord. It has many duties to perform, for it carries nerve impulses, or messages, to the brain from the body, as well as impulses from the brain to the body. It also takes care of those actions of the body which are carried on without the interference of the will, such as breathing and digestion. An odd thing happens in the medulla. The nerves between the spinal cord and the brain cross there. The result is that the right side of the brain controls the left side of the body, and the left side of the brain controls the right side.

How the Parts Are Put Together. The spinal cord and the brain consist of two substances, gray matter and white matter. In the brain the gray matter is on the outside, and the white matter is on the inside; in the spinal cord the situation is reversed.

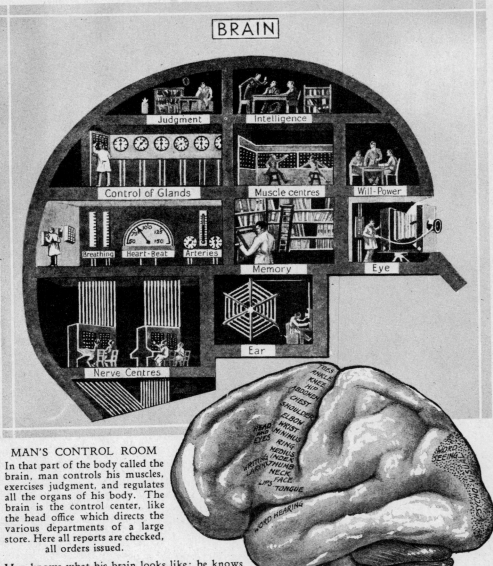

BRAIN

Judgment

Intelligence

Control of Glands

Muscle centres

Will-Power

Breathing   Heart-Beat   Arteries

Memory

Eye

Ear

Nerve Centres

MAN'S CONTROL ROOM

In that part of the body called the brain, man controls his muscles, exercises judgment, and regulates all the organs of his body. The brain is the control center, like the head office which directs the various departments of a large store. Here all reports are checked, all orders issued.

Man knows what his brain looks like; he knows what it is made of, but he has yet to find out how it works so marvelously. The parts of the brain controlling the various organs are shown here.

Gray matter is composed chiefly of nerve cells; the white, mainly of nerve fibers. The nerve cells which make up this outer layer, or gray substance of the brain, are called *neurons*. It has been calculated that at birth a child has ten thousand million of these cells. This number never increases, but the cells do grow in complexity and size. Extensions from these cells may be thought of as wires which carry messages to and from the different parts of the brain.

Disorders of the Brain. Through the brain and the spinal cord, we receive sensations, we send out nervous impulses, and we think. If disease affects a certain center of the brain, such as the sight center, then, even though his eyes are perfect, a man·will be unable to see. There are many ways in which the brain centers may be injured. Tumors may press on vital centers, infections may attack the brain, and injuries from accidents often affect parts of the brain.

Brain Development. As was stated before, the neurons, or nerve cells, found in the brain at birth never increase in number. But they do gradually develop in size and become more complex. The young child learns to walk, to talk, and to read, but does not learn everything in a single day. When he is older, he goes to school and develops his brain still more by study. Usually, when a person is about twenty years of age, his brain and his nervous system become mature.

Feeble-minded people and idiots fail to develop as normal people do because their brains never develop to that extent. Because of this varying ability of mind, we find people of all degrees of intelligence. The idiot is a person whose actions are mostly instinctive or inherited, but the genius is a person who has developed his brain to a very high degree.

In comparatively recent years, scientists have worked out ways of measuring, or testing, the mind. With these tests it is possible to find out just about how intelligent a person is. Some tests are intended to find out whether a person has special abilities, as in music or mathematics. Other tests are for character. A number of tests have been made so simple that children can readily take them. Perhaps such tests have been given in your school.

BRAKE. In principle, the brake used to stop or to slow down a modern streamline automobile does not differ greatly from the brake used on a horse-drawn vehicle. A wagon or buggy has a wood or metal block on a wheel, which the driver presses against the rim by means of a system of levers. All automobiles are equipped with flexible metal bands on the rims of one or more of the wheels, which tighten when pressure is applied to a foot lever.

Brakemen on trains formerly used a hand device. A chain fixed to a lever was wound around an axle by turning a wheel to which the chain was attached. However, this method is almost non-existent today. For modern mechanism used in stopping trains, see the article on AIR BRAKE.

BRAKE, or BRACK'EN. A member of the fern family, the brake is common in America and Europe and many other parts of the world. It grows to a height of several feet, the stalk dividing into three leafy branches. Since the plants do not fall in the winter, they provide good cover for game.

During the first World War, a chemical known as potash was in great demand. Experiments proved that large amounts of this valuable substance could be extracted from the ash of the brake. In times of famine the bitter rootstock of this plant can be eaten. Its chief use, however, is as a substitute for hops in brewing. In Europe, brake is also used as thatching for roofs and for silage. However, the brake, as a weed, creates a serious problem on the Pacific coast and in the Appalachian Mountains, where it infests pasture lands and hinders livestock grazing.

BRAN. This is a product obtained from the rough outer coat of cereal grains. Usually the word refers to wheat bran; other varieties, such as corn bran and rye bran, are referred to by their full names. Bran is an important feed for stock because it contains carbohydrates, protein, and phosphorus and because it has laxative qualities. Although not important in the human diet, except as a laxative, it is frequently mixed with flour and used in making muffins, cookies, and bread. It is also used in some breakfast foods.

BRANDEIS, *bran'dise,* LOUIS DEMBITZ (1856-1941). An Associate Justice of the United States Supreme Court for 23 years, Louis Brandeis retired in 1939. According to a law passed in 1937, Supreme Court Justices may retire upon reaching the age of 70, if they have served for ten years. Louis Brandeis was appointed by Woodrow Wilson in 1916, as an outstanding liberal.

Born in Louisville, Ky., Justice Brandeis attended school there and in Germany and graduated from Harvard Law School in 1877. In that year he began his practice in Boston, but lost friends and clients when he consistently opposed certain "special interests." He was responsible for and participated in railroad investigations, and many of his criticisms were later found to be justified. He was widely known for his progressive attitude on social questions. Among the causes he promoted were the health and safety of working women and arbitration of industrial disputes.

BRANDYWINE, BATTLE OF. During the Revolutionary War, an important battle was fought at Chadd's Ford, Penna., near Brandywine Creek, on September 11, 1777. An American force of 11,000, led by Washington, was opposed by 18,000 British under General Howe. A strategic flank movement on the part of Cornwallis forced the Americans to retreat. The American loss was about 1,000 men; the British about 600. As a result of the battle, Howe was able to enter Philadelphia.

BRANGWYN, *brang'win,* FRANK (1867-1935). Seldom is a man so talented as to be a master painter, etcher, and illustrator, as well as a designer of stained glass, furniture, tapestry, metal work, and pottery. Yet Frank Brangwyn, an English artist, was successful in all of these fields.

He was born in Bruges, Belgium, where his father was a manufacturer of ecclesiastical garments. When Brangwyn moved to England with his family, he studied art in the South Kensington school and under William Morris. While much of his work shows the influence of the work of Morris, a greater impression was made on him by his travels in the Orient, as shown by his emphasis on rich color.

He is widely known for his highly decorative murals and his spirited drawing. *Modern Commerce,* in the Royal Exchange, London, and a group for the Panama-Pacific International Exposition at San Francisco (1915) are among his notable murals; a few of his outstanding etchings are *Bridge of Sighs, Notre Dame,* and *Paper Mill.*

BRANT, JOSEPH (THAYENDANEGA) (1742-1807). In a town in Ontario, Canada, there stands the statue of a Mohawk Indian chief. The town is Brantford, and the chief was Joseph Brant, who served ably with the British during the Revolutionary War. After receiving a commission in the army, he attained the rank of colonel. Brant participated in the bloody Battle of Oriskany and led a number of Indian raids in New York, but not the one resulting in the Wyoming massacre.

When Brant was thirteen, he went with his two older brothers to take part in Sir William Johnson's campaign against the French at Lake George. After attending an Indian school at Lebanon, Conn., he became an interpreter to a missionary and acted as an agent under Johnson.

After the Revolution, Brant retired to Canada and lived on an estate given to him by the British government. The town of Brantford was named in his honor.

BRASS. Buttons, door knobs, wire screening, cartridges, screw propellers, tubes—these are but a few of the articles manufactured from brass, one of the most important alloys.

This metal, a combination of copper and zinc, has been known for centuries, having been used to some extent by the Romans. It is usually a bright yellow in color and is therefore employed in the making of cheap jewelry. It is harder than either copper or zinc, and a coat of varnish or lacquer is necessary to keep it from tarnishing. Ordinary brass contains two parts of copper to one of zinc, but reddish brass has double that amount of copper.

In the manufacture of brass, thin pieces of copper are heated with charcoal and zinc carbonate, the molten metal being poured into molds or cast into bars. Sheet brass is made by putting the brass ingots through heavy rollers. The manufacture of brass wire is described in the article WIRE.

WHERE COFFEE IS KING

BRAZIL, THE UNITED STATES OF. World center for the production of coffee and rubber, and home of the earth's greatest river system, the republic of Brazil covers nearly half the continent of South America and, with the exception of a small part in the south, lies entirely in the tropics. It is one of the five largest countries in the world, with an area of 3,275,510 square miles, some of it still unexplored. To the northeast, east, and south, Brazil is bounded by the Atlantic Ocean, while on the northwest and west, it is touched by every other country in South America, with the exception of Chile and Ecuador.

Selvas and Highlands. The long, low basin of the Amazon River extends through more than half the country's area. It is the region of the *selvas,* or great tropical forests, broken only by the rolling waters of the mighty river and occasional *campos,* or *savannas.* Within Brazilian borders, the total length of the river and its huge tributaries—the Madeira, the Negro, and others—is over 19,000 miles, of which 13,000 miles are navigable.

Theodore Roosevelt explored part of the country in 1914 and discovered a tributary of the Madeira River, nearly 1,000 miles long. Although some people doubted that he had really made such a discovery, further investigations proved that the river actually did exist, and the stream has officially been named the Roosevelt River, or Rio Teodoro. Other important rivers are the Parana and the Paraguay in the south, which together drain about one-fourth of the country. On the eastern plateau, the São Francisco is the main stream; falls interrupt navigation in it sixty miles from its mouth.

The most ancient section of Brazil, geologically, is the great plateau country, known as the Brazilian highlands, lying in the south and east. Mountain ranges and river valleys break it into a number of sectors. The most easterly mountain range, which follows the coast for nearly a thousand miles, is the Serra do Mar. Near Rio de Janeiro it is joined by the Serra Central range, which extends northward. Still farther west is the Serra da Montiqueira, containing the highest summit in Brazil, Mount Itatiaya (about 8,900 feet). This range has a northwesterly trend, and separates the sources of the São Francisco and

IN THE CAPITAL OF BRAZIL
Beautiful, and busy, Avenida Rio Branco typifies the elegance of Brazil's first city.

the Parana rivers. The Amazon tributaries and those of the Rio de la Plata are divided by mountains which run westward to the Andes Mountains in Peru.

Jungle and Highland Climate. Although Brazil is in a tropical region, the temperature is quite even in most sections and rarely rises above 95 degrees, even in the Amazon basin. The central Amazon region is surrounded by highlands: the Guiana highlands on the north, the foothills of the Andes on the west, and the Brazilian plateau on the east and south. In these sections, temperature fluctuation is greater than in the lowlands, but large areas have a pleasant climate, with tropical heat moderated by the altitude of the land and the prevailing winds.

Along the coast, the low forested plain has the hot, humid, malarial climate typical of the tropics. It is for this reason that most of the ports are purely commercial in character, providing only such facilities as are necessary to the handling of commodities. Larger residential cities are usually to be found near by, but on the plateau, where living conditions are more pleasant.

All parts of Brazil, except a small area in the northwest, normally get much more rain annually than any part of the United States receives. The very rainy season is from January to June; the dry from June to October. In the Amazon basin, the rainfall usually amounts to more than eighty inches per year and helps to produce the luxuriant tropical forests of the region. In most of the plateau country and highlands, rainfall averages from sixty to eighty inches per year. A few places receive between forty and sixty inches, and one area, that south of the wide mouth of the Amazon, has less than twenty inches. Droughts occur at times in this small section.

As in equatorial Africa, the climate of Brazil has hindered rapid settlement in modern times. The heat and unwholesome humidity of the coast districts, and the floods, forests, and malaria of the Amazon region, have held back the intensive development of this rich country.

RIO DE JANEIRO'S MAGNIFICENT HARBOR

Gray-green mountains against the ultramarine of the sea give this model city of the south a setting of unusual splendor. Rio's landlocked harbor welcomes ships from all the far-flung routes of trade.

RICHES OF BRAZIL

Coffee and rubber—millions of pounds of both—are shipped from Brazil every year. They are the country's chief resources, and Brazil is the world's chief exporter of these commodities. Above, inspecting coffee. Left, tapping a rubber tree for latex.

Agricultural Riches. Three-fourths of the world's coffee comes from Brazil, the state of São Paulo producing half of the world's supply. The northerly state of Para produces the finest quality of rubber known. Phonograph records and electrical insulation are made with a wax found only in Brazil. Cocoa is another leading product; it is raised chiefly in the state of Bahia. Cotton is also important, about seventy per cent of the nation's crop coming from São Paulo. Other important agricultural products are sugar, tobacco, and rice. Coffee, corn, and cotton, however, account for about ninety-five per cent of the cultivated area in Brazil. But Brazil has hardly tapped the surface of its agricultural wealth.

Mineral Resources. Here, again, there is a gap between resources and their use. Brazil has never fully exploited its great mineral wealth. Oil, coal, gold, diamonds, and manganese are found in workable quantities, and small amounts of talc, platinum, copper ore, agate, rock crystal, and mica are mined.

Transportation. A railroad system, connecting Brazil with Paraguay, Argentina and Uruguay, is now in operation, making the total railway mileage of Brazil about 22,275 miles. The Federal government controls about two-thirds of this mileage, the states about 1,600 miles, and the rest is privately owned. Because of the nature of the country, however, the main sources of transportation are the rivers. All coastal and river boats must be Brazilian. For long distance transportation, air lines have been established between Brazil and large cities of Europe, North America, and South America.

Developing Manufactures. In recent years, a rapid growth of the cotton-weaving industry has been taking place in Brazil, and much of the country's supply of cloth is made within its borders. Woolen goods, flannels, felts, rugs, and silk articles are manufactured at Rio de Janeiro. Flour milling is also an industry in this city, as is the making of malt beverages. Although figures for Brazil's total annual imports and exports may seem imposing, they really are relatively small for a nation of its size and population.

People and Cities. The population of Brazil is about 43,550,000—an average of about thirteen people to the square mile. Fewer than half of the people are white. One third are half-breeds; the rest are Indians and Negroes. Portuguese is the national language. (See DEMARCATION, LINE OF.)

Special inducements to colonizers have been offered by the Brazilian government, and great numbers of Russians, Italians, and Germans have settled there.

Rio de Janeiro, with a population of over 1,903,000, is the metropolis and capital city. It is located in the Federal District, on the southeastern coast of the country. Other important cities are São Paulo, Bahia (now called São Salvador), Recife (in Pernambuco), Belém (Pará), Santos, and Manáos.

Education and Religion. Free education exists in Brazil, but the illiteracy rate is high. A national board of education controls all schools. Schools for the deaf, dumb, and blind, a music institute, and an art school are maintained in Rio de Janeiro. Mining, engineering, law, medicine, and pharmacy are taught in separate institutions in various parts of the country. There are also universities, teachers' colleges, and industrial and agricultural schools.

PICTURESQUE PEASANTS
Twentieth-century merchants vie with peddlers such as these in cities of Brazil.

The Roman Catholic religion is foremost, but freedom of worship prevails, and all sects and creeds are welcome.

Government. The adoption of a new Constitution in 1934, after four years of a provisional government, marked the beginning of the Second Republic. The Constitution gave the government wide powers to regulate industry, gradually to nationalize banks and insurance companies, and to monopolize, with compensation, any form of industrial activity thought advisable. Executive power was vested in the President, who was elected for four years; he could not be re-elected.

Legislative power was centered in the Chamber of Deputies. Of the 300 Deputies, 250 were elected by direct suffrage, and 50 were chosen by professional syndicates representing agriculture, industry, commerce and transport, and the liberal professions. Forty-two members, two from each state and two from the Federal District, comprised the Senate. Important legislative powers were expressly reserved to them. They safeguarded the Constitution, co-ordinated the government, and settled disputes between the states.

All citizens, both men and women, who had reached the age of eighteen years, and could read and write, could vote. Beggars, enlisted soldiers, prisoners serving sentence, and those guilty of political activity against the state could not vote. Voting was secret and compulsory. In November, 1937, a Fascist government was established.

History. The first white man to see Brazil, according to some authorities, was Vicente Pinzon, a Portuguese, in 1500. Others believe it was Admiral Pedro Alvarez Cabral. Portugal, Spain, France, and Holland—each dominated Brazil for periods for the next 400 years. When France invaded Portugal in 1807, the royal family went to Brazil, and the seat of the Portuguese government was located there for fifteen years. Afterward, the king's son, Dom Pedro, was made prince regent, but in 1822 the country became independent, Dom Pedro being chosen emperor.

His son, Dom Pedro II, became ruler at the age of fifteen, and under his reign the country advanced rapidly; but because of a desire for a democratic government, a republic called the United States of Brazil was established in 1889. Brazil entered the first World War on the side of the Allies in 1917. An international exposition, celebrating Brazil's centennial of independence, was held in 1922 at Rio de Janeiro. Revolution broke out in 1930 under the leadership of Dr. Getulio Vargas; after its successful course, the new Constitution was set up, and Vargas was elected President. He assumed dictatorial powers in 1937. In 1945, he gave up his office, and Brazil—in its first constitutional election since 1926—elected Gen. Enrico Gaspar Dutra President. Brazil entered World War II on the side of the Allies. See Amazon; Paraná; Rio de Janeiro; São Paulo.

BRAZIL NUT, or PARA NUT. Commonly known as *niggertoe,* the brazil nut grows tightly packed in a hard, brown shell about half a foot in diameter, each large shell containing as many as twenty nuts. The nut itself is shaped like a section of an orange. The brazil nut is not only a food delicacy, but also is a source of lubricating and fuel oil. The tree on which the nuts grow sometimes reaches a height of 150 feet. It has green leaves and cream-colored flowers, and is found in abundance along the Amazon and Orinoco rivers.

BRAZILIAN "UP-COUNTRY" OXCART

FOOD *for* HUMANITY

BREAD, *bred*. No more fascinating study can be imagined than that of the bread food habits of the peoples of the earth. To the Mexican family eating tortillas of corn, to the Norwegian feasting on "flat bread" of barley, to the Japanese with their cakes of rice and wheat, to the Americans with their crisp, white loaves, bread is in truth the "staff of life." It is baked in every climate, from the equator to the frigid regions of the north and south, and is eaten in any number of forms. It may have the shape of the common white or rye loaf; or be a biscuit, roll, or cracker, but it is still bread, a valuable and healthful food. So important a part does it play in the life of nations that people have started revolutions because they had no bread.

Loaves and Cakes. Bread, no matter what form it takes, is a baked mixture of liquid (water or milk, or milk and water), and the flour of a cereal, usually wheat, rye, or corn. In the United States, Canada, Great Britain, and France, where wheat is either grown or imported in large quantities, white bread is the most common. It is lighter than other breads, has a pleasing taste, and is easily digested. Rye bread also is popular, as well as breads made of bran and whole wheat.

In many countries of Europe, black bread is made from oats or rye, and this dark and heavy bread is still popular among foreign-born people in America. In the Orient, where rice is an important crop, the flour of this cereal grain is used for bread. Roots of edible plants are ground into a flour in many tropical countries. There are still other varieties, such as bread from soybean flour, the corn pone of the Southern United States, made from corn meal, and the tortilla of Mexico and Central America, also made from corn. Ship's biscuit, or hardtack, is a bread that will keep indefinitely.

Some form of bread has been baked and eaten for centuries. The ancient Egyptians probably were the first to bake leavened bread, and they passed on their formula to the Jews and the Phoenicians. In Greece and Rome there were public bakeries where bread could be purchased; later, in the Middle Ages, each manor had a large oven where bread for many of the serfs was baked.

Until modern times, however, most bread has been baked in the home. In the pioneer days of the United States, practically all bread was baked by housewives, but as each region became settled, the custom of buying bread from large bakeries became more widespread. Today, there is little bread baked at home; even in the rural districts, many housewives buy bread at stores rather than bake it themselves. As a result, the growth of the baking industry has been rapid, and today it ranks among the leading food-processing industries.

All bread, whether black or white, baked in an electric oven, or on a rock, may be divided into two divisions, *leavened* and *unleavened*. The bread known as unleavened is baked without any yeast or baking soda to make it rise. This is the most primitive type of bread, and it is usually small, tough, flat, and gritty. It is the type of bread made by the Israelites when they were wandering in the wilderness. Leavened bread is a mixture that has been fermented, or "raised." It is the type of bread we find in our grocery stores and bakery shops, and the kind that is usually made at home.

There are several different methods of "raising" the dough for bread. The most common method is by adding yeast or baking soda to the dough. Another type, called *salt-rising* bread, is made from a sour batter of corn meal and milk. Then there is the *aerated* bread, made of water charged with carbon dioxide; and *gluten* bread, in which the starch has been removed from flour.

How Bread Is Made. The first step in making bread is to mix the dough. In making bread by either the long or the short process, that is, the sponge or straight-dough process, the method of mixing is the same up to the point of adding the flour. First the milk is heated to the scalding point. Next sugar, salt, and fat are added, after which the mixture is allowed to cool until it becomes lukewarm. Then the yeast is added. After this, the flour is added according to one of the following methods.

In the *sponge* method, a sufficient amount of flour is added to make a batter. This mixture is well beaten and then allowed to stand in a warm place until it is full of bubbles. This is sometimes called "setting the sponge" and is the method commonly used when dried yeast is employed.

When this sponge is light, the rest of the flour is added.

In the *straight-dough* method, all the flour is added in the beginning. In order, however, to have the materials well mixed, about half of the flour is put in and this batter beaten well before the remaining flour is added.

The bread from either method is now ready for kneading. The purpose of kneading is to mix the materials thoroughly and to allow air to get into the dough. Air is necessary for the growth of the yeast plant.

The dough is kneaded either by hand or by machine until it is elastic to the touch. It is then allowed to rise. The period of rising is called *fermentation,* because during this time the yeast is acting upon the sugar, producing from it alcohol and carbon dioxide. In order that fermentation may take place successfully, it is important to let the bread rise in a warm place. The temperature of the dough should be from 80° to 87° F. This is warmer than the ordinary room temperature, and hence a special place, such as one near a stove or in the sun, should be used.

During the first rising the dough should a little more than double its bulk.

The dough is kneaded again for a few moments, shaped into loaves, and placed in pans to rise again. The pan should be not more than half full, but when the dough has risen it should have doubled its bulk. This rising in the pan is spoken of as "proofing."

The short process of bread making (straight dough) takes from six to eight hours. The long process (sponge) takes from twelve to sixteen hours.

After the dough is "proofed," it is baked in an oven. During the baking, the alcohol formed during fermentation is driven off. The dough will continue to rise during the first five minutes in the oven. At the end of the first fifteen minutes, it should begin to brown. A pound loaf of bread requires about fifty minutes for baking. If a shiny crust is desired, the top of the loaf should be rubbed with fat about five minutes be-

DIFFERENT FROM MOTHER'S DAY

In the old days, housewives spent hours making just a few loaves of bread. Today, the clean, sanitary commercial bakery turns out thousands of loaves every day. The dough-mixing machine (above) can mix dough for 1,600 one-pound loaves at one batch. The dough is allowed to rise after mixing and then is baked in the oven (below), which can turn out 4,200 fragrant, nut-brown loaves in an hour. Some of the loaves are machine-sliced.

fore removal from the oven. After baking, bread should be placed where air can circulate around it until it cools.

The principle of baking bread is the same in a large commercial bakery as it is in the home. The one great difference, of course, is the fact that in a large bakery the entire process is automatic, so that the materials need never be touched by hand. In a bakery, the ovens are always kept at an even temperature, and steam is used to keep the loaves from forming a crust too fast. When the loaves are removed, they are allowed to cool; then they are sent to the wrapping machine and finally to the delivery room. Sometimes they are sliced automatically before being wrapped.

A Source of Energy. Bread is primarily an energy food. A loaf of white bread contains a large percentage of carbohydrates (starches), and also proteins, minerals, and vitamins. Approximately thirty per cent of an ordinary loaf is composed of water. Although bread is a healthful food and builds energy, it should be eaten with other foods to give best results. It is literally true that "Man shall not live by bread alone," as the Bible states.

BREAD'FRUIT. To the inhabitants of tropical Pacific islands, the breadfruit tree has an importance equal to that which the wheat field has for us. As bread constitutes a most important item in our diet, so breadfruit is of value to these islanders.

The tree grows to a height of about forty feet; its limbs, which begin to appear about halfway up the tree, bear a glossy, dark green leaf more than a foot long. Hanging singly or in clusters of two or three, the fruit itself is attached to the limb by a short, thick stem. The breadfruit is somewhat larger than a coconut. The fruit is pale green in color, the surface marked with irregular six-sided depressions; inside is a white, pulpy substance which, when ripe, becomes yellow and very juicy.

The natives gather the unripe fruit and usually prepare it for eating immediately. Sometimes, however, the entire breadfruit is baked in holes in the ground; if not thus preserved by baking, the pulpy breadlike inside of the fruit is mixed with coconut milk and eaten as a pudding.

The inner bark of the tree can be made into a rough cloth. The wood is used sometimes in building boats and furniture.

The breadfruit tree has been grown in Southern Florida. Because of the perishable nature of the fruit, however, there is no market for it in the North.

BREAK'WATER. In most coastal cities, ships and boats could not dock if there were no calm water awaiting them in harbors protected by breakwaters. A breakwater is a barrier built to keep high waves and rough seas from entering a harbor.

The usual construction of a breakwater is a line of rocks reaching from the floor of the sea or lake to the surface of the water or a little above; on this a superstructure of cement or wood reinforced by piles is erected to a height of five to ten feet above the water line.

Its location with respect to the shore is determined by the direction of storms or the contour of the coast. Often it extends from the shore for hundreds of feet, and turns at a right angle for a needed distance; or, two structures outward from the shore may converge, with their points 200 or 300 feet apart. Many consist only of long stretches parallel to the shore. A breakwater may serve as a pier, also, if wide enough for the purpose and joined to the mainland.

A detail map shows that New York, Boston, and San Francisco, on deeply indented shores, need no breakwaters; Chicago and Buffalo, and other cities with straight coast lines, require them. There is a great breakwater before the entrance to Delaware Bay; another important one faces Plymouth, England.

BREATHING. Breathing, or the passage of air into and out of the body, is the most mechanical and necessary act of all members of the animal kingdom. A human being can exist for long periods of time without food and for several days without water; but if he is unable to breathe, death occurs in a matter of minutes. When a person breathes in (*inspiration*), air enters the lungs and oxygen is taken into blood vessels of the air cells, traveling to the heart. Waste matter, called carbon dioxide, is removed, leaving the body when the person breathes out (*expiration*). Although carbon dioxide is poisonous to all animals, plants thrive on it, absorbing quantities of it and turning it into energy.

The average adult takes from sixteen to twenty breaths a minute, but exercise or physical disorder will increase the rate of breathing. In a single breath, a total of about thirty cubic inches (one pint) of air is inspired and exhaled. The act is accomplished by means of the ribs and the diaphragm, a muscle which separates the chest from the abdomen.

The lowest forms of animals breathe through their entire surface. Fish take in water through gills, absorb the oxygen, and eliminate the rest. All higher forms of animals breathe through the nostrils, pharynx, larynx, windpipe (trachea), and the bronchi, leading to the lungs. These organs make up the *respiratory tract*.

BRECK'INRIDGE, JOHN CABELL (1821-1875). Although John Cabell Breckinridge was a Vice-President of the United States, a Senator from the state of Kentucky, and a Confederate leader in the Civil War, he is chiefly remembered as one of the opponents of Abraham Lincoln in the Presidential election of 1860.

Breckinridge was born near Lexington, Ky., and was educated at Centre College. After studying law at Transylvania College, he began to practice in Frankfort in 1840, but a year later moved to Burlington, Iowa. He served in the Mexican War as major of volunteers, and was subsequently elected to the legislature of Kentucky. In 1851 he was chosen to represent his district in Congress, and in 1856 was elected Vice-President with James Buchanan, on the Democratic ticket.

Although he was a pro-slavery man, Breckinridge ruled over the Senate fairly. In the critical year of 1860, he was nominated for the Presidency by the Southern Democrats, who were opposed to Stephen A. Douglas as their party's candidate. Breckinridge received all the electoral votes of the South, except those of Kentucky, Tennessee, Virginia, and Missouri. While presiding over the Senate as Vice-President, it fell to him to announce the election of his opponent, Abraham Lincoln. Following his defeat, he succeeded John J. Crittenden as Senator from Kentucky, but left the Senate in December, 1861, because he had joined the Confederate forces.

Breckinridge served in the Southern army, attaining the rank of major general, and later was made Secretary of State of the Confederacy. After the war he escaped to Europe by way of Cuba, returning to Lexington in 1869. He practiced law in that city until his death.

BREED'ING. Even the youngest reader realizes that the best types of plants and animals are far better than those of the past. Man has brought this about by means of selective breeding—the improving or modifying of various kinds of plants and animals. By applying the principles of animal breeding, he has secured faster race horses, sheep that produce thicker wool, and cows that give richer milk. Plant breeding likewise results in specimens of greater size, improved flavor, or other desired quality.

Selection is basic in the process. For instance, if a superior wool-bearing sheep is desired, a male and female sheep with the heaviest coats of wool are taken from the original stock and paired. From their offspring, the best wool-producers are paired, and the same is done with each succeeding generation. Sometimes, it is many generations before the proper result is obtained. In plants, breeding is accomplished by cross fertilization. Luther Burbank was especially successful in crossing plants to secure improved varieties.

Animal breeding is made possible by the fact that every individual animal varies in some measure from every other, and that characters are transmitted to offspring according to certain known laws. The development of an animal is second only to its heredity in determining its value. The best specimens represent a combination of good ancestry and good types of individuals.

BREVET, *bre vet'*. See RANK.

BRE'VIARY. In the Roman Catholic Church, the regular daily religious services are contained in a book called the breviary, a name meaning *abridgment* or *summary*. It does not contain the services connected with the observance of the Eucharist. In the breviary are the prayers read or sung during mass, and those used for special services, such as funerals, weddings, and baptisms.

BREW'ING. For centuries, men have brewed beer, ale, stout, and porter. They have improved their methods and have adopted individual practices until today the manufacture of these malted liquors is regarded as a highly skilled trade. Brewmasters guard their formulas jealously so that no two brands of beer ever taste exactly alike. Their general procedure is similar, however, the variations being made only in certain details.

Generally in brewing, a cereal grain, usually barley, is placed in large tanks and is allowed to germinate, or to sprout tiny rootlets, in cold water. Sometimes corn, wheat, rice, or flaked oats are used, but these grains do not germinate so rapidly as barley. When the grain has sprouted to the proper extent, it is dried in a kiln at a temperature ranging from 150° to more than 200° Fahrenheit. Then the grain, now called *malt,* is crushed between rollers and is mixed with warm water to form a *mash.* After being boiled, the mash is transferred to tubs, and stands from thirty to fifty minutes while it changes from starch to sugar.

Having now become *wort,* the mixture is allowed to settle. Then the liquid is put into copper vessels and is boiled with hops, the proportion being three pounds of hops to three bushels of wort. After the liquid cools, one pound of yeast is added to every twenty gallons of wort for fermentation. In this state, the yeast causes another chemical change, transforming the substance from sugar to alcohol and carbon dioxide. The carbon dioxide collects in bubbles, providing the white collar of foam which is characteristic of beer.

The wort has now become beer, and, after it has been allowed to settle, the solid particles are removed and the liquor is put into casks. It is left to ripen for at least two months, after which it is poured into kegs, bottles, or cans.

Ale differs from beer in that it usually contains more alcohol. Originally, it was distinguished by having no hops. Porter is dark brown in color, and stout has more solids.

Brewing was a thriving industry in the United States before World War I, but it fell off during the emergency when grains were needed for the soldiers. It was materially reduced when the Eighteenth Amendment prohibited the sale of intoxicating liquors, although many firms manufactured "near beer," which had only a small percentage of alcohol. Beginning in 1933, when the amendment was repealed, the industry again assumed large proportions.

BREW'STER, WILLIAM (about 1566-1644). This great Pilgrim leader was born at Scrooby, England. It was probably in 1602 that a group of neighbors began the practice of meeting in his house for worship—a practice that was then against the law. They were dissatisfied with the Established Church and in 1606 formed a Separatist Church. Two years later, Brewster and these Separatists fled to Holland, where they could enjoy religious freedom.

During their exile William Brewster was one of the moving spirits in planning the journey to America. Having helped to get a land patent from the Virginia Company, he became one of the leaders of the group which sailed on the *Mayflower* in 1620. After the founding of Plymouth Colony, he was made a ruling elder and was, for a number of years, the only preacher and religious leader of the Pilgrims. He did not, however, administer the sacraments.

Man-made STONE

BRICK AND BRICKLAYING. Centuries ago, the Persian and Assyrians used brick for the construction of their temples and palaces. Today brick is employed extensively as a building material, being changed only slightly from the artificial stone required in ancient times. Then, as now, brick was made by molding clay into blocks and baking or burning it until it was as hard as stone. Baked bricks have been found in the ruins of Babylonia, where wood and stone were scarce; and even in the remains of buildings left by ancient Greeks and Egyptians, who had plenty of stone.

The Roman ruins show that brickmaking was a well-known art before the time of the Caesars. The Byzantines were the first to turn building brick to decorative account, instead of covering it with a surface material. They began an art with brick which carried on through Romanesque architecture into some of the finest medieval buildings.

In America, the art of brickmaking was an important industry of the colonists in the East, and was introduced by the early Spanish settlers as well. The adobe houses found in Southwestern United States and Mexico are a survival of this industry. Adobe brick of today is made in the same way that prehistoric people made it, as shown by 5,000-year-old samples from the Tigris-Euphrates Valley. This brick, most primitive of all types, was not burned but dried in the sun (see Adobe).

Manufacture. Modern bricks are made from clays rich in silicate of alumina, in combination with other substances, such as iron, potash, magnesia, soda, and lime, which influence the character and quality of the product. The presence of iron gives the red or yellow color and also produces hardness and strength when burned. The other substances have varying effects, depending upon the combination and amount present.

A large amount of iron produces a bright-red color, while only a small amount, eight to ten per cent, produces a dark blue. The presence of a small amount of manganese with the iron darkens the color. The presence of a small amount of iron and lime produces a cream color; with an increase of the lime a brown is produced, and with an increase of the iron, a red. Clays containing magnesia with iron make yellow brick, and clays containing alkali

BRICK BEGIN IN THE CLAY PIT. RAW MATERIAL IS MINED LIKE THIS

produce bluish-green brick, when burned at a high temperature.

The clay used in brickmaking, after it has been mixed and the stones and other impurities have been removed, is ground and molded as a soft mud, as a stiff mud, or by the dry-clay process. After being molded, the clay blocks are laid in racks and allowed to dry before being fired.

Classification of Brick. Bricks are classified according to the method of molding. *Pressed* bricks are made by the dry-clay process. *Repressed* bricks are made from soft mud, partially dried, and then pressed under heavy pressure. *Sanded* bricks are molded from soft mud with sand sprinkled in the forms.

Bricks may also be classified as to position in the kiln when burned. The *arch* bricks are the hard, dark, thoroughly burned brick in the arch of the kiln, which come in contact with the fire. The *hard* bricks are hard, deep-colored, choice brick from the inside of the pile in the kiln. The *soft* bricks are from the outside of the pile in the kiln and are light-colored, soft, and absorbent. They are used for backups (behind the surface layer) or where not exposed to freezing.

Bricks may also be classified as to form. *Face* bricks are used for exposed walls and are either *smooth, rough-texture, enameled* or *pressed. Common* bricks are the general run of brick used in chimneys, foundations and piers.

Size of Brick. Bricks of standard size are, in America, about eight by four by two and one-fourth inches, with some variations. Bricks weigh from six to eight pounds each, and from 125 to 150 pounds per cubic foot when built in masonry.

Bricklaying. One of the first principles in bricklaying is to make sure that the bricks in a layer cover the joints of the layer below. These joints are called *bonds* and to cover each joint is called *breaking bond*.

There are several methods of laying bricks. One of the most common is to lay the bricks lengthwise, with each brick of a layer, called a *course,* covering the bond of the course underneath. Another method is to lay one course of bricks crosswise, and alternate with lengthwise layers. Still another method is to alternate the course with lengthwise and crosswise bricks.

When the brick is laid lengthwise, it is called a *stretcher,* and when laid transversely, it is known as a *header.* The mortar used is composed of lime and sand and water, and should be placed between each bond and over each course.

Courtesy Brick and Clay Record

MODERN VERSION OF THE AGE-OLD CRAFT OF BRICKMAKING

From the clay of the earth to neat, trim brick. (1) Grinding dry clay. (2) Storage bins for the powdered raw material. (3) Giant stamping machine for pressing refractory brick shapes. (4) The jaws of a huge fire-brick press in close-up. With a pressure of 2,000 pounds per square inch, this machine fashions dense, tough bricks, which are then sent along to the kiln.

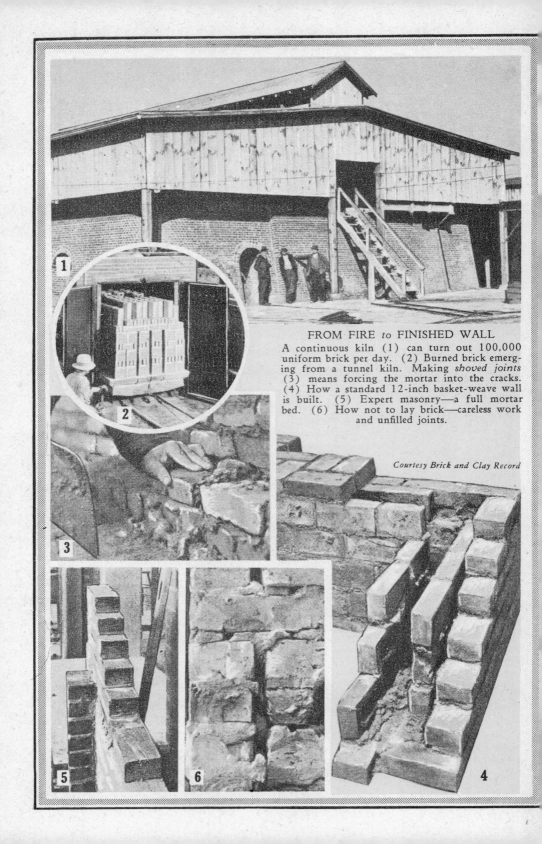

FROM FIRE to FINISHED WALL

A continuous kiln (1) can turn out 100,000 uniform brick per day. (2) Burned brick emerging from a tunnel kiln. Making *shoved joints* (3) means forcing the mortar into the cracks. (4) How a standard 12-inch basket-weave wall is built. (5) Expert masonry—a full mortar bed. (6) How not to lay brick—careless work and unfilled joints.

Courtesy Brick and Clay Record

PATHWAYS
in the AIR

BRIDGE. Traffic in many of our cities and towns would be at a standstill and a cross-country trip by motor or train would be impossible were it not for engineering structures known as bridges. Bridges are built over stretches of low land, over chasms and rivers, across lakes, and over networks of highways and railroads. To build bridges of sufficient strength to support heavy railroad trains, or streams of automobiles, buses, and trucks, requires great engineering skill.

Not only must the engineer battle the currents and tides of water, the blasts of the wind, and other forces of Nature, but he must figure to a minute degree the stresses and strains of the material with which he is working, so that the finished structure will be safe and permanent.

The Bridge in the Life of Man. Bridges have played an important part in history. In wartime they are necessary in transport-ing troops to and from battlefields. The Civil War in the United States might have ended sooner had there been substantial bridges across the Chickahominy River when McClellan's army advanced toward Richmond in 1862. Because there was none adequate to permit the transport of troops, the city was saved and the Confederates were able to drive back the Union army.

More important is the part bridges play in everyday life, in commerce and trade. Bridges make possible swift travel between cities, states, and countries. New York City's millions, on opposite sides of the East and Harlem rivers, are able to journey back and forth between Brooklyn, Manhattan, and the Bronx swiftly and easily by means of bridges. In California the great San Francisco-Oakland Bay Bridge, eight and one-fourth miles long, stretches across the bay to connect San Francisco and Oakland.

THE CHARM OF THE COVERED BRIDGE

Covered bridges preserve the quaintness of other days in many countries. Left, an old Sumatran bridge, with lashed railings and thatched roof. The old covered bridge (above) makes a truly American picture of rustic beauty. Covered bridges were once typical of New England.

From Logs and Stones to the Steel Arch. The earliest bridges were no doubt fallen logs and stepping stones on which primitive people crossed streams. The earliest man-made bridges were constructed of grapevines, trees, and timbers; but the first great bridge builders were the Romans. They principally built one kind of bridge, the arch bridge. Today there are many other kinds—the truss, tubular, cantilever, and suspension. Most bridges are built of steel or concrete or both, but there are still a few wooden ones built over small streams.

In ancient days the Romans developed the arch and found that it could be used to support the weight of the bridge. One of the oldest and best examples of the Roman period is the bridge over the Nera River at Narni, Italy, built by Augustus. However, its longest span, 142 feet, is small compared with the sweeping 1,675-foot span of the Kill van Kull Bridge, one of the largest arch bridges in the world, which connects Bayonne, N. J., and Staten Island, N. Y. (The word *span* refers to the length of the arch between two supports.)

Arch bridges such as the Cabin John Bridge at Washington, D. C., or the granite Arlington Memorial Bridge, may be built of masonry. The use of stone and brick is decreasing, however, and concrete and steel are now the most common materials. Beautiful and graceful concrete arch bridges are the Cappelen Memorial Bridge at Minneapolis, Minn., and the Hampden County Memorial Bridge at Springfield, Mass.

Fine steel arch bridges have been built throughout the world. One of these is the famous Eads Bridge crossing the Mississippi River at Saint Louis. On the lower

MASTERPIECES OF ENGINEERING

Combining beauty with usefulness, the bridge is one of the outstanding achievements of engineering. Some bridges are of the swinging type (upper left) or gracefully high-arched, as in China (upper right). Below, arched bridges adorn old towns of Saxony and Provence.

deck are railroad tracks; on the top deck is a driveway for automobiles. The bridge has three spans, one of 520 feet and two slightly shorter. Built of steel with stone piers, the arches are below the platform, differing from the Kill van Kull and Hell Gate (New York) bridges, which have their arches above the platform. Another huge steel arch bridge is the Sydney Bridge in Sydney Harbor, Australia. It has a span of 1,650 feet.

Other Types of Bridges. When wide rivers must be crossed and heavy weights carried, such as railroad trains, *truss* bridges are often built. These bridges require support at intervals for each section. The supports are piers sunk into the river; the structures between, over which traffic passes, are trusses. The New York Triborough Bridge combines suspension, cantilever, and truss construction. The truss spans are at Bronx Kills. At Metropolis,

Courtesy Popular Mechanics

GRACE OF STEEL AND STONE
Light, strong cables hold the roadway of the George Washington suspension bridge high in the air. Right, stone arches span a stream of Southern France.

Ill., a fine truss bridge used by the Burlington Railroad crosses the Ohio River.

Although the *cantilever* bridge resembles the truss bridge in appearance, it is constructed on a different principle. From piers set out from either shore of a river, arms are constructed, one reaching toward the shore and the other over the water. The arms on each pier are perfectly balanced, the river arms being joined in the center by a single truss. These bridges may have a span up to 3,000 feet, but stresses and strains and the effect of the wind are ex-

ceedingly important considerations in their construction. The bridge crossing the Saint Lawrence River at Quebec is one of the longest cantilever bridges in the world, reaching 1,800 feet from pier to pier. Another large cantilever is the bridge spanning the Firth of Forth, Scotland; each of two spans measures 1,710 feet.

Surpassed for grace only by the arch is the lacy and awe-inspiring *suspension* bridge. This type of bridge consists of a platform suspended from cables reaching from two large towers. The cables are anchored behind the tower, and vertical strands hold the platform to the cables.

The single span of the suspension bridge can reach farther than can any other type, which explains its extensive use over wide bodies of water. Navigators also favor the suspension bridge because it has only two piers, lessening the danger to boats, and because it is high enough to allow ships to pass under it safely.

Brooklyn Bridge, completed in 1883, was long the most famous suspension bridge in the world. It crosses the East River in New York City, connecting Manhattan and Brooklyn with a span of 1,595 feet. Noted for its beauty is the long Golden Gate Bridge, completed in 1937 at a cost of $35,000,000. It stretches across the celebrated Golden Gate from San Francisco to

ALLIES OF COMMERCE

Modern bridges let traffic flow two ways—along rivers and valleys, and over them. The bridge (left) is a steel adaptation of the old stone-arch type, while the bascule bridge (right) is a counter-weighted lift span for narrow streams.

Sausalito, shortening the traveling time to the northern counties of California, and providing the final link in the motor highway from San Diego to Canada. It has a clear span of 4,200 feet and a clearance of more than 200 feet above the water. The huge towers supporting the cables soar 740 feet into the air.

Other great suspension bridges are George Washington Memorial Bridge, extending 3,500 feet across the Hudson River between New York City and Fort Lee, N. J.; the Delaware River Bridge, connecting Philadelphia and Camden, N. J., 1,750 feet; the Ambassador Bridge, between Detroit and Windsor, Ont., 1,850 feet; and the Bear Mountain Bridge, across the Hudson near Peekskill, 1,632 feet. The greatest suspension bridge of all is the San Francisco-Oakland Bay Bridge already mentioned.

Movable Bridges. One type of bridge that does not have fixed supports is the *pontoon*. It is usually a temporary structure built by an army wishing to cross a river. The platform rests on anchored boats or floats. The city of Coblenz, Germany, however, had a permanent pontoon bridge across the Rhine River. When a ship approached, a section of the bridge was moved by a boat upon which it rested. After the vessel had passed, the section of bridge was replaced.

Low bridges across navigable rivers sometimes are so built as to revolve in the center of the stream. They swing around in a quarter circle, allowing a boat to pass

Courtesy Thos. Cook & Sons, Ltd.

FAMOUS BRIDGES OF THE BRITISH ISLES

The Tower Bridge across the Thames is one of London's more modern landmarks. It has a permanent passageway for pedestrians, and a carriageway which is raised for ships. Firth of Forth Bridge, west of Edinburgh, Scotland, is a noted example of steel cantilever design.

through. These are known as *swing* bridges. Often a stream is too narrow to permit use of a swing bridge because it would not leave room for a vessel to pass. A bridge which is mechanically raised from one end, and known as a *bascule,* is then used. If the space to be bridged is too long, the span is in two sections. Reaching out from piers built on either shore are the two counter-balanced arms, which meet in a perfect juncture. This is also known as a *jackknife* bridge.

Bascules are common in cities like Chicago, where the river is so narrow that a pier in the middle of the stream would be a handicap to navigation. The stately Tower Bridge of London has a bascule span. A familiar bridge throughout the world is the *vertical lift* bridge. It resembles a truss bridge when it is closed, but its main span can be raised straight up by the use of counterweights.

Drawbridges are usually associated with moats and medieval castles, but are still found on canals and narrow streams. They are opened by the pull of cables from a tower on one or both sides. Counterweights are used, as in vertical lift bridges.

Viaducts. Nearly all concrete highway bridges, other than those which cross streams, are also called viaducts. They are becoming increasingly common in our modern highway system. They carry traffic over railroad tracks, other highways, and over long stretches of low land.

Unusual Bridges of the World. Quaint, steep, arch bridges are common in Japan; some of them are equipped with steps to permit a person to ascend the arch. In primitive countries we still find rope and grass bridges which swing across rivers and ravines. These bridges are constructed on the same principle as are our suspension bridges. One of the most unusual of all bridges is the Rialto in Venice, Italy, where the platform is covered with houses and shops. The Ponte Vecchio in Florence also is like this, as are numerous bridges in India.

In the United States, particularly in New England, may still be seen the old, wood-covered bridges which were built long ago for horses and carriages. Many of these bridges are still in use; others are preserved as historical landmarks. See CONCRETE; ENGINEERING; VIADUCT.

ON CANADA'S WESTERN SHORE

Vancouver, Canada's Pacific port and largest city of British Columbia, is a metropolis of stately beauty and commercial center of a great fishing and logging province.

BRIT'ISH COLUM'BIA. On the western coast of Canada lies the province of British Columbia, a land of mountains and valleys, lakes and rivers. Larger in area than the three states of California, Washington, and Oregon combined. it is 740 miles long and 620 miles at its widest point. But the population of about 800,000 is less than one-tenth the number living in these states.

A Marine and Mountain Empire. British Columbia's shore, like that of Norway, has hundreds of narrow inlets, giving the province a coast line of nearly 7,000 miles and providing excellent navigation and fishing facilities. The province, third largest in Canada, stretches from the northern boundary of the United States to the Yukon Territory and the District of Mackenzie, and from Alberta on the east to the Pacific Ocean.

The Rocky Mountains run diagonally, southeast to northwest, through the length of the province, roughly parallel to the Coast Range near the sea. Between them are lesser ranges such as the Gold and Selkirk, on a central plateau. The two large ranges are the principal land feature of the province and have a marked influence on climate and drainage. The Columbia, Fraser, and Skeena rivers drain into the Pacific Ocean, and the Peace and Laird rivers flow eventually into the Arctic Ocean and Hudson Bay.

Between the two ranges, in the valleys of the plateau, are a multitude of beautiful, clear lakes. Along the coast are numerous islands, the most important of which are Vancouver and the Queen Charlotte group. Both have fine harbors and a mild climate. Mildness of temperature is characteristic of the western portion of the province, for

WOODLAND AND MOUNTAIN GRANDEUR
British Columbia is noted for its scenic beauty. Breath-taking snow-capped peaks, necklaced
with sparkling glaciers, sweep skyward over forests thick with noble Douglas firs. Each year,
tourists flock to the province to enjoy its magnificent outdoors.

the coast region is warmed by moist winds from the Japan Current. At Vancouver the winter temperature ranges between 37° and 60°; but east of the mountains, where the prevailing westerlies, robbed of moisture by the cold peaks of the Coast Range, blow high and dry, the seasons are dry and run to extremes of temperature: —30° to 100°. Snows remain on the mountains all year, furnishing a constant source for the streams arising in the region.

Wealth from Soil and Sea. British Columbia has very valuable mineral deposits. Gold, silver, lead, zinc, copper, and coal are mined in commercial quantities. In the province are vast forests, containing more than half the standing commercial timber of Canada. The Douglas fir is the most noted tree, many specimens growing to more than 300 feet in height. Fir, spruce,

hemlock, and cedar account for a large part of a huge industry based on timber and forest products.

In fishing, British Columbia leads all other Canadian provinces, the principal catch being salmon, halibut, herring, sole, and cod. The inland streams and lakes abound in fresh-water game fish. In various sections of the province there are deer, mountain goats, bighorn sheep, caribou, moose, bears, and other animals, providing a hunter's paradise.

Agriculture ranks with lumbering, mining, and fishing as an important industry in British Columbia. The soil of the valleys and plains is fertile, and several fruits, wheat, and other cereal grains are grown in abundance. The raising of livestock and dairy and poultry farming also contribute to the value of British Columbia's products.

CLIMBING THE "ROOF" OF CANADA

Mountain climbers find thrills and beauty among the rugged summits of the British Columbia Rockies. The view from one of the province's many peaks is an awe-inspiring sight.

Transportation. When British Columbia was first settled, water routes and rude trails were the chief means of communication. There were no railroads; so, when invited by the Dominion of Canada to become a province, in 1871, British Columbia accepted with the condition that the government would construct a railroad linking it to the eastern provinces. Accordingly, the Canadian Pacific Railroad was projected, but it did not reach Vancouver until 1885. Later, the Grand Trunk Pacific and Canadian Northern built roads to the coast. The Crow's Nest, Kicking, and Yellowhead passes through the mountains were used by the railroads.

From Wilderness to World Market. Captain James Cook, on one of his many voyages, explored the western coast of North America in 1778, and drew attention to the land which became known as British Columbia. Four years earlier, however, the Spanish viceroy of Mexico had sent an expedition there, and during the ensuing years, the area was claimed by both countries. In 1793 the controversy was settled in favor of England, by arbitration.

The valuable fur trade attracted the first settlers, and many pioneers, among them Captain George Vancouver, Sir Alexander Mackenzie, David Thompson, and Simon Fraser, explored the country. In 1818 the United States and Great Britain agreed to settle the country jointly, but when the Hudson's Bay Company occupied the island of Vancouver, the United States lost its claim, in 1846, to the land north of the 49th parallel, and the British kept Vancouver Island. The gold rush of 1858 brought more settlers to these northwest wilds, and the territory of the present province was gradually consolidated.

The province joined the Dominion of Canada in 1871, and with the completion of the transcontinental railroad, Vancouver became the third largest city in Canada. Some of the other large cities in the province are Victoria, the capital; New Westminster, North Vancouver, Prince Rupert, and Nelson. British Columbia's provincial government is administered by a lieutenant-governor, appointed and paid by the Dominion, and a legislative assembly of thirty-eight members, elected by the voters. The province is represented in the Dominion Senate by six members, and in the House of Commons by fourteen.

See the following titles for additional information:

Cascade Range	Rocky Mountains
Columbia River	Vancouver
Hudson's Bay Company	Vancouver Island
	Victoria

BRITISH COMMONWEALTH OF NATIONS.

The trapper in the wilds of Northern Canada and the sheep herdsmen of Central Australia are members of one great family called the British Commonwealth of Nations. Both recognize as their monarch the British king in faraway London. Originally, Canada, Newfoundland, Australia, the Union of South Africa, New Zealand, the Irish Free State, and the United Kingdom of Great Britain and Northern Ireland were members of this family. In 1933 the new status of Newfoundland was temporarily revoked. In 1937 the Irish Free State became the independent state of Eire, but it is still associated with the Commonwealth.

Each member of the British Commonwealth governs itself through a home Parliament, raises its own taxes, and controls local and foreign affairs. All are on an equal footing with one another and with the Mother Country.

In 1926 representatives from this great family of nations gathered in London and agreed that each member nation should be equal and free. In 1931 the Statute of Westminster put this agreement into effect. Previously, each dominion had elected its own leaders and had made its own laws but was still subject to the will of the British Parliament. Today, in each member nation, there is a British Governor-General who represents the Crown, but he cannot interfere in the governing of the dominion. The governors are simply the links between the family of nations and London.

The term British Commonwealth of Nations is often used to mean the same as British Empire. Actually, however, there are three divisions of the empire—the British Commonwealth of Nations, the Indian Empire, and the British Colonial Empire. See BRITISH EMPIRE.

BRITISH EMPIRE. No realm in history has ever matched the British Empire in size or population. Its lands and influence encircle the globe. In this far-flung empire of more than 450,000,000 persons, embracing almost one-fourth of the world's land surface, are people of every race, color, and degree of civilization. It includes black savages in Africa and white Nordics in England; Aborigines in Australia and fur-clad Eskimos in Northern Canada; Polynesians of the Pacific and Boers of South Africa. The British Empire is a league of nations and a league of races by itself.

The empire as we know it today is not very old. In 1714, when George I came to the throne, it consisted only of the British Isles, the American colonies, Newfoundland, Labrador, Nova Scotia, a strip surrounding Hudson Bay, and a few scattered posts in Asia. When Queen Victoria ascended the throne, in 1837, the American colonies had been lost, but the empire had gained all Canada, British Guiana, India, most of Australia, and a patch of land at the southern tip of Africa, as well as numerous islands and settlements all over the world. One hundred years later, the map of the world showed the additions of huge territories in Africa and New Zealand and more islands and settlements in all parts of the eastern and western hemispheres.

How to govern all these strange countries and various people has been one of the most perplexing questions confronting the British government. As a result, numerous forms of administration have developed. They fall into seven classifications.

First is the United Kingdom, consisting of England, Scotland, Wales, and Northern Ireland, administered by Parliament with the capital at London. Second are the self-governing dominions comprising the British Commonwealth of Nations. The third group consists of Malta and Rhodesia, which are self-governing colonies but under control of the British Parliament. Crown colonies, such as the African colonies of Gambia and the Gold Coast, are those possessions directly controlled by the government; they are the fourth group.

The fifth category is that of the protectorates, possessions having their own internal governments, but acting on the advice and under the protection of Great Britain. The sixth classification is India, which is an empire by itself, combining direct British control, government through a Constitution, and control by native princes. Finally, there are the mandated areas, given to the British to rule by the League of Nations.

Because of its far-flung domain, it is only natural that the British Empire should play a leading rôle in world affairs. It is very seldom that anything of world political importance occurs without the power of this vast empire being taken into consideration. Its interests are world-wide. See BRITISH COMMONWEALTH OF NATIONS.

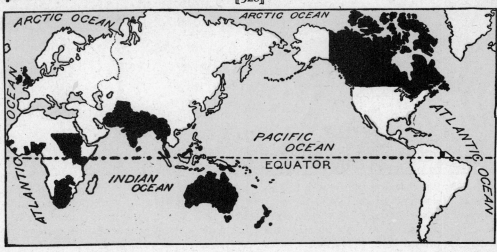

LOCATION	AREA IN SQUARE MILES	POPULATION (000 OMITTED)	LOCATION	AREA IN SQUARE MILES	POPULATION (000 OMITTED)
Great Britain and Northern Ireland ..	94,278	46,691	Union of So. Africa....	472,550	8,600
			Nigeria	372,674	19,865
Europe			Gambia	4,068	200
Gibraltar	2	21	Gold Coast and Prot...	91,843	3,441
Malta	122	255	Sierra Leone and Prot.	31,670	1,557
Asia			Anglo-Egyptian Sudan.	969,600	5,816
Aden, Perim, etc	43,400	62	Tanganyika Terr.	360,000	4,990
Bahrein Islands	250	120	S. W. Africa	317,725	267
Borneo, Brunei, and			Cameroon	34,136	778
Sarawak	83,606	775	Togoland	13,041	294
Ceylon	25,332	5,313	**America**		
Cyprus	3,584	348	Bermudas	19	30
Hong Kong	391	944	Canada 3,694,863		10,377
India 1,808,679		352,838	Falkland Islands and		
Straits Settlements	1,356	1,119	South Georgia	5,618	3
Fed. Malay States	27,540	1,777	British Guiana	89,480	323
Other Malay States	22,080	1,600	British Honduras	8,598	55
Palestine	10,000	1,261	Newfoundland and		
Africa			Labrador	152,734	294
Kenya Colony and Prot.	224,960	3,094	Bahamas	4,404	60
Uganda Prot.	93,981	3,641	Barbados	166	182
Zanzibar	1,020	235	Jamaica	4,674	1,090
Mauritius and Dep. ...	809	404	Leeward Islands	715	136
Nyasaland Prot.	37,596	1,604	Trinidad and Tobago..	1,978	432
St. Helena and			Windward Islands	521	194
Ascension	81	4	**Australasia**		
Seychelles	156	29	Australian Common-		
Somaliland Prot.	68,000	345	wealth 2,974,581		6,724
Basutoland	11,716	600	Papua	90,540	276
Bechuanaland Prot. ...	275,000	153	New Zealand, etc. ...	104,219	1,576
Southern Rhodesia	150,344	1,259	Fiji	7,083	197
Northern Rhodesia	290,320	1,392	Pacific Islands	11,450	265
Swaziland	6,705	113	Terr. of New Guinea..	93,000	484
			Western Samoa	1,130	54
			Nauru	8	3

A HERO OF THE EMPIRE IS REWARDED
Acme
King-Emperor George VI is decorating an airman for bravery in battle.

BRITISH GUIANA, *ge ah' nah.* In 1815 a new colony was added to the already vast British Empire when the Dutch, in the settlement following the Napoleonic wars, ceded to the English the territory now known as British Guiana. This is England's only colony in South America.

The territory, which was first settled by the Dutch West India Company in 1620, lies in the northeastern section of South America, just above the equator, and has an area of 89,480 square miles. Of the population of approximately 341,000, some twenty per cent live in Georgetown, the capital. Negroes, West Indians, and those of mixed races account for nearly ninety per cent of the people.

Agriculture is British Guiana's chief industry; sugar, molasses, rum, rice, balata (a dried gum), and timber are the chief exports. Mineral exports—gold, diamonds, and bauxite (aluminum ore)—in 1933 were valued at over a million and a half dollars.

There are nearly 78,000 square miles of undeveloped land available for exploration and exploitation.

BRITISH ISLES. There is probably no more famous group of islands in any part of the world than the British Isles. These islands are separated from the northwestern coast of Europe by the North Sea, the English Channel, and the Strait of Dover. Great Britain, the main island, includes England, Scotland, and Wales. To the west, across the Irish Sea, lies Ireland. The Orkneys, off the northwestern coast of Scotland, the Hebrides, or Western Islands, off its western coast, the Isle of Man, in the Irish Sea, and the Channel Islands, in the English Channel, are also included in the British Isles.

Each of the islands mentioned above is treated in this work under a separate heading.

BRITISH MUSEUM. It is said that no more complete record of man's accomplishments since the dawn of history exists than that which is housed in the British Museum. The famous reading room has probably been the scene of more scholarly activity than has any other single room in existence. The library of the British Museum ranks with the most complete and valuable libraries in the world. Its various departments, such as the department of Oriental antiquities and the department of coins and medals, boast of collections unsurpassed in the world today.

The British Museum was founded in 1753 by Sir Hans Sloane, who, in exchange for a promise that the government would pay his heirs $100,000, agreed to leave his numerous collections and his library of over 50,000 volumes for the establishment of a public museum. Montague House, the first home of the British Museum, was opened in 1759. With the years the collection expanded, and in 1847 the building in Great Russell Street was opened.

Ten years later the new library building was completed at a cost of $750,000. In this building is the famous reading room with its dome more than 100 feet in height. The room is 140 feet in diameter and provides separate desks for 200 to 300 readers. Further expansion made it necessary to build a museum of natural history which now stands in South Kensington. The Great Russell Street building has been enlarged twice.

The museum is organized into eight divisions: the library of printed books, maps, charts, and plans; the department of original manuscripts; the department of classical antiquities; the department of coins and medals; the department of medieval antiquities and objects pertaining to the history of the British people; the department of prints and drawings; the department of natural history, and the department of Oriental antiquities.

Close to one million visitors enter the museum annually, the reading room itself being used by 200,000 people every year. Of particular interest to visitors are the famous Elgin Marbles and the historic Rosetta Stone.

The administration of the British Museum is under the guidance of forty-eight trustees. It is open daily, and there is no charge for admission. To be admitted to the reading room, however, one must apply to the librarian for an admission ticket. Numerous bequests and the fact that one copy of any work published in the British Empire must be forwarded free of charge to the librarian have elevated the British Museum to its present position as one of the outstanding institutions of its kind in the world. See ELGIN MARBLES; ROSETTA STONE.

BRITISH NORTH AMERICA ACT. Each year on July 1 Canadians celebrate Dominion Day, commemorating the establishment of the Dominion of Canada by the passage of the British North America Act. This act was passed by the English Parliament in 1867 and went into effect July 1 of that year.

Passage of the act came after many years of internal strife under British rule. In 1791 Parliament had ruled that Quebec, then known as "Canada," should be divided into two provinces. One of these provinces contained the French population and was known as *Lower Canada*. This section, northeast of the Ottawa River, is now the province of Quebec. The division west of the river, called *Upper Canada,* was largely English; it now forms a part of the province of Ontario. Both Upper and Lower Canada had their own legislatures elected by the people. Each, however, also had a council appointed by the king, and disputes arose between the two governing bodies.

When dissatisfaction increased, the English once again united the two provinces, and Canada was then composed of Quebec and Ontario, New Brunswick, and Nova Scotia. By 1849, the three provinces had self-government, but the French and the English in Ontario and Quebec still were unable to co-operate. Accordingly, the three provinces drew up resolutions seeking a dominion form of government, and in 1867 the British North America Act was passed.

The act provided for a Governor-General appointed by the king; a Senate, or upper house, composed of members named for life by the Governor-General; and a House of Commons elected by the people. The act also provided that each province should have a government of its own. Ontario and Quebec again were divided, Quebec including the French population and Ontario consisting of the English. Under the terms

Courtesy French Line

WHERE PALM TREES MEET THE SEA

Colorful scenery and picturesque native ways hold travelers under the spell of the British West Indies, rich and sunny, sea-swept islands dotting the Atlantic Ocean between North and South America.

of the act, newly formed provinces could be admitted. Manitoba was admitted in 1870, British Columbia in 1871, Prince Edward Island in 1873, and Saskatchewan and Alberta in 1905.

BRITISH WEST INDIES, *in'diz*. Like stepping stones from North America to South America, the islands called the British West Indies lie scattered between the Atlantic Ocean and the Caribbean Sea, south and east of Florida. One chain of these islands, the Bahamas, stretches from Florida down to Haiti. And another, the Leeward Islands and the Windward Islands, curves like a crescent from the Virgin Islands down to Venezuela. Barbados, Trinidad, Tobago, Jamaica, and a number of other patches of land in the Caribbean complete this important cluster of British possessions.

Although situated in a tropical zone, these islands enjoy cooling sea breezes which permit whites and blacks alike to live in comfort. Because of their attractive scenery and mild climate, the British West Indies are favorite vacation spots for tourists. The chief products are fruit, sugar, vegetables, cereals, cocoa, and spices. These products are shipped to England, continental Europe, and the United States of America.

The persons living on the islands are governed by men appointed by the British government, although some of the islands have a limited measure of self-government. See WEST INDIES.

Courtesy Raymond-Whitcomb, Inc.

PEASANTS AND PEACE IN BRITTANY

Serene spires such as these that lift above the town of Quimper; and the hardy, rugged faces of
the peasants, full of the flavor of Brittany, picturesque French province. It is a popular place
for tourists, for time has dealt kindly with the distinctive customs of this ancient land.

BRIT'TANY, or BRETAGNE, *bre tahn'y*. Picturesque Brittany, a peninsula of France that juts out into the Atlantic Ocean, is one of the most charming regions in Europe. Here are found quaint peasant customs and costumes and a dialect that resembles the Welsh. Here also is a beautiful seacoast facing the English Channel, the Atlantic Ocean, and the Bay of Biscay. The land is one of natural beauty.

There is little wealth in Brittany, for the poor soil yields only small crops of grain and fruit. The natives, therefore, depend upon fishing and the tourist trade for their living. Brittany is said to derive its name from the ancient Britons who were driven there from England by the Saxons about 1,500 years ago. Before the coming of the Britons, the country had been under Roman control for five centuries. In the Mid-

dle Ages, Brittany was an independent kingdom and later a duchy of France. Today it is a French province divided into five departments, or governing districts. Its area is about 18,600 square miles. See FRANCE.

BROCK, Isaac, Sir (1769-1812). A distinguished soldier and leader of men, Sir Isaac Brock is remembered as the man who halted an American invasion of Canada in the War of 1812. An Englishman, Brock joined the British army when he was fifteen years old. He went to Canada in 1802. There he quelled an insurrection against English rule, and in 1810 he was appointed lieutenant-governor of Quebec.

At the outbreak of the War of 1812, Sir Isaac commanded a small force in a battle at Detroit. Despite the larger number of soldiers under General William Hull, he forced the surrender of the Americans and prevented an invasion of Canada. Brock then hurried immediately to Niagara to continue his campaign, but was killed in the Battle of Queenston Heights. A monument in his honor now stands on that battlefield.

BROMINE, bro'min. This very active chemical element is liquid at ordinary temperatures and dark brown in color. It volatilizes (evaporates) easily to a brown gas which is exceedingly irritating and poisonous when inhaled. The liquid produces very bad burns on contact with the skin.

Bromine is made from the brines from salt wells in Michigan and the Ohio River Valley, or from solutions of Stassfurt (Germany) salts, either by an electrical process or by treatment with sulphuric acid and an oxidizing agent. From bromine are obtained the commercially valuable bromine compounds, used in medicine. Free bromine is used somewhat in metallurgy, in the preparation of certain dyes, and as a chemical reagent. In the World War it found use as one of the tear-producing gases.

BRONTË, bron'tay, CHARLOTTE (1816-1855). The youngest of six children, Charlotte Brontë was the daughter of a needy clergyman of Haworth, Yorkshire, in England. The mother died while the children were still quite young, and they were left alone much of the time. To while away the hours, Charlotte and her sisters, Emily and Anne, penned reams of childish writings, none of which is now of value except as an indication of the amazing imaginations of the girls.

Charlotte's education was not formal, except for brief periods spent at girls' schools. She spent some time abroad and so managed to observe a little of the ways of the world from which she had been carefully guarded. That she did eventually break away from the Victorian pattern of thought in which she was brought up is astonishing.

The Brontë sisters' first venture into the literary world was a volume of poems pub-lished in 1846. It was brought out under the names of Currer, Ellis, and Acton Bell, and attracted practically no attention. In the following year, however, Charlotte's *Jane Eyre* appeared, and this book was immediately a success. It tells a passionate, stirring story, much of it woven from the author's life. Charlotte's next two works, *Shirley* and *Villette,* were also well received, but they are by no means the literary equals of *Jane Eyre.*

In 1854 Charlotte Brontë married her long-time suitor, the Rev. Arthur Nicholls, curate in her father's parish. The marriage was tragically brief, however, for she died the following year. After her death, her novel entitled *The Professor* was published. It had previously been refused by publishers, before the publication of *Jane Eyre.*

Emily Brontë (1818-1848) was the author of *Wuthering Heights,* a novel published in 1847. The book was her only outstanding work of fiction, but its expression of powerful emotion and its brooding atmosphere of mystery have kept it from oblivion. Some critics regard it as a work of genius, superior even to *Jane Eyre.* Emily was the poet of the family, and in this field surpassed her sister Charlotte. Her health failed shortly after she had achieved success, and she died in 1848.

Anne Brontë (1820-1849) wrote two novels, *Agnes Grey* and *The Tenant of Wildfell Hall.* She is also remembered for the hymns she wrote, some of which are still sung in Protestant churches. She died in 1849, only a few months after the death of her sister Emily.

BRONZE. Man's first alloy, which is a combination of two or more metals, was bronze. Thought to have come into use in Mesopotamia, about 2500 B. C., it is today widely used in the arts and in industry. Its discovery is believed to have been accidental. By chance, a small amount of tin, a white metal then unknown, may have found its way into the sandy pit where copper was being melted. Or, perhaps, the amount of molten copper was insufficient for the tool or utensil being made, and tin was added as an experiment—to see "what would happen." The result was bronze.

It was harder, heavier, and stronger than copper; it did not rust, and it took and kept a sharp edge. Although copper implements were an improvement over the unwieldy, awkward stone ones, copper was not wholly satisfactory. The metal was soft, and in tools the edges were easily bent and quickly dulled.

First used for tools, then utensils, and then for weapons, bronze, within the next five centuries, became the favored metal. Within this period, tin was discovered in Bohemia, and farmers along the Danube learned to produce bronze. The Phoenicians and Romans sailed to Cornwall for their tin.

Examination of the utensils, ornaments, and weapons found in excavations show that early attempts in producing bronze were quite by random, the amount of tin used varying greatly.

Bronze alloys with higher proportions of tin are brittle. This is true of *bell* metal, which is sonorous, and is used for bells and statues; and *speculum* metal, which is used in making reflectors (speculums). *Gun* metal is a bronze and is still used to some extent as a material for cannon. Among other alloys which have been developed are *aluminum* bronze and *phosphor* bronze. Aluminum bronze, sometimes called *aluminum gold,* an alloy of copper and aluminum, is yellow, strong, and light in weight, and is used for inexpensive jewelry and scientific instruments. Phosphor bronze is really an alloy of lead and copper. The small amount of phosphor is employed only as a refining agent, and is removed from the finished product. A hard, chemical-resisting alloy, it is used for propellers for ships and pump bearings. See BRONZE AGE.

BRONZE AGE. The last great age of man before the coming of iron was the Bronze Age. It was that period in human history which followed the New Stone Age. Before the development of bronze, there was a brief period of supremacy for the parent metal of bronze—copper. But copper is so soft that it makes a poor sword or plowshare. The Bronze Age began with the discovery that a little tin mixed with copper makes a harder, tougher metal than copper.

The Bronze Age cannot be marked off with definite dates, for it began slowly and faded out slowly at widely different times; and it lasted different lengths of time in various parts of the world. Some civilizations, indeed, went directly from stone tools to iron tools, never stopping at bronze.

But wherever it existed as a stage in the growth of a civilization, the Bronze Age played an important rôle in the development of art. Few craftsmen have produced such magnificent works of art as did the metalsmiths of the Bronze Age. This reddish-gold metal was so flexible that artisans spent much time and energy decorating nearly everything they made from bronze, no matter how practical its intended purpose might be. As a result, we have collections of thousands of pieces of ancient bronze art. It is our added good fortune that bronze is very slow to rust, so that archaeologists have been able to remove surface corrosion and restore much of the original beauty.

The Bronze Age in the Mediterranean countries began about four thousand years ago. In this age occurred the Golden Age of Greece and the peak of the ancient Egyptian civilization. But in spite of all its value—to art and to the development of tools and weapons—bronze could not last as the dominating metal because man found a harder metal. As copper bowed to bronze, so bronze went down before the clank of iron. See BRONZE; AGE OF MAN; ARCHAEOLOGY.

BROWN. Throughout the plant and animal kingdoms we find this rich color. It is the protective coloration of many animals. It is the color of autumn, the beautiful tint of woods and fields touched by the first frost. Most of Rembrandt's masterful portraits show the fine use to which brown may be put in painting.

Brown is not a primary color, but a blend of red and black, or red, black, and

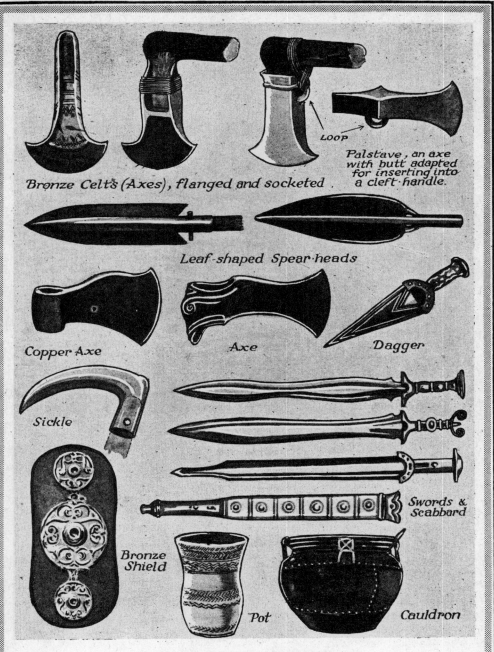

Bronze Celts (Axes), flanged and socketed.

Palstave, an axe with butt adapted for inserting into a cleft handle.

← LOOP

Leaf-shaped Spear-heads

Copper Axe

Axe

Dagger

Sickle

Swords & Scabbard

Bronze Shield

Pot

Cauldron

MAN'S FIRST METAL IMPLEMENTS

Bronze was the first metal to replace stone and bone as the material for tools and weapons. When primitive craftsmen found that they could make bronze and work it into different shapes, they were able to exercise their growing talents. The many shields, pots, and sword scabbards which have been found display the amazing skill of their makers and indicate that the Age of Bronze worked westward into Europe from Asia. And it seems entirely possible that the successive waves of migration from the East would bear the crafts and customs of the "Mother Continent" to the bone and stone workers of conquered countries.

"HIS SOUL GOES MARCHING ON"

John Brown being led to his execution after he had tried to arm the slaves. The famous song,
John Brown's Body, was written in his memory.

yellow. It can be obtained from natural mineral pigments such as bistre, umber, and Cappagh brown.

BROWN, JOHN (1800-1859). During the Civil War, the song *John Brown's Body* was sung by thousands of Union soldiers as they marched to battle. This song, which is still popular, took its name from the man who led a raid on the arsenal at Harper's Ferry, Va., in 1859, in an attempt to free the slaves.

What he tried to do was to lead the slaves in armed revolt against their masters. In order to get weapons for them, Brown and a band of followers overpowered the small armory guard and took possession of the town, holding some citizens as hostages. The expected uprising of slaves failed to materialize and a squad of marines under Captain Robert E. Lee, who was later to be commander of the Confederate forces, regained the arsenal after a fight in which Brown was seriously wounded. Brown was tried for treason and murder and convicted. He was hanged at Charles Town, W. Va., December 2, 1859.

Except for this dramatic incident, Brown's life is without particular significance. He was born at Torrington, Conn., and spent the early part of his life wandering about the country. He lived in Connecticut, New York, and Ohio at different times, and was married twice, and was the father of twenty children. In 1855 he moved to Kansas with four of his sons, and it was then that his anti-slavery activities began to attract national attention.

His raid on the Harper's Ferry arsenal was approved by some people of the Northern states, but his scheme made Southerners even more bitter toward the anti-slavery party. The song which commemorates Brown's name is an expression of the feeling he aroused among abolitionists.

BROWNING, ELIZABETH BARRETT (1806-1861). The wife of one of England's greatest poets was a great poet in her own right. Elizabeth Barrett was married to Robert Browning—and it was their poetry that first brought them together. Elizabeth Barrett was a great admirer of Browning's work. In one of her own poems, *Lady Geraldine's Courtship,* she paid Browning a compliment. When he called to thank her, there began one of the famous real-life romances.

Elizabeth Barrett spent most of her childhood at her father's country house, Hope End, near Ledbury in Herefordshire. In 1832 Hope End was sold, and the Barretts moved to Sidmouth, Devon. Three years later the family went to London. It was in 1838 that they moved into the house at 50 Wimpole Street, which is now famous as the scene of Robert Browning's courtship of Elizabeth Barrett. A well-known modern play, *The Barretts of Wimpole Street,* by R. Besier, tells the story of that courtship.

In her childhood Elizabeth Barrett suffered a spinal injury. A number of years later she burst a blood vessel in her lungs. As a result of these mishaps, she was extremely delicate. For three years, from 1838 to 1841, she stayed at Torquay in an effort to improve her health. It was there that her favorite brother was drowned. The shock to her was so severe that her life was in danger, and for several years afterward she was almost an invalid.

After her return to Wimpole Street in 1841, she wrote much of her poetry, including the poem that first attracted Robert Browning. In 1846 she married Browning, much against her father's wishes, and went to Italy to live. Except for visits to England and France, she lived in Florence, at the Casa Guidi, for the rest of her life. It was there that her only child, Robert Wiedemann Barrett, was born in 1849. She died in 1861 after fifteen years of the happiest married life.

Mrs. Browning's best-known poems are her *Sonnets from the Portuguese,* in which she expressed her love for Browning during their engagement. She showed them to no one, not even to Browning, until after her marriage. They are considered to be among the greatest love poems in English. Other works include *Prometheus Bound* (from the Greek of Aeschylus) and *Aurora Leigh,* a narrative and dramatic poem. Two volumes of poetry were edited by her husband and published after her death: *The Greek Christian Poets and the English Poets* and *Last Poems.*

BROWNING, ROBERT (1812-1889). Of all the poets England produced in the Victorian Era, none surpasses Robert Browning in vigor and clear thinking. His poems are alive and strong and, besides, have a musical lilt.

Browning was born in Camberwell, a suburb of London. He received little formal education but was tutored throughout most of his boyhood by private teachers. In his youth he traveled extensively in Europe. He began to write poetry before he was twelve years old, and, when he came upon the poems of Keats and Shelley, he determined to follow in their footsteps.

In 1844 Browning met Elizabeth Barrett, the poet, whom he married in 1846. The Brownings lived in Italy most of the time until Mrs. Browning's death in 1861. Robert Browning then returned to England to educate his son. He continued to write poetry until his death in Venice in 1889. His body was taken back to England and was buried in Westminster Abbey.

Among Browning's best-known poems are *My Last Duchess, Andrea del Sarto, A Forgiveness, How They Brought the Good News from Ghent to Aix, Oh to Be in England,* and *Hervé Riel.* But it is generally conceded that his masterpiece is *The Ring and the Book,* a long poem made up of a series of monologues. As an observer of human nature, Browning ranks almost with Shakespeare. This particular ability stands out in *The Ring and the Book,* in which the poet tells his story at the beginning and devotes the remainder to studies of characters.

Browning's best-known poetical dramas are *Strafford, A Blot on the 'Scutcheon, Pippa Passes,* and *Rabbi Ben Ezra.* His *Pied Piper of Hamelin* was written for the small son of the actor William C. Macready and is a children's classic.

Browning wrote rapidly and seldom revised his work to any great extent. It is probable that if he had been willing to rewrite and smooth out his poems, he might have attained the perfection of his contemporary, Tennyson. Besides this, Browning's work has a definitely dramatic touch, but he lived at a time when the drama was not the most popular form of writing.

BROWN THRASHER.

No one who has ever heard the song of this beautiful bird is likely to forget its rich, fine tones. Morning and evening are its concert hours, for at these times the male bird seeks a high perch and pours forth one of the loveliest songs in the bird world.

The brown thrasher, often wrongly called the *brown thrush,* lives in thickets and undergrowth, and is closely related to the catbird and the mocking bird. In spring and summer it is found throughout the United States and Southern Canada, east of the Rocky Mountains, and it withdraws to the Southern states in winter. In California and the Southwest there are several other thrashers, all of similar habits.

Rich, reddish brown above, the feathers are cream-colored on the breast, and heavily streaked with brown. The brown thrasher has a very long tail which it flirts about. The total length of the bird is about eleven and one-half inches. It spends much of its time on the ground, beneath thickets, scratching about among the leaves for hidden insects and worms. Some fruit and grain are eaten at times, but on the whole the brown thrasher does much more good than harm.

The nest is built of twigs, rootlets, bark strips, and leaves, and is usually placed in bushes or thickets a few feet from the ground. Sometimes it is on the ground. From three to six eggs are laid, grayish or greenish in color, thickly and evenly speckled with brown. The brown thrasher is shyer than the catbird and comes close to dwellings less frequently. When alarmed, it gives a sharp kissing *click* that is very distinctive.

The singing of the thrasher has been compared with that of the mocking bird of the South. Its period of singing lasts only until June in its northern habitat.

ONE OF BIRDLAND'S LOVELIEST SONGSTERS

BRUCE, ROBERT (1274-1329). The best-known member of the ancient family of Bruce was the eighth Robert—most heroic of Scottish kings. His vigorous campaigns finally forced England to recognize Scotland's independence in 1328. But long years of almost continual fighting were required before Bruce completed his task.

Robert Bruce belonged to a family of Scottish nobles loyal to King Edward I of England. But in 1296 Bruce joined Sir William Wallace in the struggle for Scottish independence. The next year, however, he was forced to make peace with Edward.

In 1306, the year after Wallace was executed, Robert Bruce began his real struggle for Scotland. First

A SCOTTISH HERO RIDES TO VICTORY

Robert Bruce, leader of the Scots, vanquished the forces of Edward II at Bannockburn in 1314.

he murdered Comyn, a claimant to the Scottish throne, and then claimed the crown himself. Successful in his plans, he was crowned king at Scone in 1306. In his struggle against England, he was often defeated and forced to hide. One time he fled to an island in the Irish Sea and was generally thought to be dead.

When he returned from his brief "exile," he gathered brave Scottish lords about him and launched a series of battles against the English. He invaded England in 1314 and advanced on the castle of Stirling. He met the army of the English king, then Edward II, at Bannockburn. Edward was routed in

one of the most celebrated of all Scottish-English battles.

Meanwhile, Bruce's brother Edward had been proclaimed king of Ireland. He met with opposition from the English, however, and in 1317 Robert Bruce went to his aid. Edward was killed in battle in 1318.

When Robert returned to England, he found that the English had advanced on Scotland again. In retaliation, Bruce conducted a five-year campaign in which he harried and routed the English frequently. Eventually Edward II was defeated at Biland Abbey in 1323. It was this event which led to Scottish independence, although it

CENTER OF COMMERCE IN BRUSSELS
Medieval Guild Houses surround the market place of Brussels, capital of Belgium. The gable
of the Shippers' Building is like the stern of an old sailing vessel.

was not until 1328 that the treaty was concluded recognizing Bruce's right to the
Scottish throne. By that time Edward III
was king of England.

Robert Bruce lived only a year after the
treaty was concluded, for he died of leprosy
in 1329. He had requested that his heart
be embalmed and given to Sir James Douglas, who was to take it to Jerusalem for
burial. But Douglas was killed in Spain
on his way to the Holy Land, and Robert
Bruce's heart was returned to Scotland and
buried in Melrose Abbey.

BRUM'MELL, GEORGE BRYAN (1778-
1840). "Beau" Brummell was the original
fashion plate—the best-dressed man in England in his day. His nickname has become
a symbol of perfection in manners and
dress. During his lifetime, his opinion in
social matters was law to his admirers.

Brummell was educated at Eton and Oxford, and later became a close friend of the
Prince of Wales, afterward George IV, who

saw to the young man's rapid promotion
in the Tenth Hussars. Connection with the
court gave Brummell influence in social affairs. He inherited a large fortune from
his father, and lived prodigally for twenty-
one years.

In 1816, having lost his money through
reckless gambling, he was forced to flee
from his creditors, and lived at Calais,
France, for fourteen years. From 1830 to
1832, Brummell served as British consul in
Caen, and in this French town he died in
misery, in a hospital for the pauper insane.

BRUNHILDE, *broon hil'da.* See SI-
GURD.

BRUSSELS, *brus' els,* BELGIUM. This
charming capital of the little kingdom of
Belgium, and of Brabant province, is situated in the heart of the country. The city
is the cultural as well as the political center of the nation.

Brussels is made up of a lower and an
upper town. The once fortified ancient

citadel, now the lower town, is surrounded by beautiful boulevards, and is the section devoted to modern commerce and industry. Here, Flemish is spoken, and the section retains the quaint charm of bygone days. The Grande Place, which is one of Europe's finest examples of medieval public squares, was originally the market place. Facing it are beautiful structures—Gothic architecture at its best—some of them dating from the fifteenth century.

In the upper town, where French is chiefly spoken, are the Royal Palace and the finest hotels and residential districts. A system of canals connects Brussels with the North Sea; it is an important railway center, and has airplane service to most of the leading European cities. The estimated population of Brussels and suburbs is over 900,000.

The capital is famed for exquisite lace, fine tapestries, and lovely carpets. Other industries include the manufacture of cotton goods, paper, and woolens; there are also foundries, breweries, and sugar refineries.

Brussels is the seat of many institutions, including the university, an academy of science and fine arts, and many learned societies. In its art gallery are exhibited some of the finest examples of Flemish art in existence.

It is thought that the Gauls and Romans founded Brussels in the sixth century. The commercial development of Brussels began in the tenth century; it was an important trade and industrial center of the Middle Ages. After three centuries of domination by Spain, Austria, France, and Holland, Belgium again became independent in 1830.

The Revolution of 1830 was a bitter struggle in the streets between citizens and soldiers. Following the victory of the people, Belgium's independence was recognized and Brussels was declared the capital. Brussels was occupied by the Germans in both World Wars. It surrendered without a struggle in World War I, but was damaged by bombing in World War II.

TOWN HALL OF BRUSSELS
This splendid Gothic building is 500 years old

BRUSSELS SPROUTS. Most delicately flavored of all the vegetables in the cabbage family are Brussels sprouts. They are hardy, cool-season plants whose enlarged buds look very much like miniature heads of cabbage.

The seed is sown late in the spring, and the seedlings are transplanted to a permanent bed when they are about six inches tall. When the small heads begin to crowd on the stem, the lower leaves should be broken off. Each plant will yield about a quart of the little sprouts. They need plenty of moisture and a long growing season. If they have too much heat, or their bed is too dry, the buds will not form compact heads, but remain tufts of loose leaves.

Wherever winters are mild, Brussels sprouts can be left out all year. Where winters are severe, the plants are pulled up with earth clinging to the roots and planted in a cellar, in moist sand. They will then give cuttings, just as in the open.

Brussels sprouts are well worth trying in the home garden, and when cooked properly are a very appetizing side dish. To prepare for the table, wash, pick off the outer leaves, and place the heads in salted boiling water. Cook quickly in an uncovered dish till tender, drain, season, and serve hot with butter or sauce.

BRU′TUS, Marcus Junius (85-42 B. C.). Shakespeare has created for us a heroic character in Brutus. And, indeed, Brutus was in real life a distinguished citizen. He was an able politician, and on several occasions governor of various provinces of the Roman Empire. He is remembered chiefly, however, for his participation in the plot against the life of Julius Caesar.

Brutus met Caesar while fighting with Pompey in a civil war; Caesar led the other side. Brutus surrendered to Caesar, and was appointed governor of Cisalpine Gaul. But it was not long before Brutus, prompted by Cassius, became the leader of the conspiracy against Caesar, and he had a personal part in the assassination.

After the murder, Brutus, with Cassius, fled to the East, took possession of Macedonia, and raised an army against Antony. About this time the triumvirs—Octavianus, Antony, and Lepidus—were preparing to fight the conspirators. They finally met in Macedonia, and after a series of battles, Brutus was completely defeated at Philippi.

Realizing that his cause was lost, he fell upon his sword, committing suicide in the traditional Roman manner.

Shakespeare said of him: "This was the noblest Roman of them all!" See Caesar, Caius Julius.

BRYAN, William Jennings (1860-1925). Three times a candidate, but never a President—William Jennings Bryan, "the Great Commoner," is numbered among the most influential Americans of his time. A staunch advocate of free trade, prohibition, and international peace, he never swerved from his convictions, despite repeated defeats at the polls. Bryan was a magnetic orator, and swayed audiences of many types, being equally effective on the lecture platform and in political rallies.

He was born in Salem, Ill., where he received a common-school education. Later, he attended Illinois College and the Union College of Law, in Chicago. Shortly afterward, he began practicing law in Jacksonville, Ill. When he was twenty-seven years old, he moved to Lincoln, Neb. Having entered politics, he soon became one of the state's outstanding Democrats, and was active during the Presidential campaign of 1888 in behalf of Cleveland.

Bryan's first elected office was that of Congressman. For two terms (1891-1895) he represented a strong Republican district, and while in Washington he delivered his first great speeches, one being against the repeal of the silver-purchase clause in the Sherman Act. In 1894, when he was defeated for the United States Senate, he became editor of the Omaha *World Herald,* a widely read newspaper.

Bryan was an alternate delegate to the Democratic Convention held in Chicago in 1896, but was seated as a regular delegate when the original delegate withdrew. An ardent supporter of free coinage of silver, at the ratio of sixteen to one, he wrote the plank on free silver for the platform. This was a measure which many, especially the conservative Easterners, believed would disrupt the finances of the nation; others thought it the panacèa for monetary ills.

During the long, heated debate, Bryan delivered his famous "Cross of Gold" speech, concluding with these words: "We shall answer their demand for a gold standard by saying to them: 'You shall not press down upon the brow of labor this crown of thorns! You shall not crucify man upon a cross of gold.'" Immediately, his name flashed across the country, and the party, adopting his program, nominated him for the highest office in the land.

Bryan traveled over the nation from coast to coast, carrying his campaign 18,000 miles, but he was defeated by William McKinley, the Republican candidate. Although he was a pacifist, Bryan wholeheartedly supported his country in the Spanish-American War, organizing a volunteer regiment which he commanded.

Defeated again by McKinley in 1900, he founded *The Commoner,* which became a monthly publication. He continued his journalistic activities by writing a series of letters for several newspapers while on a trip around the world. Bryan was a candidate for President for the third and last time in 1908, but even though he was again defeated, this time by William Howard Taft, his influence in the party continued. He aided Woodrow Wilson, in 1912, at the Baltimore convention, and helped secure his nomination. Wilson was elected and named Bryan as Secretary of State.

Disagreeing with President Wilson over World War I policies, Bryan resigned from the post of Secretary of State in 1915, on the eve of the delivery of the second *Lusitania* note. But again he showed his patriotism by supporting the administration when America entered the war in 1917.

Bryan continued in the public eye as a militant champion of his political and religious views, until his death at the age of sixty-five. He was buried in the National Cemetery at Arlington.

BRYANT, WILLIAM CULLEN (1794-1878). America's first great poet was William Cullen Bryant, who lived to see his country grow from a struggling young nation to a strong and united world power.

Bryant was born in Cummington, Mass., and as a child showed his brilliant mind and literary talents. When he was only ten, he made translations from the Latin poets; at the age of fourteen, he was the author of two volumes of poems. He entered Williams College as a sophomore when he was sixteen, but financial troubles forced him to leave at the end of the year.

One day, Bryant's father found a beautifully written poem on his son's desk. It sang of "—the hills, rock-ribbed and ancient as the sun"; and of "old ocean's gray and melancholy waste." It was the work of the younger Bryant, written when he was about seventeen. After reading it over, Mr. Bryant took it to Boston, where he showed it to the editors of the *North American Review.* They were amazed at its excellence and at first would not believe that it was written by an American, much less by a young unknown. The poem, *Thanatopsis* (from the Greek word meaning *contemplation of death*), appeared in the *North American Review* two years later.

When Bryant was twenty-one, he was admitted to the bar. He practiced law for ten years, and then went to New York. Three years after joining the staff, he became editor and part owner of the New York *Evening Post.* In time the paper became widely known for its high standards and fine literary quality. As a journalist, Bryant was a severe opponent of slavery, and his editorials were among the best antislavery writings of the day. He urged many reforms in government through his newspaper, and lived to see most of them carried out.

Some of Bryant's best-known poems, noted for their brevity, beauty, and moral tone, are *To the Fringed Gentian, The Death of the Flowers, The Crowded Street, My Country's Call, The Battlefield, To a Yellow Violet, Inscription for the Entrance to a Wood,* and *To a Waterfowl.* Other writings include translations of the *Iliad* and *Odyssey, Letters of a Traveler, Letters from the East, Letters from Spain and Other Countries,* and *Orations and Addresses.*

WHEN RAIDERS SAILED THE SPANISH MAIN
Buried treasure and death were linked in the dangerous days of the buccaneers. They marked
an era of sea adventure that live today only in song and story.

BUCCANEERS, *buk a neerz'*. The boldest breed of robbers, murderers, and merchants that ever sailed the southern seas were the buccaneers. Swashbuckling adventurers, bent on destroying the Spanish grip on the New World, they roved the Caribbean Sea and the Pacific for three-quarters of the seventeenth century, pillaging and looting the great treasure ships laden with precious metals from colonial soil, destined for Spain.

The buccaneers were by no means privateers, like Drake, Hawkins, and Cavendish, nor were they ordinary pirates, like the outlawed freebooters of the next century. Although their ambitious adventures smacked of both privateering and piracy, the buccaneers carved for themselves a cruel record of their own. They were a class and a law unto themselves, yet they had the backing of the homeland governments and shared their booty with European royalty. These raiders of the Spanish Main were made up of tough and ruthless seamen from England, France, Holland, Portugal, and other lands.

Theirs was an undeclared and ungoverned war, with no quarter asked or given. Nor was it limited to naval encounters. They raided Spanish islands in the West Indies, sacked Panama, preyed upon Peru, and established their own plantations on the territories they seized. Their ruthless commerce was enormously profitable to everybody but Spain, and the buccaneers rapidly became a large, loosely organized group of soldiers and sailors of fortune from every land, living on the spoils of their reckless courage.

Their first organization grew out of their business of supplying the ships of smugglers and others with smoked, dried meats, butchered from the wild cattle to be had for the hunting on wild West Indian islands, like Santo Domingo, Tortuga, and Jamaica. The method of curing with smoke instead of salt was a native craft called *boucanning,* from the French word *boucan,*

Courtesy Pan American Airways

THE SCOURGE OF SPAIN IN SOUTHERN SEAS

Spanish galleons, laden with treasure from the New World feared a ship such as this, for it might be manned by buccaneers, eager to board and loot.

a place for curing meat. It was a boon to sailors because of the cost and scarcity of salt, and the need for food that would keep on ships plying tropic seas. From this word *boucanning,* the buccaneers got their name.

But, however business-like they became, the purpose of the buccaneers remained the ruination of Spain. It was complicated by the roving and adventurous spirit of the men themselves. They did terrible damage to Spanish commerce, but their success in this respect was indirect, revealing to the world the corruption and weakness of the Spanish colonial system, and the wealth that lay in store for the next comer. When the Spanish colonial empire began to disintegrate, Spain's rivals — France, England, Holland—were ready and able to build their own colonial systems in lands where Spain had exercised supreme power.

Eventually the buccaneers became so numerous that they menaced the authority of the nations which had really started their plundering campaign. Under the leadership of such notorious and able brigands as Morgan, Mansfield, and Davis, these public enemies launched several serious wars in Central America, and soon brought down the wrath of European powers.

Then, too, the buccaneers were made up of many men from different nations. Internal disputes, racial differences, and mutinies eventually weakened their organization. England made peace with Spain and war with France, and the buccaneers had to take sides. Gradually, the adventurers disbanded and were obliged to assume the rôles of pirates. Growing national navies made piracy more hazardous, and so the survivors of the buccaneers gradually faded from the scene, leaving scarred ramparts and reddened hulks the only record of their reign of terror.

JAMES BUCHANAN
Fifteenth President of the United States
Administration, 1857-1861.
During Buchanan's four years in office, the North and South steadily drifted apart, John Brown's raid and the Dred Scott decision took place during his term.

BUCHANAN, *bu kan'an,* JAMES (1791-1868). From March, 1857, until March, 1861, the fear of civil war gripped the United States. Slavery was the question of the day—a country lawyer named Abraham Lincoln debated it with Stephen A. Douglas; the Dred Scott decision and John Brown's raid grew from it, to widen the gap between the North and the South; fifteen states threatened to secede from the Union because of it.

The President of the United States during these trying and tense years was James Buchanan, a sincerely patriotic but politically weak man who was unable to do anything but compromise, in an effort to stem the inevitable conflict between the states. Much had been expected of him when he took office, but, before his term was ended, he was disliked by both the North and the South for his futile attempts to preserve peace. He tried to follow a middle course, and failed.

James Buchanan was a native of Pennsylvania, having been born near Mercersburg, and was educated at Dickinson College in Carlisle. Beginning the practice of law in 1812, he became known for his ability, and was elected to the state legislature in 1814. He was at first a Federalist in politics, but on the downfall of his party, he joined the Democrats.

In 1820 Buchanan was chosen to represent his district in Congress, where he served for ten years. After a short term as minister to Russia, he was elected to the Senate (1834). In the next eleven years, as Senator, he achieved a high place in the Democratic party. Named Secretary of State (1845-49) under Polk, he helped settle the northwest boundary dispute between the United States and England. When Pierce became President, Buchanan was appointed minister to Great Britain (1853). In 1854 the Democrats nominated Buchanan and John C. Breckinridge of Kentucky for the offices of President and Vice-President.

Elected fifteenth President in 1856, over Fremont and Fillmore, Buchanan adopted unfortunate policies that cost him popularity in abolitionist and pro-slavery sections alike. He attempted to bring Cuba and Central American countries under the rule of the United States, and assumed a "do-nothing" attitude toward the all-important slavery issue. He believed that secession was wrong, but when the Southern states began to break away from the Union, he said that the Federal government had no right to keep them from seceding. Buchanan secluded himself in Lancaster, Penna., when his term was finished. He remained loyal to the Union, and died three years after the war was over.

BUCHAREST, or BUKHAREST, *boo ka rest'*, RUMANIA. "Little Paris" is the name often given this gay and fashionable capital of the kingdom of Rumania. Located on the banks of the Dimbovita River in the heart of a productive plain, Bucharest is about thirty-three miles north of the Danube.

The city is by no means little. Its population is estimated at about 648,000; it is the winter residence of the royal family, the seat of the national government, and the home of the University of Rumania. Its manufactures make it the principal market

place of the country; they include products of the metal, chemical, textile, and distilling industries. Here, too, centers the trade in grain, wool, honey, wax, wine, hides, and other produce of the surrounding agricultural region.

The community shelters many different races besides Rumanians, chiefly Jews, Greeks, Russians, Poles, Turks, and Hungarians. The businessmen of the city are mostly foreign. See RUMANIA.

BUCK'INGHAM, GEORGE VILLIERS, Duke of (1592-1628). The first Duke of Buckingham was an English court favorite of James I and Charles I. His charming personality won him favor at court, but his colossal diplomatic and political blunders finally ended with his assassination.

In 1623 he was entrusted with negotiations for the marriage of the Prince of Wales—later Charles I—and the Infanta Maria of Spain. This venture finally achieved exactly the opposite of what was intended, and brought about a war with Spain.

Three years later an expedition to Cadiz, in which Buckingham took part, was a dismal failure. Next, practically single-handed, he launched a war with France. This war ended very shortly in a crushing defeat for the duke, who was unable to provide supplies for his troops. Then for a time he concentrated on diplomatic intriguing, which succeeded in further irritating the French.

Buckingham finally returned to England, there to take a hand in domestic affairs. He was saved from impeachment on two occasions during his career, but only by the intervention of the king, whose favor he had managed to retain. But royal protection was of no avail when Buckingham set forth on a last continental expedition. This time he was fatally knifed by an assassin, just as he was boarding a ship for France.

BUCKSKIN, *buk'skin*. The pioneers in the wildernesses that are now the farms and cities of America had few needs in the way of clothing. All they wanted was

OPENING THEIR EYES TO THE SUN

When the warm sun of spring shines brightly, the buds of trees and flowers open with amazing rapidity, ending their long sleep through cold and wintry months.

something that would wear well and keep them warm. To secure it, they needed only to step into the forests with a rifle, shoot a buck deer, and dress the skin with oil or brains until it was soft and pliable. So many of the soldiers in the Revolutionary War were clothed in this simple fashion that the Continental Army was sometimes known as "The Buckskins."

True deerskin is, of course, rare now, but the name buckskin is still borne by the yellowish or grayish leather made by dressing sheepskins in the same way that buckskins were prepared. The name is also given to a creamy, closely woven woolen cloth. Trousers of sheepskin are known as buckskins, and in the cattle country a horse of yellowish color is called a buckskin.

At present the chief articles made of buckskin are gloves and shoes, which are sometimes dressed white. Indians still make moccasins of both true buckskin and sheepskin. Pieces of buckskin are used for polishing.

BUCK′WHEAT. More things than just breakfast flap-jacks come from buckwheat. This plant produces a three-sided seed which is used in brewing, in making cordials, for cattle feed, and even as a packing material. It is commonly considered a grain, because its uses are similar to those of the cereals. Buckwheat is, however, a member of the pieplant family.

Buckwheat is believed to have originated in Asia, but it is now grown all over the world. The plant has smooth stems, green leaves, and white or rose-colored flowers. One of its chief advantages is that it will grow in very poor soil. In Europe it is used largely for livestock feeding, in contrast to the many uses to which it is put in the United States and Canada. Its importance in America is increasing, its hardiness and short growing season making it very popular with farmers.

Still, the best-known use of buckwheat is in the form of flour for griddle cakes. The flowers also produce a nectar with which bees make a kind of dark honey. One of the finest fodders for cattle is the seed of the buckwheat plant, without the hull. But the hull is not thrown out, for it can be used to pack breakables. Buckwheat plants are so tough that they make good weed-destroyers and orchard cover.

At present more buckwheat is produced in Pennsylvania than in any other state, with New York a close second. More than

DRESSING UP FOR SUMMER

As frosty winds are forgotten, the buds of plants change into leafy summer dress. Green is always the popular color, and styles never change.

half the nation's crop comes from these two states, but other states are rapidly cultivating the plant.

BUD. Every leaf or flower starts as a tiny bud. It is Nature's way of protecting the young plant from the weather or from rough treatment. The tiny leaflet inside a bud has an outer coating of weatherproof varnish or coarse substance, which encases it until it is ready to develop.

The leaflet, or if it is a flower, the petal, is packed away in the bud in perfect and regular order. The folding of a leaflet in the bud is always exactly the same in every plant in the same plant family. Some leaflets are folded inside out, some are rolled one way and others a different way, depending on the family. All cherry buds, for instance, are folded together with the under surfaces out. And all maple leaves are folded back and forth like a fan.

Flower buds are easier to examine than are leaf buds. If the student of botany opens a flower bud, he will see how Nature prepares the petals for future development and how, with a strong outer coat, she protects them from damage. It is a good plan to study flower buds at different stages of growth.

BUDAPEST, *boo'da pest,* HUNGARY. Age-old capital of the Magyar kingdom of Hungary, Budapest is one of the most enchanting places along the storied blue Danube. Lying in the center of a vast plain that is one continuous grain field, the picturesque metropolis is made up of two old towns, separated by the historic river. Buda, once a fortress, crowns a hill on the west bank and is much older than Pest, the flat, more modern section on the opposite bank. The city suffered much damage in World War II. Its population is over 1,215,000.

In Roman times, the site of old Buda was occupied by a Roman camp. This camp, *Aquincum,* was not far from where the 860-room Royal Palace rises atop the citadel. Here, quaint homes and buildings of the Middle Ages contrast sharply with the more modern, active business section of gay Pest, across the river. In Pest are located the extensive manufacturing districts of the city, including the plants which make it the largest flour-milling center in Europe.

Here also are the finer residences, celebrated streets, the imposing Parliament Buildings, the National Picture Gallery and Museum, the University, and the Royal Opera House. The Hungarian Academy

Courtesy Hungarian State Tourist Department

AN ENCHANTED CITY OF THE DANUBE—BUDAPEST
The gay metropolis at night, with the Elizabeth Bridge in the foreground.

of Music, once directed by the great composer Franz Liszt, is also in the newer portion of the city.

Budapest produces machinery, cutlery, glass, and metal and leather goods. It has great commercial interests, but it is better known throughout the world for its atmosphere of gaiety, its gypsy bands, and its myriad night lights mirrored in the mighty Danube. Like Vienna, a sister city on the river, Budapest is associated with the gayety of pre-World War I days (see VIENNA). Brightly dressed peasants in open markets contrast strangely with modernistic new shops and beautiful streets and homes. The architecture also shows the influence of the earlier Turkish occupation.

Although Buda was settled by the Romans and occupied by people of many races, the modern city dates from the nineteenth century. In 1872, Buda and Pest united, following the formation of the Austro-Hungarian Monarchy in 1867, with Budapest as the Hungarian capital. See AUSTRIA-HUNGARY; HUNGARY.

BUDDHA. This founder of one of the great world religions was born in India in the sixth century B. C. Originally named Siddhartha Gautama, he became a very serious young man, a lover of solitude and a dreamer. Thoughts of religion were ever in his mind. His father, the king of Kapilavastu, a small country just north of Benares in India, grew concerned over Siddhartha's lack of interest in worldly affairs. Fearing that his son might not remain at home, he had built for him a palace of his own, and filled it with tempting luxuries.

But Siddhartha was not satisfied; he dreaded the thought of age and sickness, and feared that he might die without ever having discovered the secret of life. So the young prince went to live with the Brahmans, the learned priests of his land. After years of study, Siddhartha again became dissatisfied, and again he set out. One day he sat down to rest under a bo tree. It was a long rest, too, for Siddhartha had determined to remain until he had solved the riddle of life and the origin of evil.

SEEKER OF TRUTH

This is the colossal statue of Buddha at Daibutsu, Japan. It is called the Amita Buddha.

Siddhartha fasted and tortured himself, but all the time he was thinking. Finally the solution came to him. This life, he concluded, is merely one stage in a long series of lives in various forms, and the cause of all suffering is desire. Buddha (the Enlightened), as he came to be known, went forth to preach his doctrine, which was not in harmony with the accepted religion of the Brahmans. However, he won many converts, and his teaching became the principles of the religion we know as Buddhism.

His last days were spent happily in Magadha and in Kosala, the kingdoms of two of his earliest followers. Many of the legends concerning him have been collected, and may be read in Edwin Arnold's *Light of Asia*.

BUDDHISM, *bood'iz'm*. In many countries of Asia—Ceylon, Burma, Siam, Anam, Tibet, Mongolia, China, Japan, and Java—followers of Buddha strive to attain *Nirvana,* their idea of paradise. This ideal is an essential element in the religion called Buddhism, a belief in the value of right living that has survived in the hearts of men for twenty-five centuries.

Buddhists believe that anyone who lives suffers pain, and that Nirvana brings the only relief. But Nirvana, like heaven, can only be attained through goodness. If a follower obeys the laws: not to kill, not to steal, not to commit adultery, not to lie, and not to give way to drunkenness, and practices charity, purity, patience, courage, and contemplation, he is believed to be on the road to Nirvana. In addition to obeying these cardinal principles, a Buddhist also is forbidden to lie, speak evil, or talk coarsely, and to refrain from speaking vainly or in a light manner. Many of the precepts of this faith are similar to the teachings of Christ, and the cardinal principles are also akin to the Ten Commandments.

The religion holds that when a person dies, his soul will pass to another body. Thus, a fish or a dog can become a human being and even a high priest. According to the teachings of the faith, Buddha himself passed through many stages of life, and once permitted himself to be devoured by a lioness.

Laws of the religion were written at least two centuries before Christ, and the modern faith is founded on the writings of three separate councils. Buddha himself did not write any of these laws, but they were cherished by his followers and preserved for later writers. Since the founding of this religion, many Buddhists have become worshipers of idols, but idolatry had no part in the pure idealism of Buddha himself.

About 180,000 persons in North America practice the Buddhist religion. Over large areas of the world it governs the lives of more than 150,000,000 followers of this religion. See BUDDHA.

THE TIDE OF BATTLE TURNS
Victory for the Americans at Buena Vista.

BUENA VISTA, *bwa'na vees'ta,* BATTLE OF. Northeastern Mexico, where the war between Mexico and the United States started, fell to the Americans in 1847 in the hard-fought Battle of Buena Vista. There, General Zachary Taylor, with 5,000 men, routed the Mexican general, Santa Anna, causing him to lose 2,000 of his 17,000 soldiers. The battle began on February 22, when the Mexican forces attempted to drive the Americans from their position on Angostura Heights. The enemy almost succeeded, but poor generalship lost the engagement for Santa Anna. When the struggle was over, the following day, the Mexicans withdrew. The Americans had lost 750 men, the Mexicans probably more. This battle ended the war in the northern part of the country.

International

SYMBOL OF ARGENTINE DEMOCRACY
The domed Palace of Congress looks down splendid Avenida de Mayo, Buenos Aires.

BUENOS AIRES, *bwa' nohs i'raze,* ARGENTINA. Capital of the Argentine Republic and metropolis of the Southern Hemisphere, Buenos Aires is one of the world's most beautiful cities, and the largest in South America. It is built along the broad estuary of the Plata River. Although Buenos Aires is 175 miles from the Atlantic Ocean, the river is so wide and has been dredged so deep that the city is a great commercial seaport reached by the largest vessels. It is also an important railroad center, with many different lines converging to its terminals.

Built on a broad, level plain, the city has an area of about seventy-two square miles. It is a Federal District, like Washington, D. C., and the municipal and Federal governments share in the management. Buenos Aires is truly a New World city. Its careful planning, which includes many parks and plazas, gives it a modern, clean appearance, and its broad, tree-lined boulevards are laid out in a geometric pattern. In it are many palatial homes, as well as a large number of fine public buildings.

A few of the outstanding buildings are the Federal Capitol; the Episcopal Palace; the Cathedral; the Palace of Justice; and the celebrated Colon Theater, used principally for grand-opera performances. Many of the buildings are in the French Renaissance style, a feature which permits much variation yet preserves the unity of the group.

Of the city's many huge plazas, one of the most distinguished is the Plaza de la Victoria, which is 1,200 feet long and 640 feet wide. Like the other plazas, the Plaza de la Victoria is bordered with the beautiful buildings so typical of Buenos Aires.

But the city is by no means limited to politics and art. It is of great importance in industry, and through it passes the enormous commerce of the interior, particularly in wool and wheat. The city is also a great meat-packing center, and has factories which give work to well over 100,000 men. These firms produce furniture, leather, and shoes, textiles, tobacco, and spirits.

Buenos Aires, with a population of over 2,460,000, is a city of many races. The prosperity of the city caused considerable immigration from Northern Europe, and there are many Germans, Italians, Swedes, and French, besides the dominant Spanish-speaking Latin group. The people are educated in public schools established throughout the city, as well as in a number of private schools. There is a national university, considered one of the finest on the continent.

Once a Deserted Town. Buenos Aires was first established by Pedro de Mendoza in 1535, but the Indians were so hostile and hardships so severe that the settlement was abandoned. It was nearly fifty years before Juan de Garay re-established it. During Argentine history, Buenos Aires has been the scene of much conflict, and was important in the struggle for independence from Spain. It was not made a Federal District until 1880.

BUFFALO. Members of the wild-ox family, buffaloes are huge animals with massive horned heads. True buffaloes, or *water* buffaloes, are found along the rivers and in marshy places in the warm parts of Asia. Their liking for swampy places makes them valuable domesticated animals for the rice fields, where they save the labor of many men by pulling cultivators through the mud.

This species of buffalo is larger and more powerful than the ox. It is seven to eight feet long and five to six feet high. Its tough, blue-black hide can be made into valuable leather. Its long horns curve to the side and then back, making it possible for the animal to run through thick brush. Its feet are broad and keep the buffalo from sinking into the mud. An important food of India is buffalo milk, which is sometimes made into *ghee*—an almost liquid sort of butter.

A near relative of the buffalo of Asia is the *carabao,* found in the Philippines (see CARABAO).

Most ferocious of all buffaloes is the *Cape* buffalo of Africa. It, too, is bluish-black in color, but is not quite so large as the water buffalo. Its short horns grow from a

bony mass on the front of its head. Its favorite food is the tender plants that grow along the water's edge, and here it is hunted for its valuable hide. The hunter must be very quiet and very quick, for the Cape buffalo has a keen sense of smell to warn him of approaching danger.

Bison, or American Buffalo. Only two or three generations ago, travel across the United States was a most exciting experience. Countless numbers of American buffaloes roamed the plains, and the great excitement of the journey came when passengers began firing at scattering herds through the windows of the trains.

The American buffalo is not a true buffalo, but a *bison*. It resembles the buffalo of Asia and has been called a buffalo for so long a time that it is now known by this name almost entirely. The American buffalo is reddish brown in color. In contrast to the true buffalo, it has shaggy hair about the head and fore part of the body. It also has one more pair of ribs than has the true buffalo. The curved horns are rather short. The shoulders are humped higher than the rest of the body, and at the shoulders the animal is about six feet high. Male buffaloes sometimes weigh as much as 2,000 pounds.

Long before white men came to America, the Indians had learned to value the bison as a source of food, clothing, and shelter. They ate the meat and used the hide in making robes and tepees. A favorite food was pemmican—pounded buffalo meat mixed with fat and berries and made into cakes. The introduction of horses by the Spaniards meant, for one thing, that the Indians found it easier than before to hunt the huge buffaloes.

So relentlessly was the buffalo hunted by both Indians and whites that the animal had practically disappeared from this continent. The buffalo gave way to herds of cattle on the plains and is now found only in government-protected areas, such as National Parks and forest and game preserves, in the United States and Canada. These animals are said to be increasing in the preserves.

ONCE LORD OF THE WESTERN PRAIRIE

Before the coming of the white man, immense herds of noble buffalo like these roamed the plains of North America. Relentless hunting by mounted men with firearms threatened the species with extinction in the nineteenth century, until the Canadian and United States governments undertook its preservation by maintaining the stock on great game preserves. The head of a magnificent specimen like that shown is familiar to all, as it appears in the design of the current United States five-cent coin.

BUFFALO, N. Y. The city of Buffalo lies at the eastern end of Lake Erie where the lake flows into the Niagara River. Twenty miles up the river, Niagara Falls thunders and roars.

Buffalo is a city of parks and waterways, harbors and wharves, schools and factories. It forms one of the vital links in the chain of American commerce. Buffalo is very little farther from Chicago (523 miles) than it is from the city of New York (439 miles). In the 1940 census it ranked as the fourteenth largest city in the United States, with a population of 575,901. Including Niagara Falls and other surrounding suburbs, the population exceeded 857,000.

Eleven railroads enter the city, bringing passengers and provisions, and cargoes for reshipment. Its docks are scenes of bustling activity. Hundreds of steamers plying the Welland Canal to and from Canada, the Great Lakes system via Lake Erie, and the New York State Barge Canal, between Buffalo and the Hudson River, link the city to the waterways of the world. The Buffalo airport, too, is alive with the hum of incoming and outgoing planes that bring this air center close to the most important business centers of the west and east coasts.

General Description. From a little fur-trading settlement on Buffalo Creek, the city has grown into a port with a water front thirty-seven miles long and with more than ten miles of improved wharfage. Inner and outer harbors have been made by the construction of a system of breakwaters, one of which, built by the United States government, is the largest in the world.

As the city slopes up away from the lake, it is divided by Main Street, the most important business thoroughfare, which runs north and northeast from the lake to the edge of the city. Beautiful parks and broad boulevards with large, shady trees give the visitor to Buffalo a favorable impression of the city. Along the shore of the lake there is a beautifully landscaped park known as "The Front." Delaware Park was the site of the Pan-American Exposition of 1901. It was there that President McKinley was assassinated. South Park houses the remarkable conservatory which flower lovers always visit when they go to Buffalo.

The Peace Bridge, completed in 1927, crosses the Niagara River at Buffalo. Connecting the United States and Canada, it commemorates the one hundred years of peace between the two neighboring countries.

Buildings and Institutions. One of the most prominent buildings in Buffalo is the City Hall, which was finished in 1932 at a total cost of about $7,000,000. Delaware Park houses two splendid buildings, the Buffalo Historical Society and the Albright Art Gallery, each of which is notable both for its collections and for its architecture.

There are public schools of all types, vocational as well as academic, and many private schools of high rank, including the State Teachers College, the University of Buffalo, and Canisius College. One of the largest hospitals in the United States, the Buffalo General Hospital, and many philanthropic institutions are situated in this prosperous city. There is an excellent public library, and also the privately endowed Grosvenor Library, which is open to the public.

Commerce and Industry. Since Buffalo is so close to Niagara Falls, one of the world's greatest natural power sources, the city has available, for industry, electricity at low cost. Its favorable location with respect to land, water, and air transportation is a vital factor in the development of the city as a commercial center.

The port of Buffalo is known throughout the world, for close to 20,000,000 tons of cargo are handled each year. Shipload upon shipload of wheat, flour, lumber, ore, and fish are carried to the city by way of the Great Lakes and shipped to other cities. Giant grain elevators, with a total capacity of 50,000,000 bushels, make the city one of the nation's largest grain centers.

In Buffalo, too, is one of America's busiest livestock markets. The city is also an important iron-manufacturing center. One of the largest steel plants in the world is

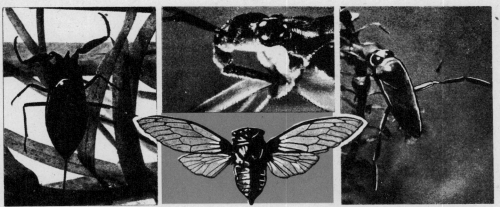

These insects have little charm for anyone but a scientist. At left is a waterbug; upper center, close-up of a waterskimmer; left, a boatman bug, and lower center, a cicada, also known as the "seventeen-year locust."

located in Lackawanna, a suburb of Buffalo.

History. Before the coming of the white man, herds of buffalo frequented the site of the present city. This fact probably accounts for the name by which the settlement was eventually known. The first white visitor to the spot was the French explorer LaSalle, who arrived in 1679. It was a good many years, however, before a permanent settlement was begun, and some of the pioneers moving westward began to choose this lakeside slope for homesites. After the Revolutionary War there was already a thriving fur-trading center.

By 1803 a definite township had been laid out, only to be wiped out by the British in 1813. After the war the place was rebuilt, and following the construction of the Erie Canal, in 1825, its growth continued steadily. It was incorporated as a city in 1832. Eleven years later, the world's first grain elevator was erected in Buffalo.

BUFFALO BILL. See Cody, William Frederick.

BUG. Most of us apply this term to any crawling insect, but the zoölogist has a special classification for bugs. Scientifically, a bug is an insect that possesses a sucking beak attached to the tip of the head and which, when winged, has its front wings thick and narrow at the base and suddenly wider and thinner at about the middle. The thin tips overlap on the back. A well-defined triangular space between the narrow part of the wings is also very characteristic of most true bugs.

Bugs are said to develop *directly;* that is, they do not go through distinctly different stages, but the young forms have at least a general resemblance to the adults. In shape, size, and habits, bugs vary so much that no very good general description can be given. They range in shape from the broad, rounded, or five-sided *stink* bug to the extremely slender and elongate *thread-legged* bug; in size from less than a sixteenth of an inch in length to nearly three inches in the case of the *giant water* bug. In food habits they range from those that suck the blood of man to those living on the juice of plants. Their color is generally some shade of green or brown, but many forms are red, black, or white.

It is probable that a majority of the bugs are either harmless or actually beneficial, since many forms feed on other insects. The injurious bugs include those that eat ripening berries and the leaves of cabbages, squash, and other garden crops.

BU'GLE. This brass wind instrument, widely used in armies for summoning soldiers to their various duties, has superseded the trumpet for military purposes. Though similar to the bugle, the trumpet is usually longer, less conical, and softer in tone. See Trumpet.

TRIUMPHS
of MAN
the BUILDER

BUILDING, *bild'ing.* The last of mankind's three primary needs—food, clothing, and shelter—is fulfilled by buildings. And the art of putting up these structures goes by the same name. Man once had nothing more than a cave or rude hut to keep out the weather and his enemies; now he has so enlarged his skill with better tools and materials that he is able to design and erect buildings to meet his every requirement. Building has become the work of many skilled craftsmen doing the job together. Their specialized skills, as carpentry, masonry, plastering, iron working, painting, glazing, and the like, make up that vital element of community life, the building trades.

This industry which uses many crafts has become so important that it affects the welfare of a whole nation. So many people are associated with it that, if the normal amount of building declines for any reason, millions of people are deprived of a regular income and the whole world feels the loss of the purchasing power of such a large group.

Great numbers of people in other industries are in varying degrees dependent upon building. For example, what would happen to the brickmaker if no buildings were built? Or the maker of cement? Or of steel? The business of building is indeed of inestimable importance to general prosperity.

In essence, this huge business consists of nothing more than the construction of buildings—from a workman's cottage to a skyscraper office building or hotel. And, also essentially, the skyscraper is about the same as the cottage. It has a foundation, a body, and a roof.

The variations in these principal features are determined by what the complete building is intended to accomplish. Small buildings have quite simple foundations, usually of brick or stone, sunk in trenches which go below the frost line. Large buildings often need foundations which require great engineering skill. No matter how much soft soil he may encounter, a builder must dig deep enough to find a firm footing for the foundations of his heavy building. Frequently this is done by driving long piles down through the earth until they strike rock. These are fastened together at the top, and make a very strong foundation. In some cases, it is too costly to force piling down to satisfactory rock, so a *mat,* or floating foundation, is constructed of great numbers of short piles bound together to distribute the building's load over a wide area of yielding soil. These are a considerable distance below the surface of the ground. The great Field Museum of Natural History, and other large buildings in Chicago, rest upon foundations of this type.

By another method, *caissons* are sunk through soft soil or water-bearing clay to the rock level. The caissons are large iron boxes (usually round) open at the top and bottom. When they reach the rock they are sealed with concrete at the bottom, pumped dry, and then filled with concrete, reinforced with steel rods. The structure then rests on these pillars of man-made stone. Sometimes these pilings or pillars must go down as much as a hundred feet before they reach bedrock.

Determining the size, number, and placing of the caissons is a task requiring careful and exact calculations. The foundations of the building rest upon the caissons and they bear the entire weight of the structure. If the building is to be made of wood, then a skeleton of heavy beams is put up on the foundation and covered with the boards and plastering which form the walls.

This same sort of frame must be constructed for very large masonry buildings. These would require enormously thick walls to carry the weight of the upper stories, were it not for the frame upon which the whole is built. This frame consists of steel columns rising from the foundation, to which are fastened braced crosspieces, or girders, forming the floors. The brick or stone walls are then "hung" to this frame, and need be no thicker than the wall of any one-story building. One of the first of this type in the United States was the ten-story Home Insurance Company Building erected in Chicago in 1885.

Such steel and masonry buildings are usually finished on the inside with hollow tiling or other non-inflammable materials and are practically fireproof. Most of these new structures depend to a large extent upon reinforced concrete. This is simply ordinary concrete with steel reinforcing wires or rods running through it, to add strength and hold it together. Floors and many of the walls of modern buildings are made of this virtually everlasting material.

Such building methods have made possible the innumerable buildings of twenty, thirty, and more stories. The celebrated Empire State Building in New York, for instance, is 102 stories high. Without its steel frame it would require walls so thick there would be no room at all inside. It is interesting to note that the cloud-piercing towers of Manhattan reflect the fact that bedrock is near the surface on the island and provides a foundation suitable for highly concentrated loads.

The third principal part of any building is its roof. And this element, like the rest of the structure, varies with the purpose of the building, and with the building's architectural style. Most small buildings, such as ordinary homes, have so-called "double," or "pitched," roofs; that is, roofs which slant downward from a ridge and project over the side walls. Tall buildings, built also according to certain styles, usually have flat roofs. Flat roofs must slant slightly to one side or toward a drain so that water will run off.

All sorts of substances are used on roofs to make them waterproof and weatherproof. On most steeply pitched roofs we find shingles made of wood or slate; or perhaps metal, and sometimes tar-paper or special composition. Shingles must slant down in order to shed water, and so on flat roofs the most common covering is a thick coating of tar or other bituminous substance covered with a protective layer of gravel or roofing material, like asbestos. Some flat roofs, particularly those used for recreation, are covered with flat tiles fitted together with waterproof cement.

Although our buildings still perform much the same functions they always have, and still consist of foundation, body, and roof, we have come a long way from the crude huts of our distant forefathers. The list of equipment which goes into a modern

MAN'S DIVERSE DWELLINGS

Throughout the world, men have adapted their houses to the climate and conditions under which they live. Upper left, a tree dwelling, one of the most primitive types, found today on the island of Papua; upper right, a grass-roofed stilt hut on the island of Celebes; center, a log cabin of the wilds of North America; below, left, Indian tepees still to be seen on the Western plains of America; and, right, kraals of South African natives.

"GRASSTOPPERS" AND SKYSCRAPERS

The remarkable difference in buildings is vividly displayed here. Upper left, a stone, grass-thatched house in Ireland; upper right, a New York skyscraper; center, a Norwegian storehouse; and, below, a modern residence.

building would fill many pages; it includes just about everything made in the way of machinery and materials, from great girders to delicate electrical instruments, and from rough concrete to alabaster. And we have specialized our buildings to an amazing degree, so that no two things seem to be done under one roof. We have hotels, office buildings, factories, warehouses, theaters, garages, churches, schools, and an endless list of others, besides the most important of all—our homes.

The art of building, of course, is not limited to just "buildings." The same type of construction also builds bridges, roads, and railways, digs subways, and dams rivers. Building, indeed, is the foundation of all progress of the world in which we live today.

Additional material is to be found in articles such as ARCHITECTURE and BUILDING LAWS, and under the names of many building materials.

BUILDING LAWS. In large communities, the way buildings are built and what they are used for directly affect the health and safety of the citizens. In order to prevent the construction of unsafe, unsightly, or unpleasant buildings, cities have building laws. For instance, in some communities it is felt that tall buildings cut off light and air, or concentrate too many people in a small ground area. Therefore the local governments have passed ordinances forbidding the construction of buildings that are, for instance, over four stories high.

The "set-back" feature of the towering skyscrapers of New York and Chicago is the result of building laws. In set-back architecture, the structure is reduced in length and width as building proceeds, and the profile of the completed edifice shows a series of long steps. The purpose is to permit as much light and air as possible to reach near-by buildings.

Building laws are not solely concerned with size. They also apply to the materials and methods of construction. In certain large cities, particularly those which have experienced disastrous fires, no wooden buildings may be erected, because of the danger of fire where buildings are close together. And many cities have established building regulations covering drainage, lighting, heating, sanitary conditions, electric outlets, maximum floor load, chimney construction, location of building line, etc.

Some require that buildings over a certain height (usually six floors) must have elevators. And the owner of the building must have his elevators inspected by a city engineer periodically, so that the machinery will never be allowed to become unsafe.

Another important phase of building covered under the laws of many cities is called "zoning." These ordinances forbid the building of business blocks in residential districts. They govern the placement of private houses in residential blocks, so that none will interfere with another, and no neighbor will find the new dwelling unpleasant. Some cities even refuse to allow builders to put up houses in certain unusual styles, because they believe variations from accepted standards may spoil the appearance of a residential section. Many communities fix a certain minimum cost for homes in particular districts, so that all will measure up to the desired standard.

BULB. In spite of its thickness and globular shape, a bulb is an unusual kind of stem. It is, in fact, an underground stem built for storage. In its heart is a bud capable of producing a root and aerial shoots, and the stem and the scaly leaves which surround it are reservoirs of starch and other nourishment for the young plant which would come from the bud.

Onions and other bulbs originated in dry climates where the growing season is short, and where plants in good times must set aside food for future use. Many of the wild flowers of the great semi-arid valleys of California are bulbous, as are many of the flowers of our northern woods. Most of them are of the lily family. So, too, is the onion, though it is the only plant of this family whose bulb-stored food is also an important food for man.

The bulb is chiefly distinguished from the other forms of underground stems by its thickness and the presence of its scaly leaves.

A *corm,* such as that from which gladioli and crocuses are grown, is often known popularly as a bulb, but it is usually thinner and has but a few scales. A *tuber* has scales, but the difference between them and those of a bulb is readily seen in the comparison of a potato and an onion. A *rootstock,* or *rhizome*, is an underground stem that resembles a root.

Bulbous plants reproduce themselves in three ways. Most of them grow seed. A few, like the onion and the tiger lily and some ferns, produce aerial bulblets which fall to the ground and germinate like seeds. Still others, of which the dog-tooth violet is a notable example, after they have stored up enough nourishment for their own future, develop other underground bulbs which become new plants.

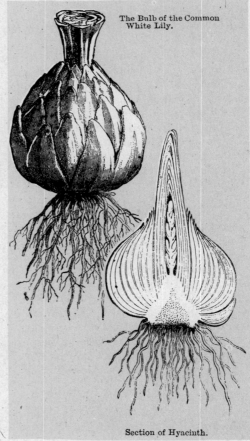

The Bulb of the Common White Lily.

Section of Hyacinth.

BULGARIAN ROSE GATHERERS   *Courtesy Travel Magazine*

Bulgaria is famed throughout the world for its attar of roses. The fragrant perfume oil is obtained by peasants from such rose gardens as the one shown here. The chief occupation of the people is agriculture.

BULGA'RIA. Proud memories of an ancient Bulgar empire still fire the sturdy people of Bulgaria, war-crushed nation once known as "the young giant of the Balkans." After the Treaty of Neuilly (1919), following the first World War, this former ally of the Central Powers became a weak and defenseless little kingdom on the shore of the Black Sea.

The Bulgarians are descended from a Turanian tribe from Asia and from Slavs, and are related to the Huns and Avars. Their langauge is Slavonic and akin to the Russian.

The Land and Its Resources. Modern Bulgaria faces east toward the Black Sea, on which are located the two main seaports, Varna and Burgas. The country is bounded on the north by Rumania, on the west by Yugoslavia, and on the south by Greece and European Turkey. Its area is 39,825 square miles. Four physical features of the land determine its climate and resources—two river valleys and two mountain ranges. Along the northern border of Bulgaria extends the valley of the Danube River. Sloping downward toward this fertile plain are the foothills of the Balkan Mountains, a range extending from west to east through the central portion of the country. In the extreme south are the Rhodope Mountains, and between the two ranges lies the fertile valley of the Maritsa.

The region north of the Balkan Mountains has long, severe winters with overcast skies, but these mountains form a high, protecting barrier from cold winds, and the country to the south of the range enjoys a fairly mild climate. In the far south the climate is like that of sunny Mediterranean lands.

Agriculture is the principal occupation of the people. The best soils are found in the Danubian and Maritsa valleys. Most of the farmers are owners of small farms, which seldom are over six acres in area. Cereal grains are the most important crops, with wheat and corn leading. These two grains and rye are widely used by the people for bread, as the Bulgarians did not submit to the corn-mush diet which the Turks attempted to force upon the peasant population of the Balkans. Among other products are rice, cotton, tobacco, fruit, potatoes, sugar beets, silkworm cocoons, and roses for attar. The growing of roses, a peasant occupation, is the basis of a prosperous perfume trade.

The mineral resources are limited, but the soft-coal mines have been developed to a certain extent, and there is a small export of this fuel. Copper, aluminum, lead, and salt are also mined, but the production is not large. The northern slopes of the Balkans are heavily wooded with beech and oak, and in this section woodcutting flourishes. Much of the timber is burned for the production of charcoal.

Cattle, horses, and swine are bred in sufficient numbers for the export of skins and live animals, but the universal domestic animal is the goat. Goat milk, soured by an artificial culture of bacteria, forms one of the chief articles of peasant diet.

Commerce and Communication. Preferring to live on their land, the Bulgarians carry on little manufacturing, and import a wide variety of manufactured products—textiles, metal wares, machinery, and other commodities. The leading exports include wheat, corn, prunes, attar of roses, live animals, eggs, and tobacco. The greater portion of Bulgarian trade is with Central Europe.

Bulgaria has a modern railroad system, and Sofia is connected with the main European rail and air routes.

Asiatic Europeans. The population of Bulgaria is a little over six million, the majority of whom are Bulgarians by race. There are many Turks, a sinister reminder of the long centuries when Bulgaria was a Turkish province. The population also includes other Slav races, Rumanians, Greeks, and Gypsies. The Bulgarians are very stocky in build, with broad shoulders, and their physical appearance reflects the solidity of character for which they are noted. Their swarthy color is more Oriental than European, but there the resemblance stops, for their character is European. They are, as a rule, devoted supporters of

Ewing Galloway

SCENES FROM SOFIA
The Church of Saint Alexander is the largest Christian church in the Balkans, and one of the most beautiful edifices in Bulgaria. Right, a Bulgarian peasant leading his donkey along a street covered with drying tobacco.

education, have high moral standards, and are thrifty and intelligent.

Primary education is free and compulsory, and only the wealthy have to pay fees in the higher grades. All the larger towns have excellent high schools, and Sofia, the capital, has a fine state university with about 7,000 students. The State Church, although Greek Orthodox, is not under the control of the Patriarch at Constantinople (see GREEK CHURCH). The great majority of the people belong to this Church, but there are a number of Roman Catholics, Protestants, Gregorian Armenians, Jews, and Mohammedans.

Government. In theory, the Bulgarian government, since World War I, has been strictly a constitutional monarchy, with the king as nominal ruler aided by an assembly and a Cabinet of eight ministers. However, actual power has changed from first one party to another. Following a complex series of revolts in 1934-35, an authoritative Fascist state was formed by King Boris, that outlawed all political parties and ruled by decree and military force until the fall of 1944, when Bulgaria broke with Germany and surrendered to the Allies. Then, under Russia's sponsorship, a new government was established that promised a return of the democratic constitution and free elections.

From Barbarism to a Balkan Kingdom. In the fourth century, the barbarous Bulgar tribes swept in from Central Asia and settled between the Volga River and the Ural Mountains. However, they were driven from there to the fertile basin along the Danube River, where, in the seventh century, they settled permanently, giving their name to the region. About 860, the Bulgars became Christians. Boris I, then king, probably chose the Greek Orthodox Church for political reasons and because of the nearness of the Byzantine capital. It was under his son and successor, Simeon, who assumed the title of emperor, that Bulgaria reached its golden age and became the greatest power in the Balkans. After Simeon's death, the nation rapidly declined.

The darkest period in Bulgarian history began late in the fourteenth century, when Islam, crusading with fire and sword, brought all Bulgaria under the rule of the Turks. Not until the Treaty of Berlin, in 1878, did a new Bulgaria emerge as a semi-independent state under the nominal control of the sultan of Turkey. Southern Bulgaria was left to the Turkish Empire under the name of Eastern Rumelia. All Europe plotted to gain influence in the new state, and in 1885 Eastern Rumelia threw off the Turkish yoke and joined Bulgaria under Prince Ferdinand of Saxe-Coburg-Gotha.

In 1909, during the Young Turk revolution, Bulgaria proclaimed its absolute independence, Ferdinand I taking the title of czar. The new ruler helped bring about the First Balkan War of 1912, in which the Balkan states united practically to force Turkey out of Europe. The Turks were vanquished, but Bulgaria soon warred against its former allies over the division of the territorial spoils. This Second Balkan War, in 1913, was disastrous to Bulgaria, its recent conquests going to Rumania, Serbia, and Greece.

In 1915, as allies of Germany, the Bulgarians crushed Serbia; but, in 1918, Bulgaria itself collapsed. Ferdinand fled the country and was succeeded by his son Boris III, in a constitutional monarchy. World War I cost Bulgaria its Aegean Sea coast, which was ceded to Greece. On King Boris' death in 1943, his six-year-old son succeeded him as Simeon II, under a regency. Bulgaria joined Nazi Germany in World War II, but surrendered in 1944. See SERBIA; TURKEY; WORLD WAR I; WORLD WAR II.

BULL'DOG. Despite ferocious looks and a well-earned reputation as fighters, bulldogs are generally good-natured, friendly animals. They are dependable family dogs and usually are perfectly safe.

A good type of English bulldog should weigh between thirty and forty pounds. Its head should be large and square, its face wrinkled deeply, and its lower jaw so much longer than its upper that the lower front

FIERCE BUT FRIENDLY
Despite their looks, bulldogs are good pets.

teeth show when its mouth is closed. The nose of the accepted, ideal type is snubbed, so that it just touches a straight line drawn from the lower jaw to the eyebrow. Such a line continued should touch the forehead.

A thick, short neck is desired. The shoulders should be wide and low, and the back should curve up to the hips, which should be higher than the shoulders. The legs should be strongly bowed, with the toes turned out and the hock turned in. English bulldogs are found in many colors, but brindle, a gray color with darker spots, is generally the most desired.

Miniature bulldogs are like those already described, but should not exceed twenty-two pounds in weight. French bulldogs are like miniature bulldogs, but have large, erect bat ears, and do not show the teeth when the mouth is closed.

BUL'LET. The projectiles, or ammunition used in small firing arms—rifles, machine guns, revolvers, and pistols—are bullets. Shaped like a cone, tapering toward the front, a bullet usually has a copper core and a covering made from a combination of copper and nickel. When fired, it travels in a spiral fashion like a well-tossed forward pass in football. The width of a bullet depends on the diameter of the gun's muzzle. Bullets for rifles are longer than those for pistols and revolvers.

Dumdum bullets, which spread out and tear the flesh when they strike, are condemned for use in modern warfare. They are, however, sometimes used in shooting animals. These bullets have a weak casing, permitting the core to widen when it strikes. A dumdum bullet wound is always large, bloody, and painful, frequently causing death.

POISED FOR THE KILL
The supreme moment of the bullfight has arrived.
The matador prepares to kill the bull and be
lauded by the crowd.

BULL'FIGHTING. The national sport of Spain, bullfighting is witnessed each year by thousands of persons in the amphitheaters of that country. It is also a favorite sport in Spanish-speaking lands, such as Mexico. This colorful and exciting pastime, in which many horses and bulls are slain, has often been criticized for its cruelty, although few human beings are ever injured or killed.

To many people, bullfighting is very nerve-racking, in spite of the color and pageantry typical of it. At a bullfight in an arena, the ceremonies begin with a parade of the bullfighters. As the band plays and the crowd cheers, the officers of the ring march in first, followed by the *espadas,* or *matadors.* They are attired in gaily colored short jackets and knee breeches, embroidered with gold and silver. They wear light silk stockings and shoes without heels, and with their small tri-cornered hats, present a dashing appearance. Most of the cheers are for them, for they are the heroes of the ring because they are the actual killers.

THE ORACLE OF THE LILY PADS
The bullfrog looks wise as he suns himself on a lily pad, but all he ever says is "jug-o-rum." His legs are a food delicacy.

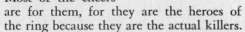

Following the matadors come the *banderilleros,* dressed like the matadors. After them come the *picadores* on horseback, dressed in yellow. They wear armor over their legs and carry short, sharp lances. The *chulos,* or helpers, follow the bullfighters. Bringing up the rear is the festooned team of three mules, or *arrestes,* used to haul the carcass of the bull from the ring. When the key to the bull pen is thrown into the ring by a dignitary, the event is ready to begin.

The bull, bred and raised especially for the ring, comes charging from his pen, furious because a pin which bears the colors of his breeder is sticking into his shoulder. The *picadores* torment him by stabbing him in the back with their short lances.

Frequently the horses are killed by the bull's horns. A trumpet then blows, and the dodging, agile banderilleros come out, enraging the bull still more by waving a red cloak at him and throwing barbs, or *banderillas,* into his neck. Sometimes, if the bull is unwilling to attack, squibs like firecrackers are set off by the darts. The trumpet blows again, and the proud matador appears.

Throwing his hat behind his back, he dedicates the bull to some high official. Then, with sword and red flag, he advances toward the bull. He attempts to kill him with one expert thrust of the sword through the shoulder and into the heart. Should he fail, the chulos make an end of the bull. But if he succeeds, the matador is hailed by the crowd and is showered with flowers and money. The team of mules then drags the bull off the field, and it is time for the next fight to begin. During a day of bullfighting, as many as eight bulls are often killed.

BULL'FINCH. Because it can learn to whistle a tune, the bullfinch has made himself very popular with bird lovers. This bright, gay songster can be heard chirping his imitative song in forests and woodlands throughout Europe and parts of Asia. He is allied to the American grosbeak. One of the few birds which can be trained to sing a definite melody, a bullfinch which has been taught several tunes is a valuable pet.

The bullfinch is bluish gray and has a bright-red breast and a black head. He has a short, thick, black beak. Being rather shy, he stays quite deep in forest shrubbery most of the time.

BULL'FROG. In many sections on early spring nights there may come from ponds or lakes a call which sounds like "jug-o-rum, jug-o-rum." The maker of this call is the bullfrog, the largest eastern frog. Bullfrogs appear early in the spring and lay their eggs during June and July.

These float in masses on top of the water, and in about four days they hatch and become "pollywogs" or tadpoles. They are full-grown, or adult, the next year, when they may reach a length of five to eight inches. Small dark spots mark the back and top of the head, which vary in color from bright to dark brownish green. The bullfrog is found in North America west to the Rocky Mountains.

Frog legs are considered a great delicacy by many. Bullfrogs are raised commercially in some sections. See FROG.

BULL'HEAD. See CATFISH.

BULLION, *bool'yun.* Precious metals— gold and silver—existing in ingots or any other uncoined form are classed as bullion. Gold or silver trinkets or dishes no longer serviceable rank as bullion; other forms include uncurrent coin and coin of foreign countries not legally circulated and valuable only as metal. Formerly, the owner of gold bullion in the United States could take such property to the government mint and exchange it for gold coin of equal value, less a small percentage, called *seigniorage,* deducted for coinage. In 1933 the United States government prohibited the hoarding of gold bullion and ordered it deposited with banks and the Treasury Department.

BULL RUN, BATTLES OF. Three months after the fall of Fort Sumter, a body of 31,000 Confederate volunteers gathered along Bull Run Creek in Virginia, about thirty miles southwest of Washington, D. C. Their commander was General Beauregard of New Orleans, a former superintendent of West Point.

They threatened the nation's capital and blocked the way to Richmond, Va., which recently had been made military headquarters. To make a show of strength, General McDowell was ordered out from Washington with 28,000 Union soldiers, mostly raw recruits.

McDowell attacked the Confederate left at dawn on July 21, 1861. At first he was successful and pressed on, only to meet the Confederate leader, General Thomas Jackson, who threw five regiments across the path of the Union advance. Here Jackson won his fame as "Stonewall." His resistance was soon strengthened by a reserve brigade under General Kirby Smith, and the demoralized Union troops began a retreat which became a rout. Shaken stragglers who gained Washington that night announced that the South had won the war.

First Bull Run was a terrible blow to the Federal cause, but it did shock the nation into building a trained army. Just about a year later, on August 29 and 30, 1862, the Union army, now better organized, had to endure another bitter defeat at this same scene, Bull Run. General Pope, to whom was credited the remark that henceforward his "headquarters would be in the saddle," followed what he took to be a withdrawal of Stonewall Jackson's command. Jackson promptly drew Pope into range of Longstreet's cannon, which caught the advance in the flank with raking fire.

The Union retreat across the creek was imperative. Union veterans did not fly in panic as they had the year before, but they were forced to fall back and reorganize. This engagement, sometimes called the Battle of Manassas, or Second Manassas (Manassas Junction is on the field), left Virginia to the Confederates and gave "Old Stonewall" a second victory on his "baptismal battlefield." See CIVIL WAR IN AMERICA.

BUL'WER-LYTTON, *lit'un,* EDWARD GEORGE EARLE, Lord Lytton (1803-1873). An English writer of many popular stories, Lord Lytton was also a successful dramatist. He was forced to turn to writing to earn a living because his mother did not approve of his marriage and discontinued his allowance. In addition to his work as an author, he also served twice as a member of Parliament. He was made a baronet in 1838 and became the first Baron Lytton in 1866.

Some of Bulwer-Lytton's most popular plays are *Richelieu, Money,* and the *Lady of Lyons.* Among his novels are *The Last of the Barons,* his greatest historical novel; *Rienzi, My Novel,* and *The Caxtons.* But he is best known as the author of *The Last*

WHEN THE REVOLUTION BEGAN IN EARNEST

The Battle of Bunker Hill, first important engagement of the Revolutionary War, was lost by the Americans, but the stout defense of the patriots gave confidence to the rest of the colonies.

Days of Pompeii, an historical novel. His books have always been popular because they tell interesting stories, even if the style is rather sentimental and affected.

BUM′BLEBEE. If a bumblebee hovers about your head, you need have little worry about it suddenly attacking you and inflicting a painful sting. Bumblebees are peaceful and never show any signs of temper unless their nests are disturbed. When these bees are disturbed, however, they inflict a sting worse than that of any other bee.

Bumblebees have thick, hairy bodies and are well known in all parts of the world, particularly in the Northern Hemisphere. Small colonies of them live in nests where about half the bees are workers (neuters) and the remainder males or females. Bumblebees collect and store honey, but the honey has no commercial value. At the end of the summer the colony breaks up and the males and workers die, leaving the females to start new colonies in the spring.

Bumblebees are chiefly of value for the aid they render in cross fertilization, which means that the pollens of two different plants are exchanged to produce a better seed. Some kinds of clover cannot be grown in a region where there are no bumblebees, for no other insect can fertilize the plants. Great numbers of bumblebees were imported into Australia and New Zealand before clover could be raised there.

BUNKER HILL, BATTLE OF. Overlooking the city of Boston stands a tall granite monument which marks the site of the Battle of Bunker Hill. This battle is considered one of the most important in the American Revolutionary War, because it aroused in the hearts of the colonists the spirit of conflict and gave them confidence to oppose regular English troops again.

This first important conflict of the American Revolution was fought on June 17, 1775. The British army under General Gage

BUNYAN'S WIFE PLEADS FOR HIS RELEASE
While he was in prison, John Bunyan began his great allegory, *The Pilgrim's Progress.*

was stationed in Boston; the American army under General Ward occupied Cambridge. When the Americans learned that the British intended to seize Bunker Hill, which overlooked Charlestown, they secretly fortified near-by Breed's Hill during the night of June 16. The next morning the British warships in Charlestown Harbor opened fire on the Americans, but were finally forced to land troops under the command of General Howe.

Twice the Americans beat back the British by their strategy of withholding fire until they saw the "whites of their foe's eyes." When their ammunition was exhausted, the Americans were forced to retreat to Bunker Hill during the third British attack, using as weapons stones and the butts of rifles. The British loss was about 1,000 killed and wounded; the Americans lost 450, including the famous patriot General Joseph Warren.

BUN'YAN, John (1628-1688). The best-known and most popular book on the spiritual life of man, *The Pilgrim's Progress,* was written by an Englishman, John Bunyan. At least part of the book was written in prison. A preacher in a society of Baptists in Bedford, England, he was imprisoned from 1660 to 1672 for breaking the severe laws against dissenters. During a second imprisonment, in 1675, his famous allegorical book was finished. It has been translated into more languages than has any other volume except the Bible.

John Bunyan was the son of a tinker and followed his father's trade. He fought on the side of Parliament during the English civil war. Largely because of his wife, he joined the Baptist society, which led to his imprisonment. Others of his works are *The Life and Death of Mr. Badman, The Holy War,* and *Grace Abounding*.

BUOY, *boo'y.* As guides to navigation in lakes, rivers, and harbors, floating objects are anchored. They are made of wood or metal and are known as buoys. The meaning or purpose of each buoy is indicated by the shape, color, number, or marking. If there is ice in the water, *spar* buoys, which are wooden poles with anchors, are used. The *can* buoy is a cylindrical can of iron; a *nun* buoy is conical-shaped.

Some types of buoys have bells, others lamps; and a third variety whistles as the waves compress and drive air through them. In the United States, white buoys indicate safe anchorage; green ones mark submerged wrecks. If there are vertical black and white stripes, the buoy is in mid-channel. Black and red horizontal stripes mean danger. Usually, red buoys indicate the starboard side for a ship entering a harbor; black indicates the port side.

THE "WIZARD" AND HIS MAGIC

Luther Burbank, master of plants, developed the small English daisy (insert) into the large Shasta of today.

BUR'BANK, Luther (1849-1926). On an experimental farm at Sebastopol, near Santa Rosa, Calif., worked a man named Luther Burbank, destined to become the world's greatest plant breeder. Today, farmers in arid regions owe him thanks as the creator of the spineless cactus, which provides food for cattle. Many others, in various parts of the world, are grateful for the brilliant array of finer fruits and flowers, which he produced through painstaking and laborious experimentation.

Burbank was born at Lancaster, Mass. On the farm where he lived, he read Darwin's *Variation of Animals and Plants Under Domestication.* This was the turning point of his life. After a short period as a factory worker at Worcester, he acquired a piece of land on which to carry out his experiments. Two years later, he had developed the now-famous Burbank potato. Formerly, farmers had been able to raise

only 200 bushels of potatoes to the acre. Now, largely because of Burbank's work, the average is about 525 bushels. The United States Department of Agriculture gives Burbank credit for an additional $17,-000,000 a year in agricultural output because of this large and excellent potato. See Po-TATO.

Because the climate of Massachusetts was not suited to his experiments, Burbank moved to Santa Rosa, where his three elder brothers lived, and began his work anew. He obtained dramatic results by *crossing,* that is, cross breeding, different forms of the same plant to produce better types, known as *hybrids.* The work involved constant selection and segregation. In guiding changes in plant life, Burbank had to remove all plants with undesirable qualities, and keep the better from the poorer.

Sometimes the proper result was obtained from one crossing, but more often it took many of them before he was satisfied. Scores of different species of berries were used in producing several different new varieties for the market. Burbank worked forty years on the development of new types of peaches, plums, and prunes, the most famous of which is the *nectarine,* a mutant from a peach.

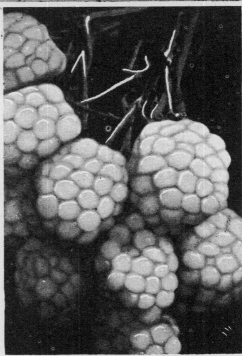

CREATED BY NATURE—
CONTROLLED BY MAN

Spineless cactus (above) is one of Burbank's achievements, now used as food for cattle; even more marvelous are his luscious, white *black*berries!

Other famous results from the Burbank experimental farm were the white blackberry, seedless apple, cobless corn, stoneless plum, and the Shasta daisy. He created a variety of wheat which grew fifty bushels to the acre, on soil which before had produced only twelve. He joined a Japanese plum to an apricot and produced the delectable *plumcot.* The *pomato,* a type of tomato which grows on a potato vine, is his creation, as well as a variety of huge black walnut and a quince which tastes somewhat like a pineapple.

A WORTHLESS COUSIN OF THE CODFISH
The flesh of the burbot, a fresh-water fish, is of little value.

Burbank was one of the most practical of men. Instead of devoting his time to botanical guesswork, he produced immediate benefits for the world. His "better fruits and fairer flowers" have raised Burbank to an honored place among natural scientists.

Burbank's wizardry with plants is to some extent preserved for posterity in his writing. *New Creations,* 1893-1901, is a series of descriptive catalogues; *Luther Burbank, His Methods and Discoveries,* 1914-15, and *How Plants Are Trained to Work for Man,* 1921, are later works. With Wilbur Hall, he also wrote *The Harvest of the Years,* published in 1927.

BUR'BOT. Shaped somewhat like an eel, with two barbs on the nose and another on the chin, the burbot is almost useless as a food, being coarse and tasteless. It is the only member of the cod family that lives exclusively in fresh water. It is found in the lakes and streams of the northern part of the United States, and of Canada, England, Asia, and Northern Europe. Its average length is about two feet; the average weight is about twelve pounds, but in Alaska it has been known to attain a weight of sixty pounds. The fish is especially active at night.

BUR'DOCK. Commonly found clinging to the clothing of people and the hair of animals, the burdock is a coarse weed which grows in the United States and Canada, especially in cattle- and sheep-grazing regions. The plant grows to a height of about three feet, although in its second season it sometimes reaches a height of nine feet. It cannot be destroyed by cutting because it is a biennial, and lives for two years; it must be dug up before it bears seed. Burdock can be recognized by its prickly flowers with hooked heads and by the roundish or heart-shaped leaves which can be used as poultices. In Japan, parts of the plant are used in soups.

BUR'GOMASTER. Although his duties are much the same as those of the mayor of a city in America or England, the German official known as the burgomaster must qualify for his position by years of study. The post is an elective one, but occasionally, under the empire, the government would refuse to sanction some choices. This title occurs in a number of plays, operas, and stories about Germany.

BURGOYNE, *bur gawyn',* JOHN (1722-1792). The turning point of the Revolutionary War is usually considered to have been the surrender of General John Burgoyne to General Horatio Gates at Saratoga, on October 17, 1777. However, one important British victory was his, that at Ticonderoga. On his return to England, Burgoyne was not at first warmly received. In fact, his command was taken from him. But later, for a period of two years, he was commander in chief in Ireland. He was an author as well as a soldier, and wrote a number of comedies, including *Maid of the Oaks* and *The Lord of the Manor.*

FRIEND OF AMERICA
Edmund Burke, who spoke for the colonies.

BURKE, Edmund (1729-1797). Outstanding as an opponent of the right of England to tax the American colonies, Edmund Burke, noted English orator, statesman, and writer made a number of speeches on this subject in Parliament. His oration on *Conciliation with America,* delivered in March, 1775, is still studied in high schools as an example of logical thinking.

Burke was born in Ireland and was educated there at Trinity College. Later he studied law in London, but eventually gave up law and turned to writing. His friendship with many of England's notables began after the publication, in 1756, of his essay entitled *Philosophical Inquiry into the Origin of Our Ideas on the Sublime and Beautiful.*

Elected to Parliament in 1766, Burke was a member of that body for almost thirty years. He took an active part in the impeachment trial of Warren Hastings, governor of India, who was accused of injustice in his treatment of the natives. Although Hastings was acquitted, Burke's oratory was heralded as being among the finest ever heard. He separated from the Liberals, among them his old friend Charles Fox, when he fought against the policies of the French Revolution. Until his resignation from Parliament in 1794, he opposed revolutionary doctrines. See Hastings, Warren.

BUR'MA. Surrounded by the Bay of Bengal, Siam, China, Tibet, and Assam, is a strange and fascinating land called Burma. It is a land of mountains and rice fields, of elephants and pagodas. The natives are happy and easy-going, not working any harder than is absolutely necessary. Burma furnished the setting for Kipling's beloved poem *Mandalay,* for Mandalay is a city in the interior of the country.

To the north, Burma is separated from Tibet by part of the Himalayas. Parallel to the mountains runs the Brahmaputra River. To the south, an arm of Burma, called Tenasserim, stretches down into the Malay Peninsula. The total area of Burma is 261,-610 square miles, which is over twice the area of the Philippine Islands.

The great river of Burma is the Irrawaddy, navigable for a distance of 900 miles from the Bay of Bengal. It irrigates about three-fourths of the country. The soil in the delta of the river is unusually fertile. Agriculture, therefore, is the chief occupation in Burma, farmers leasing land from the state. Rice leads in importance. Other products are millet, tobacco, sugar cane, oil seeds, and cotton. Iron, copper, tin, lead, tungsten, gold, silver, and precious stones are mined there. But by far the most important mineral is oil; about 250,000,000 gallons are produced yearly. Oil refining is the leading industry.

Although Burma still produces some textiles, cheap foreign goods are ruining her trade. The chief exports, most of which go to India and other parts of the British Empire, are rice, teakwood, hides, cotton, silk, rubber, oil, and precious stones. Machinery, sugar, coal, and hardware are imported.

Burma's forests are the homes of many wild animals and reptiles, including the elephant, tiger, rhinoceros, monkey, deer, python, and many others. The forests are a source of the valuable teakwood. It is in

BEAUTY IN BURMA

Such uncomfortable-looking rings around the neck may seem strange to the Western world, but to the people of Lower and Eastern Burma, they greatly enhance the wearer's beauty. Adult women sometimes don as many as 21 to 25 such ornaments.

the teakwood industry that elephants have been trained to do the heavy work. Kipling mentions them in the lines,

> Elephints a-pilin' teak
> In the sludgy, squdgy creek.

Rangoon, the capital of Burma, is situated on the Rangoon River in the delta of the Irrawaddy. The population is a little more than 500,000. Railways extend from Rangoon to other important towns, principally Mandalay, a city of 150,000, located in the heart of Burma.

The natives of Burma belong to the Mongolian race. They are an intelligent people, much better educated than are people in the other Indian states. And there is no caste system. The Burmese women have much more freedom than is usual in the Far East. They have a large share in the business of the country and are even allowed to vote. Most of the 16,825,000 people in Burma are Buddhists, the others being Animists, Hindus, Mohammedans, and Christians.

In 1937 Burma became a crown colony, separate from British India, in accordance with the Government of India Act of 1935. It has its own constitution and representative legislature; the governor is assisted by a Council of Ministers. Burma was occupied by the Japanese in 1942, but was practically freed before August, 1945.

BURNS, ROBERT (1759-1796). Whoever loves the simple verse of everyday life, knows and cherishes the songs and poems of "Bobbie" Burns, Scotland's greatest poet. He was not a man of family, or culture, or wealth. Born in poverty, forced in boyhood to work beyond his strength, he absorbed the traditions and sentiment of his native country, and phrased the old Scottish songs in words so true and tender that the world has delighted to sing them from his day to ours.

Two miles from Ayr is the small hamlet of Alloway, on the River Doon. Visitors today may see there the little thatched cottage where Burns was born, on January 25, 1759. The family was miserably poor, and young Robert had to do hard, disagreeable

SCOTLAND'S BELOVED BARD

tasks on his father's farm, tasks that taxed his strength. He had little schooling, but he read whenever he could, from morning until night, even while eating. When he was working in the fields, he carried books in his pockets, that he might snatch a bit of reading while following the plow. Out of such experiences came poems like the lovely *To a Mountain Daisy*:

> Wee, modest, crimson-tipped flower
> Thou'st met me in an evil hour,
> For I maun crush among the stour
> Thy slender stem;
> To spare thee now is past my power,
> Thou bonnie gem.

Burns' favorite book in his younger days was a collection of old Scottish songs and ballads, which had been collected and published by two Scottish writers. The words sang themselves into his mind and heart, and from his inspired imagination came new lines and phrases for the old lays.

In 1782 Burns went to Irvine to learn the flax-dressing trade, but the shop burned down during a New Year's celebration, and the plan came to nothing. His father died two years later, and Robert and his brother Gilbert tried to make a living by managing a small farm at Mossgiel. The venture was a failure, but during the unhappy struggle, for which he was ill fitted, Burns was writing down some of the poems that are today among his best works. When his plea for the hand of Jean Armour was rejected by the girl's father, he determined to exile himself in Jamaica. To obtain money for the trip, Burns published, by subscription, his first volume of poems. The success of this book, which appeared in 1786, changed the course of his life.

The literary world knew that only a great poet could have written the poems in this small volume—such poems as *Hallowe'en, The Cotter's Saturday Night, To a Mouse, To a Daisy,* and others equally famous. Burns was feasted and flattered in the literary circles of Edinburgh, and a second edition of the book was published which brought the author $2,000. The young poet bought a farm at Ellisland, married his Jean, and made a new start in life. Though he was again unsuccessful as a farmer, his poetic flame still burned brightly, and at Ellisland he wrote such well-beloved poems as *Auld Lang Syne* and *Tam o' Shanter*.

Burns had no practical ability in money matters, and in 1789 he accepted a position as customs inspector for the district. Two years later his farm failed, and he moved to Dumfries, where he relied on his salary alone for an income. Some of his most beautiful poetry was written there, but he was thrown in the company of the idle and dissipated, and a besetting weakness, his love of drink, undermined his health. Lovable, impulsive, given to moods of despair, Burns plunged into reckless dissipation, and in 1796 he died at the age of thirty-seven. His wife and four children were left unprovided for, and friends of the poet took up a subscription for their support.

"Bobbie" Burns must have felt that his life was broken and wasted, but from another viewpoint he attained the highest success anyone could desire. His poetry has given joy to countless readers. We cherish him for the love and tenderness he showed for weak and helpless things—the daisy uprooted by his plowshare, the frightened mouse, "wee, tim'rous beastie," scurrying away from the overturned nest. We admire his respect for the dignity of human character—

> For a' that, and a' that
> Our toil's obscure, and a' that,
> The rank is but the guinea's stamp,
> The man's the gowd, for a' that.

The true Burns was the poet of *Auld Lang Syne, A Man's a Man, The Cotter's Saturday Night,* and all the other poems that sing of the things dear to human hearts. By these we judge Scotland's "Bobbie" Burns.

BURR, AARON (1756-1836). In history there sometimes appears a tragic figure who has the ambition and ability to be a great man, but misuses his talents in selfish and disgraceful experiences. Aaron Burr was such a man, and today his career as a brilliant soldier and political leader is obscured by memories of his share in the death of Alexander Hamilton, and his unsuccessful plot against his country.

Burr, who was born at Newark, N. J., came from a distinguished family of educators and grew up in an atmosphere of learning. His father and grandfather were presidents of the College of New Jersey, now Princeton College. There he received his degree.

As a soldier in the Revolutionary War, he distinguished himself for bravery, and when he resigned, in 1779, he had risen to the rank of lieutenant colonel. He entered the legal profession and began his political career by being elected attorney-general of New York state. In 1791 he became United States Senator from New York.

Nine years later, Burr received the same number of electoral votes as Jefferson in the election for President, and when the contest was thrown into the House of Representatives, he was defeated only by the influence of Alexander Hamilton, who feared him as a "dangerous man." Burr then became Vice-President. In 1804 he was nominated for governor of New York but failed of election.

Blaming Hamilton for his political reverses, he challenged him to a duel. On

THE DUEL THAT BLIGHTED BURR'S CAREER

The world never forgave Aaron Burr for mortally wounding Alexander Hamilton in their famous duel. He might have become President. Instead, he died in disgrace.

July 11 of that year, the duelists met across the Hudson River from New York, and Hamilton was mortally wounded. Immediately, Burr was accused of murder; he fled to the South, but later returned to finish his term as Vice-President.

His hopes of becoming President blasted, Burr plotted to set himself up as head of a new republic or state in the Southwest. The plans were discovered, however, and he was tried for treason in 1807. He was found not guilty, but the episode definitely ended his political career. He died in obscurity on Staten Island.

BURROUGHS, *bur'oze,* JOHN (1837-1921). John Burroughs was one of those rare men to whom Nature confided her choicest secrets, and who in turn was able to interpret them for other people. He understood the birds and flowers and the habits of bees, fishes, and insects. And he was able to relate his discoveries so charmingly in poems and essays that he created a new interest in nature literature.

Burroughs was born on a farm near Roxbury, N. Y., and spent his early life there. Later he lived in a small town. He watched and studied the life about him, ever marveling at the wonders of nature. When quite a young man, he began to teach school and also to write essays about the woods and fields. His essays were so fascinating that he soon became one of the most popular writers in America.

For economic reasons, Burroughs was obliged to spend a number of years in business. For ten years he was a clerk in the Treasury Department. For several years he was a bank examiner. It was while he was in the Treasury Department that he met Walt Whitman. They became staunch friends, and Whitman exerted a lasting influence on Burroughs as a writer on nature.

Later, Burroughs bought a little farm in New York state. There he wrote many of his best-known books and essays, and many people still go there to see his house.

Among his most popular works are *Locusts and Wild Honey, Pepacton, Wake Robin, Sharp Eyes, Camping and Tramping with Roosevelt, Bird and Bough, Time and Change,* and *The Breath of Life.*

BUSH'MEN. In the great Kalahari region north of the Cape of Good Hope, in Western South Africa, dwell the Bushmen, one of the most primitive peoples in the world. These yellowish-brown natives hardly ever reach a height of more than five feet unless they intermarry with taller tribes. They are extremely shy and unite only to hunt or to defend themselves. Poisoned arrows are their characteristic weapon. They have no permanent homes, but live in caves or under any shelter they can find, moving when their water supply gives out.

The Bushmen are not intelligent enough to cultivate the land, but depend on game for a meager living. Their complicated language consists of gurgling, grunting, whistling, and clickings of the tongue, unlike any other speech known today, with the exception of the Hottentot. It is thought by some authorities that these people once inhabited all of Africa.

BUT'LER, NICHOLAS MURRAY (1862–). President of Columbia University from 1902 to 1945, Nicholas Murray Butler is a man of varied interests. He has

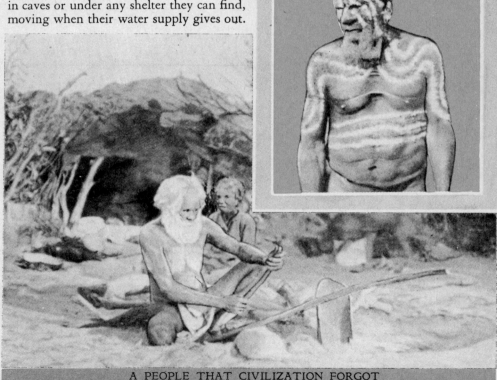

A PEOPLE THAT CIVILIZATION FORGOT
Australian bushmen, among the most primitive people in the world, still live without the benefits of civilization. One of the primitive customs is to paint themselves in grotesque designs.

constantly taken an active interest in state, national, and world affairs and has been mentioned several times as a possible candidate for the Presidency of the United States. He has been ceaseless in his efforts toward world peace. He was instrumental in the establishment of the Carnegie Endowment for International Peace. He favored disarmament and American participation in the World Court, the League of Nations, and the Pact of Paris. For these and other actions on behalf of peace, Dr. Butler, together with Jane Addams, was awarded the Nobel Peace Prize in 1931.

Nicholas Murray Butler was born in Elizabeth, N. J. He graduated from Columbus College (now Columbia University) and then studied abroad. He was made an assistant in philosophy at Columbia in 1885, becoming dean of the faculty of philosophy five years later. In 1902 he was appointed president of the university and has served in that capacity ever since.

Among other activities, he established the Medical Center, the School of Journalism, the University Extension, and the Summer Session at Columbia. He has probably received more honorary degrees from universities in the United States and Europe than has any other American; and he has also received decorations from foreign countries. Dr. Butler has written a number of books on education.

BUTLER, Pierce (1866-1939). Appointed by President Harding, Pierce Butler became an Associate Justice of the Supreme Court in 1922. He was a native of Minnesota and a graduate of Carleton College. Before his appointment to the Supreme Court, Justice Butler was a lawyer, specializing in railroad law.

BUTTE, *bute.* In the Rocky Mountain region of Western United States, the traveler often sees a solitary mountain or hill rising abruptly above the surrounding country. These prominences are buttes, formed by the washing away of soft rock and soil from around harder formations. Sometimes the word is applied to high mountains, but this is not generally the case

in the United States. The name of the largest city in Montana, Butte, comes from the fact that it is located in an area where these lone peaks are plentiful. Lassen Butte, Calif., is a volcanic cone.

BUT'TER. One of the commonest of all foods, butter is usually thought of in connection with bread, the combination forming a principal part of the human diet. As a matter of fact, the use of these two staple articles together is so general that we often refer to labor as "earning our bread and butter."

Butter is by no means a recent discovery, having been known and used as far back as history records. The Bible refers to the fact that "the churning of milk bringeth forth butter." It probably originated in Asia some time before the Christian Era, being made by putting sour milk in a bag made of the skin or stomach of an animal, and beating the bag or tying it behind or on a trotting horse.

Butter in the United States is made almost entirely from cow's milk, but in some sections of the world, the milk of such animals as the goat, camel, sheep, mare, and even the water buffalo of India is used. The liquid butter from the milk of this animal is known as *ghee.* Tibetans use quantities of butter made from the milk of the yak, their native beast of burden.

Composition and Characteristics. The composition of butter is, as a rule, 79 to 82 per cent butterfat, 12 to 16 per cent water, 1.5 to 3.5 per cent salt, and about .08 per cent casein or curd, and ash. Because of a confusion in standards for butter making, the Sixty-seventh Congress, backed by the Department of Agriculture, passed an 80 per cent standard of butterfat content in butter for all interstate commerce. Butterfat is especially important in the diet of children because it contains the health-promoting Vitamin A. There are various butter substitutes on the market, but it is unlawful to sell these as genuine butter. These products contain vegetable oils and are so labeled.

Although usually a golden shade, butter

is darker in color when made in the spring and early summer because the cows have fresh grass to graze upon. Sometimes vegetable dyes are used to keep the color of the butter uniform throughout the year. It is now believed that the natural yellow color of butter is a fair index to the amount of Vitamin A it contains. Good butter is free from unpleasant smells; it is firm when cold, and when warm is easily spread; and it does not have a greasy or oily taste.

Salt is added to butter as a preservative and to improve its taste. An ounce of salt for every pound of butter is about the standard in the United States; however, there is a considerable demand in large cities for unsalted butter, and this form is used exclusively by orthodox Jews. Market butter is judged or scored by the following scale of points: flavor, 45; body, 25; salt, 15; color, 10; package, 5.

How Butter Is Made. In foreign countries, especially, a large amount of butter is made from milk. In the United States, however, the greatest percentage is made from cream separated from the milk, since there is a smaller bulk to be handled and a much greater proportion of butter can be produced. The cream can be separated by setting the milk in shallow dishes in a cool place, or by putting it in cans submerged in cold water, but the commonest and most practical method, used in modern dairies, is by means of a cream separator, since it saves time and secures more cream.

The cream may be churned while it is still sweet, but soured cream is frequently preferred because of its flavor. In certain dairy areas, factory separation of sweet whole milk is increasing and less is being separated on the farms. Higher-grade cream and higher-score butter usually result from factory separation. While the cream is being churned, it is kept at a temperature of from 50 to 65 degrees. Churning beats the butterfat together, and separates it from the liquid parts of the milk. When the churning is complete, the buttermilk is drained. The butter is washed in water, salted, and "worked," to expel any

buttermilk or water, distribute the salt, and obtain a uniform color.

The working is done either manually or by machinery. The utmost cleanliness must be observed throughout the entire process, since butter, as well as all other milk products, can easily be tainted or contaminated. Dairy products are a natural medium for the growth of harmful bacteria.

Production. For its size, Denmark leads all the countries of the world in butter output, but in total volume the United States is first, with an annual output of about two billion pounds, approximately sixteen pounds per year for every man, woman, and child in the country. Butter manufacture is one of the nation's leading industries.

For further information, consult the following articles:

Cream Separator	Milk
Dairying	Oleomargarine

BUTTERCUP, or CROW'FOOT. From the bright golden cup formed by its petals, this wild flower received its common name. It is called crowfoot because the leaves are divided into lobes in such a way that they somewhat resemble the foot of a crow. "The buttercup catches the sun in its chalice," says James Russell Lowell in one of his poems. Many a child has held the cup, or chalice, of petals under the chin of a playmate, to see "if you like butter."

The buttercup is a familiar weed of meadows and pastures, and there are a great many species. Most of the buttercups contain very sour juices; some of us remember the mouth blisters we got from chewing the stems of buttercups. Cattle know about the burning taste of the common meadow buttercup, and leave it strictly alone when grazing. There is a good deal of variety in the way these weedy flowers grow. One species spreads over the ground by means of runners, like the strawberry. Another forms bulbs in the soil, and others grow in swamps. A buttercup that is found in ponds has its flowers floating on top of the water and its leaves growing underneath.

WHERE DIRT IS OUTLAWED

A modern creamery where butter is manufactured is spotlessly clean. The cans in which the milk is brought to the creamery are sterilized and washed by machinery (upper left); the vats that mix and stir the contents are kept at even temperatures to prevent the growth of bacteria (upper right and center); and the great churns (lower right), that produce the tasty spread for bread, are immaculate.

"CINDERELLAS" OF THE INSECT WORLD

Like the heroine of an oft-told tale, these poor and despised caterpillars are transformed into gorgeous butterflies, admired and sought by all who love beauty.

BUTTERFLY. That the most beautiful members of the insect world are caterpillars in one stage of their life history is a fact that never loses interest for us. Butterflies are well worth our study, and there is a satisfaction in learning about them in their adult stage, because most of them are harmless. A poet has suggested something of their strange beauty in these lines:

> The flash of gold of setting sun,
> The velvet dusk when day is done;
> The vivid hues of sunset skies,
> Of these, are fashioned butterflies.

Butterflies, and their relatives the moths, belong to the order *Lepidoptera*. It is sometimes difficult to distinguish between the two groups, but the feelers, or *antennae,* provide a way of telling them apart. The moths have feather-like antennae, while those of butterflies are threadlike, but enlarged at the tip. In general, butterflies are seen during the day and moths at night, although there are some day-flying moths. Usually, too, the wings of a butterfly appear to be broader and the body more slender than those of the moth, but this is not always true. Usually, again, but not always, the butterflies have more striking colors, especially on the front wings.

The Butterfly Families. Because they are more easily observed, butterflies are better known than the moths, although there are not nearly so many kinds of butterflies. They are divided into five groups, or families. These are the skippers, the swallowtails, the whites and yellows, the

THE GAYEST, BRIGHTEST OF LIVING THINGS

These are not queer tropical butterflies that you can't get for your collection, but varieties that can be found almost anywhere in a temperate climate. Most of them are easy to identify by their distinct patterns and brilliant coloring, and their picturesque names frequently are good descriptions themselves. If the sex is given, the coloring of male and female is different: (1) Peacock. (2) Common Blue (male). (3) Red Admiral. (4) Small Copper. (5) Swallowtail. (6) Orange Tip (male). (7) Brimstone (male). (8) Marbled White. (9) Clouded Yellow (male). (10) Small Heath. (11) Painted Lady. (12) Large White (female). (13) Small Tortoiseshell.

blues and coppers, and the four-footed butterflies. The last include all those that do not fall easily into the other groups.

The *skippers* are usually brownish in color, with gold or yellow markings, although some are black, or black and white. Their antennae are curved or hooked at the tip. Most skippers have a habit of flying in a zigzag manner which suggests their common name. They average about one inch in spread of wings, from tip to tip.

The *swallowtails* are all large, with a wing spread of well over two inches. They have distinct tail-like projections on their back wings, which give them their common name.

For the most part, the *whites and yellows* are medium-sized. The best-known members of this group are the *cabbage* butterfly and the *common yellow* butterfly.

The *blues and coppers* are called *gossamer-winged* and include the smallest of the butterflies, with extremely delicate and fragile wings. The best examples are the small, sky blue butterflies seen along roadways and in meadows.

The *four-footed* butterflies include all those that do not fit into any other group. They vary in size from quite small to the very largest, and include more kinds than any other family. Among them are the *fritillaries*, the *meadow-brown*, the *monarch* and the *mourning cloak*.

The Life History of the Butterfly. Butterflies undergo a complete change in the course of their life histories. They live in four different forms: the *egg;* the *larva,* or caterpillar; the *pupa,* or *chrysalis,* and the *imago,* or fully developed insect. The butterfly eggs are placed near the plant on which the future caterpillar is to feed. The eggs usually change into caterpillars in three weeks, in warm countries, but it may take much longer in colder climates.

The caterpillar is the second stage. All it does is eat and grow. The caterpillar stage lasts from about four months to as long as ten months, depending on species and climate. The caterpillar changes into a pupa, or chrysalis, enclosed in a hard, smooth budlike shell. While the caterpillars of moths spin cocoons, those of butterflies usually do not. In this stage, the insect appears lifeless, but it is nevertheless going through a marvelous transformation. After a few weeks, if conditions are favorable, the completed butterfly comes out of the chrysalis, and in two to four hours is ready for the full glory of the first flight.

The principal food of butterflies is the nectar of flowers. Life in the butterfly stage lasts only a few days. After the butterfly deposits its eggs to grow a new generation, it dies, and so the life cycle begins anew.

The Study of the Butterfly. There are many good small books which give full information on the common species, and butterflies may thus be studied conveniently. Their beauty is a never-ending source of pleasure. Some few species are justifiably destroyed by man because they damage plants. One such is the cabbage butterfly, whose green caterpillar consumes quantities of garden truck. Many species, however, are entirely harmless and afford interesting subjects for a lesson in natural, living science.

Proper study of the butterfly begins with the egg, but, as eggs are often hard to find, the amateur student may have to begin with the second, or caterpillar, stage. The caterpillar may be kept in a glass cage, in the sun. If fed and provided with a twig and leaves for cocoon building, the insect will demonstrate the marvelous changes which produce its kind.

BUTTERNUT. This familiar North American tree is valued for its wood and well-flavored nuts. These are the "butnuts" that country children like to gather and store away for refreshment on the long winter evenings.

The butternut tree belongs to the walnut family. It grows from fifty to seventy feet in height, and its bark is easily recognized by the long furrows running up and down the trunk. The twigs are coarse and contain a pith composed of many closely crowded partitions. Butternut leaves are compound, with eleven or more stalkless leaflets. The leaves are arranged alternately, the leaflets oppositely.

The nuts of this tree are somewhat like pointed eggs and are covered with a husk that stains the fingers; the stain is really a dye. In pioneer days, throughout the Mississippi Valley, a coarse brown, woolen cloth, spun at home and dyed with butternut extracts, was in general use for clothing. During the Civil War, some of the soldiers wore homemade "butternut" uniforms. The wood of the tree is the *white walnut* of the furniture trade.

BUTTERWORT, *but'ur wurt.* Growing in damp, marshy places, the butterwort has thick leaves covered with a fluid which attracts insects. The edges of the leaves curl down over any insect as soon as it lights, and the plant promptly absorbs the victim as food. Above the leaves, the plant bears tall stalks, topped with small purple flowers.

The name of the plant was given it because its leaves have a peculiar power to curdle milk. In the northern part of Sweden, the butterwort is used for that purpose. It is common in the northern parts of Europe, Asia, and North America. See Carnivorous Plants.

BUT'TONS. These practical and well-known objects first were used as ornaments or for decoration, many centuries ago. As fasteners for clothing, buttons came into use in Southern Europe in the fourteenth or fifteenth century. The first step was the adoption of a loop for fastening; the buttonhole came much later. Buttons are now fastened in three ways. Besides those sewed to garments through holes, there are buttons with shanks of metal; and a third type has, in place of the metal shank, a tuft or layer of felt or other cloth. The materials used for buttons come from plants, animals, and minerals; they include wood, gold, glass, mother of pearl, paper, plastics, vegetable ivory, shell, animal bone, steel, and many other substances.

In England, about the time of Queen Elizabeth, the city of Birmingham took the lead in button manufacture and has held it ever since. Metal buttons were made in the United States, at Philadelphia, in colonial days, and a button factory was set up at Waterbury, Conn., in 1800. An important button industry developed later in the Mississippi Valley, especially in Illinois and Iowa, where the shell of the fresh-water mussel proved to be a good material.

Some types of buttons are used for purely ornamental purposes, and others as symbols of clubs, fraternities, political grouping, and similar organizations. The American Legion, for instance, uses metal buttons to indicate membership in this organization of World War veterans. In modern costumes, some conventional uses of buttons, as on the sleeves of men's coats, may be traced back to old styles of dress in which these buttons were attached to the garment for utility. In the case of sleeve buttons, they were used to fasten back long and lacy cuffs.

BUZ'ZARD. This name is sometimes applied to the southern vulture, but belongs properly to a big, slow-moving, broad-winged bird that soars easily high in the air. Buzzards belong to the hawk family and are common in North America and Europe. Although many hawks are blamed for chicken stealing, buzzards rarely bother poultry. They are sluggish in habit, and feed on frogs, toads, worms, and insects. See Turkey Buzzard.

BUZZARDS BAY. Running southwest from the southern and western coasts of Massachusetts is Buzzards Bay. The Elizabeth Islands separate it from Vineyard Sound. The bay is thirty miles long and from five to ten miles wide. Among its harbors are New Bedford, Wareham, Nasketucket, and Mattapoisett. Today, Buzzards Bay is a famous summer resort.

BY-LAWS. These are written regulations governing an organization. They comprise the rules to be observed in all deliberative matters. For instance, the by-laws of a club will tell the secretary when and how to call meetings, and instruct the president in what order he is to conduct the business of each meeting. By-laws are usually secondary to a main body of law, or constitution, especially in social and fraternal organizations. No by-law can be opposed to the basal constitution.

In corporations, by-laws must conform in their substance, that is, not be opposed to, the provisions of the charter granted by the government under which the corporation conducts its business.

By-laws once adopted cannot be changed except by vote, and usually only after notice of a proposed change has been presented at a preceding regular meeting.

BYRD, RICHARD EVELYN (1888-   ). The name of Admiral Richard E. Byrd is honored among the names of great explorers. His is the story of a man whose daring feats have thrilled the world, and whose great love of adventure has taken him to the far corners of the earth.

He was born of a prominent Virginia family, in Winchester, Va. When he was but twelve years old, he went alone on a trip around the world. He attended the University of Virginia and then the United States Naval Academy, from which he graduated in 1912. After four years in the navy, he was obliged to retire because of a foot injury. During World War I, he served with the temporary rank of lieutenant commander.

In 1925 Byrd joined the MacMillan expedition to Greenland as flight commander. The next year, with Floyd Bennett, he made the first flight over the North Pole. For this feat, Byrd was given the rank of commander. In 1927 he and three other airmen made a transatlantic flight, but were forced down off the coast of France.

From 1928 to 1930, Byrd commanded a South Polar expedition, taking with him a competent staff of geologists, meteorologists, and other scientists. He also took with him several airplanes to be used in his explorations. A huge operations base was established at Little America, 1,100 miles from the South Pole. Elaborate radio equipment kept the expedition in touch with the outside world. On Thanksgiving Day, 1929, Byrd and three companions made their thrilling flight over the Pole.

Many other flights were made to unknown parts of Antarctica, and large areas were named. One was named Marie Byrd Land, in honor of the commander's wife. For his work on this expedition, Byrd was made a rear admiral. His discoveries proved the generally believed fact that the South Pole rests on land. See ANTARCTICA.

Admiral Byrd organized a second expedition in 1933. On that journey he spent one entire winter alone. In 1939 he commanded a third expedition to Antarctica, which was organized to make land surveys and collect scientific data for the United States government.

Byrd has received numerous medals and honors, including twenty-two citations for bravery and personal achievements. He has written several books based on his experiences, including *Skyward* (1928), *Little America* (1930), and *Alone* (1938).

BY'RON, GEORGE NOEL GORDON, Sixth Lord (1788-1824). This famous poet of the Romantic Period of English literature was a man in whom great gifts and great faults were strangely blended. During his lifetime he was considered a genius and a scoundrel. He won both the admiration and the criticism of his fellow men.

Byron's parents were separated, and he lived with his mother, who was a vain and violent-tempered woman. She fluctuated between being too kind and being too harsh with her son, with the result that he was sensitive and spoiled. His schooling began when he entered the grammar school at Aberdeen at the age of seven.

Four years later, on the death of his grand-uncle, he inherited the family title and estate at Newstead Abbey, near Nottingham. Byron spent most of his boyhood at Newstead. His schooling at this time was at Harrow. Although lame from a severe illness in his early childhood, he took an active part in school sports at Harrow, and studied rather carelessly.

In 1805 Byron began his college career at Cambridge. There he wrote his first book of poems, *Hours of Idleness*. Although this work was not without merit, it was criticised unmercifully in the *Edinburgh Review*. Greatly annoyed, Byron wrote his first important literary work, *English Bards and Scotch Reviewers,* a poem ridiculing critics.

His next success came with the publication of the first part of *Childe Harold's Pilgrimage,* begun during a trip to Spain and the Mediterranean coast. Byron was only twenty-one years old when he and a young friend started this journey, and the poem reflects the thoughts of the boy growing to manhood. The poem created a sensation, and overnight Byron became famous. He then produced *The Bride of Abydos, The Corsair, Lara* and *The Giaour,* his reputation growing with each new work.

In spite of his good looks and charm, Byron was a difficult person to live with, as he was subject to moods and had a violent temper. In 1815 he married the daughter of Sir Ralph Milbanke, but within a year his bride left him and never returned. The criticism aroused by this domestic trouble so angered Byron that he went to France, declaring that he would never again live in England.

He traveled about on the continent for a time, always moody and restless, settling more or less permanently, first at Geneva and then at Venice. He became a great friend of the poet Shelley, one of the few persons he really admired. He continued to write, first more of *Childe Harold,* then *The Prisoner of Chillon, The Dream and Other Poems,* and *The Lament of Tasso.* Next he wrote *Don Juan,* his masterpiece, and a number of dramas.

From Italy, Byron often visited Greece. He became seriously interested in the struggle for Greek independence, and took an active part in promoting the movement. He seemed to realize at last that his life had been aimless, but his good intentions came too late. In January, 1824, he arrived at Missolonghi, where he was welcomed with enthusiasm. But several months later, after riding in the rain, Lord Byron developed a fever and died within ten days.

BYZANTINE, *be zan'tin,* **ART.** When Constantine the Great removed his capital from Rome to Byzantium, in 330 A. D., he not only fortified and rebuilt the city but ornamented it with Grecian art treasures. He renamed his new capital Constantinople. From this time until the city was captured by the Turks in 1453, a style of art, known as Byzantine, flourished in Southeastern Europe. It combined the color and the architectural principles of the Romans, and the Greek use of detail and freedom. Splendor of material and ornament began to take the place of the simplicity and dignity of ancient art.

Both in mosaics and paintings, the work of Byzantine artists was characterized by the stiffness of the human figures and blankness of their expressions. But the figures were clothed in brilliant costumes, and much attention was given to small detail. The monumental Church of Saint Sophia in Constantinople was a product of a golden era in the history of this school, and is probably its supreme example. The Byzantine school also held high rank in art in Italy and other parts of Europe.

BYZANTINE EMPIRE. Known also as Eastern, Greek, and Eastern Roman, the Byzantine Empire was the successor of the Roman state that ruled the world from the Italian peninsula. The passing of the old Roman Empire and the coming of the Byzantine was a gradual transition, like the sun sinking in the west and rising in the east. When night was falling on old Rome, a new day was dawning in the land beyond the Mediterranean. From the fourth century until 1453, when Constantinople fell, the Byzantine Empire flourished, keeping the barbarians from overwhelming European civilization, and preserving the priceless culture of antiquity until it came under the fostering wings of the Renaissance.

This unusual empire, which combined Western and Oriental culture, might be said to have been founded in 330 A. D., when Constantine, first Christian to rule Rome, moved the capital to Byzantium, later called Constantinople.